THE PEACE OF THE AUGUSTANS

THE PEACE

OF

THE AUGUSTANS

A SURVEY OF
EIGHTEENTH CENTURY LITERATURE
AS A PLACE OF REST AND REFRESHMENT

BY

GEORGE SAINTSBURY

M.A. AND HON. D.LITT., OXON.; HON. LL.D., ABERD.; HON. D.LITT., DURH.;
FELLOW OF THE BRITISH ACADEMY; HON. FELLOW OF MERTON COLLEGE, OXFORD;
LATE PROFESSOR OF RHETORIC AND ENGLISH LITERATURE IN THE UNIVERSITY OF EDINBURGH

LONDON
G. BELL AND SONS, LTD.
1916

PREFACE

THE title of this book has been chosen with a special view to making that prefatory explanation, which is so obnoxious to the foes of prefaces, as far as possible unnecessary. But a little may, I hope, be added to it without offence. In the first place the writer, though he has given the usual *History of Eighteenth Century Literature* with a difference, by no means aims at supplying a " talkee-talkee " book, a series of gossiping sketches of persons and manners. He hopes to furnish an account of the subject trustworthy even for the strictest scholarly if not scholastic purposes,[1] and dealing with parts of that subject not to be usually found in similar histories; but to make it, at the same time, somewhat more attractive to the general reader by bringing out a particular and systematic view. That view is of course not new—nothing is. It was taken perhaps for the first time—with the originality of genius and with its absence of proclamation and beat of drum—by Thackeray; it has actuated to some extent the novels of Sir Walter Besant and to a much greater the poems and essays of Mr. Austin Dobson;

---

[1] As it happens, too, this period is almost the only one with which this same writer has not dealt except as a section of the whole story of English literature. The novels he has indeed handled more than once at some length, as also the criticism, but no other division save in patches and pieces.

v

it has formed part of what is real in the sometimes merely fashionable cult of Johnsonianism; it has been shared by many good wits. But it has never, so far as the present writer knows, been systematically applied to, and supported by, a survey of the whole literary work of the century; and the desirableness of doing this has long been, and is still, made evident by constant intentional and unintentional expressions of uninformed or misguided opinion.

The extreme denigration of the last century but one which was inevitably put about by the great Romantic revolt at its close, and the maintenance of which was one of the least beneficial (though not perhaps least excusable) features of the " Oxford Movement," has indeed ceased; and a certain reaction —noticeable in, and helped if not actually caused by the work of the writers mentioned in the last paragraph—has succeeded. But from work half a century old, or more, to work of the present day one still finds echoes of this denigration, no longer perhaps actively contemptuous or polemical, but still inappreciative, uncomprehending, showing that the eye of the brain is off the object. A day or two before writing these words the writer happened to come across two examples of opinion, at the two dates just referred to. The one, of extremely recent origin, was an ordinary anonymous review in which the reviewer restated the ordinary signed or unsigned opinion that eighteenth-century language was stilted, uneasy, only conventionally correct: contrasting in this respect Horace Walpole's letters with Byron's, and hinting that our present methods were better still. The other, some fifty years old, was in some words of Mrs. Gaskell's (not an unsympathetic or an unthoughtful judge) similarly contrasting—with no contempt but with some surprise—" the little power our ancestors had of putting things together," their inconsistent conventionalities, their want of introspection and the like, with the immense improvement which the middle of the nineteenth century [1] found in itself as regards these matters. Both passages came seriously " pat " to the purpose of the present volume.

It is probably unnecessary to say more. But the author may perhaps be permitted to observe that, if he has often been found fault with for paying too exclusive attention to form and treatment, that charge will hardly lie here. To omit consideration of form [2] entirely would be treason to literature ; but there are notoriously few stretches of ours which need less constant and minute examination of it than this; and the very title of this book promises preferential dealing with matter and thought and temperament. Let us hope that the promise will be kept.

G. S.

Edinburgh, *October* 1915.

---

[1] It is a deep and abiding content, for those who enjoy the *ludicrum humani saeculi*, to remember that the beginning of the twentieth century regards itself, in exactly the same manner, as an immense improvement, in these very points, on the middle of the nineteenth.

[2] The word "form" is somewhat ambiguous, and may be here misunderstood. It is not used in the larger sense of "kind" ; for the eighteenth century almost (if not quite) invented the great "kinds" and "forms" of the Novel and the Periodical Essay ; did much to Historical and Philosophical treatment ; perfected (in a sense) the heroic couplet, etc. Of all these we shall take notice. But the tendency to standardise rather than to individualise, which is characteristic of the time, lessens the necessity for detailed "form"-treatment. I have only to add now almost stereotyped thanks to my friends Professors Ker, Elton, and Gregory Smith for reading my proofs and making suggestions.

CONTENTS

CHAPTER I

ix

CHAPTER VII

CHAPTER VIII

CHAPTER IX

CHAPTER I

THE HERITAGE OF DRYDEN AND THE WORLD OF "THE SPECTATOR"—SWIFT—THE DRAMA

WHEN Dryden, by his death in the last year of the seventeenth century, at once closed the period of his own contemporaries and opened a new one in a fashion not paralleled exactly by any other man of letters, he left English literature generally in a state to which we meet more frequent parallels, but which is still peculiar. He himself, though the fact has not been commonly recognised till quite recently, if it is so now, had almost as much of " the last age " in him as of his own ; and yet he exercised a definitely modern and even " futurist " influence, as few deliberate or desperate innovators have done. His extraordinary critical faculty even overleaped the century which was for the most part disposed to regard him as the greatest of English poets, but could not quite appreciate him as a critic, and began to work again with the Romantics, ungrateful as most of them were for it. Yet, in his singularly varied command of metres, in the ubiquity of his practice in poetry and prose, and most of all in those sudden flights and flashes of meteoric verse, which, if it does not reach the empyrean of Shakespeare or Milton, goes spheres above the reach and range of any typical eighteenth-century poet—in all these he reminds us that he was born not much more than a

The relations of Dryden and his successors.

B

decade after Shakespeare's death and nearly half a century before that of Milton.

At the time of his own decease, however, the apparent state of English literature might have seemed **Apparent falling-off.** somewhat rotten to a Hamlet considerably less hypochondriacal than the actual Prince of Denmark. We are so accustomed to talk of " the great Queen Anne men," and to associate them with the first decade of the eighteenth century itself, that we are apt to forget the general literary barrenness of that decade and especially of its earliest years. Dryden was just dead, and no one " like or second " to him was left except Prior, who had only done slight things, and none of his best. Swift had indeed written *The Battle of the Books* and *A Tale of a Tub*, but he did not publish them till the fourth year of the century. Addison had done nothing of importance except some pretty College verses in the learned tongue, and some prose, also of an academic character, together with that unfortunate *Epistle to Henry Sacheverell*, of which he afterwards repented, but which shows that, at the time, earlier English literature was worse than unknown to him. Steele had done little more. Defoe had done a great deal ; but nothing in the direction of his two grand achievements—the periodical and the novel. Mr. Pope (if Mr. Pope is to be believed, which is a somewhat large proviso) had begun writing his formally marvellous *Juvenilia*, but he was not to publish them for years later. Blackmore there certainly was, and Garth and one or two others who were to be more considerable; but on its actual showing it was a day of very small things in literature, and especially in poetry. The most sanguine critic could hardly make much of any of these, and he would have needed to be a prophet if he had expected, at least with justification, very much from any others.[1]

---

[1] Some may say " Congreve ? " But Congreve was already a magnificent past. His last play dates from the last year of the 17th century, and though he outlived the first quarter of the 18th, he was then as dead to literature as Dryden himself.

Young centuries, however, are seldom troubled for want of that good conceit of themselves which, though sometimes bitter in the belly, is apparently very sweet in the mouth. This particular period had indeed, as has been shown, not much to boast of in its own achievements; but it was still in the mighty shadow of Mr. Dryden, marked black on the sand like the place of refuge afforded by a magic circle, and it was also quite prepared to be, if it was not already, proud of itself. The exquisitely absurd passage of Watts's *Odes*, as to certain nonconformist ministers, which Southey has quoted and laughed at in *The Doctor*,[1] was no doubt partly, as Southey himself suggests, due to that quaint mutual-admiration tendency which belongs to all small sects and coteries: but it was to a considerable extent characteristic of the century itself at large. If the time had not been apt to be awed by every moderately sublime Mead and charmed by each not so very seductive Bates, the lightning scathe of Swift and the venomous bite of Pope would have found not half so much to destroy or annoy, and indeed they might not have been exercised at all.

But the special form in which this Zion took its ease and persuaded itself that it *was* Zion, was not at Contempt of first so much self-admiration as complacent preceding contempt of the past. Some years before ages. it began Mr. Addison himself, as was noted above, in a composition of which he is said to have had the grace to be ashamed later, but which certainly expressed the attitude of most people for at least two-

[1] Heaven was impatient of our crimes,
And sent his minister of death
To scourge the bold rebellion of the times
And to demand our prophet's breath:
He came commissioned for the fates
Of awful Mead, and charming Bates:
There he essayed the vengeance first ["fust"]
Then took a wider sweep and brought great Gouge to dust.

(The whole may be found in Chalmers's *Poets*, xiii. 81-82.)
All these were dissenting ministers, and Mead must not be confounded with his son Richard, the really famous physician.

thirds of the coming century, had dismissed Chaucer as an " unpolished " buffoon[1] who had ceased to be even amusing, and Spenser as a dull moralist who tried to hide his dulness in his frippery. A whole long lifetime later Goldsmith was to sneer, in exactly the same spirit though in less committingly explicit terms, at Drayton.[2] We may hope to trace the progress, the fluctuations, and the gradual extinction of this contempt of preceding ages, which, starting from a not altogether intelligent adoration of the classics (most Latin but very little Greek), passed with would-be withering despite over the Middle Ages, bestowed a conventional admiration on the Renaissance, rather abroad than at home, and tempered (very inadequately) a contemptuous disapproval of nearly the whole Elizabethan, Jacobean, and First Caroline periods by an almost equally conventional, a conditional, a rather puzzled, and a not unfrequently very dubious acceptance of Shakespeare and Milton. They could not well reject these, for had not Dryden accepted both with his magnificent enthusiasm? But they did not, to use once more Desdemona's phrase which Lamb borrowed, " like them *to live with them*." To all but a very few the prince of drama and the grand-duke of epic were in spirit what their works were a little later in fact—handsomely bound volumes to lie on a drawing-room table.

This was not an altogether healthy condition of mind, and it met with its due punishment. But if all sins have their punishment, some at any rate have their solace ; if most qualities have defects, some defects at any rate foster a quality. Without this comfortable, somewhat obtuse, but feather- if not hot-

---

[1] In vain he jests in his unpolished strain
And tries to make his readers laugh in vain

. . . . .

But now the mystic tale that pleased of yore
Can charm an understanding age no more.
Account of *The Best Known English Poets*.

[2] " Drayton ! " I replied, " I never heard of him before."—*Cit. of World*, xiii.

bed-providing disposition, not a few of the advantages which the century obtained for itself (and for all time when men choose to use them) would hardly have come into being. In its own language, you cannot have the cucumber without " the stercoraceous heap." But without any more rudeness let us to the history.

In one particular direction writers had their line clearly marked out for them. Dryden, as has been The triumph said, had shown exceptional proficiency in of the heroic many kinds of metre, but he had princi- couplet. pally devoted himself to one—the stopped heroic couplet, which is perhaps more traceable to the final distichs of Fairfax's octave in his *Tasso* than to anything else, just as the original couplet of Chaucer was probably determined by his own not diminutive practice in the *Troilus*. Dryden, however, while presenting an immense improvement on Sandys,[1] Sir John Beaumont, the much-praised Waller, and Cowley, had too much of the divine freedom and variety of poetry in him to follow up the *idées mères* of this couplet—" smoothness " and " correctness "— at all slavishly or even quite faithfully. He rarely indeed exceeded the ten syllables in the line, though his principle of elision, to get these ten only, was the rational one of never sinking the metrical value, unless you can sink the pronunciation. But he did not absolutely avoid overrunning; and he deliberately engineered variety by admitting the triplet, the Alexandrine, and (in one famous [2] and not a few less generally known instances) even the fourteener. More-over, his equally powerful and subtle manipulation of word-values and sound-places, *within* the line, brought about an effect, symphonic rather than antiphonal,

[1] The priority of Drayton, Heywood and others for which some stickle (not to mention Shakespeare) is not matter of dispute or concern here. The stopped couplet itself dates from Chaucer and even earlier.

[2] Thou leap'st o'er all eternal truths in thy Pindaric way.

The Medal, l. 94.

The others are chiefly in the *Virgil.*

which gave to the couplet much more the varied value
of blank verse with rhyme than the monotony of
Beaumont's regular tinkle of answering bells.[1]

The effect was magnificent, but it was very difficult
to imitate ; and it was, as has been said, after all a
distinct " excursion out of bounds." The
ideal of the smooth correct couplet—each
answering to each, with each line, and each half
line equally responsive to its brother — was clearly
still to seek.   It was not long before it was found
once for all, and with results not so wholly or at least
lastingly " delightful " as Beaumont thought, by
Pope.   But something like it was hit earlier by Garth,
the ingenious author of *The Dispensary* (1699–1714),
a man apparently of equal talent and merit, and the
subject of a characteristically unmistakable compliment
on his professional, poetical, and moral character
from Dryden [2] and a characteristically ambiguous one
on his qualities of soul by Pope.[3]   It is not impossible,
though it is not exceedingly probable, that Garth may
have read Beaumont ; it is certain that he could not,
if he had done so and had set that excellent person's
description or prescription before him, have carried
out Beaumont's ideal more thoroughly.   The large if
not infinite variety which Dryden had achieved outshot
this restricted scope ; and though a certain block or
paragraph of verse might have all the merits of an
intricate peal of changes, his single verses by no means
regularly met " like a chime."   Garth's did ; and so,
still more, did Pope's, of which we shall speak later.[4]
The means whereby this effect was to be attained had
been already indicated, not so much by Beaumont
himself as by his predecessor, and no doubt inspirer,
Fairfax, and by his elder and younger contemporaries

Its progress.

---

[1] " One verse must meet another like a chime."
[2] " Garth, generous as his muse, prescribes and gives."
[3] " The best good Christian, *without knowing it*."
[4] In the next chapter, whither also and perhaps in some cases further some
contemporaries but not quite companions of Garth, like Lady Winchelsea, Prior,
Parnell, and Gay, may be relegated.

Sandys and Waller. They were, in brief (we may be able to consider them more fully when we come to Pope himself), reflections, as it may be called, of the folding effect of the couplet in a corresponding fold of the individual line, by the provision of a pause at or close to the middle. This necessarily gave a balance on a hardly shifting pivot ; and that balance in its turn was assisted, if not actually procured, by further corresponding arrangements of antithetic epithets and nouns in the two halves of the line. These mechanical devices undoubtedly gave the " smoothness," the " regularity," the " purity " which to ears (as ears generally were now) anxious to receive them were very delightful. From the first indeed (and Pope, who could " see a church by daylight " if ever man could, was perfectly well aware of it and sometimes scoffed at what he practised) certain dangers were clear. But these may wait awhile. It is sufficient to say that, though Garth is an interesting and valuable link for the historian, he is no great gain to the lover of poetry. Yet even he anticipates, if in a way not now more than historically satisfactory, the *nisus* (if so violent a word can be used) towards easy-chairs of literature, towards something that would rest and recreate without exciting.

But—though the comparative nullity of these opening years was to be turned into more than respect-
Creation of a able quality and quantity by Pope, by some
standard of Pope's friends, and by what may be
prose. called (though they hardly meant it or knew it) the enemies of Pope [1]—the century had, by this first decade, given what may be called a prerogative voice of no uncertain sound in favour of prose. In that region and in a much sounder sense than that in which (with much exaggeration and even some positive mistake or misstatement) Matthew Arnold described it as being so, the eighteenth century was to be the Age of

[1] Not his *Dunciad* enemies (who were mostly impotent alike for good and ill) but men like Thomson (whom he actually welcomed).

Prose—of prose in the literal and natural sense. This was its mission—to get English prose into something like the order which, with Chaucer, Spenser, Shakespeare, and Milton for teachers, English verse had actually reached, though it was for a time to refuse (or at least not to improve) the best part of its heritage here. For though it has several times been tried— once by Coleridge with the greatest possible powers misdirected by the least perfect knowledge—to maintain that a standard theory or practice of prose had been reached long before Dryden ; though Dryden had shown the way and set admirable examples of certain kinds ; he had not as yet made—though he was just about, being dead, to make—a school in prose as he had in poetry. Both these propositions need expansion and support.

It would be outside of the strict subject of this book, and probably tedious to any but a very few readers of it, to restate and discuss thoroughly the *Some mistakes about this.* fantastic nature of Coleridge's theory of a standard and accomplished Elizabethan prose — exemplified by Latimer and Hooker (two writers half a century apart in time and poles asunder in every point of style), corrupted by Sir Thomas Browne and his contemporaries, and then corrupted worse by the Augustans, till Gibbon's was " the worst of all." But some statement and some discussion cannot be avoided. It is perfectly clear — and plainness of speech may be forgiven to an " Estesian " of the Estesians who has been rebuked more than once for setting his master too high—that at the moment [1] Coleridge simply did not know what he was talking about, or that it was, as Lamb would have put it, only the most audacious fashion of " his fun." It never happened—none of it, as Mr. Matthew Arnold rashly

---

[1] It was in one of those lectures (that on " Style " to be found in the *Miscellanies* volume of the Bohn Library edition of his works, p. 275 *sq.*), which were, and in their reported condition are, famous equally for the brilliant things they contained and for the haphazard fashion of their method and construction.

observed of certain other transactions, without being able to produce the slightest evidence to prove the negative, whereas here evidence is at hand on every point. Between the style of Latimer and the style of Hooker there is little more resemblance than between the style of Cobbett and the style of Newman. Latimer indeed deserves the credit of introducing, keeping, or improving (fight might be made for all these words) a conversational element in prose; but his style was and was meant to be that of a *concio ad vulgus*, even when he preached before king and clergy. Hooker's was one of the most beautiful styles ever reached, but it was unfitted for all but very few uses; and though not monotonous, scarcely varied or vivid enough in its beauty. On the other hand, it is not merely possible but not in the least extravagant to regard Sir Thomas Browne as the greatest prose-writer in the English language, to free him from all reasonable charges of neglecting grammar in any sense but that in which grammar is a mere Orgoglio—a boisterous and swash-buckling but unreal phenomenon—of the fairyland of literature, and to extol him without limit for his unique success in adorning prose, without borrowing the jewels of verse. Yet at the same time any real critic must admit that, even more than that of Hooker, Browne's style is not a style of the average purpose, and that it is one which never could be adapted to that average purpose. What was wanted was something which would subserve this purpose, which should be "familiar but not vulgar," and which should yet be capable, without radical alteration, of having its powers raised to magnificence when needed.

Towards this consummation Dryden had been the first to show the way by his discovery of the secret of adjusting the style of prose-writing to that of well-bred and modern conversation. This had been done on a small scale but very little earlier by Cowley, and it is quite open to any one to

The definite work of Dryden.

contend that it had been done now and then by Shakespeare. But it was Dryden who first practised it on
a considerable scale, and in strict prose-writing, not
drama. Even he, however, was comparatively limited
in subject — literature and polemics, personal and
political. His very considerable narrative faculty was
exercised chiefly in poetry, and if he wished to be
splendid, as in the " wandering fires " passage of *The
Hind*, the opening lines of *Religio Laici*, and elsewhere,
he could and did " drop into verse." From this practice
of his, and from its own general tendencies, the eighteenth century was tempted to make a vicious and
unnecessary distinction, not merely between prosaic
and poetic diction (which is, to some though not to
its extent, defensible and indeed necessary [1]) but
between usages and applications of these respective
dictions themselves. It treated in poetry a great many
subjects which would have been much better treated
in prose; but for a long time, when it treated subjects
in prose, it seemed to think that if clearness and
straightforwardness of expression were attained the
Whole Duty of Prose was done, and that any further
attraction, being work of supererogation, had, according to that crotchet referred to in the Articles, " the
nature of sin," and was in fact a kind of trespass on
the rights of poetry.

Now the dangers of this limitation had been seen
earlier by Greek and Roman critics,[2] despite their
horror of " gorgeousness " in the lower harmony,
while in Byzantine times they had been formulated
with equal incisiveness and truth by the Patriarch

[1] This endlessly debated question might be settled, if critics were less litigious,
by a very simple and reasonable *Concordat*. The highest poetry can be written in
what is, literally speaking, the vocabulary of the most ordinary prose; but when
it is—for instance, "The rest is silence," or "To-morrow and to-morrow and
to-morrow," or " Put out the light,"—there is always some *additional* meaning which,
in ordinary prose use, the words would not bear. And, further, this vocabulary, in
the vast majority of instances, requires supplementing by words and combinations of
words which would seldom or never be used in prose.

[2] Especially, of course, Longinus : but there is no real exception from Aristotle
downwards.

Photius.[1] And they had made themselves evident, even during Dryden's lifetime, in the work of Lestrange, Bentley, Collier, and others.

To correct this was no doubt one of the main objects of that most notable and very largely original Degenerations Periodical Essay which—following no doubt from it, and to some extent in some externals the example the rescue of Defoe's *Review*, probably suggested in work of the Addison something like its actual first form by Swift, group. regularly set on foot by Steele, and brought to perfection by Addison—gave us *The Tatler*, *The Spectator*, and their numerous followers, immediate and later, till the very end of the century. In *The Tatler* indeed Swift himself has a direct attack [2] on vulgarisms, especially colloquial contractions and slang. But Steele's and still more Addison's way was not front [3] so much as flank attack—the indirect exposure of vulgarity and inelegance by the practice of elegant and refined writing. As in other cases, it is not so much the object of the present volume to fight old battles over again as to survey the ground from a somewhat novel point of view; and it is not necessary to give or take many blows in the Steele *v.* Addison dispute. As in other cases, also, Macaulay's maladroit emphasis provoked rebellion against it with corresponding emphasis on the other side. We might allow Steele a finer—certainly a more generous and heartfelt — sentiment, a freer spirit, and perhaps a more creative fancy; while reserving for Addison a more generally critical temperament, a better regulated if less catholic taste, and certainly more mastery of that wonderful " middle style," neither attempting loftiness nor descending to vulgarity, which Johnson, in the almost hackneyed eulogy recommending night and day perusal of it, did not overpraise.

---

[1] " The use of merely straightforward periods, without admixture, brings style down to flatness and meanness." [2] Sept. 28, 1710.
[3] There *are* of course some direct censures in *The Spectator*, such as " The just Remonstrance of offended That," etc.

The style itself is a sort of elaborate object-lesson as to the meaning of the title of this present book. The avowed purpose of these periodicals, especially of their " prior " if not in age in position, *The Spectator*, is not merely to instruct at the same time as it gives pleasure, but to instruct by pleasing—to make the pleasure not the companion merely but the instrument or vehicle of the instruction. To tastes of other times the vehicle may seem overloaded, and the instrument blunted by the work it has to do. But it was not the business of these writers to consult the taste of other times ; it was their business to form, at the same time as they suited, that of their own. Nor have they failed in the larger appeal to Prince Posterity. Miss Austen, indeed, spoke harshly [1] of *The Spectator*, but in the first place she was defending her own *domus*— the novel—against the irritating, hackneyed, canting, and silly preference of the moral essay to it ; in the second she was writing at that most dangerous of all times for fair judgment, the very moment when a fashion is going out ; and in the third literary criticism was not her business at all—she had the much more than sufficient task and gift of literary creation.

Nearly a century later, in the very act of making a selection from it, the late Mr. J. R. Green stigmatised the periodical essay generally as " a mass of rubbish." But in this as in other things he had caught far too much of Macaulay's " pistolling ways," as Lord Morley of Blackburn once justly termed them ; and he makes amends to Addison himself by extolling the " grace and ease," the "indefinable sunshiny charm " of his work, the " delicacy and refine-ment of his humour." A somewhat more catholic taste than Mr. Green's will find these qualities almost as fully in the best of Steele's contributions, and by no means absent elsewhere. It is true that Addison, like Miss Austen herself, is sometimes a

[1] *Northanger Abbey*, chapter v.

little cruel, but, as in her case, the cruelty only gives poignancy to the wit.　Addison's darts are as free from the poison of Voltaire's and Pope's as they are different from the devastating sweep of Swift's artillery. They did not even cut or pierce very deeply ; but they seldom missed their mark, and they always flashed as they flew.　Moreover their flashes illuminate a curious, various, and interesting world.　Although no doubt there were some actual " originals," the " key "-smith has found little, though he has tried to make some, scope for his tedious and rather degrading labour on this subject; yet the mass of this *Spectator* world of types is very nearly as lively as a well-recorded diary. The delightful citizen to whom " Mr. Nisby's " words were as those of a prophet, and who gratefully regaled his oracle with " marrow bones and a bottle of Brook's and Hellier " ;[1] and in a somewhat less degree the fine lady to whom Miss Kitty recited the eight best lines of *Aurengzebe*,[2] without book, are nearly as lively and lifelike as Mr. Pepys himself.　The " Coverley " papers it were vain to praise, and when " B. D." writes that as she will be fourteen shortly, " it is time to settle," and remarks on the way in which Mr. Shapeley's eyes, when they look at her, seem " to have tears in them," and wishes Mr. Spectator (whom Mr. Shapeley " admires mightily ") " could see him dance," it must be a dull mind and a narrow fancy that can want better amusement of the " middle " kind. The mightier and more soul-stirring raptures—the

The general character of the Addisonian essay.

---

[1] One of those not unfrequently gilded *Pills to Purge Melancholy*, prescribed by Dr. Thomas Durfey, tells us how greatly people suffered from bad wine in those days ; but how the beneficent
　　　　　Hellier and Brook, a method have took
by which every one may have " red port," " Vienna," " white wine," or whatever he likes, in a neat and proper condition (vol. vi. p. 340-41).　The present writer though he once began a *History of Wine*—the composition of which was interrupted by his appointment to the care of lower mysteries—does not know what " Vienna " was—Voslauer ? Tokay ? What ?

[2] Of course the famous and splendid
　　　" When I consider life, 'tis all a cheat."

voices of the mountain and the sea—are not indeed
with us; they are in fact *ex hypothesi* excluded,
and if you want them you must go elsewhere.   But
you are in a sort of Happy Valley with a pleasant
town-capital in its centre, to the streets of which you
are by no means confined.   You may make excursions
to woods and fields with a village not too far off, where
a decent meal can be obtained.   If town and country
do not fully suffice, there is literature for you—not
quite all literature, but a fair proportion both of ancient
and modern, some art (though you do not take this
very seriously), a little science, and at intervals passages
of perfectly sincere if not very enthusiastic or exalted
piety.   A "middle" style of everything perhaps; but a
happy mean enough—amusing almost always, if only
from its contrasts with or its curious anticipations of
the present, full of an agreeable decency "in the best
sense of the term" (as a late Master of Balliol used to
say when he wished to be apparently complimentary
but really meaningless), and therefore not ill to dwell
with, if not quite to dwell with for ever.

It is perhaps unfortunate, in this as in other cases,
that these essays are known nowadays almost entirely
in selections, for the most part confined to the work
of one writer, or at most two, only,[1] and that even when
the whole is given the advertisements are practically
never reprinted, though in our own days nothing is
more common than the remark that the advertisements
are the most interesting part of any paper, and many
good men make it a part of their holidays to study
carefully what in other days they have no time for.
Here these things fringe and vignette the text in the
most appropriate manner; and so set off the quaint
variety and the other-worldly character as nothing
else could do.   It may be questioned whether, except
for the abhorred "teaching purposes," even the

---

[1] There are one or two worthy exceptions, the chief of all (almost a classic in
itself) being the admirably introduced *Eighteenth Century Essays* by Mr. Austin
Dobson in the "Parchment Library" (London, 1882).

" Coverley " papers do not lose more than they gain by being artificially herded together, instead of preserving the play of their parts as constituents of the original folio.   Literature and finery, Fontange and Fontenelle, The Vision of Mirza and the Custom of Enborne, the Grecian Coffee House and Westminster Abbey, Leonora's ingenious combination of books and *bric-à-brac* and " the first perusal of the new thunder " are all infinitely more amusing and more pregnant in local and temporal colour—more distinct in the not too firm perspective of the past—than when they are taken out of their original company and cut and dried and tinned in a specimen-book at the pleasure of some modern bookmaker.   We have all done these things of course, " obliged by hunger and request of [publishers who also sometimes are] friends " ; but the best of us have always repeated the excuse of the Apothecary in *Romeo and Juliet*.   If anybody really wants to recognise and enjoy the " middle " paradise to which this volume is humbly meant to be a guide-book, let him eschew such things and fall back at least on the pocketable little volumes of the British Essayists, which give the milk unskimmed and " neat."

It is, however, known—if not to everybody, to those who have made some slight progress in acquaint-
The later and ing themselves with the history of our
minor forms. literature — that no collection of the so-called " British Essayists " contains anything like a complete assemblage of the almost innumerable publications of the kind which appeared between the first issue of *The Tatler* and the end of the century. The industry of Nathan Drake long ago got together a useful handbook to these disdained and forgotten imitators of their betters ; and the subject has recently been rehandled in those schemes of literary " research " which have for some years been fashionable.   But unless a society were formed for the purpose, it is exceedingly unlikely that the existing series from *Tatler*

to *Looker-On* will be soon supplemented. Only in the largest libraries—perhaps only in the Bodleian and the British Museum—can most of the minors be found at all; though bound gatherings of single issues occasionally (not very frequently) occur in catalogues. Some no doubt even of the contents of the regular canon which is accessible are dull; and much of Cumberland's *Observer*, with nearly the whole of the above-mentioned *Looker-On*, belongs to what is perhaps the most dismal class of all literature—writing which is a mere *pastiche* of things already old-fashioned and surviving only in the printed book. But earlier even the minorities contain additions to our panorama of the age, to the quaint and almost living picture of different things and persons, manners and customs, businesses, amusements, fashions which, two hundred or a hundred and fifty years ago, occupied the very towns and streets we live in now.

Some of the later and more lively things [1] in Addison's and Steele's own contributions to periodicals subsequent to the *Guardian* are even now familiar. Fielding's *Covent Garden Journal* and other papers have been, in name at least, saved by his novels, and in one lively but libellous instance by their connection with the "Forty-five." *The World* is far more worthy of its brilliant contributors, Chesterfield and Pulteney, Horace Walpole, Lyttelton, and others, than it suited Macaulay to acknowledge in one of his well-known blackenings of A in order to whitewash B. *The Connoisseur*, though it contains things to which Jane Austen might more justly have applied her protest than to any in the *Spectator*, is lively enough; even without its interest as containing almost our only samples of Cowper before his catastrophe. It is the custom to run down *Il Vagabondo* (as the Italians so delightfully call *The Rambler*), yet some of us (if such rash blasphemy of possible judges be permitted) would as soon

[1] Especially Addison's "The Tory Foxhunter," from *The Freeholder*.

read it as most of the respectable papers to be found every Saturday morning on our club tables. Of course in the whole batch the conventionality, the tendency to overdo the type, the avoidance, or at least the neglect of the most striking employments of light and shade, colour and value, character and idiosyncrasy, which distinguish the century, appear. But Addison himself frequently and others sometimes have transcended even this limitation, while the presence of it positively enhances the faithfulness, and so in a way the vividness of the whole picture of life. The way in which they have drawn themselves is the way in which they thought themselves; and it may be questioned whether the result is not a much truer picture—it is certainly to some tastes a much more interesting one—than all our introspection, all our analysis, all our impressionism, " symbolism," " futurism," " blastism," and the rest of our " trimmings " will give to generations as far off from us as we are from these.

Indeed as one looks over the two score and more little volumes of Chalmers's set, a sacred shame invades us at the thought of leaving such a various collection of pastime with the scanty inventory above selected. Nor can it, to any one who is not besotted with that basest [1] of limitations, the single appetite for modernity, be surprising that this storehouse held its vogue so long. Those who first went to it, for nearly half the century, had practically no prose fiction to share or drown its appeal; and even in the second half, or rather more, the novel was still a debatable and uncertain kind, not as yet fully classed, and to some extent deserving its demi-reputation by the fact that, with some few works of undoubted genius, it included not so very few

As a whole rather under- than over-praised.

---

[1] Put naïvely by a recent Radical candidate for Parliament, " What need any young fellow care for what happened in 1864 ? " It must be admitted that this, which referred to an utterance of Mr. Cobden's, was not only a frank confession but an unwitting application of the *lex talionis*. For did not Mr. Cobden himself notoriously prefer a copy of *The Times* to " *all the works* of Thucydides " ?

specimens for which even " demi-rep " itself would be too complimentary a title, and a great multitude which if tolerably respectable, were often intolerably dull. They had not " proved " the novel ; they *had* proved the essay, and its variety delighted them, and may still, if it does not exactly cause delight (that spirit comes rarely), yet furnish pleasure.   Perhaps the main drawback to this pleasure is not the moralising, which can be skipped if any one pleases, but the clumsy intrusion of those unlucky *eidola* whom convention required.   " Mr. Spectator " himself was taught by his creator to be very little if at all a bore ; but his predecessors the Staffs and his followers, Nestor Ironside, the Lizards, Adam Fitz-Adam, " Mr. Town," and the rest may be sometimes heartily wished away from the scenes and narratives which might without them be perfectly readable.   The allegorical politics are a nuisance, but they were soon dropped or kept down.   Mr. Green, who perhaps (his " doxy " being different from the present writer's) did not think the politics a nuisance, did think the literary articles obsolete, while to others they retain quite a lively interest.   Nobody can grumble at the regular " sermons," for they give themselves out quite honestly for what they are, and the reader can call on himself to hear them or not, exactly as he pleases.   And how much remains to be judiciously self-selected by the ingenious !   " Sappho " in the sixth *Tatler*, with her delightful medley (transposable without the slightest difficulty into a twentieth-century key) of pictures of our first parents in paradise as given by Milton, and by " that odious thing Dryden," whose " very fine " verses she notwithstanding relishes very much ; with an Italian fan too, the breaking of which has utterly undone her, would atone for twenty times the space of rather duller stuff that follows.   Some people have been indignant with Swift's too Swiftian treatment of that eminent feminist Miss Mary Astell, otherwise " Madonella " ;

and there is no doubt that it was a subject rather for Addison than for the terrible Dean. But the thing, especially the trials of the brawny lover with his " Platonne," is not a little amusing; and the later letter on the education of girls gives much to think, especially to one who remembers that Swift's own favourites were far from " un-idea'd." One comes close again to modernity with the loquacious " kennel-maid " (though young ladies of good birth and education did not then advertise for that honourable position by name) and her dog-adoring mistress in the 121st *Tatler*; [1] while *Spectator* No. 67 gives the sensations of indignant spectators (in the other sense) of the Tango forestalments two hundred years ago. The indignant gentleman who protests that " your Tully and your discourses of another life are the very bane of mirth and good humour " (*Spectator*, 158), might have thought the other discourse much later (No. 509, on " Party Lying ") too serious, but it has a force and freshness which make it anything but obsolete at the present hour. It may be admitted that *The Guardian* has not much that is sportive. But in the next generation *The World* and *The Connoisseur* are full of amusing things for anybody save, as the Americans put it, a very " high-brow " reader.

On one great writer of these Essays, scarcely more than glanced at as yet, something special may be said.
Swift. It may well seem to be either an idle paradox or a wanton absurdity to speak of the " *Peace* of the Augustans " in connection with their greatest man, Jonathan Swift, the most hopeless misanthropist and almost the *miserrimus* of literary history. But wait

---

[1] The 131st, on the manufacture of the awful " wine " for which in the next generation Fielding expressly reserved the vulgarism " win*d*," records one of the very few indisputable benefits of " progress." Nobody now who has the sense to provide himself with sound wine, can experience the least difficulty in doing so ; and though " win*d*" is still procurable, our hotels do not invariably supply it, while regular wine-merchants almost all stick to the honourable tradition of ' Brook's and Hellier."

a little. Compare Swift's actual " works " (remembering, but not directly including anecdote and gossip)
with those of other hypochondriacs or whatever you
like to call them. Besides his actual misanthropy—
his actual *misozoia*—to coin a more accurate word if it
does not exist, Byron's is mere mountebank's mum-
mery ; Shelley's, though real, is faint and fitful ;
Leopardi's and James Thomson the Second's suggestive, not indeed of any affectation, but certainly of
the " stool to be melancholy upon "—of the fashions
of their respective times and of certain accidents of life
and fortune. Yet in Swift's actual works there is
never any moaning or raving ; there is as little of the
inky cloak and the skull in the hand as of the des-
perado's yellow boots and fist shaken at Heaven. It
is a commonplace that children, not mere infants,
The character read *Gulliver* without any sense, without
of his any suspicion of its being other than a
melancholy. " funny book." It is not a commonplace,
but it is true that it is perfectly possible for any critic
who is *vieux routier* to dismiss or skim over the under-
meaning and take the thing as no more than fairly
sharp satire. The same is the case with the earlier
Tale of a Tub ; and even in the tremendous lines
which Chesterfield has preserved for us, there is a
certain Olympian serenity rather than a Tartarian
gnashing of teeth. Except in purely jocular pieces of
the " Mrs. Harris " kind, Swift is always *quiet* ; and
though the association of quietness and peace is sometimes deceptive, there can be very little doubt that it
is in more than one sense real. Even when—as it is
here on one of its rare occasions—the eighteenth
century is passionate to an appalling degree, it carefully
avoids tearing that passion to tatters, and making all
Its pertinence split. No matter how different—as in the
to our theme. most noteworthy cases of Swift himself
and Cowper—the characters, tempers, beliefs, associations, tastes of the individuals may be, the differ-

entia of the century remains.[1] " Offending race
of human kind " and " The Castaway " may strike
a hasty judgment as poles asunder, and, looked at
from certain unstandardised points of view, they are.
But the great law of the century—the Law of Measure
—is on them both.   Contrast them with a third utterance of a third kind of despair—Shelley's " Lines
Written at Naples " or even " O World ! O Life !
O Time ! "—and you will see the difference at once.
Shelley himself is not boisterous or bombastic or insincere, but the quiet virility of scorn or of submission
is past.   There may be less gnashing of teeth—teeth
can be gnashed without showing them much or making
a noise—than in Swift, and the *guai* may be less deep
than Cowper's, but they are far *louder*.   The tragedy
in both of these last, especially in Swift, was " too deep
for noise or foam."

This fact, this presence, to use a great phrase of
the American poet Whitman's, of " the *accepted* hells
Illustrations. beneath," accounts largely for the way in
which, for actual greatness itself, Swift
surpasses every one in his century, the nearest to exceptions being Johnson, Blake, and perhaps Bishops
Berkeley and Butler.   But it only reinforces—it does
not in the least interfere with—his contribution to
the general effect of eighteenth-century writing, which
is now being dealt with.   It has been already repeated
that in *Gulliver's Travels* itself children see nothing
but an exceedingly amusing story, and, it has been
pointed out, not with quite so much banality, that it is
quite possible to read it as such, putting aside, but not
in the least forgetting or disregarding, its terrible
indictment against what Frederic the Great, who
certainly justified his own indictment of humanity,
called our *verdammte Race*.   One generally knows
Gulliver so early, and continues to read it in the earlier

[1] It is of course more obvious still in the middle case of Gray, whose melancholy
never approaches madness.

part of life so often, that it is apt to be neglected later ;
not from any weariness or disgust, but simply from
absolute familiarity—from what is called " knowing by
heart." But take it up at any period from seventeen
to seventy or thereabouts, dismiss (it is not difficult
for any practised student of literature) the familiarity,
read it as a new book, and what a marvel of pastime
you will find ! About Lilliput and Brobdingnag there
has been hardly any controversy ; and indeed among
people of any age, possessed of the most moderate
intelligence and even the slightest sense of the comic,
there could hardly be any. The narrative is unsur-
passably told ; the satire, though just, is, as Dryden
said of his own, " not *bloody* " in the least ; and the
unceasing sallies of humour which even such, in
different ways, hostile critics as Macaulay and Thackeray could not deny, and which the latter and greater
recognised enthusiastically, are as delectable, if not
more so, at the hundredth reading as at the first. The
remark on " that delicious wine *glimgrim* " (which had
such immediately useful but ultimately disastrous
consequences), " the Blefuscudians call it *flunec, but ours
is esteemed the better sort*," might serve as a text for half
a dozen different lectures on the wonderful and Protean
thing called Humour, as might that other in Brobdingnag: " At these times my little chair and table
were placed at his [the king's] left hand *before one of
the salt-cellars*." But to praise these parts, at least, of
Gulliver, is preaching to the converted, except in cases
of which one might say, without pertness, that the
unconverted are not worth preaching to.

The Third and Fourth parts have not been so
fortunate, and the third or Laputan division has been
Some objec-
tions can-
vassed as
regards
Gulliver. from the first accused of a fault which, if it
could be proved, would be fatal from our
point of view—that of dulness. No less a
man than Arbuthnot, Swift's close friend
and almost double in humoristic faculty, began this

cry, it would seem. But Arbuthnot was a man of science, and science is undoubtedly hit pretty hard in the account of the Flying Island and its less volatile dependencies. Moreover, the said Science, like its antetype and (as some tell us) dethroned predecessor Theology, does not easily forgive, and has greatly increased in position and hardened in temper since. Yet the reclamations, even of the acutest " scientists," have sometimes laid themselves open to pretty damaging " duplies." It would be difficult to name a man of more general intellectual acuteness than the late Professor de Morgan. Yet his objection to Swift's satire, that " triangles and rhomboids are measures of two dimensions only—plane figures with no thickness," is singularly obtuse. Swift of course only referred to the superficial *shape*; and nobody with a round of beef and a sharp cook's knife could have the slightest difficulty in serving up a triangular or rhomboidal steak, as thin as sandwich material or as thick as a " porter-house " or a " Chateaubriand," or even a " Garrick," nay, a lump as deeply "*three*-dimensioned " as the rump itself. Even if the island part of the matter is dwelt upon a little too long, it would be redeemed by the lighter touches of the " flappers," etc., and more than redeemed by that wonderful and terrible picture of the Struldbrugs of Luggnagg, in which Swift's Titanic genius shows itself at its greatest. The idea of the inconveniences of prolonged old age may be a mere commonplace, and the adoption of the old Tithonus myth not beyond the reach of ordinary talent; but the treatment, and especially the ruthless, quiet, inevitable contrast of Gulliver's not exactly foolish but thoughtless imaginings with the hideous truth—*this* is the work of the highest artistry and the highest genius only.

It has, as a matter of course, been exclaimed against as horribly misanthropic; and this charge has, of equal necessity, been repeated and vociferated, almost with screams, against the delineation of humanity at large in the Fourth Part—the Voyage to the Country of the Houyhnhnms. No doubt the Yahoos are not pleasant persons in whom to " meet ourselves," as Rossetti's phrase has it, and no doubt also Swift's indulgence here in exaggerated and superfluous nastiness (without which the thing could have been made not less but more effective, and which, as physic and psychology agree, may be justly as well as charitably assigned to the physical degeneration of a brain so magnificently gifted)—no doubt this is always disagreeable and sometimes disgusting. But when it is allowed for and neglected, will anybody who chooses to contemplate man as he is, put hand on heart and say that the picture—though one-sided, exaggerated, painted with foul colours, and so on—is *false ?* If he does, cynicism and Christianity will for once unite in a mocking or grave, " Thou fool ! " The Yahoo lurks in the Greek, behind and under his culture and his art and his philosophy ; the Yahoo shows himself almost unabashed and unconcealed in the brutal tyranny, the vulgar ostentation, and the graceless vice of Rome. He is to no small extent let loose in the chaos of the Dark Ages ; and, though somewhat tamed by Christianity and Chivalry, not absent from the Middle. He triumphs alike, though masked and muffled, in the frank paganism of the Renaissance and about the stakes and scaffolds and battle-fields of the Reformation. Although still further changed and clothed and made outwardly decent, he is seldom more loathsome than in the tamed mercantile ages that follow. Frederic the Great was a crowned and cultured Yahoo ; there have been others crowned likewise before and after him. The French Revolution was the Yahooism of the Demos broken loose : and at the present day it is difficult to say whether this Yahooism is most apparently concentrated in a Trade Union agitator or in a millionaire who gives

" freak " suppers. No ! the Yahoo man pure and simple, man as he is, has always not far from him ; something of the Yahoo, it may almost be said, he has always actually latent in him.[1]

Moreover, even in this uncomfortable and apocalyptic division of the book, a sane and acute mind cannot fail to perceive and enjoy the irresistible and victorious humour with which Swift seasons, sweetens, and almost carries off the whole appalling indictment. The conclusion has perhaps a little too much of pure burlesque about it ; and was fastened upon accordingly by the shallower and baser wit of Pope for verse-illustration. But the contrast of the virtues of the Houyhnhnms and the vices of the Yahoos, with the still subtler indication of human weaknesses among the horses themselves, could hardly be made more relishing ; and the touch where Gulliver, after surviving the pestilent and unwelcome preference shown towards him by a damsel of the accursed race, admits that she was not *quite* so hideous as the rest, is perhaps even superior to the more famous one, in which he gravely deprecates disbelief of the favour shown to him by his master, as an instance of *intus et in cute* satiric knowledge of human nature.

But if *Gulliver*, with all its terrific truth of satire and its disfigurements of unnecessary nastiness, is, for size and quality, the chief actual *divertisse-* **Other works.** *ment* among Swift's works, there is no lack elsewhere of rest and refreshment which, as such rest and refreshment seldom does, will afford as much satisfaction to the pure intellect as to the risible faculties. *A Tale of a Tub*, like its nearest analogue in English (and perhaps in literature) *Jonathan Wild*, has been usually more admired than enjoyed ; because in each case people as a rule will not give themselves the slight trouble necessary to perform,

---

[1] It may be permissible to say that this passage was written with no view to the present war. How that war has confirmed it need not be said.

in relation to the food of their minds, those separating and preparing offices which are necessary in the case of some bodily delicacies—oysters, walnuts, artichokes, and the like. It is certainly not in any sense a children's book as *Gulliver* is; though there are now and then towardly children (as its age would have said) who can enjoy it confusedly, and who will clear up their confusion afterwards. Its unbroken irony, which cannot, as is in the case often if not always in *Gulliver*, be neglected or mistaken if you are thoroughly to enjoy the book; its complicated satire, political, ecclesiastical and literary as well as general, all requiring no small knowledge of the history of the time; the want of any clear definite narrative, and, as it would seem in a good many cases though not in all, its uncomfortable suggestions about orthodoxy or unorthodoxy and the like, make it or have made it a tough and bitter morsel to many. But even here, to apply afresh Hazlitt's invaluable phrase about Spenser's allegory, these things will not bite you if you leave them alone, and will leave a considerable amount of pure pastime; while to any one who reads with eyes and hears with ears and possesses a mental swallow able to take in the whole draught, this, though more concentratedly bitter than any but a few parts of *Gulliver*, is marvellously refreshing. As for the *Tale's* little companion, *The Battle of the Books*, it is almost a pity that its unique inoffensiveness to all but dead victims has made it something of a school- and college-book; for that kind of usage, though it ought not to do so, is too frequently known to injure a book's chance of being read for reading's sake at the time and afterwards. Swift may have been unfair to individuals, and though not quite so ignorant as his patron Temple, he may not have known the true inwardness (or rather absence of inwardness) of the Ancient and Modern quarrel. But a lighter, livelier, more deftly thrown off piece of writing, literature has seldom had to boast of. Perhaps one of these few occasions, however, of even better grounded boasting was given by the (as a finished thing much later) *Polite Conversation*, of which even the fact of having edited it (a fearfully disillusionising process in many cases) cannot stale the perennial freshness and charm. One does not know where to look for its like, except piecemeal in the best and liveliest comedies of older and novels of more modern literature, while it brings comedy and novel together, and so facilitates the development of the latter in a fashion quite unique.[1]

The habit, bibliographically to some extent excusable, of joining with this masterpiece the *Directions to Servants* is in many ways very unfair to Swift. He never published these "Directions" himself; he spoke contemptuously of them, and though the piece was as long (or nearly so) on the stocks as the *Conversation*, it is quite clear that it was never in any sense finished. From the fact that we have a few serious as well as many ironic observations on the subject from him, it is not impossible that he meant to turn out a sort of "diptych," which might have been an excellent thing.[2] As it is the piece is nearly the dullest and quite the nastiest of Swift's productions, this nastiness being mere filth, unrelieved by any naughty *haut goût*.

[1] In looking over this passage I am not satisfied with it. But nothing can do justice to the *Conversation*—except the *Conversation* itself. One remains at the feet of Miss Notable; and is almost ashamed to babble about the idol. Her company require no worship; but they are infinitely enjoyable.

[2] It is or should be well known that the everlasting and Protean "servant problem" has seldom presented itself in an uglier phase than during the greater part of the eighteenth century. Slavery, with its disadvantages, and (let not the modern humanitarian and democrat shriek) its advantages, had long passed; but the intermediate times—when the "household" and the "family," implying a certain bond of unity, included all inmates—were past likewise. In all establishments of anything like the upper class servants were absurdly numerous and therefore idle and inefficient; usually ill-paid, and therefore thievish and (as regards visitors) predatory, ignorant, insolent, badly-trained, corrupt in every way. The stock Jeremys and Abigails of comedy are of course not to be taken too literally. But though Swift himself kept a tight hand on his own household when he was once established in Dublin, his repeated and complaining references to "Patrick" in the *Journal*, which are evidently trustworthy, show what an almost unmitigated nuisance domestics were.

Among the smaller published pieces the attractiveness (for all those whose taste can relish literary

The smaller amontillado, olives, caviare, etc.) of the
Tracts. *Argument against Abolishing Christianity* has
always been acknowledged ; but there has been more
difference about its much later pendant the *Modest
Proposal* for supplying the wants of Ireland by
the practice of babe-eating. Probably this is one of
the cases where critical discussion is more or less
useless, precisely because hardly one of the persons
who require conversion is in the least likely to attend
to it. That Swift did not really mean to recommend
a massacre of the innocents followed by a cannibal
feast, though perfectly true, could hardly be urged by
anybody capable of enjoying the *Proposal,* and would not
be listened to by any one whom it horrifies. That
child-eating itself was in his day a familiar " shave "
from the Civil War—when Lunsford and others (see
Scott's *Woodstock*) were accused of it, and when Lacy,
the actor and playwright, made it a feature of his
amusing farce *The Old Troop*—is again perfectly true ;
but it would again argue a most peculiar absence of
humour to urge it in defence. Here the parallel
instance of *Jonathan Wild* once more comes in, and so
does that of *Vanity Fair*, whose author, in one of his
uncritical moods, was among the loudest denouncers
of the *Proposal*. But these two, though the best known
and the most elaborately worked out, are by no means
alone among Swift's *opuscula* as giving rest and
refreshment—stimulant, tonic, and demulcent at once.
The *Enquiry into the Right of Precedence between Physi-
cians and Civilians* and the *Letter of Advice to a Young
Poet* are perhaps the choicest of the others, but they
could still be added to. And while a glance has been
made already at Swift's contributions to the *Tatler*
and other periodicals, nothing like justice has been
done by it to them. The political and other articles
which have earned him, in some estimates, a princi-

pality among journalists do not indeed come specially
to the front here; though there is plenty of amusing
stuff in them, especially the famous " Bills of Roman
Gratitude and British Ingratitude," with the material
of the latter drawn ironically from Marlborough's
places and pensions and perquisites.   But there is
plenty of humour, though of the less immaculate
Swiftian kind, in the non-political *Tatler* articles, and
much more in the famous pamphlet persecution of
Partridge, which is a sort of offshoot of the plan of
Steele's paper.

Yet all this, and even *Gulliver* itself, gives place,
as regards volume of delight, only occasionally and
The *Journal* indirectly confined to satire and ironic
to Stella—its humour, to the immortal, the unique, the
uniqueness
and sup- inexhaustible, and marvellous *Journal to
remacy.* Stella*.   Here, almost for the first time,
there is not the mere perfection of Art, though the
greatest artist could have done nothing finer; but a
spontaneous overflow of nature, only unconsciously
conditioned by the irrepressible artistic genius of the
writer.   When the *Journal* was written, there was no
great novel of the domestic and everyday kind yet in
the world.   Since it was written there have been many
such; but hardly has the greatest work of Fielding,
of Miss Austen, of Thackeray himself attained the
essence of novel representation better than this " True
History " has in being at the same time a story of
actual truth—the story of a life from day to day, and
an artistic presentation of incident and character, after
the fashion of which Aristotle was really thinking
when he spoke of poetry being " more philosophic "
than history.   No other book has this extraordinary
combination of qualities.   Pepys's *Diary* and Rousseau's *Confessions* come nearest, for Goethe's *Wahrheit
und Dichtung*, though a deliberate attempt to combine
the two, is, in some fair judgments at any rate, a failure.
Delightful as Pepys is, he is essentially *mean*; and there

is nothing of that curious artistry which has been noticed in Swift, while Swift is essentially *great*. Rousseau wants liveliness and variety ; his artistry is only too conscious, and the drenches of maundering *pose* and rancid sentimentality are, at least to some, far more disgusting than those excesses of Swift's, which from the nature of the case make very slight appearance in the *Journal*. People have often tried to imagine exactly how Swift's correspondents—the rather enigmatical Stella and that shadow of a shade " Mrs. Dingley "—took these wonderful things. It is more profitable to feel, and feel again, and never cease feeling how we take them ourselves. A slice (and no small one) of history at a most important date ; a sketch of manners at a time when manners were in a curious state of transition ; a miniature gazetteer and guidebook of London and its ways ; vivid personal sketches of permanently famous folk, and pervading it all the revelation of a wonderfully gifted, a still more wonderfully complicated character and soul :—all this and more is here lighted up with constant flashes of humour, pathos, love (the two latter things so idly denied by some to Swift), pride, jealousy, and what not; and the whole made not merely life-like, but actually *alive*—written not in ink but in blood, traced not on paper but on " the red-leaved tablets of the heart " and the pulsing tissue of the brain. I have sometimes thought that the *Journal*, long before others, *is* the first great novel, being at the same time a marvellous and absolutely genuine autobiography. The rest of the century was to develop the novel itself and to give no small examples of the autobiography in letter and journal, and so finally, after a fashion which we may hope to trace, to fill a huge gap in the pastime-giving power of literature. But it may be questioned whether it ever gave us again, or whether its successors have ever given us, anything so strange, so great, so true, and at the same time so recreative as this astonishing production.

In connection with it one must almost unavoidably say something, though it would be impertinent, in the present circumstances, to say much—about Swift's actual life. There is such interest in the special matter of his relations to Stella that continued discussion on this is not only excusable but inevitable ; yet it would be almost equally impertinent to deal very fully with it here. On one point, however, despite the abundance of scattered utterances on the famous final words, " Only a woman's hair," something is perhaps still permissible. It ought to be remembered, though it rarely has been, that our actual knowledge on the subject is forbiddingly limited. We have, practically speaking, no proved and authentic deliverance from Stella at all. We have, on the side of Swift, scarcely anything that is in the least indisputable, except the certainly genuine and altogether favourable testimony of the *Journal*.[1] Outside of this we have a wild and whirling cloud of anecdote which, to any one accustomed to literary sifting, yields hardly any satisfactory evidence. Even the great and terrible four last words are not absolutely authenticated ; though there is very little room for doubting their authenticity. On them by far the wisest thing ever written is contained in Sir Henry Craik's simple comment: " It is for each reader to read his own meaning into them." But that dictum, generally indisputable in itself, expressly leaves room for individual addition. The addition, made in all humility, but after a lifetime's study of life and literature, would be in the present writer's case as follows. We are all of us sometimes fools (this will hardly be denied by any one who is not always one). But if any person—no matter how little of a fool at other times or in other ways, no matter how rare his sojourn in the House of Folly may be—if any person has seen, sees, or till the Day of Judgment shall see in

[1] For the enemy might say that the *Character* was " written to be read." The *Journal* most assuredly was not.

those four words cynicism, brutality, anything but the expression of the riddle of the painful earth in one of its forms expressed more poignantly and finally than it has been expressed by any uninspired human being excepting Shakespeare—then it is safe, with no flippancy or triumph, but with all the gravity and sadness that the thoughts of Life and Death can inspire, to pronounce that person—at the point of time and in the actual expression of his thought—not a brute, not a cynic, not anything—but an utter and hopeless fool.

　　A few more general remarks on this mightiest if in a way most miserable of our company, may still be admissible. It may seem absurd to some, *Some general remarks on* almost impudent to others, strange to many, *Swift.* if not most, to treat Swift as what the French contemptuously call an *amuseur*, even while admitting that he is so much more. But, under pardon of all three classes, this would be a very great mistake. The " accepted hells beneath," already referred to, do not necessarily destroy the amenities of the pleasant meads above ; volcanic countries are not invariably deserts of ice or snow on the one hand, of sand and *scoriae* on the other. As in Johnson's case later, though in a different manner and degree, the special character of Augustanism shows itself in what we may call the cohabitation of gravity and gaiety. In Swift's case the gravity undoubtedly turns not seldom to actual grimness, if not to positive horror ; and the gaiety, by a sort of concatenation, to extravagant burlesque and even sheer nonsense. But this is only the strongest testimony to the virtue of that Augustanism itself, though of course we must add something or allow something for the extraordinary greatness of Swift's own genius. Never, except in Shakespeare, the eternal exception, has such lightness consisted with such strength, and—at least for English and modern readers—his equal is not to be found even in the mightiest members of what may be called his own

special group. They are not many : perhaps Aristophanes, Lucian, Rabelais, and Molière are the only
ones who can be admitted, for three mighty men of
our own, Butler, Fielding, and Thackeray, can hardly
challenge admission, not because, in the two latter
cases at any rate, of inadequate genius but for certain
differences in its administration ; and Voltaire falls out
because of the constant reminder in him that he is,
though immensely clever, a " low fellow." Now
Aristophanes and Molière both lose by their dramatic
form—a form itself inferior because more dependent
upon external assistance than pure prose or pure
verse ; while Aristophanes, however well one may
know Greek, however intensely one may enjoy his
unsurpassed wit, suffers also from the hopeless gulf
traversable by no acrobatics, or aerobatics (his own
prophetic word), of archæological study, or scholastic
imagination, which interposes itself between his world
and ours. It is not from the present writer that any
one may expect dispraise of Rabelais ; but the cloudy
pillar of grotesque and jargon and what not wherein he
certainly shrouded, whether he did or did not deliberately " shelter " himself, undoubtedly mars his amusement for the general. Lucian is left, and certainly the
delight of amusement in Lucian is abundant and
intense. But he shares to some extent the drawback
of remoteness which has been noted in Aristophanes ;
and he has—what certainly cannot be predicated of
any of the others—the defect of being insufficiently
in earnest at any time.[1] Now, though it may be called
a paradox, and is certainly a neglected truth, some
earnestness is required even in fooling. By this time,
therefore, the initial apology has, it is hoped, been made
good, if not even made unnecessary. Indeed a step
in advance may be taken, and Swift may be claimed as
a whole—work and man—as one of the greatest, one of

---

[1] Except when he wrote—*if* he wrote—the great epigram on the folly of what
seems wise to men.

D

the completest, sources of interest—which of itself means, if not always rest, always refreshment—in the whole range of literature. His actual work would—supposing that we knew nothing of the man at all but only a little about the public circumstances in which he wrote—supply an immensely wide and varied range of such interest, ranging in character and quality from mere amusement to the " stronger pleasure " of intense critical appreciation. But the least curious of readers about personality, the most sluggish in hunting for biographic or autobiographic detail, can hardly refuse to acknowledge that, in Swift's case, the nature of the man does add enormously to the interest of the work. The vast amount of talk over this nature and the light thrown on it by internal evidence and external gossip, have, it has been admitted, to adopt a fine phrase of Tennyson's, not touching Swift, " made his memory confused," and it remains to a certain extent, though rather in detail than in gross, mysterious. But this very mystery is a bait to many, and can hardly be denied to be a seasoning even to the most austere. And, setting it aside, Swift's remains perhaps the most interesting study of literary character that we have. We know, as in hardly any other case, that the *Journal* and those *Letters* which have only now become accessible in a complete and orderly collection, were written with as absolute a presence of sincerity, and as absolute an absence of preparation for the public eye as those of Pope were written with the absence of the first and the presence of the second. And the wonderful and unconscious autopsy is further illumined by the work, which it illuminates in turn. To compare once more, but from a new standpoint, the knowledge which we thus possess of Swift, to the deliberately and almost ostentatiously " faked " presentment of Goethe would be absurd; but there has sometimes been a tendency to bring, of course in all cases with some admission of the differences, Swift and Rousseau into comparison, not merely in reference, such as that above, to their position as quasi-novelists. That Rousseau was not such a conscious histrion as Goethe may be granted; the famous *Paradoxe* of his sometime friend and never willing enemy Diderot might be applied curiously here. But in Swift there is absolutely nothing histrionic, strange as it may seem in such a master of irony and allegory and other forms of simulation. There was a *saeva veritas* or *veracitas* (with apologies for an unclassical form) about him as well as a *saeva indignatio*; and the former was probably as great a source of self-torture as the latter, which, indeed, it caused. Although he had some of the highest qualities necessary to the dramatist—as is shown by the admirable dialogue of the *Conversation*, and the equally admirable adjustment in value of situation, and to some extent character, in *Gulliver*—the central dramatic faculty—that of detachment from his subject—was entirely wanting in him; and fortunately so for us, if not for himself. He is at once presenter and thing presented; nay more, operator and subject, a vivisector of himself, and of humanity through himself. Retranslating into seriousness Mr. Lang's immortal parody of Emersonian transcendentalism:

> I am the ball, the bat,
> The umpire, the pavilion cat,

etc., one might apply it to Swift's operations. But these operations have the redeeming character of tragedy itself—they purge, strengthen, nay! render delightful by their pity and terror; they excite not seldom the pure comedy, not seldom the farce, the satiric drama, the entire range of the human theatre which they exhibit. The hackneyed but true saying of Swift's nearest analogue, not merely in English but in any literature—Carlyle—about every man's life being interesting if it were fully and rightly told, applies to Swift himself in the immensely raised pro-

portion of his greatness as compared with " any man."
From the supposed savagery of the *Modest Proposal*
to the infinite tenderness of the " little language "
and the laments over Mrs. Anne Long and John
Harrison ; from the profound and bitter satire of the
Tale and of parts of *Gulliver* to other parts of the latter
and not a few things done in pure though passing
gaiety ; from the relentless logic of the political dia-
tribes (one is perhaps never so near taking an unfavourable view of Johnson as in regard to these, where
his own hopeless inferiority in the very line makes his
general unfairness to Swift more signal and more
offensive) to the sheer nonsense of much prose and
more verse ; over and in all this immense range Swift
always manages to satisfy the reader in one sense, to
keep him unsatiated in another, and so still full of
intellectual appetite and artistic curiosity. Addison's
pleasant but slightly " small-beerish " manner might,
for any but strictly literary purposes, tire soon. Voltaire's unceasing and little-minded persiflage actually
does so ; so even Pope's overpolished and shallow
epigram. But Swift never wearies, for as Bossuet
said of human passion generally, there is in this greatest
master of one of its most terrible forms *quelque chose
d'infini*, and the refreshment which he offers varies
unceasingly from the lightest froth of pure nonsense,
through beverages middle and stronger, to the most
drastic restoratives—the very strychnine and capsicum
of irony.[1]

[1] Nothing, it will perhaps have been noticed, has been said above of the *Drapier's
Letters* or of the disputed *Four Last Years of Queen Anne*. But the earlier part of
the *Drapier* is almost as amusing as it is deadly ; and there are touches in the *Four
Last Years* which certainly do not help those who would deny its genuineness on the
score of the want of them. The *Drapier* partly and the *Last Years* wholly were
intentionally serious and evidently written with the most elaborate care of solid detail.
They still bear unmistakable marks of Swift's humour : but elaborate and continued
jocularity, even of the purely or mainly sarcastic kind, would have been out of
place in them, and Swift knew what was in and what was out of place as exactly
as any writer of the world. This knowledge, and the honey that tempered his
" savage "-ness are, by the way, both excellently shown in that charming correspondence, which in absence of positive acquaintance, served as a speaking-tube between
him and the Duchess of Queensberry (" Kitty "), which has perhaps never been

As, according to the plan of this volume displayed in the Contents, poetry for the most part and fiction, except in such imperfect approaches to it as the Coverley Papers and the *Polite Conversation*, are excluded from this first chapter, it may be thought strange that nothing has yet been said of what the age itself would certainly have cited as the most definitely amusing part of its literature, the Drama. But the postponement itself was neither oblivious nor in any other way accidental.

Plays, and the reading as well as the hearing and seeing of them, undoubtedly formed a large—in fact by far the largest—part of such literary pastime as existed. Indeed, seeing that theatres, at least in the provinces, were, except in their "barn" substitutes, neither numerous nor accessible, the reading of plays in the latest seventeenth and till very late in the eighteenth century, held a perhaps relatively more important position than it ever had done before or ever has done since. For a time indeed miscellaneous reading, as distinguished from that of scholars, may be said to have consisted almost wholly of plays for light and sermons for serious uses. It may be doubted, however, whether even the most theatrically given of modern readers finds eighteenth-century drama, except in a few well-known instances, or for adaptation of it to modern use, very interesting reading, while to persons not so minded its peculiarities are even less succulent. It is true that most of Farquhar's and some of Vanbrugh's pieces bear dates from 1700 onward ; but even they do not go much if at all beyond the first decade; and Congreve, as has been said, was wholly silent.

Early plays.

It is probably not necessary to enter here at any great length into the endlessly vexed and not soon, if ever, likely to be settled quality and effect of that

---

praised enough and which has sometimes been dispraised most astonishingly. But few, alas! understand the great, the beneficent, the much abused art of flirtation "in all its branches"—as inn-advertisers used to say of posting in the good days before motors.

famous onslaught on contemporary drama which
Jeremy Collier had made three years before the century
began.   In fact, whether " the parson," as Dryden
calls him in his more than half confessing reply, was
right or wrong, hardly concerns us at all.   It is more
to the point to observe that, for a very long time—as
late as Fielding's contributions to the drama at any
rate—the prudery which is supposed to have succeeded Restoration license was a very odd kind of
prudery.   And from an impartial reading of the plays,
comic and tragic, of the first half of the century, one
feels inclined to say, with some assurance, that if they
had been as coarse as that *Custom of the Country* which
Dryden, not too ingenuously, fished out of " the last
age " to defend his sins ; or as impudent as his own
Limberham or Vanbrugh's *Relapse*, they would not have
been any more refreshing.   There have of course not
been many times at which tragedy has been a source
of refreshment at all ; though when it is, " the hidden
well-water is not so delicate to drink " nor the wine of
the gods themselves more stimulating and inspiring.
But the eighteenth century, as in a reasoned panegyric
we may well allow, does not deal in such water or
such wine.   The water of its tragedy, from the Racinian
travesties of Smith and Philips to the blood-and-thunder
absurdities of the author of *The Monk* and the boarding-
school rhetoric of Home and Hannah More, through
Young's *Revenge* and Thomson's *Sophonisba* and Johnson's *Irene* and all the rest, is ditch-water, and the
wine is, as the time itself said, " stummed."   We may
simply sink this great department or compartment
altogether here.   Comedy and miscellaneous drama
should have fared, and after a time did fare, better.
Of the elements of this kind of play, furnished by a
busy, lively, varied society, it had plenty ; of the
artists necessary for dealing with those elements it
might seem, even at the beginning, in Swift and Addison and Steele to have had an ample supply, while

tradition does not seem to be extravagant in depicting
it as a true golden age of the *acting* profession in
England. But the rather subterranean and almost
uncanny agencies which determine literary history
diverted the chiefs from the subject. Swift wrote no
drama at all, though the dramatic possibilities in the
Polite Conversation have been recognised as more than
" good gifts." The comic part of Addison's opera
Rosamund, which has sometimes been rather injuriously
spoken of, is excellent and now and then has really
Gilbertian touches ; but his *Drummer* (as to the authorship whereof there was some idle bickering between
Steele and Tickell) has been apologised for by Macaulay
in that ingenious but overdone panegyric which in the
long run has done Addison more harm than good. It
is, in fact, a dull thing, and impartial admirers of the
shade which still hovers over and gives its name to
one of the loveliest walks in England, still rather hope
that it is not his.

With Steele it is different. His more irregular
and undisciplined but sometimes personally finer gifts
Steele. included a distinct dramatic faculty ; and his
rather intermittent efforts to be on " the side
of the angels " were not at variance with the reform
which to some extent followed, if it was not actually
caused by, Collier's really magnificent tilt at the
brilliant sons of Belial, who had previously held
command of the stage. His work is not free from
that somewhat liberal " taking one's property where
one finds it " which the stage permits, and which results
in various degrees of " new and original " work, from
those shown by Shakespeare and Molière to that
which Mr. Crummles exacted from Nicholas Nickleby.
But his early attempts at what is called sentimental
comedy, and his occasional brilliancy in other ways,
give his work a claim to rather more detailed treatment
than has been accorded here to Addison's.

Steele's plays ought to be read by the student of

literary history, for he is something of an origin, not merely starting sentimental and *bourgeois* comedy— a doubtful but to some tastes possible benefit—but being also largely responsible in the latter for that strange, unreal, theatrical jargon which vitiates almost all eighteenth-century drama, and which persisted, despite the equally persistent ridicule of critics, far into the nineteenth, if indeed it has ever ceased. The style of the " Heroic " plays, though softened a little by Young and others, had set the example of bombast. Steele took this, which indeed his subjects did not invite, as it stood, and added or substituted the fustian, stilted, claptrap, moralising and sentimentalising which has had itself metaphored once for all in the term " sawdust." The few funny things usually quoted— the undertaker's complaint in *The Funeral* that the higher wages he gives his men the more difficult they seem to find it to assume the proper melancholy of the mute ; the jangling of Humphy Gubbin and Biddy Tipkin in *The Tender Husband*, and the flirtation of Phillis and Tom in *The Conscious Lovers*—are good. But the conscientious person who seeks them in the originals will seek in vain for many—perhaps for any— others of the same quality. *The Funeral* itself is one of the dullest of farce-comedies ; *The Lying Lover* (one of the numerous spoilings of *Le Menteur*) disgusted its own time by the preachments which are its most original part ; *The Tender Husband*, though free from the " improprieties " of Congreve and Vanbrugh, has a central situation [1] perhaps more really disgusting than even Wycherley, or Congreve himself in *The Old Bachelor*, ever ventured on. *The Conscious Lovers*, based on the *Andria*, was the most successful of all ; but it must have been due to the above mentioned Phillis and Tom, the superior characters being " sticks " and the plot and situations improbable to a

[1] The "tenderness" consists in employing his mistress, dressed as a man, to lay siege to his wife and get compromising letters and interviews from and with her.

degree. It is also quite worth mentioning that some
of the best things, such as those above mentioned, are
repeated by the author from or in his *Tatler* and other
papers. In fact Steele is scarcely a third-rate dramatist though he is in his fashion a first-rate essayist ;
and it is difficult to be certain whether he would have
long meddled with the stage if he had not, as a political
reward, got shares in theatrical patents, and had for
his partners, and actors in his plays, persons like Booth,
Wilks, Cibber, and others who possessed the best
stage-craft of the time.

As to Steele's chief dramatic contemporaries, Mrs.
Centlivre and Colley Cibber, things are much the
same but rather worse. There are amusing
Mrs. Cent- things in Susannah and in Colley, but the
livre, Cibber, person who hunts " the real Simon Pure "
etc. up to find his context and surroundings will not find
his pains much rewarded ; and anybody who can enjoy
Tartuffe may be advised *not* to read *The Nonjuror*. Of
course the historian of literature and the student of
drama must read them, and they are not quite the
worst things that he has to read. But there is little
rest or refreshment to be found in them. The quality
exists in Cibber's *Autobiography* no doubt ; but hardly
in his plays. Even *Love's Last Shift*, one of the
earliest, the freshest, and perhaps the best, is chiefly
worth reading because it produced *The Relapse*. In
fact, nothing but exceptional genius could have made
the comedy of this particular time amusing. It was
the dregs of the " artificial " comedy of Congreve and
his fellows, entirely lacking their brilliant wit, ham-
pered by restriction of their choice of means, eking out
the writers' want of originality with endless borrowings
or stealings from old drama, foreign drama, any
second, third, or tenth-hand stuff it could lay hands on.
" Successes of occasion " like *The Beggars' Opera* do
not redeem the general dulness and disarray, but rather
throw a damaging light on them ; and curiosities of

ineptitude, like " the other [1] Samuel Johnson's " *Hurlo-thrumbo* and Lord Grimston's *Love in a Hollow Tree*, are not so much exceptions in the other direction as slightly exaggerated examples of the weakness of the whole department.

[1] The "other" in the contemporary sense. It must not be forgotten that there had been a third (or rather a first) bearer of the two names in literature—the virulent Whig parson, whom Dryden pilloried as "Ben Jochanau" some years before the actual pillory received him "flagrant from the scourge," and whom Dryden's editor Christie ineffectively tried to whitewash, after Macaulay had, more wisely, apologised for his "intemperance, intolerance," etc. But he died before the holder of the name *par excellence* was born. The *Hurlothrumbo* man, who lived to within little more than a decade of the doctor's death, was by profession a dancing-master and in literature a mere zany; but he obtained some popularity.

CHAPTER II

ALEXANDER POPE AND HIS KINGDOM

(*With a digression on " Grub Street "*)

THERE is a tendency which, being human, is like most human things not unpardonable, but like many human _{Some} things rather irritating—to try to make _{positions on} out that everything is something else. In _{Pope.} illustration of this a rather well-known Frenchman once wrote a book, not without merit, on *Le Romantisme des classiques* ; and, to append small things to great in the old manner, a distinguished American once endeavoured, good-humouredly enough, to prove " Rymerism " in the present humble writer, who had declared his adhesion to Macaulay's dictum that Rymer was the worst critic who ever lived. To rise again to the great, it is notorious that the character of Pope—not so much his personal character, for that is now pretty well beyond dispute, as the character of his poetry—has always been a favourite subject for wrangling and paradox and self-contradictions. In his own day his superiors, such as Swift, and his equals, whether jealous or not, such as Addison, had no doubt about his greatness, while the very " Grub Street " vermin, whom he foolishly provoked and persecuted, evidently regarded him with almost as much envy and secret admiration as hatred. The long and fitful battle on the " Is Pope a poet ? " question was at nearly all its revivals a battle of feints, paradoxes, and topsy-

43

turvifications ; not a few of his assailants or " discounters," such as Warton, make observations and reservations which would rather astonish those who take them, unread, as wholly on the Romantic side ; more than one of his defenders, such as Byron, adopt lines of defence which admit of dangerous flank attack ; and as has been already indicated, his latest partisans have continued the process by ringing changes on the ambiguities of words like " nature," " wit," and the like. In such a case it is perhaps best to state frankly the views of the present writer. It seems to him :

I. That to deny poetry to Pope is absurd.

II. That any one who denies him something like a chief if not the chief place in his own division of poets, unquestionable as such, will have his work cut out to make the denial good.

III. That Joseph Warton was perfectly right in his main position—that Pope was not *transcendently* a poet: though Warton frequently blundered and faltered in maintaining this.

Those who *simpliciter* deny poetry to Pope must needs deny, as a major, the definition or description of Was Pope a poetry elsewhere given ; and it is a fallacy to poet ? reply that this position ought to be generally established first. For, as Dante says, startlingly to some but with incontestable truth, " the business of science is not to prove but to explain its subject " ; or, in other words, the axioms and postulates with which we start it are not its problems or theorems. Now that Pope displayed at least two of the qualifications to be laid down as necessary for the poet—vivid expression of his actual subjects and artistic use of such metre as he actually employed—is simply undeniable. To urge that there are large ranges of subject which he perhaps could not, and certainly did not treat ; and that there was only a limited region of metre in which he was at home, would at best be legitimate in reference to the third position—his claim to poetical transcendency.   It is practically "out of order" and irrelevant as regards the first and second. Moreover, his extraordinary felicity of expression, and his wonderful command of such metre as was congenial to him, appear to have been, according to the hackneyed phrase of poets, not merely congenial but congenital.   Since he was not "the least liar" (as all poets are, according to the other tag) but the most lying of all poets and persons, we cannot accept absolutely the dates which he gives us of his precocities. But we certainly have no remains of what the elder Mr. Pope may have censured as "bad rhymes," and there is no doubt that some which must have been early are astonishingly good.   It was as if Pope had been served heir by Providence to Dryden; and had entered upon his inheritance and begun to improve it in certain directions almost before Dryden died.

To part, and what some may think (to use an ever-lastingly treacherous word) the "greatest" part, of the inheritance he did not indeed succeed.   He could not forge and wield the Olympian thunderbolt of Dryden's couplet; even had he been able to do so he could not have charged it with the massive strength of Dryden's sense.   But he might possibly claim the Apollonian darts, though it is to be feared that they could deserve the epithet of "mild" only in the hypereuphemistic sense of the Greek itself; for they were never very kindly, and were frequently poisoned.   His processes of refinement of form are extremely simple, though idle partisanship, or the mere desire to be different, has sometimes denied this.   In practice he never quite abandoned the license of Alexandrine and triplet, but he reduced it more and more; he emphasised, to the point of making a sort of continuous crease down the page,[1] the importance

Pope and Dryden.

---

[1] This is the chief point where maladroit partisanship has tried to deny what is obvious to any one with an eye and almost still more obvious to any one who has

of the central pause; he redoubled the antithesis between verbs, adjectives, substantives in the two halves of the same line; he increased the separation of the couplets; he toned off the final rhymes to as light a character as possible; and indulged very seldom in " wrenched accent " (trochees for iambs) or in tri-syllabic feet. These are the simple, almost the sole rules for the construction of the " fiddle." That the " rosin "—the application of which allows the thing in all but a few cases to escape the monotony whereunto in other hands it usually fell—is more of a secret is true; but it also is not quite undiscoverable or unanalysable.

This secret is, indeed, a sort of *secret de Polichinelle*— a position which hardly anybody has denied, though it cannot be said that everybody has exactly apprehended it. It lies in the fact that Pope, with a consummate command of one form of poetical, that is to say metrical, expression, had an even more consummate command of the manners of diction and phrase which are suited to that form; and a third faculty—less real but almost more specious than either of the others—of presenting thought—or the appearance of thought—which was once more exactly suitable to the words, and the verse, and the actual material subject. In this last point his extreme superficiality has long been more or less admitted, except by an Old Guard of partisans whose small stronghold of prejudice is perhaps impregnable, but can be simply left alone, as it has " no military importance." He practically never thinks for himself or sees for himself, while, except in some touches of personal affection and many more of personal resent-ment and spite, he scarcely ever feels for himself. It is always what somebody else has thought, the *communis sensus* of some particular nation, ancient or modern,

Pope's originality.

---

an ear. It is of course most glaring in *The Rape of the Lock*, where Pope was no doubt consciously burlesquing, to some extent, the very methods he used : but it is quite unmistakable elsewhere.

or it may be both, that Pope expresses so well, with
such admirable " wit " in the various meanings which
he himself attaches to the word. It has been recognised a hundred times that the famous couplet, the
component parts of which have just been woven into
prose, exactly describes him on the best side of his
stuff. There is of course a side not so good. Lady
Mary was perfectly right as to fact when she told how
her original admiration of the *Essay on Criticism* ceased
when she found it was all stolen from the ancients ;
except that, if she had herself known a little more, she
might have perceived that most of it was stolen or
borrowed at second-hand. Warburton knew perfectly
well what he was doing when he plastered and varnished
and buttressed with comment and exposition Pope's
well meant, admirably expressed, but sometimes almost
nonsensical and still more often platitudinous attempts
to build a mansion of Bolingbroke's half-baked bricks
and his own untempered mortar in the *Essay on Man.*
The amiable endeavours to discover in *The Dunciad* a
generous defence of good literature against those who
disgraced it become distressingly inapposite, when
one remembers that there is practically in the whole
book, whether as originally constructed or as recast
later, nothing, till you come to the fine but utterly
disconnected close, except personal and sometimes far
from honest caricatures of individual writers obnoxious
to the poet, some of them quite harmless, most quite
insignificant, and hardly any, except Curll, in any way
a " disgrace to literature." There *is* something first-
hand in that strange *Elegy on an Unfortunate Lady,*
which is the one mystery still remaining after generations of unremitting and generally damaging investigations.[1] But elsewhere, with the possible exception of
The Rape of the Lock, in the comic, to serve as pendant
to the *Elegy* in the tragic vein, the whole of Pope's

---

[1] There are some to whom this singular piece is Pope's strongest atonement
both as poet and man, for his faults as both.

work may be called translation, and not merely the
Statius, the *Homer*, and the other confessed instances.
It is always, and not merely when he has a book before
him, that he seems to be working from some brief,
carefully and extensively drawn up for him by a clever
" devil," chipping into final form a statue blocked out
by an intelligent, but himself not very original " ghost."
Carlyle, harshly but not perhaps unjustly, declared
that there was not one great thought in all the hundred
volumes of Voltaire. It would be scarcely rash to
say that there is not an original thought, sentiment,
image, or example of any of the other categories of
poetic substance to be found in the half a hundred
thousand verses of Pope. But even here the triumphant *sense* of the century saved him from mere silliness
always, and nearly (not quite) always from mere
galimatias ; while his quintessential possession of its
own peculiar form of wit infused something into the
very matter of the thought or subject which, till you
examine it rather carefully, may look like originality.

But if not wholly, yet still to some extent to be
separated from this " stuff and substance " of wit, as
well as (with the same proviso) from the,
in its own way, unrivalled supremacy of
versification above admitted, there remains—
and for our purpose remains as of supreme importance
—that wonderful faculty of mere expression, of command over diction and phrase, which has been all but
universally allowed him. His limits, even in this way,
may not be very wide ; he never delves beneath the
surface for hidden wealth of suggestion or soars into
the ether for unexpected flights of it. But, in his own
way and under his own conditions, it is almost impossible for him to make a mistake, or if he has made one
at first (the " Atticus " is a specimen) not to correct
it. The thought may be trifling, obvious, at times
rather base ; the sentiment may be plainly insincere ;
the very wit, when you roll it over a little on your mind's

The absolute-
ness of his
expression.

tongue, may be slightly vapid ; the very verse, if you go on too long with it, may impress you with a sense of monotonous mannerism. There are often bad rhymes (not including those affected by change of pronunciation) to disgust one sort of taste ; there is only too frequently bad blood to disgust another. But, with the rarest exception, the phrasing is triumphant, and those who can once perceive and submit themselves to its supremacy never rebel. One opens, absolutely at random, the *Poems*, and comes upon the following, not by any means one of Pope's " purplest " passages :

> Oh, when shall Britain, conscious of her claim,
> Stand emulous of Greek and Roman fame ?
> In living medals see her wars enrolled,
> And vanquished realms supply recording gold ?
> Here, rising bold, the patriot's honest face ;
> There, warriors frowning in historic brass :
> Then future ages with delight shall see
> How Plato's, Bacon's, Newton's looks agree ;
> Or, in fair series, laurelled bards be shown,
> A Virgil there, and here an Addison.
> Then shall thy Craggs—and let me call him mine—
> On the cast ore, another Pollio, shine ;
> With aspect open shall erect his head,
> And round the orb in lasting notes be read,
> "Statesman, yet friend to Truth ! of soul sincere,
> In action faithful, and in honour clear ;
> Who broke no promise, served no private end,
> Who gained no title, and who lost no friend ;
> Ennobled by himself, by all approved,
> And praised, unenvied, by the Muse he loved."

We do not nowadays like the rhyme of " face " and " brass " ; we are by no means avid of a series of medals recording Chancellors of the Exchequer or Secretaries to the Treasury, or philosophers or poets, or even generals and admirals ; we know that while Pollio was apparently as much of a gentleman as a Roman could be and a man of irreproachable character, Craggs was a *parvenu*, a scoundrel, and the son of a scoundrel ; we know also that, while the whole piece

from which the extract is taken was a puff introductory
to Addison's *Dialogue on Medals*, friendship between
Pope and Addison was already on very dubious terms,
even if it had not entirely broken down, and that the
legend for the promised medal is either a very careless
or (which is much more like Pope) a slyly intentional
flout to a protest in the very book against "legends"
in verse, and legends which, as this certainly would,
cover the whole side of the medal itself.   Yet all this
and some other things—there is possibly a covert blow
at Addison himself in the very last line ; the frowning
warriors rather make us smile and so forth—do not
interfere with the masterly and delightful craftsmanship
in words of the whole piece, and especially of the concluding lines just noted.[1]   The clearness without
meanness, the rhetoric without bombast, the apt variety
of not quite synonymous terms in "historic" and
"recording," the easy procession of the phraseology,
which never "brings you up" with anything strange
and yet never lets the familiarity of its words down
to the vulgar, the cunning climax of arrangement—all
these have a perennial attraction.   A person whose
sense of this kind of art has been ever so little cultivated no more tires of such a specimen of it (though
it is, as has been said, by no means of the very first
class of its author's work), than he does of a picture or a
piece of music.   Whereas, on the other hand, a person
who exclaims, "You admire *this*, when such things
exist as Prospero's speech after the masque and the
close of 'To Constantia Singing'?" needs no answer
except a silent surprise and sorrow at his obtuseness.

And of such passages there are literally hundreds
in Pope—in fact it is very rare to find a page, especially
Earliness and in the mature works, without one, and not
persistence of at all uncommon to find whole pages of the
this *A per se.* same or a superior quality.   People ignorant
of Homer in the original can, I believe, find them

[1] Afterwards actually separated as an epitaph for Craggs.

even in Pope's *Homer*, though to those who do know the Greek the constant fretting induced by the inaccuracy and inadequacy of the translation makes it readable only as a most unpleasant task. Elsewhere the gift is ubiquitous, except perhaps in the *Pastorals*, where it is not entirely absent. Even the early poems have not a little of it ; however well a reader may be acquainted with the originals of the *Essay on Criticism*, and however clearly he may perceive Pope's real ignorance or very limited knowledge of the matter, it can be enjoyed, since there is no original *form*, as in Homer's case, to dash the pleasure by comparison. The *Rape of the Lock*, especially in its first shape, but without any prejudice to the second, has radiated rest and refreshment, without losing a particle of its virtue, during its own long life and during the shorter ones of its successive readers ; the *Satires* and the *Epistles* and the *Dunciad*, and even the *Essay on Man* and the rest down to the delightful " Person of Quality " follow suit unfailingly. None of the constantly accruing evidences of Pope's rascality as a man affects this pleasure in the very least—in fact some of the proofs which are most damning morally positively increase one's æsthetic delight in the Puckish art with which he excised, vamped, and transformed prose (and even verse whenever, which was not so often, it was safe) to suit his new friendships or his new spites. Perhaps—Voltaire is certainly a companion example— there is a natural connection between the two kinds of this dexterity of fingering—that of the artist in words and that of the pickpocket or the forger. But this does not matter. The æsthetic delight remains ; and though it may be a sad fact to the moralist, it is a certain one for the student of life and literature that, even with the power of enjoying both, you may tire of far " greater " poets than Pope before you tire of him, and that you may revisit him more frequently and with far more confidence than you can revisit them.

Even yet enough may not have been said on him. Hackneyed as *The Messiah* is, and obvious as it is at Some minors. once that without Isaiah and Virgil Pope's *The Messiah.* page would be simply a blank, it is a not easily tiring or tired-of diversion to see with what gusto he sets about the work of refashioning his borrowed matter, clothing it with his own version of his greater and lesser originals' thoughts, and displaying throughout a perfect triumph of *technique*. Johnson was not merely, as he often was, prejudiced but definitely unjust (which he was seldom) and ungrateful (which he was more rarely still) in belittling the poem. For even while putting it above the *Pollio*, he ascribed *all* the merit of the improvement to the borrowings from a poet so incomparably greater than either Virgil or Pope himself as Isaiah. Pope's manner is only like that of the Roman with a very considerable difference, but it is poles asunder from that of the Hebrew. His own style of diction might easily be expected to seem hard and cold beside the delicate and almost effeminate art of Virgil, tawdry and frigid beside the splendour, the magnificence, the actually divine sublimity of Isaiah. But experience and practice tell us that though difference may sometimes imply inferiority, it never necessarily implies badness ; and then we perceive what a triumph in its own line and way *The Messiah* is—in the skilful motion of its climax, the just selection and keeping, the completeness and adequacy of the whole thing. If, once more, you confine yourself to the feeble and puerile, " I don't like this : I want something else," the piece may rank low with you ; if you ask the one question of criticism, " Has the man done what he wanted to do, and done it well ? " you cannot refuse the answer, " *Optime !* "

On the other hand there are some who—despite *Windsor* Wordsworth's vouchsafing an, it is true, *Forest,* etc. not very cordial exception from condemnation—do not find much refreshment in *Windsor*

Forest; and the "St. Cecilia" piece affords others or the same an interesting critical *lemma* in the question, "Why does Pope, who had succeeded not ill in competition with men so different from himself as Virgil and Isaiah, fail so grossly in one with a prophet and master of his own?" But there is no need of more detailed criticism. A delightful writer and true poet of our own day, himself the modern laureate of the eighteenth century, has, adopting the lesser Alexander's own phrase, declared that—

> [He] throw[s] for wit, and poetry, and Pope.

For Pope, as an exponent of wit *in* poetry, we all may throw caps and money, votes and voices. Nor is that wit of the noisy or flashy order which sooner or later tires. The salt of *mere* wit is resalted with common sense; and that again with a certain purely intellectual quality difficult positively to define, for, as granted above, it is lacking in depth, in height, in originality, in several other good things, but easy to perceive and not evanescent. And so, though he enjoyed little rest or refreshment himself, he has provided much for others.

I do not know whether the haughty and delicate souls who in opposition to Mr. Dobson, declare eighteenth-century poetry "unreadable," make any exceptions, even for Pope himself; in the nearly complete ignorance which, it is to be feared, accompanies their haughtiness and their delicacy, they seem only too likely not to make any for others. Yet how much are they to be pitied if they do not know Prior, especially with the recently recovered fragments of which the most charming but not the only charming one is on that "Jinny the Just," who—

Prior—the newly recovered pieces.

> Read, and accounted, and paid, and abated;
> Eat and drank, played and worked, laughed and cried, loved and hated,
> As answered the end of her being created.

But these additions, for which we wiser folk so much thank Longleat and the Marquis of Bath, Cambridge and Mr. Waller, are only a sort of "rere-supper," a corollary to an abundant previous entertainment.[1] That the great comic poets have almost if not quite as much idiosyncrasy in their comedy as the great tragic or serious poets in their other kinds, is a fact not much likely to be disputed, though it is sometimes left unrecognised; and there is hardly one who has more of it than Prior. With the eternal and almost unnecessary exception of Shakespeare, Prior is about the first to bring out that true English humour which involves sentiment and romance, which laughs gently at its own tears, and has more than half a tear for its own laughter. One might not have thought the lover of Cloe (unless, which is not impossible, Cloe's anecdotographers have maligned her) and the frequenter of pot-shops likely to be troubled with "fine fancies," and certainly he does not force them on us. But how airily they flit, and how delicate and varicoloured they are, from the early and gay celebration of the little Dutch chaise with its contents, literary and other, to those epitaphs which are assuredly neither morbid nor cynical merely! Prior himself may have written none too happily of Solomon, but he had at least one right to write; for no one, except Thackeray. has ever entered more thoroughly into the spirit of *Ecclesiastes*. How different is the sad and yet not in the least moping or whining morality of the poem to Montagu, a poem with its singular music infused into apparently quite commonplace metre—

Our hopes, like towering falcons, aim, etc.,

from the mere "copy-book" so often charged against

[1] We must not forget the admirable *Dialogues of the Dead* which make atonement in prose for the too well known and (as some think) far too much praised thing written with Montagu to vex Dryden. *The Vicar of Bray and Sir Thomas More* is perhaps the best, but all are good: and one of them will, if only at second hand, enable the reader to feel more on a level with Johnson and Langton by telling him something about "Clenardos."

the century ! How admirable a variant in the same
key is furnished by the *Lines written in Mezeray*, with
their strangely haunting close—

Unwilling to retire, though weary !

And this seasoning and saving "Vanitas Vani-
tatum " is not absent from things where it keeps
Their con- farther in the background—the very "Lines
firmation of to a Child of Quality " owing not a little
the old but of their savour to it. Yet with this faculty,
not always
fully recog- which, it may be admitted, does easily turn
nised quality. in other men to morbidness and cynicism,
there is no bad blood in Prior. As we have no wittier
so we have no kindlier poet, though the wit keeps
the kindliness from ever turning mawkish. The
Tales, though Johnson, unfair to Prior as a whole,
granted them his *imprimatur* as " a lady's book," are
rather out of fashion to-day. They are too naughty
for the old-fashioned and not nasty enough for modernists. But they are thoroughly good-humoured. Some
High-and-Mightinesses have dismissed Prior's love
poems as not ethereal enough—not so much suggestive
of the way of a superman with a supermaid as of that
of a man of the bag with a maid of the bar. Now
half of this is due to the tittle-tattle of the anecdote-
mongers above mentioned ; and even in the other half
there is not much justice. The "Cloe" poems
certainly do not suggest Amadis and Oriana, but in the
House of Love as elsewhere there are many mansions.
At any rate they are extremely lively, extremely pretty,
and they hit off a partnership of *amare* and *bene velle*
which persons who have confidence in their taste
enough not to bother about other people's may find
not a little delectable, and no more "nasty " than the
"nasty hard rosebud," which revenged itself by finding
such an agreeable resting-place. Prior cannot be ill-
natured. "The English Padlock " on one side is
the very incarnation of sweet and not unwholesome

temper, as "My noble lovely little Peggy" is on
another; "Down Hall" on yet a third; others (for
though ill-nature is rather monotonous, good is always
surprising when it is not stupid, as Prior never is)
on others yet.   There are people—not always bad
people—who seem to mistake Cowper's phrase, "easy
jingle" as a suggestion to take Prior lightly.   Cowper
himself did not mean it so; and it may be diffidently
suggested that if any young gentleman of the latest
block (the term is not used offensively, but is pure
Elizabethan for the fashion of hats), even after inspiring
himself by the thought (not quite at first hand) that
Tennyson does not exist and that Browning was a well-
meant but not wholly successful anticipation of the
twentieth century, that Swinburne was a musical-box
and Stevenson an ineffectual Christmas toy—if any
such will just try to imitate the jingle and the easiness—
we shall see.   While as for the longer poems, though
the whimsical inconsequence of *Alma* is sometimes a
little teasing, and though *Solomon* has (rather too
obviously) been dismissed as an instance of a clever
man trying something for which he was not fitted, it is
still lawful to take for the Muse in regard to them
Poins's wish for his sister when Scandal gave her to
Prince Hal, "May the girl have no worse fortune!"

There is indeed a singular delectableness, partly
arising from a certain strangeness and hidden quality
What this in Prior.   Some people even think, when
quality really they read of those morning walks which Swift
is. and Prior took in the Park, "one to make
himself fat and one to make himself thin," that of all
that notable set the unquestionably greatest could not
have chosen a better companion.   If he has not Pope's
intense craftsmanship, Prior has, as has been hinted,
something of the "behind the veil" touch that Pope
never even hints at.   With more delicacy even than
Addison, he has also more passion than Steele and Gay.
Arbuthnot and even Berkeley fall, the former into

lower and more unequal levels, the latter, despite his greatness, into a specialist and abstract division. Possibly, as the common theory goes, Prior may have to some extent clogged the wings of the spirit with Epicurean living; possibly, as it has been more charitably suggested, the diplomatic work (for which he was in some ways unsuited, but the duties of which he seems to have discharged faithfully enough till they called for actual heroism, which he did not possess) overloaded him. He may even have actually given the best of what was in him, helped by pleasure on the one hand and perhaps even by business as a contrasting influence on the other. But undoubtedly there is, for some tastes at any rate, in Prior a flavour of one sort, an atmosphere of Venus and Cupid and kindly sport and fun, contrasted quintessentially with a " finish " of something quite different. His own short piece on " Democritus and Heraclitus " gives a key, too much neglected, to his attitude; and he can " give a hand to each " as hardly any one else, except (once more) Thackeray, has done, and in a fashion different from Thackeray's.

What is said elsewhere in this book about Johnson will, I hope, prevent what I am about to say here from Johnson on being misunderstood. His criticism of Prior. Prior seems to me the worst and most unworthy, both of its subject and of himself, that he ever formulated, for on Fielding, where he went still more wrong, we have but verbal reports. In both cases expressions at other times show that he was speaking not his whole mind or else with imperfect knowledge. Yet this at least is formal and *ex cathedra*. Prior's very unheroic conduct at the crisis of Tory politics may have influenced him. But I should think that, as in Fielding's case also, Prior's " ease " as to what is most commonly called " morality " may have had even more to do with it. Johnson was not squeamish, his unofficial defence of Prior's own *Tales* shows that; but he did not like some subjects to be treated lightly.

Criticism by contrast is often thought to be, and sometimes is, unfair; but it is seldom more tempting

Gay.   and hardly ever more lucrative and less unjust than in the case of Prior and Gay. Contemporaries, members of the same society during the greater part of their lives, for though Gay was nearly a quarter of a century younger than Prior he survived him barely a decade; writers again mainly if not wholly of the same class of verse—there can indeed be no injustice in the comparison, and though it leaves Gay a little better off perhaps than it has recently been the custom to think him, it leaves him below Prior, in exactly the point which has been noted above as Prior's strongest. In Prior there is the Melancholy that at once transcends all art and makes all art transcendent; in Gay there is nothing of the kind, though he had his sorrows, and was quite prone enough to bewail them. He has done some charming things—" Molly Mog," the " Ode to Mr. Pope on his Return from Greece " (perhaps the best of all), the " Black-eyed Susan " song and others; while the justice of putting his larger works among the documents of our special claim will be argued presently. But one always has an uncharitable suspicion that the most brilliant of his things were struck out by contact with the superior wits of Swift and Pope and Arbuthnot; and, though he was better born than Prior, there are much more frequent approaches to vulgarity in him.

Yet those who cannot find " rest and refreshment " in *The Beggars' Opera*, in *Trivia*, and even in the sometimes now disdained *Fables* are not to be congratulated. That the " opera," besides its original suggestion, which is undoubtedly Swift's, owed not a little to the assistance of the more potent spirits of the coterie, is scarcely a matter of mere suspicion. But as marriage is sufficient to establish paternity, so is publication

enough to make authorship at least technically good.
The spirit of the whole thing ; the points made in the
famous passages, such as " How Happy could I be
with Either," the cucumber saying, and dozens more ;
the agreeable topsyturviness of the morality—do not,
as in many other cases, require the music to recommend
them.   In fact, though his ignorance is probably
disgraceful, the present writer cannot associate a single
passage of *The Beggars' Opera* with any music, as he
can in the case of dozens of earlier things and hundreds
of later.   *Trivia* is, to persons who possess the use of
the eyes of their mind, what modern picture-shows
may be supposed to be to those who can only employ
those of the body.   Nowhere do you see the London
of just two hundred years ago more clearly portrayed,
with more lively and lifelike detail.   As for the *Fables*,
that kind has paid, like others, for the enormous and
long-continued popularity it enjoyed of old by going
more than a little out of fashion.   Nothing with a
moral has been for some time popular.   But the kind
is imperishable, and the popularity will come back to
it.   Of course Gay cannot match La Fontaine ; but
he is not so far behind him as it has sometimes been
the custom of critics to say.

So, though we may agree with Johnson's " female
critic " and with himself in regarding Gay as " a poet
of a lower order " it does not at all follow that he is
dull, or really trivial, or unrefreshing.   The subtle
influence of " difference," which only repels those
critics who are " of a lower order " themselves, and
which positively attracts more fortunately gifted persons, exists in him pretty strongly.   It is not perhaps,
as it is in Prior, reinforced by the higher and greater
influence of universality ; but it exists in itself after
a fashion which, in fit cases, should be fairly compelling
or at least inducing.

A further and much stronger instance of this differ-

ence, as regards both Pope and Prior as well as Gay,
is to be found in another poet, who was thoroughly of
their time, but who, from the lateness of his most
famous composition, is apt to be thought of as belonging ┊to a slightly later generation.   Yet Young was
old enough and wrote early enough to teach Pope
something, and an important thing ; while, though he
had practically nothing else in common with Prior or
with Gay, they were all three—all four, if Pope be again
taken in—satirists.   Satire, indeed, is a genus of such
wide range that different species of it are almost as
far from each other as tragedy is from comedy.
Tragedy itself does not exist in Gay at all, the possibility of it has been here contended for in Prior ; but
it is again as an " accepted hell beneath," so far beneath
that it never emerges, but only warms and warns us
afar off.   Pope's transcendent craftsmanship enables
him once to reach it in the *Elegy*, and to show consciousness of it elsewhere.   But the poet to whom we are
now coming is not tragic, because he wrote tragedies :
indeed, the greatest of poetic moods can only be recognised in them by more than a little good-will.   He has
other claims for our consideration.

The compensations of the whirligig of Time are
almost as incalculable as its revenges ; and it would be
Young.   rash to say that Young's once almost world-
famous *Night Thoughts* will never recover
anything of their former and long-continued popularity.
It is certainly not rash to say that much worse things
have been popular since and are popular now.   Yet
Johnson, who was free from some of the reasons for
despising Young which are likely to press more rather
than less hardly as time goes on ; and who actually
thought him a poet, if not a great poet, and a man of
genius, expressly made the proviso " with all his faults."
Now these faults are very great and very curious ; and
they, as well as his merits, are worth examining.   If
the majority, or even any large proportion, of the men

of letters of the eighteenth century had been like
Young, the general title of this book would be not only
a paradox, but an impudent misnomer.[1] When a man
at seventy-nine publishes a poem on *Resignation*, it is
tolerably clear that he has had right little ease, at least
of mind, during that long journey behind him. It is
true that to a superficial reader of a mere summary of
Young's life, his solid reasons for disappointment may
appear small. For a time, in his youth, he had ill-
luck—missing, by the mere fact that there was no
vacancy till he was superannuated, the Fellowship usual
when a boy from Winchester became a man at New
College. But he was only five-and-twenty when he
was not only in a way " made " for life by becoming a
Fellow of All Souls, but made in a way then very rare.
For his Fellowship was in law, and therefore a lay one,
while he could make the best of both worlds (or both
sides of this) by the option of taking orders, as he
actually did later, with the immediate result of a rich
college living. He had, further, the very unusual good
luck of fishing out of the practically bankrupt estate
of his dead patron, the notorious Duke of Wharton,
an annuity, on evidence of claim of which one rather
doubts the validity if it were put before a court of law
or of equity to-day. He married a lady of family and
fortune ; and though he had some domestic calamities
The problems (which themselves served him as capital in
of his life the *Night Thoughts*), he died a comparatively
and poems. wealthy man. Nor had he any just cause
of complaint from the point of view of his own
Universal Passion theory. He acquired some reputation as a man of letters and a dramatist fairly early,
increased it as he went on, and died while it was still
in fullest vogue. But just as it mattered little to

[1] Quite recent publication of his letters has shown (what indeed no careful
student could be much surprised at) that he could be cheerful enough. Wharton
and Dodington were not very likely to welcome a mere Heraclitus at their tables.
But that his melancholy as defined above was real, the present writer has no doubt.
Indeed the simple and straightforward testimony of his son, given to Johnson and
Boswell in circumstances open to no suspicion, settles the matter.

Ausonius that other men thought his Crispa plain, so long as he thought her beautiful, so no doubt it would have been no matter, in a less satisfactory sense, to Young that his lot might seem to others not so hard. Probably the first check at the very opening of his career left its mark on a man who was evidently of saturnine temperament, and who, though he had plenty of wit, can, from abundant signs in his work, have had little or no humour. He was disappointed in his legal career and in politics (for he once actually stood for Parliament). The Welwyn living did not come to him till he was nearly fifty; and though there is not the slightest reason to believe his religiosity insincere, a man may be heartily orthodox and even pious without a vocation for orders. Although it is very possible that in making " copy " out of his family bereavements he exploited the agony (as is too much the way with writing fellows), there is again no suspicion as to his heart-felt sorrow. And finally there was the sting, felt still, if perhaps less commonly, of the feeling that " Promotion came not," even though the way to it seemed opened by a chaplaincy to the king. Persons of a philosophic turn, if they ever regret not having been able to take to one of the regular professions, may console themselves that this *sacra fames* of promotion spares, at least to some extent, the casual and uncovenanted worker in letters and other " outside " pursuits. The three superior faculties of Law, Physic, and Divinity have always suffered severely from it; and it never raged so furiously and so universally as among the clergy of the eighteenth century. A curate of the Adams type may have been at once too good a man to worry about it and too sensible a one to dream of its coming his way. But every beneficed clergyman seems not merely to have been always " dreaming of a better benefice "; but, when awake, to have been plaintively astonished or openly indignant at the remissness of authority in providing him with one. It is very much to be feared that discontent with the non-appearance of canonries, deaneries, bishoprics had as much as the deaths of Lucia and Narcissa and Philander to do with dictating *The Complaint*, and that a late but sane conclusion that they were not coming at all was at the bottom of *Resignation*.

Let this suffice for Young as a man, and let us return to the aspect which shows us him " with all his faults, a man of genius and a poet," with special further reference to our own business. Certainly the faults are many and great. In the first place Young—though he was a regular producer of verse in large quantities and varied forms for full half a century, and had probably written it for at least another decade before he published — seems to have started with hardly the slightest knowledge of the technicalities of his art, and never to have acquired any as he went on. By accident or by imitation he wrote (though with many blemishes even here) pretty good heroic couplet and blank verse of their respective kinds, which are not the best kinds. He chose for his amazing *Odes* metres of the worst possible sort for the purpose—metres jumpy and yet monotonous, falling short with extraordinary infelicity both of the dignity of regular measures and the charm of irregular. Half a lifetime later he chose for *Resignation*, a long poem of the most serious and even solemn nature, the ballad quatrain, which, beautiful as it can be, is far from being so in his hands, and imperatively demands shortness or moderate length in the poem containing it. His rhymes are often vicious and his phrasing and grammar, etc., clumsy and positively bad.

Luckily, however, his worst faults appear least in his most famous poems. The unbroken gloom of the *Night Thoughts* subject in *Night Thoughts*, and the rhetorical and even theatrical colour of the style, require, reconsidered. to make them popular again, a "revaluation of values," which is likely to be a very long time coming.

But, without becoming popular, literature may recover, for those who really devote themselves to it, an interest which adds to the possibilities of life. As has been said, though the expression of the poem may seem to ring hollow to inexperienced ears, there is a core of sincerity in it; and expression and thought together give powerful sidelights and correcting reagents for the general estimate of the time. Beyond all doubt Young shows, and shows early, a tendency in the mind of the time, which afterwards—indeed in his own latest days already—took the form of "Sensibility," and provided, by a rather strange way, a return to Enthusiasm. After all, the *Night Thoughts* and their curious antiphon Blair's *Grave* [1] have an uncomfortable and undeniable reality about them. We do die, and our friends die too. However we may declaim against the obvious or sneer at it, this particular form of obviousness permits no declamation and no sneering to interfere with it when the time comes. Johnson's not unmanly terror of death itself stopped the *Vanity of Human Wishes* and *Rasselas* short; it was the gloom of life alone that he dared to urge. These others, with inferior genius, went further. Grant that they had too much of the mere trappings of the subject—too much of the undertaker's and the churchyard-stonemason's shop about them. Grant that they were rather rhetoricians than poets, and that even Young, at his very best, never reaches the rhetorical perfection of that magnificent close of Johnson's *Vanity* which Scott characteristically made his private motto and quotation, and of which Macaulay as characteristically complained that the author had "not made use of his advantages." Yet their *Memento Mori* is not merely banal, especially at times inclined to charge it with banality.

But Young, at least, whatever Blair may be, was by no means only a laureate of the House of Mourning or a

---

[1] The two appeared almost simultaneously, and there is no likelihood of any plagiarism in either case.

provider of skeletons at the feast in that of Mirth. He wrote something else notable in itself and more notable still as an origin, while it is intrinsically recreative in no small degree. *The Universal Passion,* as a matter of mere literal fact, preceded, and as a matter of all but critical demonstration influenced, the most characteristic form of Pope's satire.

Of course both Young's and Pope's satiric inspirations were drawn to a great extent from Latin and French originals ; but the peculiar trend and turn of the work resulting was due to Young. Elizabethan satire had been injured by the fact that the pattern chosen had mainly been Juvenal or even Persius, and that the exaggerated moral indignation of both, and the contorted imagery and style of Persius, had been not so much imitated as caricatured. Dryden's satire was unsurpassed and unsurpassable, but it was almost wholly political. It was Young who, taking the hint from Horace, Regnier, and Boileau, but mixing, as one may fairly think, something of Addison's prose manner, produced, and taught Pope to produce, the famous style of half personal, half social persiflage, which was kept up *tant bien que mal* throughout the century, and which Byron, without much success, and a few writers down to the late Poet Laureate, with still less, attempted even in the nineteenth.

The interest of Young's satire.

Not many people, perhaps, have read *The Universal Passion,*[1] which is a pity. For it is not only, as Johnson said, a " very great performance," but what he notices as a charge against it, that it is " a series of epigrams," ought to commend it to the present day which prides

---

[1] In some editions the reading is hindered by an absurd abundance of italics. People who object to this mode of emphasis *in toto* are of course themselves absurd ; but the over-peppering of the page is extremely irritating, and it is impossible to see what is gained by printing—

Where men now *great,* from their *revenues spent.*

It should perhaps be said that the title is explained by a sort of supra- or sub-title as meaning " Love of Fame."

F

itself on its own epigrammaticity. Only, Young's
epigrams do not depend upon cheap, and sometimes
quite empty paradox. Nor need the stoutest Johnsonian, even though he go with his master in deciding
that Young " plays only on the surface of life ; he
never penetrates the recesses of the mind," go on with
him to hold that " the whole power of his poetry is
exhausted by a single perusal." Young might have
retorted that it was with the surface of life that he here
meant to deal ; and that later, in the *Night Thoughts*,
he has by no means shunned the depths. But the
fault of Johnson's judgment—a characteristic one—
lies in the last sentence. It by no means follows—it is
a false analogy and a real paralogism—that a superficial
treatment must itself be of only passing interest. Pope
is much more superficial than Young ; yet some of
those who hold Pope's poetry cheapest as poetry, would
confess that they never tire of the special pleasure
which, as literature, it is fitted to give and does give
to them. It is true that Young's is a much less artistically wrought and polished superficies than Pope's, and
so it may please less. But Johnson's error, like others
of his, arose from confining attention to the *matter*
instead of extending it, if not devoting it principally,
to the treatment.

There is in fact plenty to please, and to please more
than once. Young was writing just after the South-
Sea time, and therefore had something like a solid
background of subject on which to throw up his individual touches ; but of these last there is good store.
Nor perhaps has any poet provided such a contrast of
supply for different moods as that of *The Universal
Passion* and *Night Thoughts*.

The three poets just mentioned were not so much
subjects of Pope's kingdom as auxiliary chiefs of their
own principalities. Prior had formed and uttered his
own style certainly before Pope, even by his own

account, had got out of the literary nursery, possibly
before Pope was born. Young gave Pope some lessons
Pope's and took none from him ; while even Gay
younger shows no direct signs of influence from his
"subjects." exact contemporary and close friend. Indeed
Prior, though not to the ordinary eye showing any
trace of that rebellious or restraining influence which
will send Parnell, Lady Winchelsea, and others to a
later part of this volume, really prepared, as it has been
conceitedly put, an Asturias for those who would not
bow the knee to Pope, by his practice in the octosyllable
and the anapæst, as did also Swift. The "kingdom of
Pope" was the kingdom of the polished, carefully
"inbred," and alas! finally sterile heroic couplet. The
diction and the cadence, the trick of arrangement,
other things characteristic of the couplet, did indeed
to some extent affect other forms of poetry, especially
that very blank verse which was the most dangerous,
though often no doubt a quite unconscious, enemy of
the couplet itself ; and, by a curious survival of the
half accidental and purely personal state of things in
the first quarter of the century, people imitated now
Pope, now Prior, or Swift, or oftener Gay. Yet one
may almost say that all the verse of this class of verse-
maker either would have been couplet if it could, or
felt that it ought to have been couplet when it was not.
The curious effect, just referred to, of this upon blank
verse may first be treated, and then something may be
said of the other forms which verse, still of the school
of Pope in spirit, took, before we deal with school and
spirit generally.

Eighteenth-century blank verse has, not without
justification from different points of view, been re-
18th-century garded as a precursor of the Romantic
blank verse. revival, and as one of the most aggravated
and irritating products of neo-classic prejudices. Of
a third popular notion, that it owed its origin to
Addison's praise of Milton in the *Spectator*, little need

be said here [1] except that it has no justification at all, though this praise may have helped. Almost inevitably, the most salient and least subtle of the Miltonic peculiarities engaged the attention of his imitators first; and, unfortunately, some of these rather coincided, at least superficially, with the predilections of the age itself for artificial and conventional verse and phrase. It is possible (we have seen it done in the most recent days) by stopping your ears sufficiently, to get your fingers to confine Milton's blank verse to strict decasyllabic norm; it is easy to imitate his paragraphs, especially if you stiffen their serpentine outline and movement; it is open to the most moderate ingenuity, assisted by the advantages of what was then ordinary school education, to put one epithet before and another after a noun; to adjust inversions and to pepper your text with classicisms, Italicisms, biblicalities. The friends of blank verse at the time were nearly as convinced as was its enemy Johnson that if you did not make it "tumid and gorgeous" it was in danger of being mistaken for prose. Tumidity—of the frog-like order too often—was not difficult of attainment; as for gorgeousness, there are so many different notions as to the exact connotation and denotation of this term that some people might easily think themselves to have succeeded in being gorgeous when to others they seem only to have achieved the tawdriest frippery.

Thomson, not the originator by any means of this verse, but its first distinguished and popular practitioner, and with a touch of originality in his handling of it, was a poet of genius, though he showed that genius most indubitably in a different form. His handling of blank verse itself, though it is exposed to some of the unfavourable remarks contained in the last paragraph, is, as has just been said, by no means merely

---

[1] Anybody who wishes to know the facts of the matter may find it fully discussed in the present writer's *History of Criticism* (vol. ii. bk. vi. ch. 1), and his *History of English Prosody* (vol. ii. bk. viii. ch. 2).

a copy, and still less merely a bad copy, of Milton. But it can hardly be denied that what makes *The Seasons* attractive, as they were for so long and should be still, is much less the form than the subject—the refreshing change, not merely from town to country but from a conventionalised and arbitrary view even of town manners to a direct vision of the country itself. This is so hackneyed and " agreed " a matter that it is unnecessary to say much about it ; but if any one will compare the descriptions in *Windsor Forest* with the descriptions in *The Seasons*, he will realise the fact as not all the hundreds of critics and literary historians can make him do. Unfortunately, it was easier for his own imitators to copy his form than to inherit his spirit. Even when they stick to country subjects, as Somerville did, they seldom seem, to the present writer at least, to have found his secret, while when they changed that subject for didactics, like Armstrong and others, or for sham epic, like the impossible Glover, they became very terrible indeed. Very little of their work can be recommended to any but a student, and even he will seldom care to return to it. Except for a few passages, chiefly in Thomson himself, eighteenth-century blank verse is respectable only or mainly for two things. In the first place Thomson's own " return to nature " induced others to select the subject. In the second, it was almost impossible that some of the blank verse writers should not go to Milton himself, and find there what Thomson had missed. The full results of these possibilities we shall not find till we come to Cowper, but the possibilities themselves always existed.

The miscellaneous poetry of the eighteenth century has much more of the special quality which demands Its lyric and notice here, and it is impossible not to be miscellaneous sorry for the obstinate neglect and the too poetry. often ignorant disdain which it has for a long time met. It is of course to be found in somewhat full selection in the still, after a fashion,

famous volumes of " Dodsley," especially as supplemented later by Pearch ; and almost, though not quite
fully in the collections of Johnson, Anderson, and
Chalmers.[1] But these last require something of a
" robust genius " to cope with them, and strangely
enough nobody has been found to reprint (as might
be done in a very moderate compass) " Dodsley " itself.
Excluding not only the poets excluded above, but, from
the contributors to the actual miscellany, Dyer, Collins,
and Gray, for future dealing—excluding also, as practically self-barred from or by our general title, the
didactics which so fearfully overcast or overbilge the
poetry of the time—it may be usefully noticed, partly
according to form partly according to matter. First
we may take Spenserian imitations which at their
worst help it along as " jury " sails to bring it
to something better ; then the lyrics more or less
proper ; and then the minor couplet poems, chiefly
satirical, of the later century. Not only these last,
but almost the whole body which we shall notice,
illustrate in different ways and degrees that astonishing
influence of Pope which has been and will be acknowledged ; but other influences will have their way
sometimes, though the writers do not seem to see how
discordant these influences are. Even in the excluded
and postponed " rebels " you sometimes seem to see
that they were born in the consulship of Alexander ;
but even in the others you see notes and touches which
are heretical from the point of view of pure Popian
orthodoxy.

Some elaborate attempts have been made to impugn,
or at any rate to correct, the notion—for a long time,
Spenserian and, as it seems to the present writer, quite
imitations. rightly current—that Spenserian imitation
had a great deal to do with Romantic education : but
if these attempts are further noticed it will be else-

---

[1] Southey's *Later English Poets* (3 vols., 1807) will give further specimens if not
whole bodies of the minors and *minimi*.

where. The point of view here regards the positive merit of the pieces themselves ; and before coming to it one may properly clear away initial objections taken to the kind by Johnson in his life of Gilbert West. It may be well to give the passage :

His imitations of Spenser are very successfully performed both with respect to the metre, the language and the fiction ; and being engaged at once by the excellence of the sentiments and the artifice of the copy, the mind has two amusements together. But such compositions are not to be reckoned among the great achievements of intellect, because their effect is local and temporary ; they appeal not to reason but to memory, and presuppose an accidental or artificial state of mind. An imitation of Spenser is nothing to a reader, however acute, by whom Spenser has never been perused. Works of this kind may deserve praise as proofs of great industry and great nicety of observation ; but the highest praise, the praise of genius, they cannot claim. The noblest beauties of art are those of which the effect is coextended with rational nature, or at least with the whole circle of polished life ; what is less than this can only be pretty—the plaything of fashion and the amusement of a day.

There is an apparent moderation — a " sweet reasonableness "—about this criticism which is really engaging ; but though it is not in intention treacherous—it was impossible for Johnson to be that—it might prove so in effect to an unwary reader. The Doctor, like his almost namesake and to no small degree analogue in the preceding century, did not find Spenser's metre or his language pleasing, and cared little for his method of " fiction " ; the much earlier notice of Spenser himself in *The Rambler* shows this quite honestly, and it would have been in the memory, if not actually in the hands, of most readers of the *Lives of the Poets*. Read together, the two passages become perfectly intelligible, and are seen to be perfectly honest. But in choosing West's *Abuse of Travelling* and *Education* as examples of Spenserian imitation, the great lexicographer, whether accidentally or purposely it is impossible to say, hit upon some of the very

weakest examples of what he was attacking, and in
his very praise of them showed that he was not "at the
point of view" as regards Spenser himself.

West.

Indeed his very words here are almost
enough to show this. West, a most respectable writer
(the description is not sarcastic), was, as we know from
other sources, a real student of Spenser himself. In all
the three points specified he is nearer to his original
than most eighteenth-century imitators—not merely
the author of the wretched "Squire of Dames" and other
trumpery to be found in "Dodsley," but even, except
when Thomson's actual poetical genius bursts through
the trammels, those others who will be noticed shortly.
But he never attains what Thomson does thus attain
at times, to some degree, and what neither he nor West
himself nor Johnson nor anybody quite comprehended
—the things to which "fiction, language, and metre,"
even in their perfection, are merely instrumental, the
languid voluptuous flow of Spenser's form and phrase,
the atmosphere and substance as of dreamland or
fairyland itself, which it is Spenser's unmatched and
apparently unmatchable glory to have imparted.
Moreover he does expose himself to Johnson's critical
arrows—arrows as unerring as any such within their
own range, though the flight and even the hit of them
may show the limitations of that range itself. The purpose of "copying" does dominate ; and—certainly not
the less because it does not succeed—does prevent
the attainment of any other. Now the amusement
derived from mere mimicry, though it undoubtedly
does exist, is among the lowest, and except with minds
and tastes themselves low or undeveloped, the slightest
and most quickly satiating of all forms of amusement.
One might even add to Johnson's censure that while
no one who does not know Spenser can enjoy such
things at all, no one who does really know Spenser can
enjoy them as they are. Still, as far as that censure
goes it is lethal.

But it is more curious that an acute critic like Johnson should not have been able to look beyond the mere *tour de force* of imitation.   We know,

Shenstone.   indeed, that with some of the writers of the time this *was* the sole purpose.   We have Shenstone's confession that he began his *Schoolmistress* merely as a parody, though it turned to something better in his hands, as it was bound to do—since they were those of a poet, though not of a very strong poet.   The Spenserian stanza is an instrument of such varied power and capacity that it can be used, and ought to be used, almost independently for poetic purposes, as in the nineteenth century, with differing success, but in all cases with no intention of mere *pastiche*, Scott and Byron, Shelley, Keats and Tennyson used it.   Nor was the eighteenth quite incapable of seeing this, as it showed in at least three cases, though unluckily the least poetical poet of the three saw it most clearly. Shenstone, as we have seen, began to parody, but the magic of the thing seized him and made him write the charming stanzas about the sympathising sister in the dame-school, and one or two others.   Thomson, in *The Castle of Indolence*, seems from the first to have been unable to make up his own indolent mind whether he was serious or not.   But being a poet and a greater poet than Shenstone, the strong contagion of the form seizes on him ; and in the description of the Castle and its site, as well as in many detached passages, the chief being the well-known " Shepherd of the Hebrid Isles," he is not a caricaturist of Spenser ; he is something more than his pupil ; he is actually his descendant.   Beattie, the last, was unfortunately also the least as a poet ; but he has, in *The Minstrel*, the merit at least of entirely transcending mere copying, much more anything like irreverence or caricature. He meant to write in the stanza and in a modernised form of the language of Spenser, and to adopt to some extent what he could comprehend of his " fiction," that is to

say, his manner of telling a story. But it was not to
show that he could do it, it was because the manner
seemed to him to be the most suitable for what he
wanted to do. One may say—the present writer
would be obliged to say—" The result is unluckily not
amusing or delightful or restful or refreshing *to me*."

Thomson. But we know that it did delight or refresh
not a few generations ; almost within the
present century it has certainly, and within that century
it has very possibly, given actual delight to persons not
fools or ignoramuses. While as for the passages of
Thomson referred to above there is no " allowance " or
" compensation " required there. The first Canto of
The Castle of Indolence, with a few easily missed exceptions, is only inferior to the best things of all in its
compounding and exhibiting of the poetic Nepenthe
which Spenser's marvellous invention carries with it
for those who know how to set the charm in operation.

The central region of lyric—miscellaneous " papers
of verse " in octosyllables, anapæstic, or what not, even
including some couplet poems—employs lighter appeals,
but is for that reason much more varied ; while it is also
much more extensive. Of course one is not so rash as
to recommend " Dodsley," especially as extended by
Pearch, for a paradise of *pure* delight; and no doubt some
of the most delightful things in it—the work of Gray
and Collins especially—fall out of our present subject.
There is plenty of boredom to be found in the ten
volumes by anybody who has a morbid taste that way,
or a malicious inclination to discover weak spots.
When any lover of poetry or of pleasure comes across
the name of " John Gilbert Cooper " (an *un*worthy,
whose work is insidiously scattered about both portions
of the collection), let him instantly skip with all the
agility he possesses. And Cooper is only the Cory-
phæus of a too numerous band of boring brothers.
Their patches of the patchwork are dull enough, but

the other patches—those which are not dull—are never long lacking ; and it may be humbly suggested that the region of minor poetry which contains no dull tracts is one unknown to literary history and geography.

In ranging through these, even within the confines of this half-score of small volumes, you come almost at "Dodsley's" small things. once on those delightful petulances of Lady Mary's which culminate in the well-known duel between her and Sir William Yonge— things which should stand at the head of a never yet made collection, the constituents of which are partly, though by no means wholly, in " Dodsley " itself—the work of Chesterfield and Pulteney, the cleaner pieces of Hanbury Williams, one or two of Walpole's (though Horace in verse was a mere pigmy compared to Horace in prose), and not a few more. You arrive before long at that extremely refreshing poem on *The Spleen*, in which its quaker-freethinker-customhouse-clerk of an author put one side, though only one side, of the century so clearly and pleasantly before us. And as you go on dismissing on the one hand " the alms for oblivion " of Cooper and Co., and on the other postponing or passing as known greater things, like those of Gray and Collins, you constantly discover or recover most agreeable pieces containing lines known to everybody, but here only traceable to their origin and authorship—things of Merrick and Bramston, and others, forgotten as individuals and poets, but in a way alive here.

Perhaps there is no better reminder of that complexity of the century which is too often forgotten than the contrast of Mrs. Greville's *Prayer for Indifference* and the answer thereto of her friend the " Countess of C." In at least the central and most important stanzas of the *Prayer*, there is a deep and strong eddy of emotion, confined within almost prim form, which is rare anywhere ; in the answer there is mere triviality of both

form and thought. The amiable and semi-anony-
mous Countess evidently does not in the least understand what her friend means. Mrs. Greville's husband,
the early patron of Dr. Burney,[1] seems to have been
a typical specimen of the eighteenth-century "aristo-
crat," not exactly of the worst but certainly not of the
best kind—intelligent, fond of art, not indifferent
to letters, and a "fine gentleman" when he chose—
but fickle, arbitrary, extravagant, and proud to the
verge of insolence and considerably over that of ill-
manners.

His wife, with whom in a less scoundrelly but not
entirely different spirit from that of Lovelace and
Some selected Peregrine Pickle, he had run away when
pieces. he might have married her *nemine contra-
dicente*; and who became the mother of the famous
"Mrs. Crewe," never made him repent the marriage;
whether he ever made her do so we can guess, not least
from these stanzas. They are worth quoting, because
of the singular throb which pulses through their
polished and conventional phrase and versification:

> I ask no kind return in love,
>   No tempting charm to please—
> Far from the heart such gifts remove
>   That sighs for peace and ease!
>
> Nor ease nor peace that heart can know
>   That, like the needle true,
> Turns at the touch of joy or woe—
>   But turning, trembles too.
>
> Far as distress the soul can wound
>   'Tis pain in each degree—
> 'Tis bliss but to a certain bound—
>   Beyond 'tis agony.

---

[1] In whose daughter's *Diary* a good deal may be found about him, including
the record of a memorable and disastrous evening when he and Dr. Johnson, by
Greville's own desire, were brought together, and when the fine gentleman, after
engrossing the fire and being obliquely but justly rebuked for it by the Doctor,
"ordered his carriage." It should perhaps be said that the *Prayer* is not in
"Dodsley" proper but in the first volume of Pearch's continuation.

The context tones this down a little, and the piece ends with the again characteristic ironism :

> Half-pleased, contented I will be,
> Contented—half to please.

Even in this there is the concentrated neatness and adequate restraint which few deny to the Augustans, with a half-concealed intensity less often allowed to it. But of the central passage quoted, a hasty person has been known to say that there is more true passion in it than in the whole of the works of my Lord Byron.

In this somewhat informal review, however, one should not omit, while thinking of special pieces and of bards who " count " only *par intérim*, individual poets in special or mixed styles, whose work is sometimes to be found in " Dodsley," sometimes outside of it. There is the work—flowing too freely from the tap, but almost always a " good creature," whether in smaller or stronger beer—of John Byrom, whose three best-known things (the pleasant lines, as early as the *Spectator* period, to " Jug " or Joanna Bentley, daughter of the awful Aristarch himself, idol of the youth of his college, and mother of Sir Fretful Plagiary; the famous Jacobite toast on King and Pretender and " God Bless us All " ; and the delightful verses—in " Dodsley " these—on the combat between Figg and Sutton) may be supplemented by not a few others, if people will take the trouble to look for them. There is Anstey, whose *New Bath Guide* is excellent fun to the present day, but in whose numerous other works the feet of the explorer, unless he is more on study than on pleasure bent, had better *not* stray. There is Christopher Smart,[1] who when insane was almost a great poet with that *Song to David*, which was—appropriately in a way—"scrabbled" on the walls

Other poets.

---

[1] One's usual contempt for Mason reaches its deepest point when one finds him writing to Gray about Smart (to whom they were both personally well affected) : " I have seen his *Song to David* and thence concluded him as mad as ever." Fortunately for " Skroddles " he was not himself in the slightest danger of any *furor poeticus*.

of a madhouse, was almost lost to sight, except in fragments, when it was published, and was only recovered
in recent times.   Nor was he an utterly small one
when he was sane.   Between the scum and the dregs
of the stuff attributed to Hanbury Williams, there is,
as noted above, some clear and pleasant liquor to be
found ; and though the verse of John Hall Stevenson,
Sterne's " Eugenius," is scummier and dreggier still,
with the bitter of even its cleaner parts more acrid than
refreshing, every now and then one comes on something neither foul in scent nor merely nauseating in
taste.   The really or nearly first-rate pastime of the
political verse on both sides in the last years of the
century must be postponed.   But a little should be
said of a few typical poets of the century.   Thomson
and Shenstone again, Akenside and Churchill will
perhaps suffice.

Perhaps no one, with the possible exception of
Milton, has been worse served than Thomson by
the modern habit of using for quite, or
at any rate moderately young children
English classics instead of ancient as instruments of
linguistic and literary " drill."   The older fashion of
making such children " get by heart " passages of our
poets had much more to say for itself.   It stored the
memory with things worth remembering ; and as it
was not accompanied by elaborate technical exposition,
it did not leave any " strap-marks " to accompany and
gall that memory.   On the other hand, having been an
old classical master as well as more recently an, in one
sense, older professor of English, I cannot but think
that the few and too often half-hearted advocates of
classical education make a grave mistake in forgetting
this.   Latin and Greek, while they perform the dis-
ciplining which is so necessary far better than any
modern language, and especially than English, in consequence of their initial strangeness and the impossibility of " scamping " them, can and do interfere in no

Thomson again.

way with the future enjoyment of our own and other
" easy " literatures. " Can, or at any rate does, any
ordinary public school boy in adult life read Thucydides
or Aeschylus with his feet on the fender ? " ask the
modernists disdainfully. " If you plague unwilling
boys with Latin and Greek early they will not read in
this fashion later " say the well-meaning but unwise
advocates of a partial surrender. Well, I should
personally be very sorry if my fender and my eyes could
not even now and as long as I live employ such an ever
delightful and interesting *medius terminus*. But I do not
see how the later franchise is likely to be extended by
curtailing the initial admission to it ; and I do see that
the enjoyment of English classics is hindered, while
this " initial franchise "—the knowledge of the actual
language—is in no way helped, by too early drilling
in the literature. For Sixth or even Fifth form work,
when childish recalcitrance and inability to understand
are over, and for University study, there cannot be much
harm in " English literature " work if wisely guided.
If I were dictator I would have none of it, or only a
little " getting by heart " and fair instruction in the
general history of the subject, before.

In particular, as was said above, eighteenth-century
writers suffer much from being used in this way, and
Thomson perhaps most of all. Putting aside a few
classicalities, any child can read him with ease as far
as his mere wording is concerned. But the stiffnesses,
the " stilts " of his diction are likely, and all the more
likely the more they are brought to close knowledge,
to revolt a young reader, and he can seldom be made
(unless he is an unwholesome little prodigy and prig) to
understand the historical and literary reasons of the
thing. If they are forced on him he is likely to hate
them all the more, while there are few compensations.
Sooner or later, afterwards, he begins to like Shakespeare and Spenser, Coleridge and Shelley and Keats,
Tennyson and Browning, Swinburne and Morris and

Rossetti, for themselves, and Thomson goes even lower in his estimation.   Yet even *The Seasons* and still more, as has been said, *The Castle of Indolence*, read with an open mind, have plenty of charms for a spirit of any native catholicity or for one disciplined by study of a wiser kind than that condemned above.   The beauty of the description—when you have no memory of being bored about the derivation of "irriguous" or by demands to point out the passages most inconsistent with Spenser—is plain enough ;   and an intelligent " grown-up " can very well understand the things for himself and as well pardon them for the interest of the undertaking.   And then the interest of *The Seasons* themselves, the quaint and positively piquant combination of unerring recognition of natural beauty with still conventionalised composition and colouring, becomes no small pleasure ;   while, as has been said more than once, the person who cannot enjoy at least the first canto of the *Castle of Indolence* cannot enjoy poetry as such, and has no right to enjoy Shelley or Keats.   Of *Liberty*, indeed, the enjoyment—except that of mild laughter at its hollow rhetoric—can, save in a very few passages, be slight ;   but one or two of the shorter poems [1] have a truth and a melody to which the ear of the present day seems to be too often insensible, perhaps because the accompanying tongue cannot produce them.

Shenstone is a point of greater danger for us : in fact some partisans of the eighteenth century would
Shenstone.   probably condemn it as rash, if not positively
again.   contrary to the laws of war and poetry, to attempt the defence of so weak an outpost.   Yet it may perhaps be made good ; and if it can be made good it will strengthen the general position immensely. Shenstone is a most curious figure.   He is sometimes actually included among those " rebels," or at least

---

[1] Especially "Tell me, thou soul of her I love"—a strong suggestion of a harpsichord, played low in a room faintly scented with *pot-pourri*.

reformers, who would not bow the knee to Pope and Popistry; and there are reasons for this. In his prose essays he has left some of the soundest dicta on poetical subjects to be found in the critical literature of the entire century.[1] Even in his verse, he is obviously making perpetual " tries " at pure poetry, and shows nervous attempts—too weak to be called struggles, but not too faint to be recognised as at least velleities—towards rejection of didactics and the couplet, and towards attainment of the imaginative in subject and the complicatedly melodious in form. But, as a general rule, he has chiefly succeeded in making the worst of both worlds. Johnson, despite a considerable prejudice in his favour as a member of the same college—one of the Pembroke " nest of singing birds "—was revolted by his pastoralities in literature and by his dilettante potterings with " prospects " in life and land. The more decided of the earlier Romantic pioneers found him weak and tame, and when the Romantic spring at last came up and broadened to the long Romantic summer, these uncomplimentary epithets began to seem themselves too tame and weak for the frippery, the artificiality, the rococo tawdriness of Shenstone's verse. For at least a hundred years people have as a rule refused to take him seriously, and have regarded attempts to do so as instances either of inferior taste or of merely freakish paradox. At the best he has been allowed the parallel of " Dresden china," and rather of that inferior variety which the French call *faux Saxe* than of the genuine article.

Yet this is distinctly unfair, and where it is not the result of mere ignorance or neglect, it can only be that of partial or wholly defective judgment. Shenstone

---

[1] " Rhymes . . . should consist of syllables that are long in pronunciation." . . . " The words 'no more' have a singular pathos, reminding us at once of past pleasure and the future exclusion of it." . . . " Every good poet includes a critic; the reverse will not hold." And in several places he condemns the rigid iambicism and "elision" of the time.

G

himself, as is evident from the history of his life and
the irrefragable evidence of his letters, was not in any
sense a strong man ; and it is evident also that he
suffered from that confusion of half-seen ideals which,
though not invariably, is often associated with want of
strength.   The consequence was that, in a perfectly
just application of the phrase which Matthew Arnold
(one fears one must say it) absurdly applied to Shelley,
he " beat his wings " more or less " ineffectually " in
this and that direction.   But he *had* wings, and he
could flutter and sometimes flit if not exactly fly with
them.   The charm of his diploma-piece, the *Pastoral
Ballad*, is one of the most oddly compounded philtres
in poetry.   But those who are insensible to it, show
that there are callosities in their sense of poetic beauty.
It is very conventional, it is sometimes nearly silly ;
it is never much more than pretty and what is called
" winning."   But then there are so many things and
persons in life and letters that are not pretty and not
winning at all !   Further, there is truth under its
artifice, both of feeling and of expression, and that
artifice itself is, on any sound criterion, not far from
artistry.   Above all (and this applies to a large number
of his other poems, though the mixture of success and
failure is more evident there) there is a quality which, at
other and what we are pleased to call greater times of
poetry, seems to be hard to attain.   Compare Shenstone with the Haynes Baylys and the Alaric (Attila)
Watts's of the nineteenth century, and you will see in
him not merely superior poetic powers, but something
in method and manner which is not due to individual
so much as to temporal quality.   The sense and the
wit, sometimes worn something fine, the solidity and
the elegance of the earlier time kept it from the mere
drivel of the later, when this was not great.   Shenstone,
with a not contemptible supply of actual music, has
combined with it, not merely something of an obscure
echo, but something of a perfume, something of a

faint individuality of line and colour, which no time will give to any one who is not a poet, and which some greater poets have not been able to reach at other times.

With Akenside and Churchill we pass to a very different division—some would say a more characteristic one—of the poetry of the century. In neither of them is there anything of the germinal character of Shenstone and even of Thomson—they have no sign of the past[1] or of the future. Akenside is, in his peculiar and sharply limited way, an incarnation of the more specifically eighteenth-century qualities, except playfulness; Churchill emphasises not so much the century's sense of its own conception of art—in which he is often deficient—as its vigour, its acuteness, and the bad-blooded variety of its wit. Both are satirists of almost the first class in a certain kind or rather in two kinds—for Akenside never sinks from indignation to mere ill-nature, and Churchill seldom makes the corresponding ascent. Both have *animosity*, but they have it in different senses of the word.

Akenside is a particularly curious study, though it may perhaps be seldom that the study passes into delight, and still seldomer that delight itself makes the study easy from the first. It is interesting to consider what he might have been at other times ; but the decision will probably vary, not merely with different persons, but even with the same person at different times and in different moods. From the curious fancy which he had for remodelling his poems, more than one of which exists in widely different forms, it might seem that he was not satisfied with his own work ; yet even in spite of this he is entitled to the praise—a great one within certain limits—that he always seems to have done, satisfactorily according to specification, what he meant to do *at the time*. He

Akenside.

---

[1] Dryden, whose influence is very strong on Churchill, being (see the opening of this book) not counted as " past," though he himself had much of the past in him.

never writes bad verse, at least according to the theory
of verse which was obviously his.   He never uses inappropriate language—with the same proviso.   And
he never talks exactly nonsense, though his devotion,
not merely to that strange Whig theory of the century,
in which it is very difficult to detect any principle except
that of being different from the Tory theory, but to
a sham Republicanism, makes him sometimes come
near it.

On the other hand, except in the satiric line, he does
not seem to know what the subjects of poetry should
be ; or what, granting any subject as possible, the
treatment which will make poetry of it should be ; and
he is always a rhetorician rather than a poet.   But as
a rhetorician in verse he is most remarkable.   Only to
an actual student of its kind can his largest and best-
known work, the " twice-laid " *Pleasures of Imagination*, be recommended.   But among his rather chilly
odes that *To the Evening Star* at least should be read
for pleasure—the subject (to borrow Blake's so different
language for it) has " washed his dusk with silver."
The *Hymn to the Naiads* is a most curious example of
rhetorical art in verse.   But the *Epistle to Curio* (which
he altered into an almost worthless *Ode*) is perhaps his
most striking thing.   It is an address to Pulteney,
before that remarkable statesman had resigned " patriotism " for a peerage ; and when the anti-Walpolian
Whigs, with some Tories, expected indefinable things
from him.   Macaulay has laughed at Akenside's
poem for being unpractical, and so it is ; for its author
had, as has been said, adopted the windy, theoretical
republicanism of the " Harmodius, Aristogeiton,
Brutus, and Deuce knows who "[1] kind, which required the French Revolution to put an end to it in
blood, and in mightier laughter than that of Thomas
Babington.   But in itself it is a really splendid thing ;

---

[1] With apologies to Mr. Browning's—
  " Who is Dante, Boccaccio, Petrarca, St. Jerome and Cicero."

one must go to Juvenal at one end or Victor Hugo at the other to surpass it for what may be called pulse and rhythm of satiric verse, the cool and stiff heroic couplet being for once red-heated and almost molten by a passion unknown to Pope and a sincerity rarely affected by the Olympian muse of Dryden. The mere man of the world, the merely practical politician, the historian who knows the facts of the case and attends only to them, may be tempted to smile at its almost fanatical earnestness ; but the judge of literature will, in its own way and division, give it a mark of no common whiteness.

" Whiteness " and Churchill are terms which do not inevitably suggest each other ; while on the other

Churchill. hand Churchill's actual merit as a satirist— he had no other and hardly attempted to have any other—has sometimes been exaggerated. But he was not very black as a man, and as a writer he was decidedly clever. The merit of fertility which Johnson, whom he had lampooned, allowed him with magnanimous and only very slightly contemptuous equity was something ; he had but a little time in which to do what he did,[1] and though perhaps he never did it quite consummately, he generally did it rather well. In particular there are few writers, except the greatest, in whom that strong *sense* of the time, which is so important, appears more clearly. Churchill abuses this sense no doubt ; he employs it quite as often in the service of Falsehood as in that of Truth ; it does (as it did not in Johnson, for instance) get between him and the higher and nobler things. But when he said, as he probably did say, on his death-bed (though the saying was naturally denied by those who were largely responsible for his ill-fate), "What a fool I have been ! " it was to moral not intellectual folly that he must have referred. Whether there is much positive delight to

[1] The whole of his important work was done in little more than three years from the *Rosciad* in 1761 to his death in the autumn of 1764.

be got out of him is a question the answer to which, by different explorers, will probably be very different. His real or assumed ill-temper, the desultory snapping as of an ill-conditioned dog in which he indulges, and the rarity of passages condensed and intensified (like that of Akenside just referred to) by an alliance of enthusiasm and art, may disgust some, and at best fail to attract others. But others still may find a certain pleasure in " The Bruiser," as Hogarth's admirable adaptation has immortalised him—the bear with his formidable hug, the prize-fighter with his fist ready to defend himself and attack others at any moment, with all the resources of science of the lower, but not quite the lowest, satire.

The more anecdotal side of literary history in the eighteenth century has been glanced at in the last paragraph ; but it might have been drawn upon more freely in those which preceded. The famous picture of Thomson wandering at early morn in his sunny Richmond garden and biting at the peaches, with his hands in his dressing-gown pockets, has shocked the moralist, and disgusted the nicer taste which figures to itself what the bitten fruit must have looked like afterwards. But the sun and the wasps would soon put that at least partially right ; and the image is one of a quiet voluptuous content which is not unfascinating, and a great deal of which is to be found in the earlier century. Indeed Thackeray has actually, in the later half of the succeeding one, drawn a more mannerly pendant.[1] In the same way the Mephistopheles of shabby suggestion may spoil the Leasowes. But " make the betht of them not the wortht " ; let there be no mould on the statues or breach in the benches ; let the

---

[1] The unheroic narrator of *Lovel the Widower* who sallies forth in his dressing-gown at early morn ; but he " picks " a strawberry or an apricot as season may be, and puffs a cigarette. One thinks (with relish) of the youthful twentieth-century critic detecting " Victorian " primness in this—in blissful innocence and ignorance of the fact that nobody knew the contrast on both sides better than Thackeray himself—or so well.

streams be mudless and the bosquets nicely clumped, and (with a few added conditions of Phyllis and Chloe and Florence wine and the like) one might not soon tire of scented time in such a place. Even in such a partly ugly and mostly ludicrous scene as that " Supper according to the Manner of the Ancients," [1] the original of which Akenside is said to have actually given, there is something refreshing for fit moods—the moods of high jinks and actual jokes—especially as recounted, not shared.

It may be possible therefore, without making a " doxy " of the not " widowed " but immensely Return to over-husbanded baggage Paradox, to take generalities. a view of strictly eighteenth-century poetry, even of the most characteristic kind, as it is generally thought to be, very different from any that has been usual and even from some that have been unusual. It is almost needless—and might be quite so were it not desirable for completeness of statement— to say what the usual view or views for the last hundred years, or nearly so, have been. In the general critical estimate (with uncritical readers it has, as a rule, dropped out of sight altogether or been merely kept in view as a subject of early and obligatory study) it has been dismissed with more or less indulgence [2] as hardly poetry at all ; as at best " prose and sense " put into verse always smart, sometimes smooth, and sometimes also stronger, still seldomer dignified. Surprise, and even a sort of surprised resentment, has often been shown when any one who enjoys poetry older and younger pays any attention to it as actual poetry. If, from this centrical or centripetal tendency, there have been eccentric or centrifugal divagations, they have almost wholly taken one of two directions. The most usual and the most sane has been an attempt

---

[1] Vide *Peregrine Pickle*.
[2] " Stiff and formalised "—I find it knocked off in these words by a reviewer on the very morning on which I copy them here.

to vindicate for the eighteenth century a sort of converse " return to nature," in expression at least, a revolt against " metaphysical " extravagance, " false wit," " Euphuism," and the like. While recently some of the husbands of Paradox (whether right- or left-handed it is not necessary to say) have deprecated comparison with the poetry of other ages altogether, though they have not very clearly indicated what standard of estimate they wish to substitute. It must be obvious, or rather it ought to have been so, that both these views or sets of views, the favourable as well as the unfavourable, sin against the central law of literary criticism, which bids you, in almost the oldest utterance of Greek poetry and philosophy combined in the mouth of an historic person, " find *the whole* " or at least search for it.

The indiscriminate-condemnation theory or theories cannot be justified, because they overlook the fact that every age has a right to the poetry as to the other things that it desires and deserves. The attempts at apology, when they are pushed too far, when they rest on verbal quibbles such as the ambiguity of the word " Nature," and especially when they deprecate comparison altogether, commit the perhaps worse sin of ignoring the continuity of literature and of poetry itself. The decriers forget, or implicitly deny, that there are many mansions in poetry ; some at least of the apologists forget, or by implication deny, that the whole of poetry is one street which leads from the lowest forms of animate or inanimate nature to the foot of the throne of God. (If the older metaphor of chain connection be preferred, with " links " instead of " houses," it will equally hold good.)

In order, therefore, to judge this or any age or period of poetry fairly and correctly we must look at both house and street, at both link and chain. By doing so it will no doubt be found that there is as usual something of truth in, or at least some excuse for, each and

all of the views referred to. But it may not be impossible to come, as a total result, to an estimate which,
whether anybody may have anticipated it or not—few
things are new—at any rate differs pretty distinctly
from any that has been summarised or even alluded to
as yet. If we can effect this it will be no small justification for the attempt of the book generally. For if
the views of the extreme contemners be correct you
might as well look for rest and refreshment in the walls
of Balclutha, or in some demoniac's habitation, empty,
swept, and *un*garnished, as in this poetry. While if
those of the extremer partisans or paradoxers be wholly
true you might justifiably convert the imperative of
the tag into an indicative, and say, " Quaero aliud
diversorium."

The points which seem to have been insufficiently
considered in all the views hitherto glanced at are as
follows :

First : Insufficient—perhaps in the case of the new
construction put on " return to nature " incorrect—
Erroneous notice has been taken of the *positive* qualities
conceptions of of eighteenth-century verse, of the indica-
this poetry. tions it gives of what that period actually
desired and deserved in poetry, and of what it actually
attained or at least aspired to.

Secondly : The services which it rendered, in the
general history of English poetry, to the general
development of that poetry, have been misestimated.

Thirdly : Its exact relations to the periods before
and after it have been neglected.

Each of these points may, with every effort to avoid
prolixity and to secure precision, be handled in turn ;
while it may not be improper to add a few words on
the general character of the delight which it can give
respectively to the critic, to the student, to the lover of
literature, to the mere reader, and so cumulatively to
the fortunate persons who, as everybody should do in
his way, combine these conditions. For, after all, the

critic who is merely a critic almost deserves the ob-
jurgations heaped on him by enraged authors ; the
student who is merely a student is a poor kind of
creature ; and the reader who reads simply to get
rid of time, which he does not know how else to
employ, is not much above Watts's sluggard ; while
even the lover who does not see the faults as well
as the beauties of the beloved object belongs but to a
feeble folk, and does but " touch the hem of Nature's
shift."

In regard to the first head, and perhaps of most
importance in regard also to the whole question—of
Discussion of such importance indeed that it may be given
them. a considerable *lemma*, a digressive argument
in support—is the demand that due attention should
be paid to the fact that there *is* eighteenth-century
poetry—that the period itself paid very considerable attention to verse, and ranked it exceedingly high
in the scale of literature, putting no doubt its own
construction on the question what poetry was, but,
subject to that practically universal condition, quite
acknowledging its primacy. In fact it is no freak to
say that, rank for rank, poetry has hardly ever received
more, and rarely so much, honour. From *The Cam-
paign* at the beginning to *The Village* not very far from
the end, astonishing relative position [1] was gained by
poetical efforts which, even when we put aside the
altered " exchange," as we may call it, in their poetical
value for quality, strike us as no such very great things,
in their own currency and mensuration, for bulk or
weight or face-value. If it was an age of " prose and
sense " only, it seems at least odd that so much importance should be attached to verse and decoration of
sense. Nor was this mere traditional docility. Locke,

---

[1] Johnson mentioned, as a thing positive and beyond question, that Goldsmith
would have got much more money and many more readers for *The Vicar of
Wakefield* if he had been known at the time of its appearance as the author of *The
Traveller*. There have been times—it is a question whether the present is not one
of them—when a new *Traveller* would have found its only chance of being bought,
or even read, in the fact that it was by the author of a new *Vicar of Wakefield*.

one of the century's acknowledged teachers, had expressly flouted (or rather, for that word hardly expresses
the rather owlish gravity of the Lockian manner,
denounced) poetry as idle and pernicious. But the
century would have none of his estimate in this case.
Although it did not thoroughly understand them, it
accepted even Shakespeare and Milton, in whom (it
might be said) lies not only the subject but the spirit of
all verse. It regarded Dryden, whom it understood
better, very much as we should regard Shakespeare and
Milton rolled into one. And for anybody who would
give it verse after its own manner it had not unfrequent
rewards, dignities, " places with pinsions," and almost
always praise, if not pudding, given in the most liberal
fashion.

But some one perhaps may interjaculate " Grub
Street ? " One may thank him, for he has in the
Aristophanic phrase " given a handle," and
of the aspects of literature of the eighteenth
century which most need handling Grub Street is one.
To say that " Grub Street " (that is to say, the supposed time and place of poverty, persecution, and
contempt which fell upon literature, and especially
poetry, between the golden age of preferment under
Anne and the very late openings for profit by periodicals and public buying and so forth) is altogether a
figment and a mystification would be excessive ; but
that the popular idea of it partakes, to a very large
extent, of mystification and delusion is a simple verity.
We can produce strong evidence against the truth of
this notion, and what is more, we can destroy, or largely
invalidate, the evidence called in its support; while (and
this is perhaps the most important point of all) we can
trace and expose the origins, progress, and general
fashion of its growth. Perhaps, indeed, this last point
should be taken first. " Grub Street "—that is to say
the idea of a sort of regular community of men of letters

"Grub Street."

existing [1] in want and tyrannised over by booksellers, capriciously patronised, and neglected at intervals by "the great," compelled to do sordid and sometimes disgraceful tasks for scanty bread, etc., etc.—was very largely due in the first place to the satiric but not spiteful ingenuity of Swift, Arbuthnot, and Gay. It acquired solidity, if only as a butt and victim, from the selfish spite of Pope. Then Pope's great influence, seconded by the special fancy of the century for types and stock characters, made it a useful subject for writing. In the third place the eccentricities and misfortunes of some individuals, but above all the favourite and towering figure and the widely known fortunes of Johnson, seemed to corroborate it. Last, but by no means least, the peculiar idiosyncrasy and the immense popularity of Macaulay fortified it and established it to such an extent that even the wider study of the time, from Thackeray to Mr. Dobson, has hardly shaken, much less upset, it with the general, although experts may know it to be an exaggeration, if not a falsification, and may now and then have pronounced it to be so. A little fresh discussion of each of these stages may not be superfluous.

The importance, and what it is hardly too strong to call the crime, of Pope in the matter are both excep-

Perambulation and examination thereof.

tional. The mere selection of the "poor poet" as a satiric butt is of course as old as Juvenal, and no doubt much older; even in English it was getting into its third century by Pope's time, and the original "Scriblerus" jests [2] were not much more than amplifications of an old

---

[1] The special or central *time* of its supposed existence may be said to be from the death of Addison to the pensioning of Johnson—say in round dates 1720–1760.

[2] Attempts have sometimes been made to blame Swift expressly as an originator of the persecution, in consequence of his contemptuous and sometimes savage references to pamphleteers, and the too famous incident when he hindered a man of his pardon (not, by the way, for pamphleteering but for rape). This is, no doubt unintentional, confusion and almost prevarication. The dangers and hardships of *political* writing were well-established things long before those of Grub Street ; and though the same individuals might and probably would suffer from both, there was no real connection between them.

trick. But Pope's poisonous and self-torturing spite was not satisfied with this, and he must needs represent the whole corporation of letters, with hardly any exceptions beyond the narrow circle of his own friends and associates,[1] as a mere College of Dulness, and, not content with this, must exult and triumph in its supposed degradation, suffering, and contempt. It is impossible not to be reminded of the finale of his own most brilliant (and not perhaps quite most unjust) piece of personal satire on Addison, and not to regard, half with laughter and half with sorrow, the attempts made by persons not so far below Atticus himself, to represent the *Dunciad* and the scraps of similar matter in other poems as a noble defence and vindication of the dignity of literature. There was not the slightest danger, in Pope's time or before or after it, of the sort of Twilight of the Gods of Letters described in the splendid but hollow rhetoric of the *Dunciad* close. The writers whom he specially attacked, with the capital exception of Cibber, were dull enough, but they were of no mark or likelihood, and, but for the *Dunciad* itself, they would all— with the exception, not this time of Cibber, but of Theobald, saved by the very drudge-work on Shakespeare which made Pope hate him—be forgotten ; their very names would have been as much " alms for oblivion " as their works actually are. But it suited Pope to vent his spleen upon them, and in accordance with the habit of the time he could not rest without making individuals types, or from representing and revelling in the dinnerlessness, the rags, the degradation, not so much of Gildon or Welsted, of Corinna and of Curll, as of *the* poet, *the* playwright, *the* essayist, *the* publisher, *the* anybody and everybody who had anything to do with literature.

[1] It is usual, and it is just, to credit Pope with freedom from that jealousy of "beginners" which men of letters, more generally amiable and respectable than himself, have sometimes shown. It is, I say, just ; but it may be feared that the Devil's advocate might suggest that these beginners had not attacked Pope, and that he hoped to retain them on his side.

Somebody has spoken of the " wicked charm " of a popular epithet or nickname.   This charm is great ; Pope and Macaulay on it. but sometimes, at any rate, it is not so powerful or so wicked as the effect of an easily followed example.   The eighteenth century caught up " Grub Street " ; it may even be said that Grub Street itself caught itself up.   Not only did

The Muse find Scroggins underneath a rug,

but Scroggins consented to find himself (or perhaps, in his blindness, other people of his class) in the same situation ; and yet other people took him and them as being found there.   He, and persons much superior to him, paid the just penalty.   Nothing in literary history is more curious than the way in which, in times of somewhat sophisticated civilisation especially, " writing fellows " forget the simple police warning that " what you say will be used against you "—except perhaps the correlative phenomenon that every age forgets at once to guard against this, and to apply critical correctives to its own application in regard to predecessors.   But we are not here dealing with literary history at large ; and it is only desirable to apply these correctives briefly in the present instance.   As far as Johnson is concerned, dealing with the matter, important as it is, will be better postponed till we deal with him as a whole.   We may pass here with advantage from Pope, the originator of the mischief, to Macaulay, the crystalliser of it.   Very long, in all probability, will it be before the conception thus arrived at is *un*crystallised and dissolved ; though already some good has been done by the effort of divers persons, living and dead, to produce this desirable result.   But a little may perhaps be done here to assist in the *de*crystallisation and dissolution.

As for the interval between Pope and Macaulay, there was nothing, as it has been already said, that the eighteenth century loved so much as a type ; and the

type of the "Distressed Poet"—warranted by the
classics, thrown up no doubt to some extent in fact by
the high-placed failures of Addison, Prior, and even
Steele in the earlier days, illustrated by Churchill and
Goldsmith later, and not discredited wholly by still
later persons who tended towards the more modern
"Bohemian"—gave it what it wanted. Hogarth
helped, if not directly, in design ; [1] the novelists saw
their prey ; the dramatist could not miss it ; the
philosopher and the divine of the period found their
awful examples ready. The type was really a Boojum ;
but it was useful for so many purposes that it could
hardly fail to be taken for a Snark.

But let us turn to the facts and confront Macaulay
and the (part if not whole) fiction with them. Everybody knows, or should know, the famous and brilliant
passage in the Essay on Johnson which deals with the
subject.[2] Of Johnson himself, as has been said, we shall
speak later. But in the context Macaulay mentions
Savage and Boyse [3] as his only definite examples of
the pure Grub Street type of which he has left such a
striking picture in the general *manière noire*. He adds
Fielding, Thomson, and Collins as persons who were
at least arrested for debt ; he specifies Churchill as a
late example of the company. As he does not mention
Chatterton we may for the present leave him alone.
Churchill has been dealt with and none of the others
really dwelt in Grub Street. It may suffice here to
deal with Savage and Boyce,[3] the sole real examples of
the Grub Street period proper, except Johnson, that
Macaulay produces.

Is there anybody who, having critically and dis-
passionately read the works and the lives of these two

---

[1] "The Distressed *Musician*" embodies much of Grub Street.

[2] The biography in the *Encyclopædia Britannica*, which, though relieved of the
extraneous and rather discreditable cavillings at Croker, is on the whole inferior,
contains a rather more subdued reference to the subject.

[3] These spellings seem to be quite optional ; but the *s* is sometimes preferred
because a well-known musician and one or two other minor poets usually have
the *c*.

persons, believes that "Grub Street" had anything
whatever to do with their misfortunes? The real
Grub Street was no doubt their proper
place; but it was quite unnecessary for the
ideal one to exercise its maleficent spells on
them. Savage was probably a measureless
liar, certainly an unmitigated ruffian, and even more
certainly a very indifferent poet. *The Wanderer* is a
caricature of all the very worst faults of eighteenth-
century poetic diction. *The Bastard*, which is short
and relatively strong (it is here that the famous line—

The Grub Street "pattern pieces." Savage and Boyse.

> No tenth transmitter of a foolish face

occurs), bears most suspicious marks of assistance from
Pope, to whom Savage acted, for a time, as a sort of
âme damnée. The " Volunteer Laureate " Odes to
Queen Caroline and other similar things could hardly
be surpassed for bathos by the unkindest parody of the
regular laureate manner, and the few lyrics are worse
than the couplets. Savage had read Dryden, and
sometimes gains from the reading a certain rhetorical
strength which is not merely Popian; but of original
power he has little or nothing.

It may, however, be granted—if anybody taking a
really critical view chooses to insist on it—that this
strength, in happier times and circumstances, might
possibly have shown itself to better purpose. But
" conditions," as the old phrase (which we have kept
in " ill-conditioned ") went, like his—in other words
Bohemianism *plus* brutality—must have met no very
different end. Macaulay's other example, Boyse, is
more fatal still. It is neither mere Zoilism nor mere
bravado to say that to the *eidolon* of Grub Street, and
to that only, Boyse owes whatever reputation he
possesses. It is not a little noteworthy that Johnson,
who knew him as they sojourned together in the partly
fabulous regions, and whose charity was inexhaustible,
never put him in the British Poets, or wrote his life;

while he did, according to one version of the story,
make a most unsavoury comparison of him.   The only
" life " that we do possess is made up by the honest
journey-work of Chalmers from the gossip of Nichols.
The most that a charity, which would fain be not very
far behind the Doctor's own, can do for Boyse is to
hope that the worst things recorded of him—his
reckless bringing of an indulgent and respectable
father to ruin, shame, and death, and his connivance
at the misbehaviour of a worthless wife—are not true
or only partially true.   The facts remain that he was
a shameless begging-letter writer, a persistent rejector
of the various good chances which divers people very
surprisingly put in his way, a lazy literary hack—industry being the only thing that makes acquiescence in
hack-work pardonable.   Turn to his verse—to call it
poetry would not, as in the case of Savage, be questionable, but utterly absurd—and the very quotation of
him for any purpose other than the rebutting of previous mention becomes inexcusable.   He had the
impudence—supported perhaps, as impudence often
is, by a knowledge of his time—to write a poem on
"Deity," which some people praised.   This poem on
Deity consists of couplets like this :

> In diff'rent individuals we find
> An evident disparity of mind—

which, if it had been intended for caricature, might
have required notice of Boyse different from that
which is now being written.   It would be really at
home in Canning's *New Morality*.   This precious
pièce de résistance, in the fare he offers, is supported by
a tolerably abundant collection of minor " copies of
verses," [1] a very large proportion of which consists of
translations.   But the stuff, whether translated or

---

[1] It is rather a pity that this ingenious euphemism has somewhat gone out
of fashion.   There are few times in which it is not applicable ; and our own is
certainly not one of them.

original, is mere ditch-water; there is not a piece,
among the hundred or so reprinted in Chalmers, which
goes above the level of an inferior prize poem.

If Grub Street had really been responsible for
quenching the ignoble race of gutter-scribblers like
these, one might take a new view of the matter, and say,
" All honour to Grub Street ! "   But the facts of the
case forbid any such solution of the tables in laughter.
No time and no place, no rate of payment and no
system of society will save a man who alternates idleness with debauchery, and who treats gifts and pensions
as the typical sailor of old times is said to have treated
his prize-money, by simply trying how quickly he can
drink, muddle, and otherwise chuck it away.   On the
other hand, no supposed or even real misfortune will
turn tenth-rate " Balaam " into work of genius.   But
it was an addition to the original sin of the " Grub
Street " myth that it actually made some good folk
accept this impossible and mischievous metamorphosis.
Your Grub Street hero was *ex hypothesi* a genius, who,
partly by his own ill-guiding but more by unfavourable
social conditions, came to grief.   The amiable illogic-
ality of the general simply converted the proposition,
and took it for granted that a man who drank, guzzled,
muddled, and in unspeakable ways dissipated what
gains he had, was a man of genius.   As a matter of
fact what men of real genius are there, except Johnson,
Goldsmith, and Chatterton, on whom the Grub Street
curse can be pretended to have fallen ?   In all three
cases everybody who knows anything about the matter
knows that Grub Street had nothing, or hardly anything, to do with the matter, and anybody who does not
know will find the necessary facts and arguments in
their places here.

Indeed one may go further and, not in the least out
of mere freak, argue that Grub Street was not too stingy
or hard, but a great deal too liberal to its supposed
denizens.   *The Wanderer* and *The Deity*, at most other

times, would have been simply unnoticed or have made
sport for the reviewers ; and it is by no means certain,
shocking as the statement may seem to some, that *The
Traveller* itself does not admit of pretty rough handling.
That, in the Grub Street time, men-of-letters-of-all-work
who chose to bestow on that work itself, and on the
ordering of their lives, that modicum of decent industry
and common sense which is required, no matter what
a man's business or profession may be—that such men
failed to secure an adequate livelihood between 1720
and 1760 is a demonstrable untruth.   If such persons
as Macaulay selects " never knew comfort " it was
simply because they never chose to know comfort.
Savage himself might have, it is confessed, enjoyed it
if he had not been a ruffian and a wastrel of an altogether exceptional type.   Boyse, with brains which,
to judge from his work, would not have overstocked a
decent usher at a private school, might have done
hardly less well but for his own folly, laziness, and
vice.   While on the other side, men like Dr. John
Campbell,[1] who was merely a typical bookmaker of the
better class, never knew anything like hardship, and
made incomes which, comparing prices, habits of living,
and other things of the kind, were certainly equal if
not superior to anything obtainable in the same way by
the same brains and methods in more recent times.

We may take it, then, as fairly proved that the
eighteenth century had no contempt for poetry, as it
understood poetry.   The next question is,
18th-century   What was the worth of that understanding ?
poetry tried
by a general   Was eighteenth-century poetry merely prose
touchstone.   after all ?   What has been said about Pope
should have answered this question already in a
considerable degree ; but the answer may at once

---

[1] Campbell was born in the same year with Boyse and a year before Johnson ; so
that he comes into exact chronological comparison with them ; and, considering that
he began as a lawyer's clerk, he can hardly be said to have started with any particular advantages.   A little more may be said of him later.

be summarised and extended with a certain anticipation or forecast here.   It is impossible, except on the
most one-sided and arbitrary theories of poetry itself—
the theory that in it " all depends upon the subject "
doubled with the further theory that only a limited
class of subjects are suitable, and triple-mailed with yet
another that the treatment, as well as the subject
generally, must be of one kind and not of another ; it
is, let us repeat, impossible, except on a counter-
doctrine as arbitrary and as uncatholic as the strictest
house of eighteenth-century critics themselves—to dis-
qualify this poetry as merely " measured (and sometimes rhymed) prose."   Allow the widest exclusion of
partially and practically " romantic " poets, such as
that which has been actually exercised in this chapter,
and there remain things—not merely show-pieces like
the close of the *Dunciad* and that of *The Vanity of
Human Wishes* (which, though undoubtedly rhetorical,
are rhetoric thoroughly brought under the species of
poetry), and things like Prior's best, (which though they
may lack " high seriousness," are essentially poetic
utterances of the comic spirit)—but hundreds of various
examples onward and not always downward, which will
stand the test.   " What test ? " somebody asks.   Why,
the only catholic test-question of poetry—Is this the
vivid and consummate expression, in metre, of an impression furnished by object, event, passion, imagination, fancy, or whatsoever humanity can be, do, suffer,
or experience ? [1]

It is sometimes one's duty to animadvert upon the
Partly   limited conceptions of this all - important
metrical.   agent of metre which the century entertained.
This has to be done ; but it should never be done

[1] This will be found not so very different from what is perhaps the nearest
approach to the impossible *definition* of poetry—Hazlitt's : " The natural impression
of any object or event, by its vividness exciting an involuntary movement of imagination and passion, and producing by sympathy a certain modulation of the voice or
sounds expressing it."   The last clause has been frankly clarified into the one word
" metre " ; and the first has been made more precise by some omission and some
addition.

without a corresponding and deliberate acknowledgment of the benefit which accompanied these
restrictions. It is not too much to say that the
poets, from Dryden to Johnson, knocked a real sense
of regular rhythm into the English head. So few
people have given themselves the trouble to understand
what English prosody really is ; how entirely it differs
from that of every other known language as a result of
its blended character ; and how very long and difficult
the evolution of the new compound was, that they
most naturally enough fail to see this. Twice already,
though the principles of evolution had never ceased to
show themselves, the discipline of practice had failed.
Chaucer had brought it up to the utmost perfection
possible at the time ; but he was no sooner dead (nay, as
some of Lydgate's and Occleve's early productions must
have been written when he was alive, we may say he
was *not* dead) when things got into chaos again, save in
the school-learnt and artificial dialect of Middle Scots.
The great Elizabethans, from Wyatt to Spenser, did
get things into regular shape, from the more advanced
condition of the language, while Shakespeare once more
perfected the " escapements " of prosodic liberty.
But, once again, the general sense of rhythm was not
strong enough, and the loose and flaccid couplets,
the chaotic blank verse, the occasional anarchy (attributed traditionally to Donne) of the early and middle
seventeenth century showed it. Milton did much—it
must be repeated over and over again, that in Shakespeare and Milton all the art of English verse is dis-
closed as was all the art of Love in the *Romance of the
Rose*. But the transcendental union of order and
freedom in both was too much for the average man,
and he could not yet interpret or follow it.
    From various symptoms in his very extensive range
of metrical practice, it is probable that Dryden *could*
have shown, had he chosen to do so, nearly as much
varied mastership in both ways as the two greater poets

whom he followed, and whom he has celebrated so magnificently. But something kept him from doing this, and it is by no means certain that it was not a beneficent something.   For a time the spirit of poetry could do without extremely varied metre ; it was high time for the method of poetry to be disciplined once for all in regular rhythmical correspondence.   This was done, and done thoroughly, in the three or four generations between the Restoration and the French Revolution, so that when the spirit woke again to bolder flights it achieved that magnificent order, tempering freedom once more, but never mastered by it, which gave us Coleridge and Keats and Shelley, Tennyson and Browning, Swinburne and Christina Rossetti.   Another century of the combined exercise may have loosened this discipline a little, as is shown by a few strayings after dissonant and unrhythmical hexameters, fantastic and cacophonous " bar " measures, sheer prose *vers libres*, and the like.   But the public ear at large has not been really spoilt, and that it has not been we owe to the sober, staid, sometimes, it may be owned, to the most catholic of us, unsatisfying and even irritating goose-step tramp of the eighteenth century.

It will probably, however, be a long time indeed— if, in the unfortunate dissidence of the forces which might, if united, bring the end of that time about, it ever comes at all — before the importance of rhythmical considerations can be beaten into the heads of Englishmen after the fashion in which it seems to have existed in those even of Latins, and the understanding of which seems to have been part of the birthright of Greeks.   " Never mind about the manner, tell me about the matter " will still be the patter-demand.   This demand, if it means complete separation, is of course unreasonable and the compliance with it would be in fact impossible. You can, to some extent, consider manner apart from matter ; you can never entirely reverse the operation

But of manifold composition.

with any result satisfactory to literature. But it is
possible and perhaps desirable to avert the consideration from the technicalities of form, and to consider what, assisted by them and in the combined
result, a given period has produced in substance. He
must be either a very thoughtless person or one very
limited in taste, who, when he has really given himself
the slight trouble necessary to know it, ranks the production of the eighteenth century low. That production cannot as a whole be fairly summarised till
we have seen, in direct line, the complements, " separ-
atist " rather than definitely revolting, which are to
be dealt with in later chapters. But the actual characteristics — the wit, the wisdom, the full - sounding
rhetoric, the unsurpassable neatness, and other things
which have been already set forth are admirable and
delectable things in themselves : and when you compare
them with the products of any other country at the
same time they become more admirable and more
delectable still.

Yet the comparison must be taken in the right way,
not the wrong, if the real value of the eighteenth
century—intrinsic and as a part of the general history
of English literature—is to be perceived. The attitude, not merely of the true student but of the true
amateur in all æsthetic matters, should emphatically *not*
be that indicated by the text—

> A bumper of Burgundy fill, fill for me ;
> Giving those who prefer it champagne !

but—

> A bumper of Burgundy fill, fill for me ;
> (Without prejudice as to champagne).

There are as many mansions in the Kingdom of
Literature as in that of any kingdom of earth or Heaven ;
and we cannot have one of them shut up or marked
for condemnation. Of a dozen material analogies for
the poetry of the eighteenth century which suggest

themselves, none is perhaps more suitable than that of a " clear canal " broadening itself here and there into " as clear a lake," where the waters settle and calm themselves from the rather tumultuous flood of the seventeenth and the latest sixteenth, till fresh influences quicken and stir them to fill new rapids and waterfalls in the nineteenth.   But the river as a whole, from fount through stream and lake and fall to what unseen, unknown ocean awaits it, is ours: and no part of it should we fail to explore and to enjoy.

CHAPTER III

THE NEW PARADISE OF THE NOVEL

THE subject of this chapter would, almost by itself, justify the title of this book. Persons at once ingenious and ingenuous have sometimes wondered how the world beyond ever got on without novels ; yet it is certain that it had to get on without them, save in verse or in beggarly and roundabout substitutes, for more than two thousand reading years, though the romance came to the (partial) rescue, first in prose then in verse then in prose again, in the last thousand or thirteen hundred of these. How the novel in the full sense actually came about in England (as it did to some embryonic extent) *before* the eighteenth century, there is no room and perhaps no need to tell here ; it is enough [1] to say that it was not till the alterations of prose style, effected in the last third of the seventeenth by Dryden and those about him, that the prose novel could well have been written. For it deals with ordinary life and incident, with character, with a great deal of introduced conversation, and—in story, in talk, in comment, and everywhere—with all sorts of miscellaneous matters. For the treatment of all of these, except for the rarely required purpose of impassioned eloquence and for that (hardly to be required at all for another century) of elaborate semi-poetical description, the stately and magnificent but cumbrous and involved

---

[1] The account may be found briefly put in *The English Novel* (London, 1913). Repetition has been, as far as possible, avoided here.

diction of the earlier period would have been entirely inappropriate; the less gorgeous but more flexible and handier style of Dryden, especially as it was further developed in different directions by his disciples Addison and Swift, served perfectly.

But these two great Successors did more than further perfect the instrument: they practically applied it to the work. Dryden himself had shown (as, for instance, in the slight narrative and conversational framework of the *Essay of Dramatic Poesy*) what he might have done if the time had come, and the idea had struck him. Addison, in the " Coverley Papers " of the *Spectator*, made a much farther step. Defoe—in that singular and rapidly written group of which *Robinson Crusoe* is the best known and *Moll Flanders* the most " novelish "—went still farther; and Swift, though in two different books, *Gulliver* and the *Polite Conversation*, advanced perhaps farthest of all before the appearance of the mighty quartette, to whom the actual origination of the complete English Novel is usually and in the main justly ascribed.[1] It is indeed necessary (and the present writer, as to some extent *particeps criminis*, may frankly acknowledge that it has not perhaps always been sufficiently done) to warn the reader as to the very considerable body of prose fiction, mostly translated but sometimes original, which actually exists before 1740 and *Pamela*. Everybody who has dealt with the subject ought to have been aware of the fact that this body was large, though perhaps nobody quite realised its bulk till Mr. Arundell Esdaile recently published, for the Bibliographical Society, his invaluable catalogue of *English Tales and Romances from* 1475 *to* 1740—a list filling no less than 325 quarto pages. Yet perhaps, after all, this long muster-roll does not yield much, in point of distinctive

The preliminary "studies"—Addison, Swift, Defoe.

---

[1] The present writer is not disinclined to call Bunyan the first English novelist; but he, as well as Aphra Behn, Head, Neville, and one or two others to be glanced at presently, falls out of our story for substantive mention.

character, beyond the items already recognised by every competent person who has dealt with the subject —*Euphues* and the *Arcadia* and the minor Elizabethan pamphlet-novels, the romances of chivalry of the seventeenth century, Neville and Head and Aphra Behn and a few more earlier or later. Many of these books, in fact most, were translations; and all, whether translations or not, save the versions of *Don Quixote* almost alone, wanted the " That ! " or rather the many " Thats " which constituted the full novel, whether it be of the non-romantic or the romantic, the historical or the purely quotidian, the ordinary or the eccentric kind.

But it would be a gross unfairness to the third of the great eighteenth-century precursors of Richardson not to admit—not to insist—that he did far more to establish it as the staple literary refreshment stall or ground of the nation and the literature than Addison with his finer and more delicate literary art, and Swift with his immensely greater genius. After all, the Coverley Papers are not a novel; they are but the materials of one. Much has to be added in the way of mere connection; at least one indispensable figure, the Widow, has to be called out of her present " Mrs. Harris "-like condition into actuality, several more minors are wanted, and those who exist require more development and interaction. In short, not only is the meal for the hungry novel-reader not dished up and served, but it is only half-cooked and even not yet " caught " in parts. So, too, in the *Tale*, in the *Battle of the Books*, and even in *Gulliver* the interest of narrative fiction is not the main one; in the first two it is, intentionally at least, quite subsidiary. The *Polite Conversation* stands to a complete novel as it were on the opposite side of difference when compared with the Coverley Papers. It is evident that Thackeray's mouth (to speak in something like its own language) watered over it. It has a heroine—in fact, though she is naturally less refined, there are touches both of Ethel and of Beatrix in Miss Notable, whose Christian name one fondly guesses at. It has a good deal of character already, and of character easily developable ; it has perfect dialogue ; description, even at that time (as a score of periodical papers show) could have been thrown in amply by more than one eminent hand ; and it only wants a story, whether of the complicated plot kind or of the loose and " chronicle " variety, to be poured in on all these finished things, as a cook pours gravy into a pie, to jelly its parts together.

The former sort nobody then living in England had yet shown himself able to supply ; only one person living was able (and not yet shown himself to be so before Addison's death) to supply the latter in a fashion which was practically new. This was (it should hardly be necessary to say it) Daniel Defoe. That strange polygrapher—who tried a hundred things in the less exquisite kinds of literature, some of them almost as new, touched nothing in which he did not show talent, but accomplished nothing else that could in the least challenge genius—was the first Englishman, and almost the first modern European to compose, on the great scale, prose fiction which should possess an interest of *story*.[1] That is the one point on which it is necessary to dwell here. It is not merely idle bravado to reverse the famous Johnsonian dictum as to Richardson, which has so often to be quoted or glanced at, and say that if you read Defoe for anything else but the story you would hang yourself. His style, though not without vigour, is without much attraction ; his characters, though they have life have little individuality, and no depth, or colour, or charm ; his descriptions and inventories, though they add to that strange verisimilitude which has been so much discussed in him, have rarely any other merit ; plot he has

[1] It may seem impious, but is hardly even improper, to question whether the interest of *Don Quixote* itself is purely a story interest.

next to none ; and his dialogue, though once more deserving the praise accorded to his description, deserves no other, for it has none of the various gifts of humour, irony, quaintness, passion, and the rest which give zest to book-talk. But he is, to children and grown folk alike, what the Pied Piper of Hamelin was to children only—he makes you follow him wherever he goes. The voyages and the solitudes and the terrors and the triumphs of Robinson ; the immoral or rather non-moral Odyssey of Moll Flanders (for Moll might have been as strictly moral a person as Borrow's apple-woman thought her but for circumstances) ; the curious duplicate of this Odyssey in the life of that very interesting boy and rather contemptible man Colonel Jack ; the adventures of Singleton with his remarkable success—one cannot say in making the best of both worlds, for to alter Mr. Midshipman Easy slightly " that's when he's *been* tried above," and we have no report of that trial [1]—but in retaining the profits of scoundrelism after returning to a life of honesty ; even the intricacies which bring retribution on that disgusting[2] creature Roxana—all these have the mysterious power of *absorbing* the reader, of making him forget time and work and trouble and even other pleasure, in the mental contemplation of these unreal beings who are yet so profoundly real, though they live and move and have their being only in his own and their author's fantasy. To Defoe this power, on the greatest scale, was first granted ; he was the first magician except Cervantes to exercise it, in more than miniature, without the aid of poetry in form.

The source and nature of this strange pleasure are, like the source and nature of all pleasures and all things, unknown ; and the various speculations on the

[1] One rather fears, recognising the presumption of judging even a two-hundred-years-back neighbour, that he may have had experience of that very uncomfortable " logicality " assigned by Dante to the Adversary and his representatives.

[2] Disgusting, not because of the presence of vice but because of the absence of passion in her. It is curious how different the effect of this absence is in her case and in Moll's.

subject as usual only " push ignorance further back,"
if indeed that phrase of the great sceptic is not itself
too positive, seeing that the ignorance does not retire,
it simply changes ground.　It is of course akin to
that quite as unintelligible interest which a good many
people take in the actual performances, speech, and
existence of their actual fellow-creatures: but it contains mysteries of its own.　Again, people have risen
up early and gone late to rest enquiring why things
which would bore, disgust, shock, terrify, or simply
excite little or no attention in life, excite and delight in
art and especially in literature ; and they have found
out nothing at all.　Enough that the pleasure exists.
But it is not idle or superfluous to invite notice—not of
course for the first time—to the fact that it begins now
to exist, and that men begin to avail themselves of it,
in a new and a much more extended way.　It had
always existed as regards poetry ; it had long existed
as regards romance—that is to say, a somewhat limited
range of exciting incidents not unfrequently raised to a
higher power by supernatural or improbable adventure, with, in the better examples, a strong tinge in spirit
of the poetry which had been its earlier form.　Even
as regards ordinary life, and to some extent character, it
had existed for some four or five hundred years in short
tales—*fabliaux*, *novelle*, *nouvelles*, what not—as well as,
with certain extraneous and partly mechanical re-
inforcements, in drama.　But it now began to exist on
the largest scale and with the most varied circumstance.

　There can be no doubt that Defoe's celebrated
circumstantiality had a good deal to do, and that following of this always has had a good deal to do, with this
uncanny process of, as the French call it, " enfisting " the
reader.　We laugh at the " more-by-token " method ;
and it sometimes is, and perhaps is always in danger
of being ludicrous, even in fiction, while its association with " button-holing " makes it formidable and
detestable in life.　Yet its power is great and strange.

It is more easy to understand the persuasive effect of
repetition, " What I tell you three times is true," than
that of mere multiplication of circumstance ; and yet
this last, though less aggressive, is more subtle than
the other ; it nets, if it does not knock down. Robinson Crusoe's bags and his barrels, his plantings and
burrowings and makeshifts for this and that utensil ;
the elaborate operations whereby the wicked elder
brother makes himself master of Moll Flanders'
virtue—a fortress not of itself requiring much bom-
bardment ; the obtaining, division, loss, recovery,
trouble in keeping, of Jack's illicit gains ; the
meticulous marches and conflicts of Singleton's journey
—contain hardly anything supremely interesting in
itself or individually, and much which, taken singly,
would have next to no interest at all. Nor, as was said
above, are we deeply concerned about the personages
or characters, though Jack's childish innocence, while
it lasts, makes him, by its force of contrast with his
surroundings, perhaps an exception. But it all helps,
if it does not solely constitute, the true *mimesis*—the
unreal-real re-creation which gives the things their spell.

So far, however, the novel does not part company
with the romance, though it relinquishes some of the
romance's *viatica* for the journey. But it is
already adopting, from the slightly degraded
forms of that romance, the " picaresque "
narrative, and carrying still further, the
use of strictly ordinary materials. Of course there
has been some change of what is strictly ordinary
between the reign of the first George and that of the
fifth ; but the change is merely relative and propor-
tional. What has been called " the no-time and no-
place of romance " disappears. Crusoe's island may
be neither confidently Juan Fernandez nor definitely
Fernando Noronha, but it is not an island of romance ;
while all his other sojourns are discoverable on the map
and in the gazetteer to the satisfaction of any court of

What these gave, and what they did not give.

law. The uncanny exactness of Singleton's explorations has gained rather than lost interest since the whole journey has been atlassed. As for the resorts of Moll and Jack and the Cavalier [1] they are mostly in named places, to which we can go to-day if we like ; and the manners (as we know from other sources) are rather truer to life—inasmuch as there is less of the influence of the " printed book " in them—than those of any story of to-day. Nothing is heightened ; nothing (in the rhetorical sense of the term) " amplified."

It has sometimes been regretted that Defoe's imagination (for it would be absurd to deny him this faculty) was so low and prosaic ; but this is hardly wise. The earth, not the air, was to be the special scene of the novel's operations. It might rise meteorically now and then, but it was better that it should walk steadily at first, and this Defoe taught it to do. He left, of course, a great deal more to be done ; indeed the novel is, in its very essence, the most unfinishable of all kinds of literature. Drama, unless it borrows the aid of poetry, soon comes to the end of its tether ; poetry itself is infinite in treatment, but by no means so in subject. But the novel, by the very fact of dealing with ordinary life—which, like the grass to which it is so often compared, is never alike in two instances —retains a practical infinitude. The mere changes of manners and other externalities of life provide the novelist with constant new subjects ; and within these larger phases the life of one nation is not like that of another, nor that of any town, nor that of the streets within the town and the houses that form the street, nor of the individuals who inhabit the house. We come constantly, in this interesting age, to instances where its practice unwittingly upsets its principles. It was an avowed principle of the eighteenth century that you must generalise and conventionalise, that you must not

---

[1] This is not the place for renewing the probably hopeless enquiry, " Was he a real Cavalier or an invention ? " In parts at least his adventures are of first-rate novel *quality*.

"count the streaks of the tulip." Yet it almost invented, it certainly first developed and popularised, the novel, the very postulate of which is that no two tulips have the same number of streaks or the same arrangement of them.

In regard to the four greatest novelists who, between 1740 and 1760, extended Defoe's operations by pro-
The four ducing and solidly "patterning" the novel
constructors. in no small variety of kind, it is not the main object of the present writer to criticise them in the ordinary sense, still less to compare them for purposes of preference or ranking. If we enumerate and analyse, not too minutely or techni-cally, the nature of the delights they brought, that will do.

There has always been a good deal of controversy about all of them, though less about Smollett than
A point to be about any other. But a larger part of this
slightly controversy has busied itself about a matter
handled, and or set of matters with which brief dealing
not returned here will suffice, namely, their "moral"
to. character. This (except in regard to Sterne, who even for that time went out of his way to invite objection, and to certain passages of Smollett which do not now exist in any ordinary edition) did not trouble their contemporaries much; though a point in refer-ence to Fielding and Johnson which is not a hackneyed one will be taken up later. But the rapid exaltation of the standard of "propriety" in the later part of the century soon began to make people take exception to the lower if freer level of situation, thought, and to some extent phrase in the great quartette. Early in the nineteenth prudery—though men of such un-blemished character and high intellectual position as Scott and Southey stood out against this—increased and multiplied; and you find even a writer of such skill in their own craft and of such almost masculine sense and humour as Miss Ferrier indulging in positively

I

violent language [1] on the subject.   Half a century later
still, the American critic Lanier, in whom some have
seen genius and who certainly had talent, echoed the
protests voluminously ; and though it is rather the
thing at the present day for novelists to be " improper,"
there have not been wanting persons of unquestioned
" light and leading "—even of avowed partiality for
the eighteenth century generally—who find the coarseness of these great " amusers " by no means to their
taste.   A slight examination of the facts of the case
may, as has been said, suffice, but some must be made.
For one does not want to recommend " refreshments "
which derive their attraction from being put on the
Index.

As regards Sterne, though attempts at defence have
been made from Goethe (a not entirely impartial judge)
to persons still living, it is really hardly necessary to
call upon prosecuting counsel to reply.   Passion and
voluptuous beauty at one end of the scale, frank and
abounding fun at the other will excuse much, will
indeed sometimes make excuse unnecessary.   But
Sterne has nothing of the first ; and his best comic
efforts stand in no need of unclean assistance, or use
it in a fashion which is hardly offensive.   Nobody but
a very feeble vessel, an overstarched precisian, or an
absolute fool need be ashamed of laughing at the
limited liability association of the Abbess and Margarita in accelerating the paces of that lazy quadruped ;
but in other instances (the proportion of the two kinds
being about twenty to one) there is no hearty fun at all,
but a sniggering attempt to tickle and excite certain
nerves which are in a state of unhealthy neurosis.
Almost every one has recognised the futility, and for so
quick-brained a person the foolishness (if it was seriously
put forward) of his analogical self-defence about the

---

[1] She makes one of her characters in *The Inheritance* describe the works of our
present authors as " noxious exhalations " which are "already passing away." And
not only the context, but many other passages, prove that this was her own opinion.

unconventional displays of small children. For this conduct is unconscious and therefore innocent ; Sterne's is conscious in the highest degree, and therefore guilty.

It is, on the other hand, by no means certain that much purely ethical disgrace rests upon Smollett, though he was the greatest offender, by far, in actual coarseness and from the æsthetic point of view. His insertion of the original form of the Lady Vane episode for money is ugly enough ; but, somewhat paradoxically, it becomes less ugly when we look at his own practice on after occasions, which shows at least that his poverty was not consenting to what his conscience disapproved. He had a rough, coarse taste, which his medical education and his sojourn in the " hells-afloat " of the time had made rougher and coarser ; he was one of the savagest of satirists, and satire had always given itself the extremest license in this direction ; while, lastly, every one acquainted with Scottish literature, except a few to the manner born who have let patriotism blind them, knows that, almost from the earliest time, its license of matter and expression had been astounding.

In the cases of Richardson and Fielding there is matter for closer argument, though not perhaps much room for argument that should be really profitable. The old contrast of Richardson's morbidity and Fielding's breezy health is sound enough ; and it is also perfectly true that Richardson, quite as much as Fielding, introduces " inconvenient " situations, though in actual language both are decent. Against the scandal caused in some respectable minds by the rather generous license of actual conduct allowed to Tom Jones, and even to Booth, by Fielding, there may be set the feeling, most certainly undergone by persons little, it is hoped, less " respectable " than those previously mentioned, not merely that Pamela's virtue is a matter almost wholly of prudential calculation, and that she seems no more offended, shocked, or disgusted at her master's attacks on it than she would have been if they had been playing cards together and he had endeavoured to win her money—but even that the divine Clarissa's chastity, though of course of an infinitely higher and more refined type, is not quite so much "sun-clad" as it is sun-spotted by a singular reluctance to escape the danger once for all; by a tolerance, only less than Pamela's, of what she should have regarded not merely as an attempted injury, but as an unforgivable insult; and by that shiftiness and dislike of plain truth which some even of her admirers have admitted. It seems in fact to some that if Fielding goes too far in the direction of Smollett, Richardson comes much too near to that of Sterne in a kind of unmanly sensuousness. But this being said, enough has been said on a perhaps unavoidable but in very few instances delectable side of the matter.

The other sides, or most of them, are delectable enough, though the rarest and most refreshing delight is not to be found in Richardson. *Pamela*—

Richardson.

at least if its mostly dull afterpart and afterthought be omitted, or rather stopped short of—is so very much the liveliest story which had been, at its date, vouchsafed to the English reader that we cannot be surprised at people buying four editions (a number equal to at least forty now) in not much more than four months. In later days the more ambitious character of the author's other books, the admitted limitations to the charm of the heroine, and perhaps a rather snobbish reluctance to take an interest in a little person of no " quality " have been against it ; but it remains the only book of Richardson's which you can read for the story without the exercise of an almost painful agility of mind to discover exactly when to skip, and of hand and eye to conduct the skipping. The old motive of " the quest " is briskly carried out ; the characters, if not exactly diploma-pieces, are sufficiently hit off, bustled through effective incident, and made to talk in a human manner. It is a novel, and it is no wonder that it acted like a bit of already fermented dough to set further fermentation going, and to introduce the enormous mass of novels which the last seven quarters of a century have seen.

Thus the example of *Pamela* was followed and bettered, not merely in the peculiar and (to her author) Especially in painful way, which will be noticed soon, his first-born but generally. Her younger sister and *Pamela.* brother—*Clarissa* and *Sir Charles Grandison* —may be of higher quality and may offer more voluminous attractions, but it is to some of us very satisfactory that they have found far fewer imitators, especially in point of scale. Richardson had, of course, shown his much-talked-of knowledge of the human heart in *Pamela* itself and Pamela herself. But the future " Mrs. B.," and " Mrs. B." when she attained that dignity, are, though by no means simpletons, persons of comparatively simple motives and aims—to keep physical purity until one can part with it at the legal rate of exchange, and to enforce possession of the price under safeguard of documents properly stamped and filed. " Mr. B.," on the other hand, at first merely wishes to get what he wants without paying that rate for it, then he consents to buy when he cannot steal, and afterwards wants to withhold some of the purchase-money. The minor characters play up fairly, but that is all. In *Clarissa* and in *Grandison* the scheme is immensely enlarged, the *dramatis personæ* multiplied, almost more than in proportion, and in all the major characters and not a few of the minor the analysis of motive, thought, and action is carried to a much higher pitch. The results in part give us, no doubt, some fine artistic work ; to some judges of distinction they have seemed to do so even in the wholes. Others have been less fortunate and severer in their " findings "—to employ two different but

connected senses of that word. The present writer
has read both books in parts several times and may do
so yet ; he has read each through once ; but nothing
would induce him to do *that* again, except the want and
the offer of money, official duty, or the absence of
another book in prison, on a wet day in a country inn,
or under other circumstances when one must read or
die. Even in these latter cases he thinks he might be
enough like Lord Foppington to prefer his own
thoughts for at least a considerable time. Yet it is
quite certain that many persons, to whom the writer is
not such a fool as to consider himself superior, and
some to whom he is just wise enough to acknowledge
his great inferiority, have found rest and refreshment
in these two books. And it is a matter fortunately
outside of all personal considerations and individual
judgments whatsoever that the elaborate analysis displayed in them is in itself capable of affording almost
infinite satisfaction to numbers of the most different
tastes. It is in fact a sort of borrowing, with extension
and alteration, of the dramatist's instrument of the
soliloquy. Richardson adopted the nearest and most
obvious prosaic substitute on a larger scale, the letter—
while he further made use of a kind of *reportage*, not
so much (though he has something also of this) in the
circumstantial multiplication of detail like Defoe's, as
in the recording of conversation almost and sometimes
quite *in extenso*.[1]

He also varied his scenes a good deal, if he did not
avail himself much [2] of elaborate outdoor description—
that was not in the way of the time—still less of those
indoor " settings " of which, except Smollett, who had
ideas of it, no eighteenth‑century novelist made
much as yet, and which was practically introduced
by Scott. Thus, if he never perhaps produced a

---

[1] Diderot, in his famous glorification or apotheosis of Richardson, admits and
makes a merit of the recounting of scenes, such as a dinner-table conversation,
totidem verbis—as if they had actually been overheard.

[2] He did to some extent.

really perfect novel, he presented his readers and provided his successors with a very large stock of novel materials and methods, while, as has been said, in *Pamela*, as it first appeared, he did something more.

The novelty and volume of the entertainment provided, the power unquestionably displayed in the providing, and (in the case of the later and *Fielding.* larger books) the strength of the appeal to the nascent taste for " sensibility," account quite sufficiently for the reception which Richardson's books found. Yet it is difficult to believe that the average reader of the better class *s'amusait franchement*,[1] to quote once more a phrase of Emile de Girardin's, which occurs very frequently to those who know it. But, except in one case perhaps, the quality or faculty of frank amusement certainly could not be denied (except by persons with very poor and unhappy brains, or of a cast of mind too much sicklied with moral preoccupations) to the work of Richardson's great successor, parodist, and superior, Henry Fielding. We know indeed that in one famous instance, just referred to in a note, this frankness of his was used against him—that the absence of parade and ceremony, the self-sufficient and careless ease of his methods, was taken, or pretended to be taken, by Johnson as a proof of shallowness and superficiality. Yet Johnson himself supplied the most destructive reply to his charge by admitting that he had read *Amelia* through at a sitting, an honour which, as we know, he very rarely bestowed upon books. And (at one time at least) he had not read *Joseph Andrews*.

---

[1] The utterly "damning" quality of Johnson's thousand times quoted (and intentionally, of course, the reverse of "faint") praise seems to have been too little realised. If the reader of a story for the story feels inclined to hang himself the author of that story ought to have first turn at the gallows. A psychological treatise has no business to masquerade as a novel. And we know as a matter of fact, from Fanny Burney, that the Duchess of Portland—Prior's "noble lovely little Peggy," and if not a blue stocking, a woman of sense and cultivation, found Richardson, and said that her friends found him, "heavy" and "depressing."

Here also, as in Richardson's case, though the ways of the two men were so different, the pure story-gift *Joseph* was never better displayed than in its first *Andrews.* exercise. How strong this gift was in Fielding might almost be seen from the way in which it has got the better of the natural cramping effect of parody itself. Generally speaking, to enjoy a parody, it is necessary to be pretty well acquainted with the thing parodied.[1] This familiarity may have existed in the first readers of *Joseph Andrews* ; but it certainly has not usually existed in their successors. Yet nobody can find the slightest difficulty in comprehending or appreciating the adventures of Pamela's brother, however little he knows about those of his supposed sister, though this later knowledge may add a little to the piquancy of some of the episodes. Indeed there is a common theory, not worth discussing here, that Fielding forgot all about his own starting-point, and only remembered it—not to extraordinary advantage—at the very end. But the *liveness* of the whole, the spontaneous, artless (though so artful) reality, carries everything off. It is a question, though to some people it may seem a blasphemous one, whether the elaborate and ostentatious analytical and synthetical processes of Richardson do not leave a taint of the laboratory—a trail of the "research student"—over *his* most successful creations. Joseph and Fanny themselves, though early subjects of the bad little cherub who watches over good young heroes and heroines, escape harm to an unusual extent ; while evil influences are present in decreasing measure, and good in increasing, through the Towwowses and Trullibers, through Betty and Mrs. Slipslop, till, in the sublime, the unprecedented, the rarely equalled, and the never surpassed figure of Parson Adams, the evil ones disappear altogether. Never since Cervantes in any literature,

---

[1] See Johnson as quoted above (p. 71) on the imitators of Spenser. The necessity is all the greater the less "serious" the copy.

never since Shakespeare in English, and hardly out
of these two in modern books, had there been such a
pure creation, such an example of humanity, not so
much copied from life into literature, as passing direct
from literature into life, as that admirable and almost
adorable student of Aeschylus, practitioner of cudgel
play, and servant of his Master. Of course the thing
is not a faultless monstrosity: there are some faults in
it, the effect of insufficient practice, especially the
tedious " inset " of Mr. Wilson's experiences.[1] But
these things themselves pleased the groundlings of
Georgian times, just as Shakespeare's word-plays
pleased those of Elizabethan, and as other things
unnecessary to mention please those of our own. They
are, unlike Richardson's shortcomings and undue pro-
longings, easily negligible, while the rest is pure and
perpetual delight.

It would be foolishly and indeed childishly pro-
vocative to give the same description to *Joseph's*
Jonathan successor in publication, though probably
Wild. (for more reasons than one) forerunner in
composition — *Jonathan Wild* — without proviso or
reservation. A very large number even of well
qualified persons—perhaps even a very large majority
of them—do not seem to find in *Jonathan* delight of
the intensest kind, if they even find delight in it at all.
To the general it is much worse than caviare ; it is
more like asafœtida, without even pungency to recommend it. Some, not dull themselves, have found
it dull ; some, whose gust is as a rule fairly or even
more than fairly catholic, have found it disgusting.
Perhaps the most curious thing is that some (to take
yet a further class) who have no objection to what are
called " grime "-novels in general, who relish and revel
in the modern variety, do not seem to be able to
" taste " this curious little piece. Now the present
writer as a rule positively dislikes, and is distinctly

---

[1] And even these are relieved by Adams's "groans" and the occasions of them.

bored by, the grime-novel, whether it presents itself in the lower examples of the old picaresque style, or in our modern "realistic" productions. Yet to him *Jonathan Wild* has always been, from his first reading of it, in a measure rather increasing than decreasing, a real joy. It is of course not a book that one reads extremely often, for obvious reasons; not that there is, to any one who can taste it at all, anything distasteful in it, but that its quintessenced and sustained pungency requires a fresh palate, rested and standardised with less high-flavoured food, to enjoy it thoroughly.

The delight which it affords is almost as purely intellectual as any which can be, at the same time, æsthetic. There is a certain interest of story, and in this it is distinguished from its great and perhaps only predecessor in the same line, the *Tale of a Tub*. And its interest is not concentrated on a prolonged history of one character, as it is in the chief of its successors, *Barry Lyndon*. It has no passages equal to the greatest of Swift's, but its character and its story make it more strictly "delectable" as a whole; while it is superior to Thackeray's own rather overpraised attempt in equality and concentration. It is true that a Devil's Advocate of good qualifications for his post might urge that Fielding has not exactly carried out what seems to have been his own intention. The satire is ostensibly, as far as the *parabases* [1] and comments go, moral, and to some extent political. But those who most enjoy *Jonathan* pay hardly any attention at all to the political bent, which is trite and capable of a good deal of *retorsion*. As for the moral one, the important constituent of it, the virtuous Heartfree, is, if not exactly a nuisance, a very scanty contributor to the interest: while the other characters are so frankly destitute of all notions of morality that they do not fall under the jurisdiction of

---

[1] *Graecum est* and some call it pedantic; but it is the only single word in any language for those episodic addresses, from the author to the reader, which are so characteristic of Fielding and Thackeray, which irritate some people so much, and perhaps delight others all the more because of the fact of this irritation.

that court. With the exception of Miss Theodosia (who is a kind of magpie or grey-hen), they are all studies in unrelieved black. But their black, though unrelieved, is marvellously *nuanced*; and they are so utterly human in their inhumanity that a fresh scale of values arises under which they justify themselves, and by help of which the surpassing irony—never excessive, never inadequate—of style and treatment can have free play. Even such a transient, though not in the least embarrassed, phantom as Miss Straddle is arch-real; how much more Jonathan himself and the divine (or at least superhumanly detestable) Letitia, and the rest! The gravity as well as the easy supremacy of art with which the manipulator of these diabolically alive puppets handles them; the absence alike of savagery and of mere amusement in his vivisection, preparation, and exhibition of them; the perfection with which this artistic object, certainly the actual one, whether it was the conscious one or not, is achieved, make the thing absolutely unique. The only other novelist who has come near to it in complete dispassionateness is Miss Austen.

When we get [1] to *Tom Jones* there is more prospect of agreement. Tom has shocked some persons who
Tom Jones. have been spoken of already, and he has disappointed other persons of whom something may be said later. The last person of importance who did not like him from one point of view was probably Colonel Newcome. The persons, whether of importance or not, who have disliked him more recently from the other point of view, it is unnecessary and might be disagreeable to specify. In

---

[1] The provision of delight by Jonathan's companion in the Miscellanies of 1743, *A Journey from this World to the Next,* is by no means small. There are scores in it of those sentences piercing life to the joints and marrow, and laying the whole thing bare at the particular point, which are characteristic of Fielding. But it is pretty obvious novice-work—imitative frequently, dull sometimes, with at best anecdotes in place of story, and traits in lieu of characters. No one who has rejoiced in the novels should fail to read it, and not many fit readers will read it only once; but it is not a good *introduction* to its author.

that middle region of appreciation which, as with mountains, is also the highest, there is no doubt about his history. The thing could not have been better done ; though some people might like " The Man of the Hill " omitted (as he can be without affecting the general merits in the least, being merely a parenthesis), and others would bring against Blifil something like the objections which have been hinted above against Heartfree. It is almost a pity that the comparative study of literature was rare in the eighteenth century ; for the delight which, in a creditable number of cases, was excited by the book would have been infinitely increased. One such student indeed there was ; but Gray, though he liked *Joseph Andrews*, had apparently not enough manliness to see some of Fielding's real merits, and in respect to this is said to have actually agreed with Johnson—the poles meeting for once—as to his inferiority to Richardson in constructive psychology. It was still more unfortunate that there was no one like Dryden, in whom genius played the part of knowledge, to say, as Dryden himself said of Chaucer, " Here is God's plenty."

For it indeed is " an abounding book." One can afford, for many reasons, to leave almost untouched that question of its eminence as a construction which has been settled for all time in the minds of all competent judges by Gibbon, Coleridge, and Scott ; while recent attempts to dispute the settlement have merely settled the attempters' own position as critics. Moreover, except to special natures, excellence of construction is perhaps the least delight-giving merit of a novel. It may indirectly contribute to satisfaction ; it may even be, as some contend, indispensable thereto ; but you do not, until you are a very sophisticated person, appreciate it or enjoy it directly. The interest of the incidents ; the narrative faculty shown in setting them forth ; the truth, liveliness, and freshness of the characters ; the efficacy of such description as there is ; the

point, variety, suitability, and what not of the dialogue
—these are what give the direct pleasure of novel
reading. And Fielding here puts the whole plant of
the pleasure-giver in motion, as no novel-writer—not
even Cervantes—had ever done before.[1] The shapes
arise—shapes gracious, or comic, or villainous, or
ordinary-made-extraordinary, of almost all kinds—
Sophia and Mrs. Waters and Lady Bellaston, the
Squire and his sister, Black George and Blifil, Thwac-
kum and Square, Partridge and Allworthy and the
rest. They group themselves into the companies, they
adjust themselves to the scenes, that come so naturally.
They pose (though in one sense the word is inappropriate enough) before the backgrounds of the park-lands
of Somerset, or of the Upton Inn, by Sabrina of the
degenerate and muddy countenance, or of the country
roads and of the town streets, "as answers the end of their
being created." [2] They talk to the same purpose—
always like men and women, if not of the special world
of to-day, of one which is only that world in somewhat
earlier garb of garment and phrase of speech. To
use one of the few emphatic vernacularities which have
fortunately never gone out of fashion, and, it may be
hoped, never will—they are " all right." They pass,
and all's well ; only not quite so well as when they
were actually passing.

But then these *parabases*, which so do torment our
modernest critics in Fielding and in his greatest
Fielding's successor ? For my own part I have always
"parabases." considered this objection as one of the
feeblest in all that critical history with which I am
fairly well acquainted. Of course, if the question is
left at mere *liking*, there is nothing to say. I have no

---

[1] He has not of course the tragic and romantic background and "underground"
which exalt and set off his great predecessor and master in the comic prose epic
after so unique a fashion : but this is his only inferiority, if indeed it is an inferiority
at all and not only a difference. Also, though it is a bold word, his work has some
elements of pleasure which are not in *Don Quixote*, while it is free from some of the
less delightful points in *Don Quixote* itself.

[2] *Vide supra* p. 53.

more right to quarrel with their dislike than they with my liking. But when they say, not that the things are displeasing to them, but that they are faults of art, then I have a right to demand proof. I have never received it. It is said that these digressions are faulty because they "interrupt the muffins "—becaus : the serene development of plot and character is entirely broken into by them. But is this really the case, save with those whose souls, as Dryden well put it about another cavil, are " heavier than their senses ? " It is true, for instance, that the Meredithian *ambages* of style and phrase do delay and interrupt reading. It may be that, as the Meredithians themselves say, the interruption is worth suffering, that you ought to discipline yourself to digest the knotty knarry insets, and that pleasure as well as profit will result from the digestion. It may be so. But interruption itself—except possibly but doubtfully in the case of some persons of portentously rapid intelligence, probably if not certainly in that of a larger number who bolt the phrases whole— is there. With the Fielding-Thackeray digression it is different. In Fielding himself it usually occurs unblushingly but obligingly at the beginning of a chapter —you can skip it with hardly so much exertion as that by which you avoid or overstep a stone in your path. It is in fact little more than the prose equivalent of a Greek chorus, or even of those lyrics which, in some modern plays, are left to the discretion of the actor or the reader to put in or leave out.

Another objection, brought more frequently against Thackeray than against Fielding, but sometimes applying to both, is that the things are impertinent sermonisings—intrusions of the author's own thoughts, sentiments, and opinions ; excesses of the heresy of instruction, etc. etc. This is an even less exquisite song than the other. In the first place their essential " skippableness " covers them from this attack also, in the second the objection betrays both bumptiousness

and critical paralogism. One need not be the meekest
man on earth, or the least self-confident, to have a very
shrewd suspicion that, on the whole, the opinions,
sentiments, judgments of a man of genius may be at
least not improbably worth attending to, and will be
still more probably well expressed. But there is more
to say, and nobody is arguing—at least it certainly is
not being argued here—that a bad parabasis is a good
thing. "Prove all things ; hold fast to that which is
good " is the motto of good criticism as well as of good
religion. Prove Fielding as much as you like, you
will practically find him good throughout.

The general approval which, *exceptis* not too cere-
moniously *excipiendis quibusdam*, rests upon *Tom Jones*,
does not shelter *Amelia* quite to the same
extent. There is in its favour that singular
and already quoted admission of Johnson, Fielding's
most formidable enemy—an admission increased a
little in interest by the fact that some have seen in Dr.
Harrison (the book's good if somewhat humoursome
half-hero) strong traits of the other Doctor himself.
But some readers at all times have found it lacking in
excitement and sustained interest ; while bold bad men,
for a generation or two, have thought Amelia rather
mawkish in her perfection, and Booth a poor weak
creature alike in vice and in virtue. Except from a
rather sentimental point of view it is difficult to get up at
first the enthusiasm which one feels for *Joseph* and for
Tom—which here and there some may be found to feel
for *Jonathan*. But only think what one's opinion
would be if their gracious sister existed without them !

And the " abundance " remains. The faults of
Amelia's faultlessness, and the charms of it, must appeal
at once to any one who by nature can see either or both.
They want no critical exposition: they simply shed it
and remain as they are. You can understand the
whole of Booth, and that means (not to go to the entire
length of the proverb) that you can pardon most of

Amelia.

him. The others—Miss Matthews, Colonel Bath, Colonel James, that not wholly agreeable but wholly human sister of Bath and wife of James, Harrison and his prig of a son, so apparently different from but so fundamentally alike those later academic prigs of ours— these and the minors of all sorts give you room and verge enough for the cult of the Comic Spirit in almost every direction.

Finally, there is the incomparable *Voyage to Lisbon*, perhaps the most unique swan-song in the world, with its quaint minute Dutch painting, its heroic endurance and quiet exhibition of pain, its glances now and then at things that the author has rarely or never touched before—which completes one of the great Works and Days, gives the result of the Hour and the Man at one moment, in the marvellous story of English literature and of English men of letters.

One of the most curious ineptitudes on this subject is the judgment of Walter Bagehot that the parallel of

Bagehot on Fielding and Thackeray.

Fielding and Thackeray is wrong because Fielding had " a bold spirit of bounding happiness " and Thackeray was " a victim of sensibility who could not help wondering what the footman behind his chair would think and say "— with more to the same effect. From this judgment, a more recent writer has said, " there can be no loophole of appeal." Well, it is not necessary to look for loopholes when the door stands open, and the real judgment (for Bagehot's is an indictment or an advocate's plea, not a judgment) is " No case." In the first place there is an evident confusion between the personality and the craftsmanship of the two authors. Nobody but a native of Paraguay [1] would say that Fielding and Thackeray were wholly, or even to any great extent, alike as men ; the point always drawn by critical experts is the companionship—and the almost

---

[1] " O people of Paraguay ! how long will you continue idiots ? " (*Dr. Francia, their dictator, as reported by Carlyle*).

exclusive companionship—of their creations in life-
likeness. Moreover Thackeray's sensitiveness to the
footman's thought was only part of that astonishing gift
which made him always know what " the other fellow,"
footman or financier, duke or cook, *was* thinking.
Fielding had the same faculty, but here Johnson's
injurious comparison between him and Richardson
acquires some value. He did not care to lay its
processes — the stages of the analysis — bare as
Thackeray did. But the fact is that Bagehot, though
one of the numerous whims or crotchets of the
most crotchety of centuries has recently "taken him
up," was, with all the acuteness of his mind in
divers ways, the variety of his interests, and the often
considerable charm of his writing, a *very* amateur
critic ; and like most amateurs, rather prone to set
himself against accepted judgments in order to show
his own originality.[1]

But what deceived Bagehot may help us to clear
our vision in a way specially suitable to the purposes
of this book. Undoubtedly an eighteenth-century
writer, as compared with a nineteenth and still more
with a twentieth, had a certain capacity for that " taking
of short views " in which a critic who belonged to both
eighteenth and nineteenth found a shield against
distinct *un*happiness. Men then " cultivated the
garden," and did not trouble themselves much to look
over the garden walls. It is an entire mistake to think
that Richardson did this ; his sentimental and analytic
psychology never goes anywhere near the infinite or
even the unusual. But what Fielding could do was
to make the common garden plot not common by
bringing it under the species of the eternal and the
universal. He never potters or higgles ; but his motto
is always *age quod agis*. He lives in no fool's paradise,
but he does not look out for stools to be melancholy

[1] And after all Bagehot's judgment is only an application of Lady Mary's dictum
that her cousin " could feel happiness with his cook-maid."

K

upon. Not all humanity is in him ; but everything that is in him is human.

The attractions of Smollett, whether they are of a lower kind or not (and few competent judges, except Smollett— contrasts of some difficulty in and about him. Scott, who had both patriotic and professional [1] reasons for partisanship, have denied that they are), require more discriminate handling. To one not unimportant class of humanity Smollett is probably the most attractive of all the four great eighteenth-century novelists, if not of all those of the eighteenth and early nineteenth, except Scott at one end and Defoe at the other. The delight of boys in *Roderick Random* and its successors has been enthusiastically proclaimed by Dickens and other great persons ; while many myriads (the term is not in the least rhetorical, for there have been some thirty generations of boys from ten to sixteen since Roderick swaggered into the world) of small ones have felt what these others expressed. Smollett hardly ever preaches or reflects or advocates. He will still be telling of *doing*, and this doing, though, as Thackeray acutely remarked, it is seldom invented but usually observed or experienced, is of the liveliest kind. His characters, if not subtle, are thoroughly " lived." His descriptions, especially of interiors, are perhaps better than those of any one before him, not in extraneous talkee-talkee and word-painting, but in vivid staging and stage-furnishing of his actual scene. His horse-play amuses boyhood ; his nastiness does not disgust it ; the spice of quarrelsomeness, advancing towards ruffianism in some cases, corresponds to the rough-and-

---

[1] He evidently saw that gift of Smollett's for "interior" drawing in the novel which has been and will be noticed ; and which he himself was to inherit and use far more effectively. (Also his purely narrative excellence, for which see below.) Lamb (*teste* Hazlitt who, however, says he converted the heretic) was inclined to agree with Scott. But Lamb's judgment was notoriously as uncertain at some times as it was consummate at others.

tumble ways of healthy youth, or at any rate does not offend them. There is nothing intricate or cryptic in him. And even in *Humphrey Clinker*, which seems to maturer estimates infinitely his best thing, and to which the above indirect sketch would do some injustice, there is enough of the simpler attractions not to fail to please the simpler tastes.

Those of us, however, to whom the gods have not shown their love with the killing kindness of the proverb, do not (unless we have caught the trick of that cult of the ugly which has been fashionable for nearly a generation) find it possible to like Smollett's earlier work quite frankly. Roderick Random is a scarcely tolerable young cub, and Peregrine Pickle is a quite intolerable young blackguard, without their author or creator being, to all appearance, at all aware of the two facts. He seems to have thought Roderick an honest and rather a fine young fellow ; Peregrine a "young blood" and nothing worse: whereas, in the case of "Perry" at least, all the beatings that ever fell on the guileless and guiltless body of Don Quixote, *plus* those inflicted on Sancho, would not have been sufficient to expiate his executed pranks and his attempted crime. For sheer nastiness nobody of genius except Swift (for that of Rabelais, and still more certain things in Cervantes himself, fall out of real comparison) has ever come near Smollett. His extreme license in other directions (unfortunately in one case at least made worse by the fact that he took money for giving it scope) put the first edition of his second book on the *Index Librorum Prohibitorum*, and in numerous other cases goes near the line. Moreover the one excuse of such license, that it is prompted or at least accompanied either by passion or by humour, never applies in his case. In no single instance does he show the slightest conception of what passion is ; the humour of such histories as those of Miss Williams and Lady Vane is what Carlyle used to call a "ghastly *minus* quantity," though he can of course show this all-saving quality elsewhere. Although he seems personally to have been one of those " whose bark is worse than their bite," the barks, or rather the snarls and growls, are so continuous that until one comes to *Humphrey Clinker* itself, almost all the inhabitants of his world seem to be, if not exactly devils, human beings who are either malignant, or feeble-minded, or both.

Nevertheless, Smollett's powers of amusing are very great, except in *The Adventures of an Atom*, and perhaps in the unlucky *Journal*, where the everlasting grumble becomes merely a bore, though the book has some merits. Even *Sir Lancelot Greaves*, which has been fallen foul of by nearly everybody, is quite good reading if you consent to sink, or take for granted, the improbability of an English eighteenth-century Don Quixote extending his adventures much beyond a day or two, without the law coming down on him. But any one who refuses to make this concession is of the class of persons who really have no business with novels at all. In this " worst," as the common phrase goes, of his intentionally amusing books, Smollett still shows that singular narrative faculty which is his great gift : and, as it happens, its very opening scene is a really admirable example of the other gift of " interior " painting which has been mentioned, and which nobody had had—or at any rate had thought of using—to the same extent before.

In the other books this narrative gift, and this faculty of placing and staging as well as telling the story, have of course a much better chance. However often you may have read *Roderick Random*, however much the details may sometimes make your gorge rise, and its spirit and temper may disgust you in less physical ways, it is impossible not to recognise the manner in which chronicle or panorama—for there is no real central action—is carried on before your eyes, afloat

A master of narrative and of amusement.

and ashore, abroad and at home, in town and country, but always with extraordinary craftsmanship in the mere way of telling. The larger, more varied, and even less connected *Peregrine Pickle* shows no falling off in this respect ; though it sometimes seems to be on the point of passing into a sort of *Arabian Nights* congeries of separate Tales, with a few connecting characters, it never loses " holding " interest. An English Scheherazade would have been quite safe if her sister had had it at her finger's ends and divided it skilfully.

It is perhaps impossible to say the same of *Ferdinand, Count Fathom* as a whole. Smollett's stock of observation and experience, though far from exhausted, was getting low ; and his invention did not supply him with anything much more than the stock picaresque machinery. But that his narrative faculty, when he has anything to narrate, is as good as ever is shown by the famous opening scenes, and by passages now and then throughout.

To say that he gave himself time to recuperate and restock would be somewhat misleading, for though the novels from *Random* to *Fathom* followed each other with some rapidity, and nothing of the same kind appeared, except the short and slight pastiche of *Don Quixote*, for a considerable period, the author was occupied by an unceasing and exhausting round of practice, journalism, historical bookmaking, controversy, foreign travel, with more bookmaking in translation. But the reservoir of experience and observation is one which, in fit cases, fills itself insensibly and automatically ; and by the

Illustrations chiefly from Humphrey Clinker.

time when in his last days at Leghorn— a broken man, but a man of genius still—he began *Humphrey Clinker*, the unfailing narrative gift (which, though he tried it in the rather dangerous letter form, was equal to the occasion) found plenty of material to work upon. It has been a fashion

of critics, rather surprising in more ways than one, to
regard Smollett's heroes—at least Roderick, Peregrine, and Matthew Bramble—as consciously or unconsciously autobiographic or self-picturing at different
times of his life.   That, in the first two cases, this is an
uncommonly bad compliment is not quite so fatal to
the truth of the theory as the simple fact that neither a
Roderick nor (still less) a Peregrine could possibly
have grown up into a Bramble.   Some of their extraneous faults or follies he might in youth have been
guilty of ; but as they are both fellows without even a
trace of gentlemanliness, and he is a thorough though
eccentric and " humorous " gentleman, that transformation of the entities or identities is impossible.

As to one of the minor delectations of this very
delectable book, some more of the critical mistakes,
which seem rather to cluster round Smollett's complex
and slightly enigmatic personality in life and letters,
may seem to have been committed.   The misspelling
of Winifred and her mistress has been called
" original," which it certainly is not, being clearly
taken from Swift, though, like the kiss in *Mademoiselle
de Maupin*, " reviewed, corrected, and considerably
augmented "—a process, by the way, to which it was
itself subjected later by Dickens and by Thackeray still
more.   The Fadladeens of criticism have of course
objected to this device, or at least dismissed it loftily,
as childish, mechanical, and rather to be despised.   To
happier judgments it is a great promoter of happiness.
But of course it derives only a part, and a small part, of
its charm from its independent existence.   Many writers
since Smollett have tried it ; and when they have not
been able to " live up to it " in other ways they have
failed miserably and to extinction boringly.   It is
because here, as in Swift to no small extent and in
Thackeray to the greatest extent possible, it is accom-
modated to the characters, and so heightens and distinguishes them, that it gives so much pleasure.   And

this is the more remarkable because one of the great advantages which *Humphrey Clinker* possessed over its predecessors is exactly this point of character. Character in its proper—or at least its " properest "—sense had never been Smollett's forte. He could do excellent " character-parts " of the theatrical kind—his sailors especially, in *Random* and *Pickle*, are justly famous. He had, if not exactly originated, borrowed from drama also, and greatly improved the " national " character part, as in the Morgan of *Roderick Random*, and he was to repeat this with still greater success in the Lismahago of *Humphrey Clinker* itself.

But if Lismahago be compared with Morgan, the advance, to be charged of course to some extent but not wholly to the fact of compatriotism, is very noticeable. Morgan, though a most lively type, is much more of a type—the " Taffy " of the stage from Fluellen through his debased successors downwards. Lismahago, though intensely Scotch, is also very largely individual. He is very nearly, if not quite, on a level with Richie Moniplies and Dugald Dalgetty, if he falls short of the Baron and the Antiquary. It is curious by the way that Scott, unduly as he exalts Smollett, is actually unjust to Lismahago, saying little more of him than that he was " perhaps not a caricature," though, or because, he himself knew the assigned original.

But the rendering of the eccentric, though it pleases the great popular vulgar on the one hand and, in consideration of the difficulty of bringing it off completely, the small critical vulgar on the other, never yields but a minor triumph to the " purged considerate mind." It is, as all the best judges have seen, and as some of them have specifically acknowledged, the " making of the common as if it were not common," the casting of the glory of sunlight or the mystery of moonlight on the obvious, the forcing of the reader to disregard the ordinary and feel it extraordinary, which is the real achievement of the artist in fiction. Smollett

could not do this as Fielding could, and therefore he is
inferior ; he needed some touch of the eccentric itself,
be it " humours " or bad-spelling, practical jokes, *haut
goût*, satire, " seasoning " of some kind to make his
common market meat go down. But he has never
applied these more successfully, and hardly ever less
excessively, than in the case of Matthew Bramble ; and
though Matthew's sister and his maid take a little more
advantage of the spice-box and the salt-cellar, they can
scarcely be said to rely on it. Moreover, this happy
adjustment pervades almost all, if not all, the minor
characters, incidents, and scenes. With the slight
allowances for man and time specified already, there is
hardly a more entertaining book in English fiction than
Humphrey Clinker.

Personalia in criticism are sometimes deprecated or
condemned altogether, and are still oftener regarded
with suspicion and dislike. Of course they,
like all other things, may be overdone or
done in the wrong manner. But as, after
all, criticism is worthless if it is not based
upon personal experience, the discouraging of the
recital of that experience seems as strange as it would be
in the case of scientific experiments. It so happens
that the present writer can give a rather exceptional
record of the kind in the case of Smollett, especially
from the point of view from which Smollett is being
chiefly treated here—mainly as an *amuseur*, which term,
though its intention in French has usually been
derogatory, has been unintentionally cleansed by rash
application of it to Dumas. The duty, if not the sole
duty, of an *amuseur* is to amuse ; and if he fails to do it,
or, having done it, fails to continue to do it, he may be
said to fail generally. Now in some cases the continuation is secured in a partly illegitimate way. A
book or an author becomes a habit ; and as in the case
of other habits, *usus concinnat amorem.* The defects as
well as the merits become familiar and agreeable ; the

*In it and in
others a
champion
amuseur.*

whole is regarded like the " old slippers " that so did revolt the high-toned mind of Miss Gabler.

But when books are read at long and irregular intervals, so that the influence of different ages, moods, and circumstances are brought to bear, the total result should be a " corrected " and *pro tanto* final one. The present writer was very familiar with Smollett in his youth, and say up to the age of five and twenty. Then, in one of those accidents which are among the fates of books, he read him very little (certainly less than Fielding) for another five and twenty. A commission to edit him then brought about a most thorough reading and re-reading for the construction of prefaces, and the revision of proofs, and then naturally enough even *Roderick Random* and *Humphrey Clinker* fell out of hand for a time. Of late, and practically in old age, they have been read again, both for literary purposes and for mere pastime. The estimates of youth, of middle age, and of what one may hope is not yet second childhood, have of course varied somewhat ; an entire absence of variation would only prove the want of sensibility of the testing instrument. But as regards the pre-eminence of narrative faculty which has been chiefly held up here, Smollett stands this severe test remarkably. You may dislike more and more—or at least as much as ever—the callous selfishness of Roderick, the positive brutality and malice of Peregrine, the unbroken grime (till his not very probable repentance) of Fathom, and the patches of mere nastiness which disfigure even *Humphrey Clinker*. You may quarrel more (this deponent doth not, but others may) with the excessive improbability of *Sir Lancelot Greaves*. But this will not affect—it at least has not affected in the present case—the delight in the unfailing spring of narrative power which almost all the books, the first and last especially, show ; and you may even feel inclined to admit that as a *mere* tale-teller Smollett really does deserve the title of best of this great bunch of four. Fielding of course, as has been argued, has other and higher merits to which Smollett cannot pretend, and when he chooses he can run Smollett hard, in fact can bring off a dead-heat at least even here ; but he very often does not choose. Richardson notoriously cannot tell a story, or rather he simply will not, and deliberately clogs or deluges his action with talk. Sterne ostentatiously proclaims that he has no story to tell, though he manages to inset infinite storylets, which he tells sometimes very delectably. But Smollett, save on the rare occasions when he too chooses not to exercise his power, tells consummately. It was probably a recognition of this faculty, as well as an innocent compatriotism, which made Scott rank him decidedly too high as a whole ; it is certainly this which has always made him the delight of ingenuous youth ; and it is this which should excuse, or at least counterbalance, his faults to those who, though " age " may have " clawed them into his clutch," have not forgotten that they " had ever been such " as their youth was once. His part of the " Paradise of the Novel " is no doubt a *Paradisus valde terrestris* ; but his way of initiating it gave the truest impulse to the attainment by others of the paradisal quality of amusement, of refreshment, and (hurly-burly as his books are in some of their scenes) of rest.

In turning to the fourth member of this great group, one may experience no slight feeling of relief at having got over the most, indeed the only, irksome part of the matter already. We have not

Sterne.

to consider the point—formerly confessed and now avoided—whether a " nice " judgment in the old sense of the adjective must condemn Sterne ; we have only to see whether he can be found " nice " in the more modern acceptation which precisians have in vain protested against—*i.e.* " delectable." It may be said plumply that the person who does not find him so is profoundly to be pitied. It is of course possible, even

without taking into account the outrages on Mrs.
Grundy at all, to find plenty of what Sterne himself
would call " stop-watch " objections to him ; and even
some which will hold valid in a much higher court
than that of stop-watch criticism.   What was said
not long ago of Smollett applies *mutatis mutandis* to
him.   He relies far too much upon eccentricity, and
this eccentricity is sometimes of an even lower kind
than Smollett's.   He has purely mechanical tricks with
typography—dots, dashes, etc.—sheer "clowning," not
at all of the Shakespeare-clown fashion, with blacked
pages and even with end-papers stuck in the middle of
matter, with blank spaces and so on.   His deliberate and
monotonous discontinuity or total absence of story is
(in *Tristram* at least) sometimes a mere bore: and
the " sensibility " which so charmed his own day has
altogether ceased to charm not merely our day but
many a long day before ours.   All this is known and
well known—*archi-connu*—not to be contested or even
talked about much by anybody who is not writing for
mere instruction, or else taking the idle and childish
line of denying patent facts to get credit of paradox
and epigram.   But it cannot be truly retorted that the
same objection applies to the eulogy, or at least the
reasoned eulogy of him.   Since the late Mr. Traill's
admirable book a good deal of new matter has accrued
about the man ; but unfortunately new knowledge
about the man is apt rather to burden afresh that
uglier side, of the account of which we take no more
notice.

There are, on the other hand, many signs that
Sterne is little read. There have, of course, been new
Much read at editions of him—the present writer is represent day ? sponsible for one, and there have been
others since.   But in common with all eighteenth-
century writers, save perhaps Johnson, he seems to
have slipped once more out of the favourite reading of
persons who busy themselves " pastimeously " with

literature.   To anybody who has felt the pulses of literary history long and carefully, it may seem not improbable that the recent " slump " in eighteenth-century values is part of that curious and very amusing anti-Victorianism, of the absurdity of which its victims do not seem even yet to be conscious.   Thackeray and those about him down to men living recently, such as Sir Leslie Stephen, and others still with us, " took up " the eighteenth century, so there must be something bad about it.   Or, if you take it up yourself, you must take it up in a new way.

For us let it be sufficient if we can stand on the old way, and perhaps clear it a little of rubbish which may have accumulated on it, and make it out a little freshly. Not indeed that much labour is required.   Sterne is inviting enough to any one who does not allow himself to be frightened off, either by the moral taint or by the artistic or inartistic tricks already mentioned.

One thing may be and ought to be said, nor can it be said too strongly.   Sterne founded and evidently meant to found the modern eccentric novel. The eccentric novel earlier If anybody dislikes the eccentric novel— and later. thinks it a mistake or a bore—he has only got to keep away from Sterne.   He may abuse the kind as much as he likes ; but in this initial example, almost more than anywhere else, it so clearly puts out the sign warning, " If you don't want eccentricity, seek another inn," that he has only himself to blame if he enters.

It is possible that some one may say, " But the eccentric novel had been invented long before by Rabelais."   The eccentric *romance* had been written by him, and for the matter of that it was much older than Master Francis himself, and goes back to the *chansons de gestes*.   But there is perhaps no point in which the difference between romance and novel— often difficult to define exactly, and dangerous if too roughly insisted on—is more clearly marked than here.

If not a certain extravagance, at any rate a certain inherent exemption from the ordinary bonds of time, space, and probability generally, belongs of right to romance. How did knights subsist when they were dungeoned for months or years, with nothing (apparently) but their unpleasant companions, the live toads and snakes, to eat, before the Sultan's daughter came down and set them free? Where did Sir Guyon get that extremely handy " iron lock " with which he temporarily at least silenced Occasion? especially when he had lost his horse and any possible saddle-bags? Did the Palmer keep a sort of small Army and Navy Stores in his wallet? These questions, which the somewhat dull scorner asks half seriously, and wholly with offensive intention, the really critical lover of romance dismisses with perfect unconcern.

We don't know and we don't care. Therefore to exaggerate these improbabilities to the point of bur-
Sterne's new lesque is a perfectly easy thing, and was
methods. done by very inferior creatures—authors of *Audigiers* and *Tournaments of Tottenham*—throughout the Middle Ages. It is indeed not an easy matter to add and infuse the wisdom and the wit, the scholarship and the poetry (yes! the poetry), the intense and intricate knowledge of human nature which Master Francis so consummately displays, and by dint of which, and of a certain *generosity* and transcendence even in the use of things not convenient, he comes out æthers above Sterne's region of sniggering innuendo. But as a work of art—it may be again and unhesitatingly affirmed—the eccentric novel is a much more difficult thing than the eccentric romance. Here the basis has to be ordinary common life, and this has—to coin a necessary word—to be *eccentrified*. Directly upon the attempt to do this there follows the danger of mis-doing it or over-doing it, with the perhaps still greater danger of letting it run into ordinary life so as to spoil its ordinariness. Some people, not having thoroughly

comprehended Sterne, may question whether he has escaped these dangers, but, except perhaps in regard to the mechanical devices above admitted, it may be fearlessly maintained that he has. Mr. and Mrs. Shandy, My Uncle Toby, the Widow, Trim, Dr. Slop himself, even the " supers," like the cathedral dignitaries, are no doubt surrounded with a sort of mist of extravaganza and caricature by their adventures, their combinations, the author's cap-and-bell comment and digression, by this, that, and the other stroke of fantastry. But each one is, in himself or herself, a possibly and not in the least improbably actual being, such as anybody who has gone through life with his eyes open has known. They are in fact much more intrinsically true to actual life than many, if not almost all, the characters of Dickens. Take—the illustration has been used elsewhere—even such a mildly Rabelaisian episode as that of the Abbess and Margarita. You will find it vignetted, arabesqued, and burlesqued into the extraordinary and the " improper," but it remains in itself perfectly credible and convincing. It is really questionable whether the realism of the presentment, here and elsewhere, is not as unquestionable as its sentimentality or its fantastic handling. Sterne's method and object do not require or indeed permit him to force this realism of his figures home with the irresistible completeness of Fielding, or to present the analysis of them with the pitiless [1] minuteness of Richardson. But it is a question whether he is not really more of a realist than Smollett.

There may not be very many to whom this contrast of veracious underdraught and fantastic travesty is perceptible, or delightful when pointed out, but it is quite certain that it lies at the root of much of Sterne's actual attractiveness. That attractiveness, in itself, is

---

[1] This stock epithet for analysis may be saved from some at least of its banality in this instance by reflecting that it may be applied in two ways. Richardson's admirers have described him as pitiless to his personages ; some of his critics admit that he is so to his readers.

rarely denied ; it is the " but " that is Sterne's enemy. The way in which his scenes, sometimes corrected and finished as punctiliously as a steel engraving, some-times shaded off on all sides into a sort of halo of mist, impress themselves on the mind, is unique. Dickens had one of not the least of his flashes of genius when he made such an apparently unlikely person as Sam Weller speak of " the gentleman in the black silk smalls as knowed the young 'ooman as kept a goat." This dramatic-pictorial faculty is, in combination, very rare, and its effectiveness depends no doubt to some extent on the want of continuity in Sterne—on the way in which the shapes arise, grow vivid, flicker, faint, and disappear, speaking all the time, when they do speak, in strictest conformity with their presentation. Probably the effectiveness is also due in part to the fact that there is after all very little of it. Although *Tristram* was actually and originally dribbled out over a long series of years, and of cunningly small and widely printed volumes, both it and the *Sentimental Journey* will go, without " diamond " type, into four still smaller—two of moderate size, and even one somewhat but not excessively " squeezed." The stuff which they contain could not, in fact, be hastily produced, and probably could not have been produced at all except in Sterne's actual " twenty years of shooting, fishing, playing the flute," and occasionally performing the light duties of an eighteenth-century parson, followed by nearly half the time of travel, society, and what not. Nor could he, as probably, have produced much more if longer life had been granted him, nor will any wise person wish that he had done so. Of the good strong ale, and generous port, and subtly-flavoured claret, and wisdom-giving amontillado, and inspiring champagne, and ineffable burgundy of Fielding and Scott and Miss Austen and Dickens and Thackeray and other great novelists, one never can have too much. But Sterne is not a drink or a wine either of barley or grape—he is a liqueur—agreeable but not perhaps exactly whole-some, artistic but certainly artificial. And it is only a yokel who wants kümmel or goldwasser, chartreuse or curaçoa "in a moog."

In a certain sense, however, one may be said to be preaching to the converted and kicking at open doors in praising or recommending the four great novelists of the eighteenth century. There is at any rate a well-known kind of critic who is apt to assert haughtily that such things may be taken as read—a phrase which, by the way, has at least two meanings. But these great names, in a rather deleterious sense, overshadowed ten times their number of writers, who deserve more or less to be read, not merely for purposes of study, yet who are practically unknown to the general, and per-haps cannot be said to be well known even to the elect. In speaking thus one is not of course referring to books like *Rasselas* or the *Vicar of Wakefield*. Many people are obliged to know these in one sense of obligation, and almost every one is obliged to pretend to know them in the other. But they are more interesting from the literary point of view, and as part of their authors' works, than as novels. *Rasselas* notoriously has little more story to tell than the Knifegrinder had—in some ways almost less—and full as the *Vicar* is of delight-fully told incident and delicately "set" character, its quality is perhaps rather dramatic than strictly proper to fiction. The extraordinary power of the close of *Vathek* has secured it, and must always secure it, a success of esteem—to what extent the book is actually read and enjoyed one had perhaps better not enquire. The sensational character of *Caleb Williams* keeps it, or till very recently did keep it, on railway bookstalls: and motives more intelligible than respectable secure occasional reprints of *The Monk*, while the quite re-spectable enthusiasm of individuals has sometimes done

The minorities —not always so minor.

the same for *The Fool of Quality*, Mrs. Inchbald's books, and a few others. The critics, and her inclusion in the still charmed circle of Johnson, to use a phrase perhaps too vernacular to apply to a lady, "keep Miss Burney going," after a fashion.

But even that spell has not extended to two of Johnson's older friends of the same sex who were novelists—Mrs. Lennox [1] and Mrs. Sheridan, though their works are well worth reading. Who reads that very amusing book *Jemmy and Jenny Jessamy*? A foolish prudery is believed to have begun, and an almost more foolish insistence on up-to-dateness has continued, the exclusion of that charming thing *Peter Wilkins* from the boy's bookshelf. Everybody is supposed to know the *Castle of Otranto* ; one wonders how many people could stand an examination on it? Mrs. Radcliffe is still a name not infrequent on the pens of reviewers at least. One wonders again how many could tell, and attribute each to its proper heroine and context, any three adventures of Adeline, Emily, and Elena?

There is of course the excuse that the books are, at least in many cases, not easily attainable, except by going to large public libraries—and the present writer most frankly admits that he never reads books in any other place than his own house when he can possibly help it—or by hunting them up in catalogues, which is troublesome and somewhat though not very expensive,[2] while it sometimes provides very undesirable copies. For the things were read eagerly enough once, and are apt to bear tokens of the fact. I believe living authors of the baser sort grumble at the present rage for reprints of old work. But that rage, while repeating

---

[1] She has however a place in Mr. Austin Dobson's delightful *Eighteenth Century Vignettes*.

[2] Even the "very" must sometimes be admitted. The last copy of *Miss Betsy Thoughtless*, which the writer saw in a catalogue before writing the above words, was priced at two and a half guineas ; and Madame d'Arblay's unreadable "dotage" of *The Wanderer* has been known to fetch, in a disgustingly bad copy, money enough to buy half a dozen fresh ones of *Vanity Fair*, or *Esmond*, not in the cheapest editions.

issues of the four great ones, Miss Burney, and one or two others, has left untouched scores of novels, the worst of which is a better thing than the average six-shilling article of the present day.

These books (which, not of course to the novel gormandiser who spends whole days on his gormandising, but to the intelligent voluptuary who regards novels as things to be digested at leisure after his or her day's work, would probably provide an entire year's supply, even in the case of fairly rapid readers) may be divided into three classes. The first, rather thinly peopled, comes before *Pamela*; the second is contemporary with, but evidently to some extent and ever more and more influenced by, that book and the other work of the Four; the third is composed of the productions of definite " successors " and pupils from Fanny Burney onwards.

The first group, as has been said, are but a scanty folk, and it may be added a rather feeble one. Even by diligently searching Mr. Esdaile's above cited catalogue, which ends with the year before *Pamela*, one can fill out but a scurvy company. The political fictions or semi-fictions of Mrs. Manley are scarcely more than outside documents for historical students of the period: and the curious philosophical novel of *Gaudentio di Lucca*, though good wits have attempted to " take it up " from time to time, and though it has actually been attributed to the great Bishop Berkeley instead of to its obscure but actual author Simon Berington, is scarcely a refreshing production. Even the most satisfactory figure of the time in the department, Mrs. Eliza Haywood,[1] note-worthy here by two books published long after *Pamela*, was affected, in certainty, rather than probability, by the new examples of Richardson

---

[1] The production by which she attracted some of Pope's coarsest but not cleverest satire in the *Dunciad* was a following of Mrs. Manley in political semi-fiction, and not a novel proper—or even improper.

and Fielding. No one who has read *Idalia* and
any of its earlier companions on the one hand, *Miss
Betsy Thoughtless* and *Jemmy and Jenny Jessamy* on the
other, has failed to be struck by the extraordinary
difference between the two groups. The earlier ones
are only recommendable, and may well be only
tolerable, to students, being jejune tales in the French
manner, without zest of incident, subtlety of character,
liveliness of dialogue, or any other legitimate novel
attraction.

The advance as to all these things in the two later
novels is extraordinary. It is true that neither the
unlaboured and dæmonic lifelikeness of
Fielding, nor the elaborated verisimilitude
of Richardson, is to be found in them ; but to say
that is simply to say that they are obvious adventures in a new kind by one who, though she was
evidently a craftswoman of remarkable talent, was
not an artist of genius. Miss Betsy herself, if not an
absolutely live girl, is more like one than any previous heroine of fiction other than dramatic, except
Swift's Miss Notable, who is at least more than half
dramatically presented ; and there are characters in
both books (especially Lord and Lady Froth) who are
more vivid still, though their vivacity may be little
more than episodic. *Miss Betsy Thoughtless* has been
extravagantly described as " the first domestic novel
in English," and the indebtedness of *Evelina* to it has
been much over-estimated by Dunlop. But great praise
—praise even greater than this because thoroughly
just—is still due to it. Stimulated no doubt by the
examples referred to,[1] Mrs. Haywood seems to have
perceived that the " heroic " character of the French
tongue and older romances, and the " picaresque " of

Mrs. Haywood.

[1] To whom it is perhaps just to add Marivaux. That curious writer was undoubtedly much influenced by Addison ; but I have never shared the general
tendency to underrate his reflex effect on the English novel. That of Le Sage is a
thing "which nobody can deny," but it was still very mainly in the old picaresque
vein, as was also Scarron's.

the Spanish, French, and English, might safely be
abandoned for something corresponding to the comedy
of more or less real life which had now held the stage
for nearly a couple of generations ; discarding the
Congrevian tendency to stop action in order to fire
volleys of wit, availing oneself of the greater length,
scope, and variety of means provided by continuous
prose, and discarding likewise the conventions, stock
language, and other artificialities of the stage. She did
not of course do this perfectly, or she would have been
a genius ; she did do it in these two books to a very
great extent, and therefore she deserves the assignment
of talent, and they deserve what they do not now get—
the reward of reading. No doubt it is easy—con-
temptibly easy — to pick holes with their speaking
names, " Thoughtless," " Forward," etc., and still
easier, though even more contemptible, to talk about
obsolete manners, stilted diction, and the like. The
fact remains that, to any one of fairly catholic tastes,
Miss Betsy Thoughtless and *Jemmy and Jenny Jessamy* are
quite as good reading as any but the few very best
novels that the twentieth century has yet produced, and
much better reading than the enormous majority of the
others.

If, however, the little troubles, partly self-sought
or brought, of Miss Betsy, and the light though not
loose loves of Jenny and Jemmy, seem trivial

Mrs. Lennox.

to any persons of a serious turn to-day,
comedy of a more ambitious kind and something
like tragedy await them in the work of Charlotte
Lennox, heroine of Johnson's quaint all-night
revel of apple-pie and bay-leaves (Mycerinus could
hardly have turned night into day for long on that
regimen), and Frances Sheridan, whose " right to
make her readers suffer so much " he praised not
faintly under the guise of censure or question. *Arabella* (an alternative title which has the merit of not
" giving away " the *donnee* of the novel as *The Female*

Quixote does) is an exceedingly clever book not quite " brought off." Nothing of the charges—exaggerated but not wholly undeserved—which have been levelled at Smollett's *Sir Lancelot Greaves* can possibly fasten on it, for the Scudéry romance (devotion to and almost perversion by which is the heroine's mania) was a real thing, and a fairly fresh influence still. Moreover Arabella herself really fulfils the *sine qua non* of a heroine—that you can fall in love with her,—even if she does not attain to the highest state of those with whom one *has to* fall in love. The book was unfortunate in being succeeded by a still cleverer duplicate *Quixote* in Graves's novel, to be noticed presently ; while, actually before the century closed, Miss Austen had satirised a third variety of romantic extravagance in *Northanger Abbey*, with genius to which neither Mrs. Lennox nor Graves could pretend. These things do not matter much to the really critical, who know that, in literature at least, a good thing is not made bad by a better. And though even such elect must admit positive faults in *The Female Quixote*—superfluous argument, insufficient story - interest, and not much of that of character outside the heroine's—these faults do not prevent it from being both readable and enjoyable, especially as a change from the monotonous flimsiness of the average [1] twentieth-century novel.

The faults admitted are rather more noticeable, and the counterbalancing merits rather less, in the Sarah Fielding, Mrs. Sheridan, and Dr. Shebbeare. work (*David Simple*, *The Governess*, etc.) of Sarah Fielding, who had to double the parts of her brother's and collaborator's sister and of Richardson's friend, though she " held by the blood of her clan " not ill in point of humour. But for one great fault, not exactly

---

[1] I must beg leave to insist upon this word. If the twentieth century can follow up *Sinister Street* as the nineteenth followed up *Waverley* and *Pride and Prejudice* exactly a hundred years before, the reproach of its first decade and a half will be more than taken away. Nor do I limit the benefit-exception to Mr. Compton Mackenzie. But the *average* is simply boring.

identical but connected with that which earned Johnson's oblique compliment to *Miss Sidney Biddulph*, Mrs. Sheridan's novel would rank, in point of actual interest above Miss Fielding's, and perhaps above Mrs. Lennox's. The "suffering," however, to which the Doctor alluded, and which is certainly inflicted to an unmerciful extent on the heroine, if not on the reader of the book, is too prolonged, too unbroken, and at the same time too little exalted by passionate and tragic intensity, to be sound and pleasure-giving art. A good girl who is persistently ill-treated and hardly ever resents it, is a figure, one fears, in which the gods take warmer interest than men do. But the book shows power ; and though in more ways than one—length, letter-and-journal method, and dabbling in unhappiness—Richardson, of whose " seraglio " the author was a member, and to whom she dedicated her novel, has much to answer for in regard of it, it remains one of the documents of the early and powerful hold which women took of the novel.[1]

Philanthropists, and those faddists of another type who are never happy unless they can trace in literary work some connection with matters historical, political, social *et omne quod exit in-* " al," have sometimes had a good word for Shebbeare's *Lydia*, because one of its personages, Canassatego, a virtuous Indian, is a sort of link in the queer chain or chains, most oddly assorted otherwise, in which Aphra Behn, Rousseau, Bernardin, Chateaubriand, Wilberforce, Clarkson, and Mrs. Beecher Stowe figure as celebrants of the merits of the noble savage and injured person of colour. To some who are proof against this irrelevant attraction it seems a very dull book. The author had more brains than character ; but even his brains were not those of a novelist.

---

[1] One does not forget " Aphra " of course, and she is mentioned above. But when you call for others, nobody but Aphra comes before the eighteenth century, in English at least. The immediate example for most was, no doubt, Madeleine de Scudéry's.

In the same year with *Lydia* appeared the first, and
in the next came the beginning (for it took nearly
Amory. ten years in all to appear) of the principal,
novel work of a person to whom the attribu-
tion of " brains " without the qualification of " cracked "
might be and has been seriously questioned.   But it
may be doubted whether anybody really understands
the eighteenth century, as it was and as it might have
been, until he has read *John Buncle* through, and has
at least acquired some notion of the contents (it will
be observed that the requisition is qualified) of the
Memoirs of Several Ladies, both the productions—at the
close of a long and obscure life—of Thomas Amory.
Hazlitt's praise of Amory has brought upon subsequent
critics the danger of being thought merely " to say
ditto " to that great master by those who do not know
the ins-and-outs of the subject.   But few who do know,
though they may agree with Hazlitt's general conclusion, will accept the singular and not a little discussed
label of " the English Rabelais."   Both Rabelais and
Amory are eccentric ; but they are so almost in two
different senses of the word, and even bating the
demurrer of ambiguity, their departures from the centre
are in the most diverse directions.   They are both
lovers of sensuous (the precise might say sensual)
pleasures ; and they both express their love with that
" gusto " which Hazlitt himself admired and exercised.   But here the resemblance ceases or almost
ceases.   It is impossible to conceive Rabelais as being
for one moment ignorant of the ludicrous side of his
thoughts or words ; if we laugh we always laugh with,
never at him ; and the only danger is that we should
fail to get to the innermost " onion-coat " of his manifold and labyrinthine irony and humour.   In Amory,
on the other hand, there is no secondary meaning
whatever.   His greatest absurdities are set down with
an ultra-scientific matter-of-factness, without the very
slightest touch of tongue in cheek or wink in eye.   His

wildest extravaganzas of description have the sobriety
of a road-book. Actual madness has usually been
postulated as the only possible explanation of this
singular *diathesis* ; and Amory probably *was* mad in a
way diametrically opposed to Blake's way, as unpoetical
and unspiritual as Blake's was spiritual and poetical in
kind. In fact *John Buncle* and the " Prophetical "
books should be read in some connection if any one
wants to survey the eighteenth-century mind and its
possibilities, in abnormal as well as normal conditions.

Moreover, *Buncle*, though it perhaps requires in most
cases the exercise of that art indispensable to pleasur-
able reading—the art to skip now and then—is very
good stuff for a competent skipper, and can be read
by some not without pleasure from end to end, save
perhaps in its " Christian Deist " arguments. The
author's wives, and his meals, and his travels and his
sometimes distinctly acute excursions into criticism of
various kinds, do furnish forth a plenteous " treat," as
his time would have said. The earlier *Memoirs* have
been already recommended with a most cautious and
conscientious proviso. Much more skipping is required, and perhaps the reader for mere amusement
had better let the book alone. But the possible and
gentle chosen, to whom this little guide-book is humbly
offered, may not find it too much of a choke-pear,
especially as it will help them to " orientate " more
definitely its author's place in the history of the eccentric novel. Amory can, even when he began to publish, have owed nothing to Sterne: and it is probable
that what he published had been, in part at least,
written long before it appeared in print. He is thus
an additional instance of the fashion in which the mid-
eighteenth century not merely started the novel proper,
but actually laid out its future courses in far more than
one or two directions. Nor should it be forgotten
that he was a man born earlier even than Richardson,
and that he appears to have known Swift when both

were inhabitants of Dublin.   The " strong contagion "
of the greatest of Deans, on all his familiars who had
any genius to bring out, is well known.   And genius,
very limited and much distorted if any one likes, but
still genius, may be fearlessly ascribed to Amory.

But a much greater loss of unmixed " rest and
refreshment " than that experienced by any non-
The Spiritual reader of the books noticed since we took
Quixote. leave of Sterne, is his who does not read
The Spiritual Quixote, by the Reverend Richard
Graves, undergraduate (too late for Johnson, but contemporary with Shenstone and Whitefield) of Pembroke College, Oxford, Fellow of All Souls, and rector
of Claverton, almost a suburb of Bath, from the middle
of the eighteenth century to a point well within the
nineteenth.   During his life of nearly ninety years
Graves knew many good men, and showed abundance
of good wits, writing not a little in various kinds of
verse and prose.   But he never did anything so good
as the book just mentioned, which is partly a satire on
Methodism and partly a picaresque novel of the usual
kind, but which adds to these two characteristics,[1] in
which it follows its great original though with independence, those of a really interesting story, requiring neither moral satire nor comic adventure to
make its interest.   For this interest is derived from
well-told narrative and vividly sketched character, with
those little touches of speech, description, and so forth
which give what Galt (*vide infra*, p. 176 *note*) called
" likeliness."   It has been said, and the saying can
be well supported, that both Scott and Dickens knew,

---

[1] Some who love *Don Quixote* more well than wisely may exclaim at the attach-
ment of the frequently uncomplimentary epithet "picaresque" to that great and
immortal book.   But therein show they their want of wisdom even more than
their possession of goodness.   No one of Cervantes' personages is exactly a *picaro* ;
but almost the whole body as distinguished from the soul of his work is picaresque
in kind.   It may, or may not, be superfluous to add that both *Don Quixote* itself
and *Gil Blas* ranked almost as English novels at this period and till some way on in
the nineteenth century.   They were certainly far more read, in proportion to the
possible number of readers, than they have been since.

and did not disdain to utilise their knowledge of, Graves, and in more than those places, which they have thus honoured him by drawing upon, he had anticipated them in that indefinable verisimilitude which is the one thing needful to the novelist, and which perhaps only Fielding had mastered more thoroughly and earlier. For a book that is to be amusing without being flimsy, and substantial without being ponderous, *The Spiritual Quixote* may perhaps be commended above all its predecessors and contemporaries outside the work of the great Four themselves: while there is at least one unblushing criminal who confesses that he had much rather reread it than either *Clarissa* or *Sir Charles Grandison*. If the reprinter has not already got hold of it the sooner he does so the better.

The popularity, the praise, and even the solid profit which novels almost from the beginning [1] brought to their authors necessarily attracted adventurers into the new literary field. The number of novels written in the third quarter of the century (extending that period a little so as to run up to but exclude the appearance of *Evelina* in 1778) was very large. It will, however, scarcely repay even the connoisseur-amateur of novels to extend his perquisitions far beyond a certain limited though not very scanty list of already proven wares. It took but very little time to show—what intelligence could have easily foreseen, and what wiseacreism soon availed itself of to discredit the whole class—that though some novels might be far from rubbish, and some of them quite worthy to rank with the greatest literary work of the past in other prose kinds, a good many were only fit for the rubbish heap. This is,

The state of the novel about 1775.

---

[1] Six hundred pounds is no doubt " dirt cheap " for *Tom Jones*, if we look at what more recent novelists have received for work not possessing a hundredth part of its merits. But it was a very large sum at that time, when Johnson maintained that no author could count upon more than ten shillings a sheet " communibus sheetibus " for his work. For *Amelia* Fielding received a thousand ; and even *Joseph Andrews*, written in the very dawn of the new novel day, and by a man only known as a somewhat third-rate playwright, had brought him nearly two hundred.

has always been, and no doubt always will be more or less true of the majority ; and there was more excuse for the fact then than there has been at any time since. Although masterpieces had been produced, the conditions of mastery, even in what we may call a pass degree, were by no means well understood—they seem in some cases to have escaped the very masters themselves. It was long—it was very long indeed—before novelists ceased to be perturbed by that most unreal of bogeys on the threshold—the haunting fear that the reader will ask how the writer came by his information. And this fear had much to do with the often awkward letter-and-journal form, and everything to do with the childish preliminaries of manuscripts turning up in this way or that ; superfluous narrators who are introduced only to be got rid of or to clog the story ; and all the other silly tricks which two great " instaurators "—Scott in the Introduction to *The Fortunes of Nigel* and Miss Austen in *Northanger Abbey*—have satirised. They cumbered themselves for nearly as long—during the special time mentioned almost without exception—about unnecessary services of more or less unusual incident (proper enough for romance, but superfluous in novel), about laboured comic episodes and tedious didactics, about all sorts of superfluities and supererogations. They were too often tempted to borrow stage tricks, stage conventions, and, worst of all, stage lingo. Never, during the whole century, did they arrive at any understanding of historical treatment, especially of any fashion of reproducing the manners and the language of old time convincingly. And not unfrequently, extending the already pretty loose and large but not necessarily objectionable license of the time, they resorted to the obvious and time-dishonoured bait of " inconvenient " scene and subject. Even of the greatest Sterne notoriously makes this a main engine of attraction in his peculiar way ; Smollett had actually to purge his work of its worst parts, and has left not a little which had much better never have been there ; Richardson, though he goes about it so gravely that some hold him guiltless, is really a sinner.   Fielding, despite a general but quite uninformed notion, is really the cleanest of all the Four, at least in his three principal and generally read books, just as he is the freest from all other tricks and manners just censored.   But at the other end of the scale more than one book " too widely known " (as Macaulay observes demurely of the most notorious [1] of all) relies upon sheer pornography : and others, such as the novel-work of Dr. Dodd, forger and Magdalene chaplain, go exceedingly near it.

There may be some dispute whether the traditionally if not actually well known *Chrysal* of Charles *Chrysal.* Johnstone comes under the damnatory purport of the last sentence.   It can perhaps only be saved by the acceptance of a very doubtful plea of Carlyle's, for the most objectionable of his heroes, that a certain acidity or acridity in the treatment of " inconvenient " things has a purifying or at least sterilising effect.   *The Adventures of a Guinea* (to give the book its other title) cannot be refused such praise as may be due to the exhibition of undoubted brains. But they are brains which are accompanied and actuated by very bad blood.   What Swift seems to those who do not understand his greatness Johnstone is—a Timon soured and embittered, without even Timon's indifferent excuses for his misanthropy.   Great part, moreover, of the very peculiar attraction—it is to be hoped rather limited in respect of the number of the persons attracted—exercised by *Chrysal* is moreover derived from a practice early indulged in by some of the greatest of novelists, and never since wholly disused,

---

[1] Since paradox became the trick of the time there have not been wanting discoverers of redeeming merits of style, narrative faculty and the like in this.   The present writer, who is not in the least squeamish, is entirely unable to discern these. It would be interesting to find a person who, on his honour and conscience, would declare that the work in question would still be interesting if the subject were not obscene.

but to some of the most enthusiastic admirers of some
of its greatest practitioners a very doubtful one—the
" key " appeal, as it has been called, that is to say, the
introduction, under less or more transparent disguises,
of real persons, scenes, and incidents of the novelists'
own time.   That this practice sometimes gives additional life and force to the book need not be denied ;
but there is a criterion which at once admits this, and
confers immunity from what may be called the ethical-
æsthetic [1] objection.   If the book retains its full story-
interest when the reader is ignorant or careless of the
origin of the characters, the artist has earned his
exemption, and if not, not.   It can matter to no
judicious admirer of the Marquis of Steyne that there
was a certain Lord Hertford who had some of the
characteristics of that formidable nobleman ;   nor,
though the mere facts are a little more interesting, does
it add to the actual attraction of Becky or of Blanche,
that eyes which fortunately still behold the light once
also beheld a possible original of " Lady " Crawley,
and that an admitted model for the creator of *Mes
Larmes* once travelled with Thackeray himself on
the South Western Railway from Southampton to
Waterloo.   But as for the mere key-novel, if you do
not know that there is a lock it is generally very dull,
and if you have not got the key it is irritating as well.

Frank Coventry's *Pompey the Little* (a title which
requires no great intelligence to interpret as concerning
Pompey the a pet dog) is also a " key-book " ; but it is
Little and quite possible to read it without troubling
Peter Wilkins. oneself about the key at all, and the reader
will have a pleasant and amusing novel of manners with
a university touch about it (Coventry was a Cambridge
man) which is agreeable, and unluckily too rare in
eighteenth-century books.   For the references there to

---

[1] As the present writer has always been a steady protester against those who
would confuse Art and Morality this phrase may seem inconsistent, but it is not.
Art has its own morality—a pretty severe and complicated one.   It is sometimes
called " Taste."

university life are not very numerous ; are sometimes, as in the case of *Humphrey Clinker*, by persons who had never been in Eden; and are too often conventionalised in various ways.[1]

The occultation of *Peter Wilkins* has already been deplored in passing, but that most agreeable book is not thus to be dismissed. It is said, let us hope falsely, that twentieth-century boys will not read a book that has not an aeroplane in it ; and though there is much flying in *Peter*, it is unfortunately performed by natural and not artificial " aviatics," which might sink it lower still with the luckless young gentlemen in question. But the adventures themselves, at least in the earlier part, are very well told (the almost unknown author, Robert Paltock, ranks next to Swift and Defoe in this department), and the heroine, Youwarkee, has been, by a catena of the most respectable and at the same time unpuritanic authorities, pronounced almost as charming a heroine of the simpler and kindlier sort as can be found anywhere. She is in fact a savage Sophia or Amelia, from whom, perhaps, her creator may have taken a few hints (though in Amelia's case he must have been very quick about it), but who would certainly welcome her as a sister. Now the fictitious persons who can be ranked as sisters or brothers to Fielding's characters are not exactly numerous.

One cannot speak with so sweet a mouth, or in anything like so unqualified a style, of a more ambitious *The Fool of* and in a sense more highly reputed per-*Quality.* formance, Henry Brooke's *Fool of Quality*. Brooke's case is different from his compatriot Amory's, for he certainly was mad, in the ordinary sense of the word, during the later part of his life, and there is no evidence that Amory ever was. Henry, Earl of Morland, the " Fool of Quality," is

---

[1] Tom Warton's *Progress of Discontent* (in verse) is the most genuine-looking thing perhaps ; but it is very brief. Some lively but scandalous touches in *The Connoisseur* merely concern the escapades of undergraduates in town.

essentially a gentleman, a term one can hardly apply to
Buncle ; and he has, perhaps more than any of the more
deliberate and self-advertising copies of the Knight of
the Rueful Countenance, that peculiar and exalted
knightliness which the marvellous genius of Cervantes
has known how to combine with his hero's insanity.
But Don Quixote, even in his most didactic moments,
is never dull ; and in his most deluded ones is never
exactly silly, while he is sometimes (another miracle
of combination) marvellous wise.   Now neither his
" quality " nor his virtues prevent the " Fool " from
sending his folly into deserts of dulness and quagmires
of absurdity, while he is a past-master of the worshipful
Company of Knife Grinders as to " story," and, though
often a good, is hardly ever a wise fool.   Nevertheless
the book has been enthusiastically admired by some.
Wesley abridged it ; Charles Kingsley actually reprinted it in full in the hope that his enthusiasm might
be shared, and it undoubtedly has great merits.   Its
style is excellent, and it has been compared, in the
flashes of its best parts, to work of the highest or of
very high merit—*John Buncle* itself, Borrow, Mere-
dith—especially, as the juxtaposition of these three will
suggest to the cunning, in a singular combination of
carnal exuberance in fighting, eating, drinking, and
so forth with philosophical reflection and intellectual
subtlety.   If anybody possesses not merely the art
of plain skipping which has been praised before, but
that of skipping-*cum*-skimming, which is the higher
degree of it, he will find plenty of pasture in *The Fool of
Quality*, though he may never be able quite to rise to
Kingsley's yoking of it with the *Faerie Queene*.   If it
were not for its great length it would make a good
pocket or table book, and if it were not that its best
things are not easy to extract from their chaotic context such a book might be (perhaps it has been ? [1])

---

[1] I do not remember to have seen Wesley's abridgment. But this would
certainly have been made *edificationis non voluptatis causa*.

drawn from it. But it offers very few of the ordinary attractions of a novel as such.

The present writer has made some detailed attempts elsewhere [1] to deal with the much written of but perhaps never satisfactorily dealt with character and genius of Frances Burney; and he does not propose to repeat any kind of polemic here further than to say that she has been both under- and over-valued somewhat oftener than she has been impartially judged. The fact is due to various causes, but the most important of these are connected with a curious and almost unique other fact. For the great reputation and positive popularity obtained by her first novel, when the eighteenth century had almost its last quarter yet to run, was revived and much increased by the publication of her *Diary*, nearly a long lifetime later, when the nineteenth was not far from completing its first half; and again by the supplement of the *Early Diary*, forty years later still, when more than a century had passed since *Evelina* appeared. This very un- usual condition of what may be called stages or relays of stimulus to interest in her, was assisted at other intervals by incidental " flappers " (to speak Laputan), by connection with Johnson, by one of Macaulay's most *con spirito* if least controversial essays, and by other things, reminding one of the scratch eights that pick up and quicken a university boat in training. For the purpose of our title it would be foolish not to confess frankly that the *Diary*, both as originally published and as since supplemented, is *uberrimum et fructuosissimum* —much more so than the novels. Of these last in- deed, the latest, *The Wanderer*, has been, with practical unanimity, pronounced unreadable ; and though one has seen a protest or two against this judgment, this really must be put down—to avoid unceremonious " disabling of judgment " straight off, or the perhaps

Madame D'Arblay.

---

[1] Especially in the volume entitled *Essays in English Literature*, 1780–1860, *Second Series* (London, 1895), pp. 203-236.

even more offensive suggestion of deliberate and perverse paradox—to one of those effects of association which count for so much. The previously mentioned " wet day in a small country inn," with absolutely nothing else to read or to do, might render *The Wanderer* not quite unwelcome; and if one read it before and after a particularly good dinner, or while the effect of a letter imparting some particularly good news as to love or war, politics or property lasted, its defects might be less obvious. But " it by itself " is simply a clumsy and immensely long ado about nothing, without any of its author's former command of character-parts if not of character, and written in one of the vilest lingoes of Frenchified Johnsonese that Reality ever indulged in to triumph over Nightmare. *Camilla* is considerably less bad, and has parts in it which are positively good, and which make it quite readable as a whole. But it is a declension from *Cecilia*. This has nothing against it except the excessive length, which Richardson (perhaps on Scudéry models) had introduced, and a slight beginning of pomposity of language. These make it not nearly so delectable as *Evelina*, the eldest of the family, not merely of Miss Burney's novels, but of that much larger and fairer herd which was successively re-mothered by Miss Edgeworth, Miss Austen, Miss Ferrier—

(. . . in *novel*-reign
Maid-mothering is not held a stain),

and a long line of maids and matrons down to Miss Braddon, who died but a day or two before these words were written.

Justice, it is hoped, has been done to Mrs. Haywood, Mrs. Lennox, and Mrs. Sheridan ; but Time ^{The advance} was not so kind to them as he might have ^{made by her.} been ; and they had not, as their men contemporaries had, genius enough to neutralise his grudge. The stages of " modernness " are very difficult to mark off. The most important one comes at the Restoration, and from thence onwards the pace is quickened. Addison is more modern, not perhaps in definite style but in thought and subjects, than Dryden; Chesterfield is more modern than Addison. But Horace Walpole and Lady Mary are more so even than Chesterfield, and, especially when we turn to Miss Burney's *Diary*, we find her, as her age would warn us, still more so again. She is not so modern, at least in point of diction, in the novels; indeed the fatal mixture, above mentioned, of two of the most incompatible things in the world, Johnsonism and Gallicism, in the later ones, and a certain primness (for there is no Johnsonese here) in *Evelina* itself, are not in their favour. But from the very first she had, as no one of her sex had had before in degree, and in a way quite different from that of those who had come near it, a grasp of the externals of a modernising society, especially in the middle (and rather lower than higher middle) class.

One does not know that Lord Orville and Sir Peregrine and Mr. Villars and Mrs. Selwyn are extremely striking in their verisimilitude—they are still " academies," and the low comedy of Madame Duval and Captain Mirvan is not much less conventional than Smollett's. But the Branghtons and Mr. Smith are new because true, and true because observed. In their mere outline there may be still something of the conventional " cit " of the stage and the periodical. But Fanny could not help filling in and half-obliterating that outline with the actual lines and colours which she had seen in Poland Street, Lynn, and elsewhere. And the result was the *grand prix* of the novel—Life. It was not the universal life of Fielding, or the analysed and re-created life of Richardson, or the rough and tumble of Smollett, or the " eccentrified " and sophisticated but still living curiosities of Sterne. But it was something that could be very much more largely multiplied than their manners—a true *mimesis* or artistic re-creation of actual human types and individuals, which the artist, which even the craftsman could follow, varying his models ever in every country, time, and circumstance. The person who should attempt to ingratiate himself by paradox nowadays must indeed be careless of his company ; yet one may say that (though everybody should read *Evelina*) the gifts of Miss Burney as a novelist are to be sought rather outside of than in her novels. It is in the *Diaries*, and perhaps especially in the Early " Diary," which was never subjected to the cold shade of her late primnesses, that her astonishing faculty of catching and rendering true ordinary life, from wigmakers to princesses, is best shown. She put something of this—less in each as she went on—in her novels, and it served as their passport-flavouring. In the *Diaries* we have it neat ; it is not timidly and almost grudgingly administered seasoning, but solid fare or a thirst-quenching draught. Macaulay has " put in his thumb and picked out a plum " here and there, from the Johnson period, deftly enough. But even there he left a great deal unpicked, and his unfortunate eagerness to make a Whig trump card of the hardships of the Court sojourn, and to palliate the Whig persecution (though Heaven knows Toryism had little to pride itself on here!) of that ill-chanced hero Warren Hastings, made him leave out a great deal that he might have taken. He might have made real fun out of his hastily dismissed " half-witted Protestant minister," " Mr. Turbulent " or M. de la Giffardière, whose " half-wits " do not appear in the *Diary* quite so clearly as his whole insolence (he was one of the polyglot riff-raff whom Queen Charlotte liked to have about her). Macaulay might also have done much more than he did with " Mr. Fairly," a very questionable gentleman, who fooled Fanny to the top of even her bent with sentimental-literary flirtation, and then " planted her there " for a rich wife. But even in these two

Comparison of her novels with the *Diary*.

characters, though Fanny has given rather fatal testimony in them against her own good sense, penetration, and power of taking care of herself, we see that touch of genius which she possessed. The French refugee, petulant, vulgar, not indeed stupid or even silly, but essentially coxcombical ; the amiable, well-mannered, English colonel,[1] gentlemanly as far as externals go, entirely incapable of brutalities either à la Pickle or à la Lovelace, but weak, selfish, sentimental, and rather " sloppy "—are there " in their natural," as clear and well defined as the more popularly appreciated sketches of the abominable Schwellenberg. The conversations are up to the lives, they are indeed far in advance of those in the novels ; and anybody who chooses may see that the Princess Augusta of England spoke of the Princess Royal of France, a century and a quarter ago, exactly as any girl of the gentler class, would speak of another girl of that class now, unless the more modern damsel talked slang.

Moreover, Macaulay did not know the Early " Diary," which, being, as was said, in a more virgin condition, gives us perhaps more indisputable evidence as to Miss Burney's novel-writing and other faculties than either the novels themselves, or the " official " and censored issue of 1842. We may have nothing in it— though we sometimes have " ekings " of the same accounts—quite equal to the stories of the greater St. Martin's Street parties, or the Court scenes, or the Hastings trial. But we see still more of Poland and St. Martin's Streets in their every-day aspect ; we get curious glimpses of Fanny's earlier love-affairs ; we have more than glimpses of that singular household of the Rishtons (her half-sister Maria Allen [2] and her husband) and accounts of journeys, to the West chiefly,

---

[1] One ought perhaps to remember that we have not got *his* version of the matter. His conduct in the King's illness seems to have been admirable and his general reputation of the highest. It is a dangerous thing to flirt, even within strictly primitive limits, with a " little character-monger," and then to ride away from her, even in such a fashion as no Court of Honour or of Love could severely blame.

[2] This Maria's letters read like those of an actual novel-heroine.

but sometimes also to Lynn, which are full of novel material of the best and most vividly reported kind. At Bath, in Devonshire, at Gloucester, in Worcestershire, and elsewhere, Fanny " gangs amang them taking notes " in a way possible and permissible only to a Devil-on-two-sticks or a novelist. " Mrs. Brilliana " and Miss " Lilies-and-Roses " are as certainly genuine portraits as anything can be ; and yet their proper place is not in actual cathedral towns or actual baronet's houses—it is in the realm of the novel. And, contemplating them, one sees how that realm and its possibilities were, if not exactly exalted, extended, varied, made more subservient to the " general joy " by this shy, not very pretty, not in other respects very clever little creature, who did not even improve her one talent as she might have done, but who had it, and imparted it to others who could improve it to the utmost.

While, therefore, there is, from the actual literary facts of the case, no great reason to acquiesce in Macaulay's idea of shelf-fuls of brilliant novels being lost to the world through Dr. Burney's mistaken and rather selfish ambition and the cruel kindness of the Royal family, there can be no doubt at all that her uncomfortable exaltation, as well as the actual popularity of *Evelina* and *Cecilia* and the friendship of men great in letters and politics, and the position which this gave her in society, helped to raise the status and popularise the profession of novel-writing, almost as much as the actual merit of her work enlarged the scope and extended the province of the novel. Very few years indeed passed before the questionable creatures, Purpose and School—to which Rousseau and Sterne had already opened the way in the case of Sentimentalism and moral or immoral theory—began to lay hands from all sides on the new kind. The mischief which they have done since, and the rubbish which they have contributed, ought not to blind us to

the fact that, in stimulus of production and variety
of production, there was, for this early period, if not
some antidote to their bane, at any rate some advantage
mingled with their mischief. In the last twenty years
of the century novels became more and more abundant ;
definite and considerable varieties, such as the Terror
novel and the Revolutionary novel, arose in groups,
while both in them and in other sub-varieties or non-
descript individuals, a curious resurrection of romance,
though for a time of an inferior and bastard kind,
endeavoured to assert its ancient right to the dominion
of prose fiction.

There is no reason to question Horace Walpole's
title to be the leader in this reaction, or to refuse to
The Castle *The Castle of Otranto* the corresponding
of Otranto honours of priority. But certainly no
and the
Romantic stranger Moses ever led children of Israel
reaction. or Jacobel back to a land flowing with the
old milk and honey ; and few more rotten craft
have ever carried any discoverer to his goal. Age
and fuller acquaintance with his life and literary work
may indeed very largely temper the contemptuous
dislike which " warm youth " may have excited in a few
persons by no means Macaulayan in general views, but
who have imbibed it from Macaulay, or even arrived
at it independently, in regard to the deviser of Strawberry Hill. His *Letters* would by themselves almost
justify our general title ; and the rest and refreshment
that you get from them renews itself, if not exactly
from moon to moon—indeed in the leisurely after-day's-
work reading which suits them best, a single month
will hardly suffice for degustation of the sixteen volumes
—at any rate from year to year without the slightest
staling. But we shall try to do justice to them later.
The important thing here is to note how every fresh
reading only confirms the sense that Horace had no real
love for things mediæval in general, and no real understanding of romance in particular. His fad *was* a fad

pure and simple, and might have dated and directed itself in any other way and time where he could attain the credit of singularity and originality. There is hardly a single genuine and unguarded expression of taste, throughout his immense body of writing, which is sincerely Romantic when he is not " speaking in character "—talking " Strawberry." But it was his fad, and he played and lived up to it as well as he could, which, as he was a very clever man, is not saying little.

It is true that the *Castle* itself is emphatically a "Sham Castle," as a well-known feature of Bath is frankly called, that it is indeed much more so in literature than " Strawberry " itself was in building. Not only does it not make *us* shudder or wonder (which after all are not essential effects of romance), but it does not make us dream, which is almost an essential one. Still, it made *them*—as it would appear from testimony equally indubitable in fact and respectable in origin— do all three, and in doing so *omne tulit punctum* for the time. We put it beside a book of the *Morte d'Arthur* or one of the *Faerie Queene*, and we find it ludicrously and disgustingly wanting—a complete failure in what we wish it to be. They put it beside the work of Mr. Pope and Mr. Addison, and found in it a calm ignoring of the pure reason to which they had been accustomed, and of which they were tired ; an attempt, bold and new, at the imagination, or at least the fancy, of which they had been so long deprived. Further, it coincided with those other and more wisely guided but less popular tentatives in the Romantic direction, which will be dealt with in a later chapter. But it was some time before it served as a direct pattern. Clara Reeve's *Old English Baron*, more than a decade later, was the first of any mark, and when, as in the last quarter of the century, it had a very numerous family of children or grandchildren, their kind was vitiated, first by the same faults and more of the same which characterised itself, and secondly, by a curious cross of foreign influence, which, however, had originally been derived from the same source. The *Castle of Otranto* had appeared just at the time when the German Romantic movement, revolting against the French and generally " neo-classic " influences which had so long dominated Germany, was partly exhuming its own mediæval literature of folk-lore, ballad, and what not, partly absorbing greedily whatever English thing it could get from Shakespeare downwards. It fastened eagerly on *Otranto*, and proceeded to develop the pattern with not a little of the passing genius, which for not quite a century dominated the Hercynian darkness, but still more with that curious mixture of methodic and mechanical ability with positive stolidity and silliness, which has, since the Renaissance at least, been an abiding characteristic of those who dwell between Rhine and Vistula.

Of the terror-and-mystery novel (the " novel of suspense " as some call it, adopting from Scott a label doubtfully intended as such), the chief writers—almost the only ones now known, except to special students—were Mrs. Radcliffe and " Monk " Lewis. But in the eighteenth century it enjoyed an enormous popularity, securely registered and irremediably ridiculed in Miss Austen's *Northanger Abbey*.[1] In Lewis's hands (as it had done in those of the Germans) it admitted real *diablerie* and permitted great licence of situation and action ; in Mrs. Radcliffe's and in most, though not quite all, of her minor followers', it was strictly "proper," and employed a curious, ingenious, and, at the time, highly relished machinery, which has been accurately enough called the " explained supernatural." Both these methods of applying the supernatural element

The development of the "Terror" kind.

---

[1] It is said that the apparently burlesque titles (*Horrid Mysteries*, etc.) of the rubbish in which the innocent Catherine and the less innocent Isabella revelled, are certainly genuine in part and probably in whole. The practitioners were extremely numerous ; and the practice, even in its original form, continued far into the nineteenth century—almost until the further developments spoken of above.

were revived in the sensational novels of the third quarter of the nineteenth century and sporadically since. The first is not justly chargeable with what has been perhaps not unjustly called the "school-boy naughtiness" and extravagance of *The Monk*. Bulwer and Mrs. Oliphant, to name no later writers, showed that conclusively; George Macdonald more than conclusively. But few complete examples exist in which the enormous difficulty of handling the pure supernatural in prose and at length has been mastered. The "explained supernatural," though something not quite unlike it occurs in the work of Wilkie Collins and others, has, since the attraction of its first appearance and its startling contrast to things known and popular passed away, been itself little popular, either with the public or with critics. Some at least of the former do not like to be cheated of their wonders; many of the latter regard such a much-ado-about-nothing as inartistic.

Yet Lewis may be read, once at least, not without amusement; and there is a cheerful cut-and-come-againness about the innumerable persecutions and palpitations of Mrs. Radcliffe's heroines, the perils of her heroes, and the luxuriance of her descriptions, sometimes in themselves no bad examples of the new and promising if rather novice-like devotion to the "picturesque" which is not to be denied or belittled. But she suffers, and others of this and other schools suffer still more, from that want of self-criticism which is the almost inevitable penalty of emancipation.

The other chief group, which is ticketed with more or less appropriateness as "Revolutionary," does not escape *The revolu-* (as how should it?) some silliness, and it prob-*tionary novel.* ably did a good deal more mischief than the "Terror" kind. But it was written, as a rule, by persons of much greater ability—the mere ruck of novel-writers having little inducement to try it. Holcroft, Godwin,

Mrs. Inchbald, Mary Wollstonecraft, Bage, were none of them " the first-comers " ; their books would no doubt be more purely delectable if they were free from the sentimentality and the anarchic purpose which they inherited from the French *philosophes* ; but, on the other hand, the absence of that purpose might have prevented them from being written at all, and in most if not in all cases it does not entirely stand in the way of delectation pure and simple. Probably Holcroft, at least in his later novels, *Anna St. Ives* and *Hugh Trevor*, is the worst offender ; but the much earlier *Alwyn* is free from this offence, and has much of the liveliness of his dramas. Probably not one in a thousand of the many thousands who have enjoyed Godwin's *Caleb Williams* has derived any part of his enjoyment from the undercurrent (sometimes much more than " under- ") of Godwinian dissatisfaction with society ; and it is certain that some of the minority who do not enjoy the book would like it much better if this undercurrent were turned off altogether. That Pecksniff - and - pinchbeck Plato's other chief novel, *St. Leon*, derives its appeal partly from the " Terror," or at least the supernatural motive, and is not indebted to either this or the revolutionary sentiment for its chief attraction—the character of the heroine Marguerite, said to be studied from Mary Wollstonecraft herself. The undoubted power of Mrs. Inchbald's *Simple Story* and *Nature and Art* may have been, as in other cases, to some extent excited by the fermenting atmosphere of the time, but has no necessary or exclusive kinship with it. That curious person, Robert Bage, has been of late years for the most part overlooked altogether, passed by with slight and slighting mention, or definitely depreciated by critics. But as he happens to have had Sir Walter Scott [1] on his side he can afford to echo as to others

---

[1] Scott's criticism in general is often put aside as too good-natured. Some allowance perhaps has to be made for this—but to push it to a disabling extent is a gross error. In relation to his own province especially his *expertise* was fully equalled by his acuteness.

the famous, " They say.　What say they ?　Let them
say."　Bage had imbibed from his French teachers,
among other forms of " free-thinking," an inclination
towards *grivoiserie,* which sometimes neglects not merely
the limits of strict propriety, but those of fairly easy-
going good taste ; and his most ambitious books,
Hermsprong : or Man as He is Not and *Man as
He is,* which Scott did not give in the " Ballantyne
Novels," are sometimes rendered tiresome by his
purpose.　Nor need anybody spend much time,
trouble, or money in questing for the very rare and not
very beautiful *Fair Syrian.*　But the other three, which
Scott did give, *Mount Henneth, Barham Downs,* and
James Wallace, are books well worth reading, and full
of a salt which, if not always Attic, seldom lacks some
kind of savour.　If Bage had lived fifty or sixty years
later he might have been a very considerable novelist.

　　Minor groups—such as those children's books which
now first began to be written, and which included the im-
Minor groups. mortal [1] *Sandford and Merton* ; as the abortive
　Vathek.　historical novels, which failed of life by reason
of the inability above noticed ; as the beginnings of the
" fashionable " kind, and the riff-raff of the " Minerva
Press "—need not detain us ; while it would be impossible to deal with individuals like Cumberland's *Henry,*
an odd, not quite brainless, but of course unsuccessful
attempt to double back on Fielding, or with the works
of Mrs. Opie, Charlotte Smith and others.　In fact,
most of these belong as much to the nineteenth as to
the eighteenth century, and throw forward rather than
backward in character.　Only, before concluding the
chapter with more general considerations, one must
allow oneself the pleasure of a word or two more on that
almost entire and perfect chrysolite *Vathek.*　Description and praise of it would be equally superfluous ;

---

[1] This word is not used in the cant ironical sense.　*Sandford and Merton* is uncommonly good reading for "those who know," and we shall see it again (*v. inf.*
p. 267).　With regard to *Vathek* no one should fail to supplement the old texts
with the " Episodes " recently published by Mr. Lewis Melville.

nothing in that way need be said except the old, "Let
him that has not read it read it at once! and let him
that has read it read it again and again." But it is not
superfluous to point out that *Vathek* is essentially of the
eighteenth century itself. It was suggested beyond
doubt by Anthony Hamilton, who, Englishman as he
was, first achieved the blending of the Eastern wonder-
tale and the French satirical *fabliau*, and by his pupil
Voltaire. But Beckford strikes out in it a line
discarding the mere playfulness of the seventeenth-
century element which survives in Hamilton, and
substitutes, in part at any rate, a graver wisdom and a
tragic tone for the thorn-crackling laughter and the
random-thrown fireworks of Voltaire. Yet even the
magnificent close has a precision and a lack of mystical
vagueness which differ from anything of pure nineteenth-century origin. The Ancient Mariner has not
told his tale; while on the other hand no touch of
German extravagance or childishness drags it down
to the level of the Terror school that was so soon to
follow. Beckford was, in fact,—whether he was born
so or only played up to the ideal of the part with consummate success—the typical *milord Anglais* of foreign
eighteenth-century observation or imagination. He
wasted much substance and did some foolish things in
living or in playing so, but he produced, not only
Fonthill, a mere rococo folly the end of which was its
own moral, but *Vathek*—a possession and delectation
for ever in itself, and a sign of the actual nature, as
well as of the approaching change, of the time which
produced it.

There is of course a temptation to lengthen this
chapter, because its contents support the title and
Some remarks purpose of the book in the most obvious and
on old and incontrovertible manner; but this is not a
modern novels. history of the Novel. Enough detail has
probably been given, though it may not be ill to
repeat that actual exploration of eighteenth-century

fiction will be rewarded by the discovery of many things that are restful and refreshing enough, though not mentioned here. But it is still more proper to insist on the general contribution to the literature of pastime and recreation that the century made by its practical discovery of the long elusive novel proper ; and on the way in which the fact of that contribution was in no small part due to the actual characteristics of the time. Business-like even in its amusements, it saw that there were what have been later called by-products in ordinary life which could be utilised in this way, and it utilised them. At first it seemed rather to ostracise Romance, but that unbanishable thing recovered its citizenship before long, without taking any partisan vengeance on its younger sister the novel, entering, on the contrary, into partnership with her. Nor, at this time, did the two together threaten, as they certainly have threatened since, the older pastime of dramatic fiction.

There was therefore made at this period an immense dead lift—an almost uncountable augmentation—of the power of literature to delight. The amiable and respectable old heresy that you must have instruction as well was not given up, though in the best examples it wrought little harm. But delight of a literary kind, while not being withheld even from the keenest intellects and most sober tastes, was tendered to the *vulgus* (let us not say the vulgar) in a fashion which had no earlier parallel. More cheaply, more easily, for longer time, and with a singular faculty of renewal, the novel gave to the world of readers, from Johnsons and Lady Marys [1] to school-girls and shop-boys, a pleasure which nothing but the theatre had given before in kind, and in giving which it left the theatre behind, in all the respects just glanced at and many others as well.

[1] Lady Mary delighted in novels and had boxes of them sent to her in Italy.

One slight objection may be guarded against in conclusion. Of late years there has arisen a school of novel-criticism, largely of American origin, but with numerous recruits or disciples of English birth, which shakes the head over the excessive simplicity of the methods of the English novel from Fielding onwards. Novel-writing, according to this, is not only a difficult thing (there need be no controversy there), not only a complicated thing (there is still no need for positive contradiction, though one may scent war), but a thing to be conducted according to an intricate set of rules, involving perpetual prohibition, insisting on thrust in carte before you thrust in tierce, inevitable location of the " brown tree " in the proper place, use of the stop-watch and the measuring tape, and in fact all the old *patati* and *patata* of conventional censorship in other kinds. It is all very pretty and very scientific ; and as some of the doctors and doctresses of the school are venerable and others engaging, the application of that terrible talisman or touchstone, " By their fruits ye shall know them," would be not a little disagreeable. But one remembers the result and fate of former attempts at codification in matters extra-literary as well as literary. To one thing especially which also came " Eastward Ho ! " there seems a strong resemblance, namely, to those " American Leads " at whist with which the Wise Men of the West indulged us, as some think, so calamitously, a generation or so ago. They were very ingenious, they were to a certain extent logical deductions from, or generalisations of, observed successful practice ; they fortified the sense of proceeding *secundum artem*, and seemed to solve the problems they raised. But they deprived the best game in the world of all its frank and fresh enjoyment as well as its scope for individual genius ; and by degrees they killed it, and handed over its kingdom to a vastly inferior successor. There may be small danger of the parallel proving itself an omen ; let us avert that by all preceptist and practical means. But it certainly has some interest as a parallel.

For (let it be peremptorily and unblushingly asserted and reasserted) the business of the novel is in the first, second, and even third place to *interest*. It may interest by the simplest process of mere legitimate amusement, or by the most complicated one of absorbing attention to passion, character, dialogue, and (perhaps) plot. It may, legitimately again, add to these attractions of description, style, and so forth, though if it ever attempts to substitute such attractions for, or to let them predominate over, the sheer interest of story and character, its achievements in this respect have, to use an admirable phrase of the Articles, " the nature of sin." The objects set before it by the school of criticism just glanced at too often not merely bear a sinful colour but are plain and overt sin itself. For attention to them too often actually interferes with the interest in the case of the plain and honest consumer, and substitutes for it, in the case of others, the morbid satisfaction of a previously unhealthy and not always genuine appetite. The proper pleasure, the " *indigenous* pleasure," as we may almost translate Aristotle's famous phrase, of the novel is excluded for an alien and artificial voluptuousness.

That the eighteenth century never mistook the object of the novel would be too much to say. Not merely its earlier but practically all its novelists were in a manner pioneers and experimenters ; and they sometimes let wandering stars guide them into wrong roads. Moral intention—the most dangerous misleader of the novelist, except immoral intention—led Richardson and many others astray ; " sensibility " did the same ; nay, except that we would not miss the " sad lucidity ' of the wisdom expressed with such dignity of form in *Rasselas* for anything, and in whatever shape it chose to present itself, one would be hard put to it to defend *Rasselas* as a novel. But on the whole the blessed common sense of the century was justified also of this, its special child.   The eighteenth-century novel did not mean to accomplish the driving of pigs into or out of clover, or the squaring of the circle, or the performance of any Kehama-like intricacy of ceremonies and sacrifices, or the mystifying of the reader with any sort of cyphered jargon.   It meant to *interest*—by amusement, by excitement, by suspense, by pathos, by sarcasm, by every legitimate means and perhaps in some cases by means not wholly legitimate, morally or æsthetically.   It fulfilled its intention for its immediate readers: and a much larger part of it than is generally thought is capable of repeating that fulfilment for even a fifth or sixth or any generation that is not reduced to the grovelling necessity of declining any literature not strictly adjusted to its own daily life.[1]

---

[1] Perhaps it may not be wholly wicked or wholly irrelevant to add a note.   The fallacy of "rule before work" which has been countered above, was perhaps never better illustrated than by some naïf remarks of John Galt, the writer who, much more than Burns or Scott (for they were not of a mere parish, or province, or even nationality, but of the whole world) shows us Scotland as it was while still in a manner a separate country.   Galt wrote not a few novels, including two or three of great merit but not strictly belonging by chronology to the present book, though eminently of it by spirit.   Of these, even in his own day, *The Annals of the Parish* was recognised as by far the best.   This annoyed Galt.   He acknowledged that it perhaps had more of what he called "likeliness" (meaning at the time "life-likeness") than others ; but he urged that it had no plot such as a novel ought to have.   Those critics who have been mentioned above—and who not unfrequently put their opinions with a delectable metaphysicality and *Marivaudage* of lingo before the public at this moment —extend their technical requirements far beyond "plot" which indeed they sometimes despise.   But they all agree in disparaging and belittling that "likeliness" or "life-likeness" wherein lies the conclusion of the whole matter.   It was the eighteenth century which brought this life-likeness into novels ; and for so doing may it and the Lord be thanked !

CHAPTER IV

JOHNSON, BOSWELL, AND GOLDSMITH

THE volume of existing writing about Johnson is so immense that it may, from different sides, be regarded as impertinent and as idle to add any more. But it is quite certain that without something on him this book would be in the state of that presentation of Shakespeare's most famous play which it is no longer lawful to mention except by allusion. Johnson is not only by common consent one of the most striking figures of the eighteenth century, but he is, from a certain side and in a certain sense, *the* eighteenth century—in its strength and in its weakness, in what must be admitted to be its glory, and what has sometimes been harshly and uncritically called its shame, though it might justly be styled " limitation." It is quite certain that no one who has not arrived at a tolerably distinct and achromatic view of Johnson can, except by mere accident or pure intuition, understand the eighteenth century at all. And it is hardly rash to add that, if you understand Johnson thoroughly, if you recognise his defects, comprehending also, as is necessary to their full recognition, the qualities opposite to them, and so appreciate his qualities, with the circumstances, causes, and conditions of both, only that part of the eighteenth century which is directly concerned with the idiosyncrasy of individuals will remain for you to find out. Now it is one of the not very numerous patches of

Necessity of and apology for writing about Johnson.

common ground in this matter that the idiosyncrasy of individuals is not the most remarkable point of the century. Therefore, even if you aspire to, and in part deserve, the somewhat idly framed and sometimes questionably given title of *Johnsonianissimus*, you will not necessarily be the complete master of our *Sette Cento*. But you will not be very far off such mastery.

On the other hand—a phrase just used may have prepared the acute reader for the caution—the cult The various attitudes towards him. and even the passionate study of " the great lexicographer " is not without dangers— nothing that has once become, in whatever aspect, a fashion, fails to breed them. It was in his own latter time, though he had not a few enemies and some not despicable ones, notoriously the fashion to regard him with " a foolish face of praise," and to speak of him with a tongue nearly as foolish as the face.[1] Then, though rather less rapidly than usual, came the reaction under Romantic influence ; his style was abused and his critical attitude pooh-poohed. Next, the great duel of Macaulay and Carlyle over the body of Boswell's *Life*, recalled and in a manner fixed public attention to him ; though the quarrel itself rather concerned the biographer than the biographee, both writers, in their widely different ways and capacities, admiring Johnson himself, even if Macaulay joined some unintelligent satire with his admiration. For the past eighty years the good omens have shamed the ill, perhaps in rather increasing measure ; but the pestilent "fashion" has returned, and men, Johnson's characterisation of whom would have been very delightful to third parties, but very inconvenient to the persons themselves, have " taken him up." It is even a little frightful to think what that characterisation would have been in the case of the defunct head of a distinguished college ; it is infinitely

---

[1] The "green goose," Boswell, of course has exaggerated both for us ; but he seems to have had not a few to keep him in partial countenance who were neither geese nor green.

amusing to draw up various fancy specimens of it as it might have affected a living essayist and politician.

Very little shall be said here on the character of the famous book—not of his composition—by which Johnson is generally known. Even before Macaulay's love of antithesis, and his hatred of Croker, prompted him to write his famous essay—certainly ever since— Boswell has been a temptation to that lowest of literary vermin, the cheap paradoxer ; but let him not tempt *us*. The inspired-zany theory, and the devout-hero-worshipper-with-a-few-personal-flaws theory, and all the rest shall rest, in the other sense, as far as this book is concerned. One thing is clear, that Boswell was a great artist, for he set himself to do a most difficult thing, and he did it consummately. That the eighteenth century produced his books [1] would be almost a sufficient justification of the title of this. Except when a man wants poetry, there is no book in the world, not even Lockhart's *Scott* (perhaps the only near second) which is so certainly good to read, in gross and in detail, through or at intervals, at night or at morn, to rest from other work or to put yourself in training for it. But though Boswell's life was wholly passed in the eighteenth century, though he has provided such an astonishing mirror of part of it, he was not himself in the special sense *of* it, save in quite unimportant ways. Even Pepys, between whom and Boswell such extraordinary likenesses (with as many great differences) exist, was more of his time than Boswell was. But Boswell's subject, as has just been said, *was* his time to a very great extent.

Boswell himself, not at all improperly in the circumstances, and basing himself (as he had almost a full **Boswell and** right to do) on one of Johnson's own in-**Pepys.** numerable *obiter dicta*, that as to autobiography, has regretted that Johnson did not write his

---

[1] Taking the *Tour* as independent of the *Life*, which it, of course, is ; though one always thinks of them together.

own life. The general *dictum*, and so again in a way Boswell's adoption of it, has been endorsed by Carlyle, who indeed did not carry it out in his own case, but went unfortunately far towards doing so by those " Reminiscences " which have excited only less controversy than Boswell's actual book. Here one may doubt. Autobiography in the full sense is no doubt thinkably or theoretically possible, and in another sense might be theoretically priceless. A perfectly genuine and full autobiography would have the value of a physical autopsy and more, though it would in almost any case, except that of persons who were of no mark or likelihood, be somewhat terrible.[1] We have it, to a certain extent and for a limited period of life, in the case of Pepys, and are very glad to have it ; but the instance itself pretty nearly decides that we are perhaps better without more of the kind. It decides, however, more than this. The Clerk of the Acts of the Navy rarely thought of anybody but himself ; and by a curious though quite logical consequence he rarely did injustice to them, simply because he was one of the most purely (if not always prettily) " objective " persons who ever lived. But most men do not live to themselves as Pepys did, and few men have had their relations to other people so entirely unaffected by really " passional " considerations.[2] And the two chief examples of actual autobiography by great men of letters are " awful examples " indeed. We say, and we say justly, that the author of the *Confessions* was, though a man of genius, a hopeless cad ; and that the

---

[1] FitzGerald applied this term even to Thackeray's creative analysis. Later, and as they have been hailed, more intricate analysts in fiction have ceased to be terrible and have become merely tedious, as Richardson was earlier. But the exposition of a real human heart, not of a merely vulgar kind, can never, whether in fact or fiction, be true without being tragic ; and therefore full both of pity and terror.

[2] Although we know from an amusing passage that he was once " in love with [his] wife," and though it may be contended, with not too much paradox, that he was scarcely ever quite out of love with her, it would be quite ridiculous to apply the phrase to any other of his numerous or innumerable connections. They were not even philanderings or flirtations or fancies—they were merely accesses of *concupiscentia carnis*.

author of *Dichtung und Wahrheit*, also a genius, was a
" cultured," but rather priggish, snob. Yet if Rousseau had not been a cad and if Goethe had not been a
snob, what could they have done with the passages
which earned them these just designations? They
must simply have left them out. In other words, the
picture would have gained by the omission of ignobility,
but it would have lost by simple concealment of the
truth. A perfect autobiography would be an anticipation of the Day of Judgment. Without being a simple-
ton or a sentimentalist, one may not feel quite equal
to that, either in one's own case or others.

The two famous "quarto MS. volumes"—into which
Boswell, with his usual inconceivable shamelessness,
The possible confesses to have peeped, which he thought
Autobio- of stealing (in which case Johnson, with
graphy. his also usual and equally incomprehensible
tolerance, did *not* kick the Peeping Tom from his
presence, but did confess that he himself should
have gone mad), one of which in the sad last
days that odd person Sir John Hawkins, apparently
with a good object, did remove, whereupon Johnson,
having recovered it, forthwith burnt it with its companion—might have contained an actual autobiography
fuller than the sketches we have, and certainly must
have supplied more or less exhaustive materials
therefor. In form they were probably scattered
jottings of the *Prayers and Meditations* kind; but less
strictly "divine" in character, and wider in range.
Probably also a large part would have been occupied
with those valetudinarian details of which the letters
are rather unnecessarily full, and of which Mrs.
Thrale complained with rather better reason than her
complaints usually possess. The curiosity which
regrets their loss need not be—though it is most likely
to be—ignoble; but there are two inferences, or at
least suggestions, which seem to be warranted by the
facts known. It is probable that Boswell derived

from his spyings some warrant for that curious digression, just at the end, about Johnson's morals. It is nearly certain that, if he did so, he had found nothing worse, in the good old schoolboy phrase, to play the sneak about.

To some extent this self-revelation is actually provided, in Johnson's case, by the publication, disputable but on the whole justified, of the *Prayers and Meditations* themselves on the other side, and by some curious fragments of anecdotic reminiscence like the delightful Bet Flint story (though this wants expansion), the story of the early conjugal tiff in the "First Ride Together," the exquisitely tantalising glance, in University College Gardens, at "Phil. Jones, who loved beer, and did not get very forward in the Church," the solemn reference to the occasion when the same fortunate College "saw" the Doctor consume three bottles of port, and the like. But these do not go very far; and as every biographer has before noticed, Boswell's own searchlight is only turned on the last third, and rather less, of Johnson's life, with the comparatively scanty details gathered from various sources as to the earlier two-thirds and more, while (as has also been laboriously calculated) the biographer's personal communications with his subject did not amount together to anything like a year of days. To want anything better than Boswell is certainly irreligious; but considering Johnson's very large acquaintance, not merely at the last but at all times of his life, a man beginning earlier than Boswell and taking pains might certainly have found out more, especially as the supply of sources must have been immense.[1] The century in general lived much in public, and no representative of it more so than John-

The Johnsonian legend.

---

[1] Hawkins has been defended as well as denounced; and Boswell was obviously prejudiced against him. But he himself was as obviously a dull dog, whether in or out of his "shoes and st*aw*kings," and he certainly "sinned his mercies" of opportunity. His book, too, is dryness itself: but not with the dryness of wit or wine.

son, owing to his horror of solitude. The worst of the actual deficiency of detailed information as to his life before he was fifty has been the inevitable creation of a legend, for the shaping and determination of which Macaulay is no doubt more responsible than any one else, but for which it is perhaps usual nowadays to put too much of the blame upon him without at the same time taking care to avoid swallowing the legend itself.

Whether the " Grub Street " experiences and characteristics form a really considerable part of the personality is a point on which a negative answer has been more than hinted at earlier, argument in support of it, as far as he is specially concerned, having been then expressly postponed. It may now be given—not, it is hoped, too tediously. Everybody knows, and it cannot be necessary to quote nor paraphrase, Macaulay's [1] vivid picture in a sort of diptych, first of the supposed conditions of Grub Street generally and then of Johnson as he emerged upon society, the greatest but the last representative of Grub Street itself—the faults and foibles of the type being (with the essayist's well-known faculty of suggesting something perhaps a little more or less than the truth) represented as not merely characteristic of the " Street," but as being caused or brought about by residence there, and strange to a generation for which Grub Street no longer existed. But let us, once more, examine the details of this picture a little.

In the first place there is the very considerable fact that Johnson never came within very many miles of the shadow of Grub Street till he was twenty-eight—at

---

[1] It is said to be a not uncommon foible of " writing fellows " to imagine that everybody knows all they have written. To this I can plead "not guilty." But if anybody should unfortunately read into the above remarks (and perhaps others in this book) an intention to treat Macaulay with the sciolist impertinence too common for many years past, let me firmly disclaim it. A paper in *Corrected Impressions* (London, 1893) puts what I think of Macaulay perhaps most succinctly. It will be found to contain much more praise than blame ; and in many other places I have protested against low estimates of him both as a verse- and as a prose-writer. But that his inveterate habit of over-colouring, over-emphasising, dropping all cautions, provisos and the like, made his critical and historical estimates subject to heavy discounts and offsets, cannot be denied.

which time a man's manners, habits, and so forth
are pretty well fixed. In the second, comparatively
scanty as is our information about him
during this time, and indeed during the subsequent period (almost as long) before Boswell
met him, it is quite certain that these
manners and habits in his case *were* formed, and that
they were such as were likely to interpose the most
serious obstacles in the way of success, no matter at
what time he had begun his career, from the days of the
Elizabethan University Wits to the first quarter of the
twentieth century. It is all the more glory to him, and
it is no discredit to his time, that he did finally make
his way against such a constellation of inauspicious stars
as that which governed his whole life, till he was in
advanced middle age, and did not abate all its malefi-
cence even then. But Grub Street had uncommonly
little to do with it. Before he ever saw Grub Street he
had shown signs of some of the worst physical and
mental consequences or symptoms of that constitution
which used to be called scrofulous, and is now, I believe,
called, by the learned, tuberculous. Although possessed
of enormous bodily strength and undaunted courage, he
was (as we are reminded, sometimes very specially *ad
nauseam*, in all writings about him) awkward in shape,
purblind, disfigured in countenance, and—worse than
all—afflicted with incurable melancholia. His education, though not exactly neglected, was irregular ; and
his family circumstances, though there was always
some property, were frequently close to want. Although
he seems always to have been regarded as a boy of unusual parts, he, somehow or other, never seems to have
had any chance of the numerous small endowments
which then passed youngsters from school to University,
with a much fairer prospect of continued subsistence
than exists at the present day. Above all, indolence
and irritability of temper were, as they always continued
to be, his constant companions—companions by them-

Its connection with " Grub Street " dis- cussed.

elves sufficient to ruin any man's chances in the profession of letters, and not likely to improve them in the
time of patrons. When he at last got to Oxford it is,
after all that has been written on the matter, even now
entirely unintelligible how he could have expected to
stay there till he took his degree: and he had to leave
prematurely from simple want of money. Whether he
had or had not made the proper use of the time he had
there we cannot say, for the evidence is not conclusive.
He had admittedly dawdled at home without doing
anything particular for two years before he went, and,
after he left, his bad luck, not quite unaided by injudi-
cious conduct, kept him dawdling for some years more
before he went to London. He admittedly quarrelled
with his actual patrons, and gave other possible ones
the idea of an ill-conditioned and impossible person.
He married at six-and-twenty, without any assured
income, a woman nearly twice his age, with hardly any
fortune, and sank what money she had on a most
unpromising adventure of a private school. And then
he went to " Grub Street " with twopence-halfpenny
in his pocket. Even supposing that Grub Street was
the malevolent and maleficent monster that it has been
depicted as being, need it have exerted much of its
fiendishness to prevent a man of this stamp from at
once attaining affluence or even comfort ?

If I have been so unfortunate as to convey to any
reader an impression unfavourable to Johnson, let me,
in a passage intended to refer to what follows
as well as to what precedes, remove that
impression at once. I do not believe that
there is any one now living, or any one who ever lived,
less guilty of the intention to produce it than I am.
I think Johnson one of the greatest of Englishmen,
one of the greatest of men of letters, and one of the
greatest of *men*—not less great because he had an
abundance of human infirmities. But fear and favour,
and deference to fashion, and refusal to face the truth are

The reasons
of Johnson's
poverty.

accursed things, both in life and in literature—perhaps nowhere more accursed than in criticism, which is not the least department of literature. I want to set down the facts, and I am bound to say that I see in these facts little of anything that throws special blame on the eighteenth century, or that supports the notion of Grub Street as a cause of Johnson's misfortunes. A great deal has been made of Lord Gower's amiable description of a man for whom he was trying to obtain a degree as a preliminary to employment, as " starving by translating for the booksellers." Now it so happens that we have, at this very time, some facts and figures bearing on the case. They show that Johnson in eight months, from August to April, received all but fifty pounds for translating Sarpi (" Father Paul "), a translation which never was finished or published. It is not a magnificent or munificent sum. But in the first place there must be certainly more than one man of letters now living, as certainly not possessed of genius like Johnson's, but holding at the time no higher position in letters than Johnson then held, who has received nothing at all for considerable amounts of work on books, which for this or that reason not depending on himself, never were published ; and sometimes for books which were. In the second place, translation has almost always been shockingly underpaid. It is not so very many years since I was informed by a writer of distinct talent, and, I believe, quite trustworthy, that *five* pounds was what he and others were wont to receive for the translation of an average French novel ; and I could fortify the instance by not a few others in regard to different kinds of literary work. But there is something more to add.

Living in England was, at the time, extraordinarily cheap. It is in regard to this very period that Johnson told Boswell the well-known story about living on thirty pounds a year ; and though he drew attention to the impossibility of doing so at the time of their con-

versation thirty years later, he does not seem to have
denied it at " Temp. of tale," as the old illustrations to
books are legended.   Now fifty pounds in eight months
at this rate would carry a man through more than a year
and a half—more than double the time of working—
even if he did nothing else.   Of course the calculation
is not intended to be Shylockian.   Johnson was
married ; he seems always to have helped his mother ;
he must have bought some books, and so forth.   That
he would have been as cheap at five thousand a year as
many modern Cabinet Ministers would have been dear
at five hundred or the fifty itself, is the present writer's
heartfelt belief.   But taking the facts into consideration ; taking his own repeated and well-supported confessions that he always worked hastily, against the
grain, and with long intervals of by no means enforced
idleness between ; adding perhaps the one rather unpleasant fact of his life, the reception of subscriptions
to the Shakespearian project without doing anything for
them, and without even keeping regular account of the
subscribers ; remembering also that though he made,
owing to his own peculiar way of working, little profit
of it, he actually received £1500 for the Dictionary in
the Grub Street or anti-Boswellian period,—can we as
critics—that is to say as judges—declare in honour and
conscience, after examination of the evidence, that it
was the out-of-jointness of the times, and not the faults
of nature and of will in the man, which brought about
his penury ?

Two other things, the one wholly, the other mainly
to Johnson's credit, have still to be put.   The most
affluent man of letters could not have been less—very
affluent men of letters have often been very distinctly
more—apt to haggle and higgle about fee and reward
than he was.   Ridiculous as the ten guineas paid for
London may seem, it appears that he would have
accepted a smaller sum, except that " he would not take
less than Paul Whitehead."   At the other end of his

career the price paid for the incomparable *Lives of the Poets* was certainly far too small,[1] but he seems to have been quite satisfied with it. And so in other cases. Indeed, in a well-known passage Boswell says that far from joining the clamour against booksellers (*i.e.* publishers) which every author has heard, and in which too many have themselves taken part, he declared " the trade " to be as a rule not only just but generous. In fact he was both too proud and too indolent to bargain. One may admire him and feel inclined to imitate him ; but it is evident that when a man behaves thus, the gratification of his pride ekes the stinting of his cheque. To which it may be added yet further, that Johnson's indomitable independence, his just scruples, and his curious predilections stood in the way of his fortune. It is known that he might have had one good country living ; and it is almost certain that he might have had his choice of many others had he consented to take orders. But he would not do so, partly because he doubted his worthiness, and partly because, in both cases being no doubt quite sincere, he hated living in the country. On the whole, unbiassed judgment must decide that it was rather a great and surprising stroke of luck that he at last got a pension, with the minimum of obligation to do anything for it, than that he had to wait for it, or for something, so long. No national or royal money was ever better bestowed ; but hardly any has ever been bestowed on a recipient who had gone less out of his own way to meet the guerdon, one may almost say, who had done so much to make it unlikely.

But enough and too much of this :[2] let us turn to his genius and its legacy.

---

[1] £200. He eventually, not at his own instance, got £400, but it was the opinion of good judges that, had he bargained, the booksellers would have given him £1000. Considering that they had given Smollett double the sum for his merely creditable compilation, the *History of England*, one need not doubt that they would.

[2] It has been said purely with the object, not of reflecting on the man, but of doing justice to the time.

Of the great characteristics of Johnson there have been many statements, but perhaps only one real opinion, or to put it otherwise, one common *His greatness.* denominator of judgments, present when they are true and absent when they are false. It is the acknowledgment of his magnificent common-sense, passing into, and tempered by, a melancholy wisdom, higher in its sphere but more restricted in its operation than the common sense itself. It has been said that not the slightest novelty is claimed for this statement, any more than for the other statement that the lady in black velvet and diamonds, whom Johnson himself remembered (or made himself remember) as " touching " him in his childhood, is dead. But it is questionable whether a large number—whether perhaps the majority of the Doctor's critics—have kept in mind the position in detail as well as they have asserted it in general. The most conspicuous instance of this is of course again Macaulay, who never showed either his inordinate love of startling contrasts or that unlucky Philistinism of Whiggery which was equally characteristic of him, so much as in his " look on this Johnson and on that." " This " was in Macaulay's view, a noble, charitable, high-minded, moral and religious philosopher ; " that " was a drivelling idiot, or at least a fantastic and eccentric crotcheteer, who believed in ghosts, held the doctrine of Divine Right, fasted on Good Friday, and declined to go to public worship in Presbyterian regions. There is no need to elaborate the proposition, or to demonstrate the fact that many persons, equal or perhaps superior to Macaulay in purely intellectual qualities, have shared Johnson's principles and practice in all these points. But Macaulay, though the most conspicuous, has been very far from the only offender in this kind. There are not a few professed " Johnsonians " who smile superior or stand surprised at his politics ; there are others who except his literary criticism, peremptorily

or apologetically, from their praise of his wisdom ; yet
others to whom his attitude towards country and town
is the stumbling-block ; and so on and so on.

Yet it is not difficult, if only that doctrine of his own,
which should be the one guide in this matter—" Clear
your mind of cant "—be not merely written on fore-
head and wrist, but graven on heart and brain—to
" go solid " for Johnson, putting aside the petty
personal deficiencies which are due to ill-breeding, ill-
fortune, and disease.   Even his bearishness and irritability were not only partly due to the last-mentioned
cause, as constant features of " scrofulous " diathesis,
but have been grossly exaggerated.   His rough side
was not as a rule shown to those who met him
" manful under shield," [1] or to those who frankly sub-
mitted to his authority.[2]

As for all the rest, it is perfectly possible to hold
views very different from Johnson's on many—it
ought to be possible to hold them on all—
points strictly controversial ; and yet to
maintain his almost unrivalled claims to
possession of the lower sense and the higher wisdom
mentioned above.   Except *Ecclesiastes*, *Rasselas* is probably the wisest, though with that same exception it is
almost the saddest book ever written.[3]   Melancholy
is here not terrible as in *Gulliver*, because resignation,
which is absent in Swift, is present in Johnson.
But if this melancholy is not " hateful as the gates of
hell," it is at any rate as solemn and as sorrowful as
the gates of the grave.

Yet it is never exaggerated, in at least a subjective
sense ; that is to say, though Johnson's view of life

*The variety
of its
simplicity.*

---

[1] Unless of course they "took the offensive" in another sense.

[2] Boswell himself may seem to supply an exception ; but the incredible folly of
some of his remarks, and the fly-like teasingness of his general attitude, excuse
anything.   The case of Goldsmith is more dubious ; but Boswell's testimony here
is not seldom suspicious, and it must be admitted that in the " Poor Poll " moments
Goldy and Bozzy were too much on a par.

[3] Renan's description of the *Koheleth* as a " livre *aimable* " is a curious instance of
his shallowness of thought.

may be too exclusively sombre, his view of the gloomy
side of life is never false, and is true to fact as well as
to his own perception of fact.

Perhaps there has been no time at which the contemplation and degustation of this blend, of common-
sense and uncommon yet widely different wisdom, were
more sovereign and specific than they should be at present. The flighty idealism and the mere materiality
which between them characterised the greater part
of the nineteenth century might, indeed could not fail
to profit by Johnson ; but his formula was not then
so clearly " indicated " as it is for our present mixture
of self-conceit, contempt of the lessons of history, fads,
crazes, affectations, and worst of all " rotting." An
elaborate analysis of this last curious and very disgusting feature would be rather out of place here, but
as it constitutes the main difference between the
And the eighteenth century with the greater part
motive. of the nineteenth and the latest nineteenth
with the twentieth, something must be said of it. To
define strictly is of course difficult.[1] It is opposed
utterly to " high seriousness," but it is equally and in its
quintessence opposed to true humour, though it may
perhaps claim to be related, on the wrongest side of
the most unclean blanket, to wit. Cheap epigram and
idle paradox are its sword and shield ; " don't-care-a-
damnativeness " its coat of mail ; ignorance its helmet,
and bad taste its stink-pot or hand-grenade. The
crank and the quack and the pure " rotter " alternate,
combine and blend in such a portentous fashion that
it is often difficult to identify or to separate them.
There are popular writers of the present day of whom
you cannot so much say, altering the famous line to
suit, that " every inch that is not crank is quack," as

---

[1] This might come near : "A habit of adopting and expressing views likely
to shock simple folk ; of ostentatiously flouting popular morality and conventional
reverence, etc. ; and of resorting on every possible occasion to what Tourguénieff
—marking and hitting the game early—called 'the reversed platitude.'" The thing
has probably always been a measles of cleverish undergraduates : but it only recently
became an endemic *lues* among grown-up folk.

that crankery and quackery have been forced into each other's fibre by a *plusquam* hydraulic press, the mass having then been saturated, as far as possible, with " rotting " ; while others exhibit more or less of the three constituents by themselves, and yet others, escaping these severer manifestations of the disease, exhibit a dreary adhesion to mere theory and formula.

To all this[1] the temperament, principles, and method of Johnson form the complete antithesis and absolute antidote. He had abundant humour, with more than sufficient self-will, and Boswell has recorded, with a fidelity tempered by imperfect comprehension, the Johnsonian habit of arguing or " taking the other side " out of a spirit of contradiction and caprice, which sometimes approached that of pure Puckish mischief. Yet this never in the least approached " rotting " in its constitutional and malignant form, and can only be confounded with it by those who can look solely at the surface. It was in fact hardly even a fringe—it was a mere detachable and but occasionally worn lacing—to the garment or armour of massive though not in the least stolid sense and wisdom. Even the silly objection to " the obvious," which has become a sort of mark of " rotting " itself, can fix no hold on Johnson because of the special characteristic of his sagacity—the revealing and restating, as if they had been obvious, of things previously mistaken or denied. His aphorisms and deliverances generally are not so much—

What oft was thought, but ne'er so well expressed,

though they have a good deal of that too, as—

What all should know, but none have yet observed,

and the number, bulk, and variety of them are astounding.

---

[1] It has been the fashion, for a few months past, to say that " the war " has killed " rotting." Such a kind goeth not out with one year's trouble (mostly of other people) or two ; and there are signs enough that the state of our Denmark is far from sound yet.

It is true that though the diffused admiration of him has never wholly ceased, and has perhaps even (and so far fortunately) rather increased of late, thorough appreciation of his wisdom is not to be attained without a little difficulty. Boswell is no doubt a great stand-by, and his occasional summaries or collections of detached *Johnsoniana* are not merely valuable storehouses, but no mean works of art—the occasionally "green-goosish" comments which the collector himself appends themselves contributing, though no doubt unconsciously, a positively artistic advantage of contrasted setting. But it is to be feared that the letters, which contain almost more of this wisdom, are not uncommonly skipped; while even these letters require supplementing by the aid of his minor and miscellaneous works, which are very seldom read at all.

If this latter is the case, it is no doubt very largely, if not mainly, due to the hasty acceptance of a far too *The common* common dictum, that Johnson, though a *views as to* great conversationalist, was not really a great *Johnson's* *speech and* writer. Perhaps also some defenders of his *writing.* style have done him less service than they intended by over-exalting it for general use, and as a contribution to the main progress of English; while others of them have not fully appreciated the characteristics of the style itself. No doubt Macaulay's description of it is one of the worst parts of his essay—so strangely compounded of good and bad. What he describes is not really Johnson's elaborate style at all; and the chief characteristic which (not indeed inventing it, but accepting it and "passing it on" with his own unique power of effective "vulgarisation") he fixed upon—that of using Latinised diction—is very far indeed from being the real *differentia*. Johnson did, whether from the character of his favourite studies; from conscious or unconscious imitation of Browne; from a desire to lift English out of its drab vulgarity in the second quarter of the

o

century; or from other reasons too many to mention—
he did indulge in such diction; but it seems to have been
at least as common in his praised conversation (though
he sometimes " translated " both ways there) as in his
discredited writings; and it never was the staple or
secret of that writing at all. This staple or secret is
to be found in the elaborate rhetorical *tesselation* of his
phrase—by which clauses and sentences were balanced
against each other, and built up into larger sentences
and paragraphs on a system of almost mathematical
or military exactitude, file being drawn up against
file, and squadron against squadron, while both the
constituent clause - members and *their* constituents
of substantive, adjective, and verb were balanced
or " dressed " against each other in pairs, triplets,
even quaternions of strictest equivalence and equili-
brium in rhythm and thought. This Palladian
architecture of style is no doubt more imposing than
delectable; and the artificial " art " of it sometimes
invites Queen Gertrude's protest to Polonius, except
that " matter " is never deficient. But it is by
no means omnipresent; and it may be doubted
whether it is ever very conspicuous in his really best
passages.[1]

To bolster out this chapter with citations would be
mere bookmaking, and quite out of keeping both with
the plan and the scale of the book itself; but one
instance of the singular faculty of putting a case once for
all may be allowed. There is probably no question
on which more vain breath—few even upon which
more serious difference of opinion—has been vented,
than the question whether an advocate may undertake a cause which he knows or even suspects to be
unsound. It is believed to have actually troubled
some sensitive but surely rather neurotic consciences;
it has helped to create or feed a sort of popular

---

[1] There is, as every student knows, a great deal of it in *The Rambler*; some but
rather less in *Rasselas*; and comparatively little in the *Lives*.

prejudice against a great profession; and it went near to spoil some excellent novels in the case of Anthony Trollope, not to mention others. Johnson pricked the bubble once for all in a single sentence, though he enforced it with others. " Sir, you do not know it [the cause] to be good or bad till the judge determines it." This is the kind of thing that the " rotter " derides as " obvious "—the fact being that it is only the " short title," or compressed conclusion, of a long and complicated argument; while certain sentences of more modern writers, which their admirers look upon as original, simply turn out on examination to be mere cobwebs of jargon.[1]

But one may go farther and say, not in the least for the sake of paradox, that even where Johnson went wrong in selection of point of view, and consequently in view itself, he was almost invariably right, granting his own position and stock of definitions, axioms, and postulates.

There are perhaps no points on which more plausible—at any rate on which more frequent—objections

His most challenged criticisms on— are taken to a high estimate of Johnson's judgment in general, as well as his literary sense, than in regard to his critical opinions of Milton, Swift, Fielding, and Gray;[2] but (with possibly one exception) a thorough and impartial examination will lead—not certainly to agreement with his results, but to complete understanding, and therefore at least partial allowance or exculpation, of the methods by which he attained them. The exception (which may be anticipated, if not from the reader's own knowledge, from what has been said earlier in this book) is, of course, Swift; and there one has certainly to confess, though not, according to the principles of this discourse, to avoid. There is in fact no satisfactory

---

[1] A somewhat longer example of Johnson's combined acuteness and equity is to be found in the string of replies, strictly orthodox in their Anglicanism, to Boswell's putting of the commonplace " Protestant " objections to Roman Catholic doctrine.

[2] Prior might be added, but his case has been already dealt with.

way of accounting for Johnson's almost invariable injustice to this mightiest of his immediate predecessors and elder contemporaries ; and the only way to account for it at all, as it seems to the present writer, is by supposing a sort of " clot " of minor prejudices mischievously obstructing the flow of equable judgment. Johnson (one may think unjustly) suspected Swift of irreligion, and felt the always sensitive nerves of his intellect and his faith quiver at such arguments as those of that *Tale of a Tub*, which, in another mood of petulance, he used to deny to its author because it was too good.   He did not like, and cannot be blamed for not liking, Swift's foulness of language.   Like many other practitioners of ornate style, he thought Swift's a plain one, neat perhaps but poor and beggarly.   He probably thought Swift's scholarship insufficient.   Moreover (a point of the first importance to which we may return in connection with another of the four persons named above), he pretty certainly felt some fear of his own melancholy view of life passing, as it did in Swift's case, into unmitigated misanthropy.

But these things might, it may well seem, have remained scattered, and, even if combined, have prevented, it may be, full appreciation, but not provoked that depreciation which is undoubtedly the worst blot on his criticism—if they had not been conglutinated by the subtlest and most maleficent of all influences—a fancied private grudge. Johnson is said to have denied that Swift (as there was perhaps too much chance that he might have been if they had ever met) had been personally rude to him ; but one may very much question whether " Sherry " was as dull as Johnson would have had him to be by nature, when he suggested that the Doctor thought Swift had neglected to enforce the application made by Lord Gower for a Dublin M.A. degree to Johnson. Boswell, for once doing justice to his legal education and profession, ingeniously dismisses this as " not

Swift.

proven "; but if not *probatum*, it is in the very highest
degree probable. Johnson was on the whole a just
man, but he was almost excessively human. Everybody must have observed in his fellow-men, and he
must be a very excellent or a very obtuse person who
has not observed in himself, at least a tendency,
requiring to be guarded against, to exaggerate not
merely personal offences, but personal neglects, slights,
and other *misères*.[1] It is hardly too much to say that
presumed negative injuries of this kind rankle in
sensitive dispositions even more than open and positive
attacks or affronts. That the belief would have made
Johnson unjust to Swift without the different causes
of dislike mentioned above, there is no reason to
suspect; it would at most have made him unsympathetic. But it gave, unluckily, the point of attraction
to which they all gathered, and which, by assembling
and coagulating, made them a formidable and a
maleficent whole.

In one of the remaining three cases, Milton's, one
might almost " deny the major " or rather the, in this
case, more important " minor," for John-
son's estimate of Milton's poetical value on
the whole was high and almost of the highest. But
in details he was of course often very, and sometimes
very unjustly, hostile. Here the personal element
could not possibly come in; in the other two, Fielding's and Gray's, it might, but we may here echo
Boswell's phrase, and say " there is no sufficient
evidence that it did." We may dismiss these first in
part. The praise of the *Life* of Savage in *The Champion*, which has been attributed to Fielding, is pretty
certainly not his; and Johnson, who at the time was
likely to be well acquainted with London journalism,
probably knew its authorship.[2] But this only pre-
cludes positive ingratitude; and so far as I know or

Milton.

---

[1] Of course actual saints do not require even to guard against this: but a good
many people are not saints. [2] Apparently it was Ralph's.

remember, there is no other point of personal contact between Johnson and Fielding. Gray, we know at least from anecdote, did on one occasion speak somewhat rudely of Johnson,[1] but not in a fashion which Johnson himself is likely to have much resented, even if he did hear of it, which is nowhere said or insinuated. So the coast is, on one side, clear.

On other sides Johnson's judgment on details is once more easily accounted for, and little as we may agree with him, certainly not blameworthy. He had a perfect right, if he chose to do so, to think Milton's politics detestable, and his personal character by no means attaching. The only question is whether he "carried over" these opinions into his opinion of Milton's poetry, and allowed them to colour it unfairly in detail if not in whole. But there is, again, no reason —certainly no necessity—for thinking anything of the kind. Milton was, most prominently at any rate, a blank-verse poet, and Johnson did not like blank verse. Even in his blank verse Milton admitted licenses which Johnson (though some of his own allowances practically justify them) thought excessive, if not absolutely to be barred. Where Milton does not use "blanks" he uses, as in *Comus*, *Lycidas*, the choruses of *Samson*, mixtures of metre, and of rhyme and no rhyme, which again were offensive to Johnson, and contradicted the general principles of prosody in which he had been brought up. He thought the sonnet both trivial and un-English. In point of matter many of the most beautiful passages in these pieces, as well as in the *Paradises* and almost the whole of *L'Allegro* and *Il Penseroso*, consist of descriptions of nature, for which Johnson did not care. Therefore,

---

[1] Bonstetten told Sir Egerton Brydges that he was walking in London with Gray when they saw Johnson before them, and Gray said, "Look! look! there goes the Great Bear." Nicholls adds that the poet disliked Johnson and "declined his acquaintance"—how, when, and where we know not. Johnson was not wont to thrust his acquaintance on anybody. But the same authority expressly affirms Gray's admiration of Johnson's understanding, goodness of heart, and generous charity. See Tovey's *Letters of Gray* (London, 3 vols., 1904–12).

admitting Milton's greatness as a poet, he condemned these parts of his poetry.

Now, it may be said, all these dislikes were wrong. Be it so ; the present writer at any rate does not share so much as a single one of them, whatever may be his opinion of Milton's politics and his religious views, of his temper and his character generally. But let it be remembered that even Cardinal Newman, who will scarcely be considered a reckless Hedonist, an upholder of the right of private judgment in all things, or a maintainer of the doctrine that truth is what each man troweth, candidly confessed [1] his belief that there is no criterion of poetry except the pleasure which it gives to writer and reader. If Johnson did not like some characteristics of Milton's poetry he had a perfect right to say so, especially as he at least could give reasons why he did not like it, reasons depending on a coherent if questionable theory of poetry itself.

With respect to Fielding, it must have struck many people, as it struck Boswell, that the confession as to

Fielding. reading *Amelia* through without stopping, outweighs the repeated but fantastic depreciation of its author.[2] To adapt the old Roman story, a novelist who makes an " *un*gentle " reader, and such a reader as Johnson (who, notoriously, seldom read *any* book through), " come down " in this way, *is* a great general ; and there is no more to say. But the specification of fault-finding, itself rather fantastic, in particular the famous remark—about Fielding telling the time and Richardson's taking the watch to pieces [3]—is a paralogism which, in another's mouth, Johnson would have torn to ribbons. But Richardson

[1] In the Preface to his own collected *Verses on Various Occasions*.

[2] To which must be added his other confession that, when he spoke, he had not read *Joseph Andrews*. The two, taken together, reduce his expressions almost to a consideration and condemnation of *Tom Jones* exclusively. What will be said presently makes this even more probable.

[3] Fielding did *not* only tell the time, he made the watch that told it ; and if Richardson knew how a watch was made, it is most deeply to be deplored that he actually produced such clumsy turnips.

was Johnson's friend and benefactor, while his works were of a nice morality. Fielding was a " vile Whig," as his greatest admirers, who may chance also to be very strong Tories, must sadly admit. There is another point to which the present writer, many years ago, was, he believes, one of the first to draw attention. Johnson once confessed that " wherever young ladies are there is always temptation," and he undoubtedly may have considered that Fielding took this temptation of young ladies a great deal too lightly.

There remains Gray; but here the circumstances in regard to Milton reproduce themselves to no small extent. Gray was a Whig, and as we see from his letters, though not in the least on any such principle as that on which Johnson was a Tory,[1] a decidedly violent one. His most intimate friends were Horace Walpole (of whom Johnson spoke with good-natured contempt, and who was never tired of abusing Johnson) and Mason (whom Johnson was quite right in thinking a miserable poetaster). Further, it is constantly forgotten that Johnson actually gives the *Elegy* praise more valuable than volleys of dithyramb. For the rest, Johnson's criticism of him was from his own point of view justified; and even if allowance be made for this point of view as wrong, distinctly damaging. He said that Gray was " dull, but dull in a new sort of way," and called him a " mechanical " poet. Gray is not dull to us; but will any catholic and historically-minded lover of poetry deny that very much if not most of his interest outside the *Elegy* (which, remember, is not in dispute) is derived from " his new sort of way," that is to say, from his contrast with the average verse of his time ? If Gray had written about

Gray.

[1] There is perhaps no greater proof of that unlucky shallowness which marred Macaulay's great gifts than his denial of Johnson's "conviction" of Toryism. If ever political faith was "whole and smooth and sound," logically connected and logically carried to an end, it was Johnson's. Indeed the argument that he "thought one form of government as good as another," *i.e.* for the individual, shows that Macaulay did not understand the question, or begged it.

1650 or 1850 instead of about 1750, should we rank his actual verse, except the *Elegy* and that marvellous stanza of the *Ode on Vicissitude*, very high ?   Then, again, will any critical admirer of Gray place his hand on his waistcoat and deny that Gray, with the same exceptions, and hardly these, *is* mechanical—in diction, in versification, in almost every respect of technique and architectonic ?   Was there ever a poet less spontaneous, less inevitable ?

It is indeed, as has been said elsewhere of Johnson, one of the most interesting and attractive things about him, that even when he is wrong he cannot help being right too in some measure, degree, aspect, or connection.   The famous and curious quotation from *Julius Cæsar* which Ben Jonson criticises, but which cannot be found in the play—

> Cæsar did never wrong but with just cause—

has been applied to Johnson very defensibly, except of course in his moments of pure perverseness.   Nay, even when the famous spirit of contradiction is on him, or when he is playing the " Swiss of argument," and taking up a side for mere luxury of indulgence in whim, though you may sometimes come upon a paralogism more or less deliberate, you will seldom meet an instance of positive delusion or unconscious fallacy. His mental vision had qualities exactly the opposite of those of his bodily sight.   He may see narrowly or at a wrong angle, but he always sees, and sees clearly what he sees.

Common sense salted and spirited with humour ; inflexible principle combined with utmost charity ; *Some end-words.* wide knowledge without pedantry (the notion of Johnson as a typical pedant probably still survives, but only in the poorest wits, unenriched with even the slightest knowledge) ; curiosity again tempered by a wholesome scepticism which applied to all things provable, while it respected things where proof is not in place ; pride, in that sense where pride is no deadly sin—indeed no sin at all—because it has been tried seven and seventy times in the fire of suffering, and purged of all the dross of vanity ; a courage mental, moral, and physical, utterly fearless of every person and everything but God and God's doomsman Death ; other good things that could be catalogued almost to weariness,—all are to be found in Johnson, and most of them are, as has been said, specific for the opposite qualities so common in our day. Nor is it even in the least degree true that presentation of these, in a restful and refreshing manner, is confined to the *Life*, delightful as that is, and much as we owe to its author. The charm is to be found in the letters, of which that Life itself largely consists, but which occur in some bulk outside it ; in the *Lives of the Poets* eminently ; in the *Journey to the Western Isles* almost equally ; in *The Rambler* and *Rasselas* for all those whose intellectual range goes a little beyond halfpenny picture-papers and the six-shilling or sevenpenny novel; in the *Prayers and Meditations* for those who are not superior to religion ; in the very pamphlets and miscellanies for those who deserve to find it. Those who wish to feel and see the things of ordinary and sometimes not ordinary life that are, who are not too proud to be warned of the consequences of these things that will be, let them give at least a small part, and that at frequent intervals, of their days and their nights to Johnson, with a certainty of gaining delight as well as profit from the study.

It is perhaps, though there are many subsidiary attractions in him, this perennial life-wisdom which makes Johnson such a specially *dulce refrigerium*, and the shadow of his great rock so welcome a refuge in a waste and sweltering land of paradox and mirage, of crankery and quackery, such as that in which we have been sojourning for more than forty years now, till, as has so often happened, war has come once more to strengthen and sober and arouse us, if at the eleventh hour we will. It was natural enough that his qualities should have been belittled, because they were obscured, in a time of enthusiasm and excitement like that of the quarter-century of revolutionary war and Romantic revival which began not long after his death. It was perhaps excusable that, except by voices in the wilderness like Carlyle's, he should be half-patronised and half-poohpoohed by the generation which succeeded, of which Macaulay was a tolerably typical representative, and which believed, as sincerely as it could, that if you had Free Trade, and a vote, and publicity, and peace for the time being, and competition with adulteration as an admissible form of it, and so forth—all was and would be and must be well. But the new wars (because their lesson was learnt imperfectly) from 1854 to 1871, and the extension of franchise from the unstable middle-class half-way house to the more and more unfittest, and Darwinism, and *Essays and Reviews*, and the dechristianising and democratising of the Universities, and the promiscuous extension of a misunderstood education, and the repauperising of the poor, and the plundering not merely of the rich but of all who work honestly and honestly save, with all the rest of what calls itself " modernism," —these things have brought about once more a new relation between Johnson and the times, the relation, as has been said so often, of patient and specific.

Sooner or later, in thinking of Johnson, one always comes or returns to the close of the *Vanity of Human Wishes*. In this magnificent descant—to *The Vanity of Human Wishes.* find anything finer than which in its kind we must go to the books of *Ecclesiastes* or of *Job*—a fresh side of that peculiar quality of the eighteenth century which we are trying to bring out emerges. Johnson was an intensely melancholy man. But his melancholy did not take the form of misanthropy or of rebellion ; and he was also intensely religious. Yet this gorgeous rhetoric of resignation is, though not in the least insincerely, not very ostensibly Christian, or if so, Christian-Stoic rather than Evangelical or Catholic. But whichever of the three it be, or whatever else than any of them, the quietness and confidence which are the strength of the century (a "strength," in the old sense of "stronghold," from which it could never be dislodged till it wandered therefrom of its own motion) remain prominent. He watches "the torrent of his fate," and throws no bridge —even no duckweed—of gloss over it. He hopes for little or nothing in this world, and interglimpses at least the possibility of despair as to the other. But he neither whines, nor rages, nor attempts to jest the matter off. In this philosophical melancholy, as even in those private theological exercises which we rather unfairly know, he remains sane, steady, unshakable. The most Romantic of all the Classics—affected even sometimes himself by the excess which is the defect of the Romantic quality—he still keeps the secret of the century, and in the very trouble of his soul lets no public avowal of trouble escape him. We know from accounts which, whether wholly friendly like Boswell's, or partially so like Mrs. Thrale's, are equally indiscreet, that in private, or even in society, this placidity was not always his. We know from the published (but not personally published) *Prayers and Meditations* above referred to, how very much the reverse of placid was the mood in which he contemplated Life, Death, and Eternity. But even under this rather pitiless and unfair light he shows, to a judgment which combines criticism with charity, no weakness, no hysterics ; and the works which he published himself never lack that dignity which necessarily involves quiet. A nineteenth-century Johnson is difficult to imagine, a twentieth-century one is, so far as we have gone, impossible. In the seventeenth he would have been quite different, whether his religiosity had taken the form of enthusiastic and mystical devotion, or that of almost fantastic philosophy. Only the eighteenth could produce, and only the eighteenth did produce, him ; and had it produced nothing else it would stand crowned among the ages.

The suitableness of different members of the Johnsonian circle for appearance here varies of course very much. Few of them, in what we have of theirs and know about them from others, are quite uninteresting ; some are in both respects of the highest interest ; of some we can only pine for " more." A hint of such pining has already been given in reference to Bet Flint, the heroine of that sudden lifting and dropping of the veil which naturally aroused the curiosity, as well as the surprise and laughter, of Mrs. Thrale and Miss Burney. Personal acquaintance with Bet would no doubt have had to be conducted with caution ; but a full record of her life, in the style of this fragment, would apparently have been a *Moll Flanders*, with considerably more piquancy in it. In fact, if Johnson has been condemned to any labour in the " milder shades " (in which, like many if not most good Anglicans, he was inclined to believe), conceived and directed by a more humorous spirit than Dante's, it may have been the writing of novels—as much in the spirit of Democritus, as his only actual story is in the opposite vein. But of the friends who are not mere " shadows on glasses," those who minister more or less substantially to delight are not few. Of Boswell, as has been suggested already, we need hardly speak. Although he is in some ways very eighteenth-century, just as he is in others very much of a Scot, neither his Scotticism nor his eighteenth-centuriness can be said to be of his essence, and still less of the essence of his book. He tells us about eighteenth-century people from Johnson downwards, but in doing this he is, so to speak, at one remove, to

Those about Johnson.
Some dark stars.

say the least, from forming part of the eighteenth
century. It is his portion of the universal—small and
peculiar as it is—that makes him such a peerless
reporter of the particular. The distinction may seem
wiredrawn, but for the writer it exists, and he may not
overstep the wire. And after all it is enough to say,
and an immense thing enough to say, that large part of
the delight in, and the knowledge of, the eighteenth
century that we enjoy is derived through, if not from,
that lucky luckless fool of genius, the much abused,
much praised, much written about, seldom perhaps
wholly understood James Boswell of Auchinleck.

That there was a certain similarity between
Boswell and Goldsmith may have been part cause
Boswell again. of the scanty affection that existed between
Goldsmith. them; as well as their rivalry for Johnson's intimacy, and the fact that one was an Irishman
the other a Scot. But this similarity was entirely
personal, and not in the least literary. In Oliver there
is nothing of that comparative second-handness, that
" one stage removed " quality which has been noticed
in James. He is essentially a part of the eighteenth
century, not merely an evidence about it; and it is
further noticeable that while, when Boswell ceases to
be a reporter and endeavours to entertain us with the
" sprouts of his own brain " and the anecdotes of his
own conduct, he approaches nearest to that mere zany
which unkind and inappreciative critics have deemed
him, Goldsmith's very best things are his own and
nobody else's; the very meaning of the famous comparison of the Angel and the parrot is that though
he may have talked nonsense about himself he never
wrote it. Probably, if we knew nothing about him but
from his works, we should endorse, with less hesitation
than we sometimes do, the words of Johnson, who knew
both his works and his life best, " a very great man."
It is quite certain that we must, putting this (so to
speak) eavesdropping and spy-work aside, pronounce

him a very delightful writer. Except when he endeavours (generally "for a consideration") to be learned, or philosophical, or critical, which were the three very last things that the gods had made him—if indeed they ever made him any of the three at all—he is like that bee which he took for his emblem on one occasion, only that he is all honey and no sting. To praise any of Goldsmith's work specially may seem impotent or stupid, at best or worst the mere "shop" of a lecturer on literature. But, as in other cases, one may without impertinence doubt whether the presumed acquaintance is quite as thorough as the required admiration is ready, and also whether the *variety* of Goldsmith's excellence is quite universally known by familiarity with it. Everybody knows *The Vicar of Wakefield*; certainly a good many schoolboys and schoolgirls do. The same may be said of *The Deserted Village*, and to a smaller extent of *The Traveller*. Some play-goers have seen, and more play-readers (who, it is believed, still exist as a perhaps small but perhaps also not despicable class) have read *She Stoops to Conquer* and *The Good-natured Man*. A generation or so ago all educated persons did know *The Haunch of Venison* by heart ; do they now ? *Retaliation* has been kept reasonably alive—perhaps by good men's efforts and its subject. But do many people read *The Citizen of the World* and the more unequal, but in parts even better, miscellaneous *Essays* ? Will everybody—will ten per cent in reasonably cultivated but not specially bookish circles—rise to the bait of " Mr. Rigmarole " ? Perhaps the audacious sciolism of *Animated Nature* and the *Histories* has deservedly expelled them from those sacred (the word *sacer* has several meanings) courts—the schools of modern England ; but if any wise elder person were to seek to refresh himself with the unsurpassed narrative and admirable quality of their style, would he find them easily without rummaging the grubbiest corners of the second-hand book-shops ?

Not, of course, that he ever, from his own day to this, lacked the praise and the love of the competent ; His amiable amusingness. nor that he has failed to be " took up " (as Lady Clavering says) even quite recently, and, according to the ways of recent paradoxing, sometimes from points of view where he least deserves it.   People have even tried to make him out a critic, which, as has been said, is the very thing he is not ; and, from the very nature of almost all his faults and even some of his merits, could not have been.   He was now too good-natured and now too much under the influence of half-innocent and wholly childish fits of jealousy to possess the critical *ethos* ; he was always too careless and (it must be said) generally too ignorant to possess the critic's equipment.   But as an " amuser " in the very best sense of that unnecessarily degraded term, and as something more than an amuser, he has few superiors in anything like his kind. In fact he is practically unique, or (the parallel is of course no novelty) belongs to a species of which La Fontaine is the only other individual.   Neither *The Traveller* nor *The Deserted Village* is first-rate or even high second-rate poetry, though there is in both fine rhetoric, which is possibly not wholly Goldsmith's own.[1]   But it is possible to read *The Traveller,* and quite easy to read *The Deserted Village,* over again—in the second instance at least over and over again—despite the damaging associations of old learning and even of modern teaching, despite the want of poetical intoxication, despite the often banal and in part sometimes actually unreal thought.   Some people at least never get tired of *Retaliation* and its almost inseparable companion in fluent anapæsts ; if Goldsmith was defrauded of his actual savoury meat, he has left a spiritual haunch of which no treacherous friend can deprive future ages, and the relish of which is

---

[1] Johnson certainly contributed something ; there is every probability that he at least revised much.   The peculiar tone of stoical melancholy is eminently his, and it appears nowhere else in Goldsmith.

enhanced by the presence of the so—in the flesh—
obnoxious contributors to the *Snarler* and the *Scourge*.

For some three generations, indeed, *The Hermit* (or,
as most people call it, " Edwin and Angelina ") has
His remark- provoked, if not inextinguishable laughter,
able range. an irrepressible smile ; but to any one even
slightly tinctured with that most precious injection,
an enjoyment of literary history, it is for some
thing more than mild amusement. Why was Dr.
Minor forced, or at least induced, to write in the
style that Dr. Major ridiculed and caricatured ? is
a question the answer to which should both delight
and profit, while it is easy enough to find.[1]

The prose and the dramas—they are prose in more
than the mere fact that they are not verse, indeed
some heretics have dared to wish that Goldsmith had
written them as companion tales to the *Vicar*—require
no allowances, except those indicated above ; intelligent skipping, or benevolent excuse, when Goldsmith
gets out of his depth or rather (for he has depths of
knowledge of human nature) into his shallows. *The
Good-natured Man* is probably the least interesting of
the three, because it has more of the conventions of
its actual form ; and the *Vicar* is of course the best,
because it combines an approach to tragedy with
comedy, while the others are comic merely. But in it
the mixture of sense, " sensibility," and stingless
satire, in the others the mixture of two at least of these,
and in all the *mimetic* faculty—the gift of representation
of human action and actors which drama and novel
alike require, ought not soon to pall. An entire
character perhaps, as distinguished from a character-
part like those of Moses and Tony, Goldsmith could
not quite draw ; if you compare the Vicar with
Parson Adams the difference will jump to the eyes.
But his flashes and vignettes of verisimilitude are
unceasing.

[1] The answer, though perhaps unnecessarily, should be found in Chapter VIII. *infra.*

P

It is perhaps for this reason that some readers affect the *Essays* (including under this term the *Citizen*

Power of his "Essay" quality. of the World) most of all. No troublesome and question-begging construction is required; the genius can be indulged and relaxed at pleasure. When it is absent, or not eminently present, the place can be neglected for a better exhibition of it elsewhere. The " Reverie at the Boar's Head " especially, often and highly as it has been praised, can hardly be praised too often and too much. It is perhaps the highest point reached by Goldsmith in the intellectual range, and it is not much lower from the artistic side. Those who find it a little too abstract (though there are concrete touches enough) or too markedly ironic, or in other ways too severe, have plenty of compensations from the usually admired Beau Tibbs downwards. Perhaps nowhere, indeed, does one find the peculiar level-headedness, rescued by wit from banality, which has been more or less generally allowed to the century, better illustrated than in these papers ; and a curious experiment may be made by comparing them with the work of two other writers in very much the same kind, Addison fifty years before and Leigh Hunt fifty and more than fifty years afterwards. The result may surprise some people, and of course may not be agreed upon by all. But, to the present reader and writer, Goldsmith seems to be less out of date, not merely than his earlier but than his later competitor. Addison was no doubt a wiser man than Goldsmith, and though a less agreeable, he was possibly a greater writer ; but even for persons accustomed to " horizontalise " their reading, and free from that distressing inability to enjoy anything out of their own time which has been so often mentioned, he possesses a certain aloofness, a quality somewhat of the mummy. Leigh Hunt was, for more or fewer years, actually the contemporary of living men who are not yet Struldbrugs ; but his triviality emphasises his out-of-dateness, and he has neither the attraction of antiquity nor that of idiosyncrasy to recommend him. Now that "standard" quality which the eighteenth century so eminently possesses, and which makes it "of the centre," despite its deficiencies in certain ways, displays itself in Goldsmith after a fashion which saves him from both these inconveniences. It is perhaps most eminently present in that remarkable style of his which is so charming and so difficult to characterise— more so even than Addison's own. Johnson, Burke, Gibbon, his own contemporaries, can be analysed in this respect with no difficulty ; you know, if you have some patience and a little skill in such processes, exactly what makes them what they are, and what you yourself like or dislike in them. Goldsmith defies analysis, and therefore synthetic imitation. Even Thackeray, who could write, if not like Addison, like Steele, and also like a contemporary of Goldsmith, Horace Walpole, so as to deceive the very elect if he had attempted the trick, never attempted to imitate Goldsmith, and merely resembles him in perfect naturalness. Indeed much though we talk of "return to nature" as not effected till late in the eighteenth century itself, and in a manner against its grain, it may almost be said, and the saying is less of a truism than it may seem, that when that century is not conventional, few centuries have less of convention. It was much too fond of assuming *personae*, but, when it dropped them, the human *res* remained in a curiously normal and unsophisticated condition, nor was that condition ever better shown than in Goldsmith.

It has been observed elsewhere that "those about Johnson" include, in the widest sense of the term, with a few exceptions and recalcitrants, most of the noteworthy men and women of the time. But a good many of them have found or should find better niches in other chapters. Not only the just mentioned and mighty names of Burke and Gibbon, but Mrs. Thrale,

Garrick, and others fall out here in this fashion.   Some,
perhaps, would wish Reynolds to figure.   But we are
not here dealing with the arts of design ; and though I
am quite willing to pay to the President's literary performances all reverence duly exigible, I cannot say that I
find them either specially restful or specially refreshing.
Few other members of the Club have left us much that
could be so designated, and the hosts of minors must
stand out.   But it is indubitable, though it is not
entirely explicable, that for about thirty years, from the
appearance of the *Dictionary* to his death, eighteenth-
century literature is centripetal and centrifugal to
and from Johnson, as if he were a sort of maelstrom.
His influence interrupts, and in interrupting on the
whole helps to mature, the somewhat crude romantic
tendency of Gray, Shenstone, Percy, Macpherson,
Walpole, and Hurd ; it keeps apart, blights, or in this
and that way affects, other essays of premature innova-
tion, such as those of Chatterton.   The most inconceivable but, if conceived and satisfactorily executed,
not one of the least delectable of Imaginary Conversations might be, in the hands of a genius, one between
Johnson and Blake about the year 1780.   But Johnson
wrought his own work, and he wrought it nobly : while
if that work itself may not seem exactly of the kind
indicated in our title, he can claim an overpowering
makeweight in the *Life*,[1] which without him could
never have been, and which actually preserves most
of the salt and savour of his authentic utterances.

---

[1] One of the curious touches which have made the profane describe Balzac as
oscillating between a genius and a *commis voyageur* was his making Gautier give him
half the pay which "Théo" had received for an article on him with the plea—
logically unanswerable—that but for himself, Balzac, it could not have been written.
The proportion on which, following this principle, the profits of the *Life* ought to
have been, if possible, divided between subject and writer is an interesting problem.

CHAPTER V

LETTERS, DIARIES, AND THE LIKE

THE subjects of the following chapter have often—
perhaps too often—been regarded as the typical, or at
A *Non-*" De-
batable Land,"
yet perhaps
not enough
honoured. least the most representative, exponents of
those characteristics of the eighteenth cen-
tury which have chiefly attracted attention,
if not always of a wholly favourable,
yet of a grudgingly allowanced kind. " The eighteenth century " (to amalgamate different opinions and
points of view of this general tenor) " may have
failed in producing and in appreciating the highest
literature ; and its thought, especially in poetry, may
have been shallow, its knowledge sciolist, its manners
coarse, and its sentiment absurd ; but it certainly did
introduce into one range of letters an urbanity and ease
which had not previously been known, and which
perhaps did not survive it very long." This book has
been, and if it may be will be, something of a demurrer
to the limitations of this judgment ; but the admissions
of the judgment itself have too much in common with
our title-purpose not to be taken advantage of. The
names of Lady Mary Wortley Montagu, of Chesterfield, and of Horace Walpole hardly need suggesting to
any one in the slightest degree lettered ; but there may
be something not wholly hackneyed to be said about
them, and about others. Some of them—of the minors
more particularly—were also of " those about Johnson," as indeed a majority of men and women of letters,

for more than half the century were ; but they figure
here in a different orbit or relation.   With Lady Mary
he had nothing or next to nothing to do ; [1] with Chesterfield he had slight but too notorious and unfortunate
dealings, which may themselves be dealt with presently ; from him we have nothing about " Horry "
but a piece of good-natured slighting,[2] which would
have annoyed its object extremely, while Walpole's own
abuse of Johnson shows him at his worst, though some
have endeavoured to excuse it as loyally filial.[3]

The eldest of the three has perhaps been the subject
of the least discordant, as well as of the least dis-
obliging, judgment.   It is true that we have
from the youngest a tissue of lampooning
notices directed not against " Lady Mary's "
wits—Horace Walpole had himself far too much wit
for that—but against her character and (what is perhaps
more fatal) against her appearance, habits, and behaviour during the later part of her life.   But she was
an intimate friend of Horace's detested sister-in-law,
Margaret Rolle, Countess of Orford ; and there were
other reasons likely to arouse that personal spite which
was the worst feature of his character.   Pope's attacks
are still more largely " discountable " ; for though we
may not know exactly what happened between the two,
it is pretty clear that he made a fool of himself,
clearer still that she did not let him make a fool of her,
and certain that she aroused thereby another spite,
which was to Horace's as vitriol to white-wine vinegar.

Probably she had not much heart—not many people
of her generation and station had ; and the next had
to go through the stage of " sensibility," or sentimentality, before it could revive the real organ from its

*Lady Mary
Wortley
Montagu.*

---

[1] Speaking under correction, but with the aid of the excellent and not too
labyrinthine index to the *Globe* edition, I do not think her name occurs in Boswell.

[2] He owned that Horace "got together a good many curious little things, and
told these in an elegant manner."   Of course he did not know the *Letters*.

[3] Johnson was not only, as a Tory, strongly opposed to Sir Robert generally, but
his early anonymous satire, *Marmor Norfolciense*, was one of the bitterest of the anti-
Walpolian skits.

torpid state. Yet her marriage, though it ended in an unquarrelling estrangement from a husband of whom in his later days nobody has a good word to say, seems to have been originally a love-match. Her alleged misbehaviour to her sister, and anything more than imprudence in her relations with that enigmatic French-man Rémond de Saint-Mard, seem "not proven." If she did not love her son, she did not love one of the worst-blooded, if not one of the worst-witted, scape-graces and scoundrels in Europe; and there is no doubt about her affection for her blameless daughter, though it may have been of a rather dispassionate kind.[1]

Nevertheless there is no doubt that, for a time at least, she was charming as a woman, and at no time was she other than charming as a writer. Her verse flashes with the very best paste in Dodsley; and, for its purposes and in its place, we do not care to test it for pure diamond quality. In prose the famous letters have found few detractors, though somehow it seems to me that of late years she has found fewer eulogists than formerly, and than she deserves. If this means that she has fewer readers it is a pity, because it would be an additional proof of that apparently *incapacitating* effect of modernity which is noticed elsewhere in this book, and which seems to be making it more and more impossible for people to take an interest in anything but the " cackle of their bourg " and their day. The brilliant and varied pictures of scenes and manners, both in her earlier and in her later time; the occasional shrewd literary criticisms (she was, it must be remem-bered, Fielding's cousin, and had other literary blood in her); the unfailing acuteness (sometimes no doubt passing into " cuttingness ") of her remarks on men

---

[1] Of course the contrast-comparison with her great predecessor in letter-writing, daughter-study, and Mary-ship, cannot be missed. One of the points in it is that nobody has anything bad to say of Lady Bute, and nobody (save her mother) any-thing good to say of Madame de Grignan, putting aside that beauty which, in itself, her mother seems rather to have exaggerated. Lady Louisa Stuart, Lady Mary's grand-daughter and Scott's friend, seems to have had not a little of her grandmother's talents without any of her weak points.

and things ; the easy, fluent style, neither slipshod nor
stilted ; the interest in all manner of things which
brought about her famous introduction of inoculation,
and lasted through her life—all these merits and others
make her perennially readable.   There may be, as in
the entire group—with hardly more than such an
exception which is no exception as Cowper—too much
"light without love ; " a somewhat hard intellectualism,
which, if there were nothing else on the earth, would
make rather arid pasture.   But, as it happens, the
literary earth is a ζείδωρος ἄρουρα, bearing many
other kinds of food for those who choose to take them.
Lady Mary is not " adorable " [1] like her French predecessor ; but she is very frequently admirable and
always enjoyable.   She never " wrote herself out " ;
the later letters (sometimes idly doubted as questionably genuine) are as good as the earlier, and even show
a certain progress.

Lady Mary's junior by five years, Philip Dormer
Stanhope, fourth Earl of Chesterfield, resembled her
Lord Chester- very much, not merely in experiencing and
field.   showing the influences of the same time,
society, and general circumstance, but even in personal (though not physical) characteristics.   Seldom
indeed has any literature (not even the French, to
which both, no doubt, owed something) produced so
striking a pair in the same time, the same social position,
and the same departments of literature, but in different
sexes.   He wrote less verse than she did, but what he
did write was " verse of society " of the highest merit.
Like her, he had wide interests, and his work in connection with the adjustment of the Calendar may rank
with hers in combating smallpox.   As a woman, and
also owing to other circumstances, she had not his
political chances.   He did not indeed make the most

---

[1] One sometimes wonders how much of H. Walpole's cult of Mme. de Sévigné
was due to his dislike of her successor. But quite impartial judges have felt the
spell.

of these, for reasons out of our range ; but he was at one time a very considerable figure in that region, and his administration of Ireland has nearly always—and quite justly—been eulogised. That he was a gambler all readers of *The Virginians* know ; but so were most of his contemporaries. Horace Walpole's constant girds at him (due partly to the usual filial or would-be filial partisanship, partly to jealousy as of a rival wit), are accompanied by that obvious though unwilling admiration which is the highest possible compliment. But he has suffered, partly from the traditional stigmatising of his famous *Letters* as immoral ; still more of late from the effect of Johnson's almost more famous, and certainly now better-known *Letter* to him.

In respect to this, and to the estimate to be held of Chesterfield in regard to it, the present writer finds himself in the unfortunate position of being in a minority—perhaps of one, certainly a minority—against all or most recent critics. The *Letter* is of course a magnificent piece of English rhetoric ; it is saved from the worst sense of the term " rhetoric " by its obvious sincerity ; when you compare it not merely with such stuff as " Junius," but with all save the very best things of Burke himself in somewhat similar kind, it towers above them ; and (though perhaps all its admirers do not see this) it is perfectly free from the snobbishness reversed of a protest against the neglect of an 'umble man of letters by an 'aughty haristocrat. It is nothing so little as it has been taken to be—a sort of trade-union protest of authors against patrons instead of employers. Johnson writes not merely with sincerity, he writes with dignity, but does he write with justice ? or has his intense and passionate personal pride " presented " Chesterfield's conduct as " more hideous than it " was ? Was that conduct [1] even hideous at all ?

The unlucky incident with Johnson.

---

[1] The facts are generally known and they (at least Johnson's views of them) are stated in the *Letter*. But some readers may perhaps be reminded that Johnson had had an introduction to Chesterfield and had, after attending his levees without much

I own I cannot see it. The patron system was undoubtedly a bad one, and this was one of its natural results. We have abundant accounts—not merely in such "realistic" eighteenth-century fiction as Smollett's, but in more or less trustworthy records of actual fact—of these levees. If they were painful to the nobler and more deserving among the clients, they must have been a horrible nuisance to all but the vainest and most empty-headed of the patrons. They were often so crowded that the most ideal Mæcenas ever excogitated by flatterers could not have attended to everybody; a large proportion of their constituents were the scum of "Grub Street," and access to, or exclusion from them—civil or uncivil treatment at them—were necessarily to a large extent, if not wholly, in the hands of servants. Now, though no doubt there were exceptions, there is overwhelming testimony that the eighteenth-century serving-man, from foot-boy and groom to steward and major domo, was "in a *loomp*" bad—extremely bad.[1] He was venal, insolent, idle, and almost certain to be particularly inclined to exercise these amiable qualities at the expense of poor men of letters—a class whom he probably did not more despise for their poverty than he hated them for their superiority in some ways to himself. That Chesterfield did not go out of his way to relieve Johnson from these disadvantages is probable enough ; in fact, we may say, certain ; and from what *we* know of Johnson that was a great pity. But Chesterfield did not know what we know ; and for all he did know, Johnson might have been—to take once more the stock-examples—a Savage or a Boyse. It seems to be pretty clearly established [2] that the old notion of his having made offensive references in writing to John-

---

or any notice or result, discontinued the attendance. When the *Dictionary* was about to appear the Earl wrote two exceedingly flattering articles on it in the *World*, and the *Letter* was Johnson's acknowledgment.

[1] See above on Swift's *Directions*.

[2] The "respectable Hottentot" of the letters was evidently Lyttelton not Johnson.

son's manners is unfounded. So when he wrote the
World " puff " of the *Dictionary* there is not the slightest
reason to believe that the writing was due to a sense of
guilt, a fear of retaliation, or a desire to " curry favour."
Chesterfield, though he had little or none of the absurd
morgue which a few of his compeers showed, was a very
proud man, and though he affected pococurantism, was
a sincere admirer of literature. On the other hand,
Johnson had shown *his* pride, properly enough, in
discontinuing an attendance which, whether degrading
or not in itself, became so by indifference to real or
even presumed neglect. But, when the olive-branch
was offered, it would surely have shown truer mag-
nanimity, not indeed to receive it with effusive and
humble gratitude ; but also not to reject it with toga
wrapped round body, and gesticulating hand - play.
If he could not cordially accept the offered hand, or if
his own was not light enough (as perhaps it was not)
for a half-ironic expression of thanks, with a " better
late than never " touch in it, he should have left the
matter alone. In any of these three cases he would
have kept that position of equality in letters with the
Earl which was the point of importance. His actual
conduct does not seem to me to have established any
superiority, except that of the professional rhetorician
over the amateur.

　　Chesterfield himself, however, was only an amateur
in the sense of not writing for money. He was a much
Chesterfield's greater master of English than either Lady
real quality. Mary or Horace ; his wit was, as has been
said, acknowledged by friend and foe ; and he had
far greater intellectual power than some of those
who have sneered at his *petit - maîtrisms* and his
homilies on " the Graces." His prophecy of the
French Revolution—not the only one of course, but
by far the most weighty and well-reasoned—is or
ought to be well known ; and a great many maxims of
singular practical insight might be extracted from his

works. But his chief claim to attention, from the special point of view of this book, is of course the *Letters* to his son and godson, though the few personal " characters " which he left are his chief exploits in style. His work, even more than Lady Mary's, seems to have rather dropped out of sight lately, or is only referred to with commonplace and probably second- or third-hand sneers.[1] To anybody with even the slightest catholicity of taste and (one might say) intelligence of judgment, the *Letters* are most curious and interesting things. It is constantly forgotten that they were never in the slightest degree intended for publication, that their publication was unauthorised, illegal, and a piece of blackmail. Chesterfield was far too acute a man not to see that, as public matter, they might bring some ridicule, and were sure to bring some odium on him. But they were written with absolutely private purpose, and adapted to that purpose with the practical ability which he showed in regard to politics and to the " Calendar " matter. Whether young Stanhope was a hopeless lout, or merely a person of ordinary or a little less than ordinary talent and manners, does not matter a jot. His father evidently knew that he was no genius, and that wit must do a good deal to help nature if he was to " make a figure." And he set himself to supply and apply that wit with all his own wits and all his energy. That his ideal—if it *was* his ideal [2]—is not the highest, or a very high one, must of course be granted ; but much as he himself hated proverbs, something about " silk purses " occurs here. That his morality was not that of an anchorite, or even of a Henry Fielding, is certain likewise. That if we look up for poetry, enthusiasm, sense of mystery, the

[1] It it is by no means unlikely that Dickens's absurd caricature in *Barnaby Rudge* of " Sir John Chester " did the real Chesterfield some harm, with numerous but ignorant readers. The Knight is a villain—a term which nobody could apply to the Earl ; a coxcomb and a fribble, which only fools would transfer to Chesterfield ; and above all a selfish and unnatural father, while Chesterfield was exactly the reverse.

[2] For any one, that is to say, of higher qualities and capacities than those of the person with whom he was dealing.

higher charity, and a good many other things, we shall not be fed, is even truer. But his pattern of a man of the world—neither hero nor saint, but at the same time neither a ruffian nor a cad, nor, except on extremely strict lines of judgment, a rascal—has something to say for itself; and, in some respects at least, might be copied by our intensely self-admiring twentieth century, with considerable advantage. And this is not the main point, nor is—though it has more "mainness" about it—the fact that this was the ideal of an important part of humanity for a considerable time. The main point is the singular dexterity and the unwearied zeal with which the rather thankless task is carried out. The varied adaptation (a point for which all fathers are not famous) of the style, tone, and substance to the boy's and young man's advancing years; the mixture of kindness and authority; the effort (with no mere condescension in it) to make the letters interesting and amusing as well as instructive— are all extraordinary things. The more recently published sequence of letters to young Stanhope's legitimate supplanter, the godson who succeeded to the title and estates, are less interesting, though they show something of the same characteristics; but no one really knows Chesterfield till he has read those to Dayrolles, to Chenevix, and to Madame de Monconseil. Here we find, not perhaps to the intelligent, "another Chesterfield," but a side or sides of the same, which it had not been necessary, or indeed desirable, to exhibit in the correspondence with the boys. There is a deeper wisdom, a wider range of subjects, less detail of an amusing kind, but also no triviality and no schoolroom monitions—every now and then something approaching to sentiment. It would be the cheapest and silliest paradox to deny that Chesterfield's faults are eminently those of the eighteenth century; it would be hardly wiser to assert that its merits which are not small are not eminently his.

The last of the trio, Horace Walpole, so often
mentioned already, has undoubtedly fared best with
Horace posterity as far as reading goes, and no
Walpole. wonder—for he is perhaps the most variously
and the most voluminously amusing of all writers
outside the novel.[1] The sixteen volumes of the
latest and most complete (yet still not complete)
edition of his letters—that of the late Mrs. Toynbee
for the Clarendon Press—is one of the most remarkable " stand-bys " in the sense of our title to be found
in literature. It is so vast, so various, so unfailing in
interest that though it is difficult to imagine anything
more different in tone from any possible " Song of
Repentance "—Romantic or other—you feel inclined
to do with it what Heine's Herr Ulrich did with his
Liedchen von der Reue, and " when you have brought it
to an end, begin it all over again." Even a single
reading of it will supply the evening requirements of
a man who does not go to bed very late, and has learnt
the last lesson of intellectual as of other enjoyment—
to enjoy *slowly*—for nearer a month than a week, and
perhaps for longer still.

But as concerns its faculty of satisfying and re-
satisfying without satiating, this curious collection has
other sources and resources besides its mere bulk,
though that is so great that the first volume becomes
almost unfamiliar before we have reached the sixteenth. The variety above mentioned is one of these,
and the most obvious. But there are others—two
especially—which in increasing degree are less open
to the charge of obviousness. The first is the strange
character—stranger the longer you examine it—of
the writer. The second is a peculiarity—most germane to that of the century generally—of the writing.

---

[1] His own novel-writing has been previously treated (*v. sup.* p. 166 *sq.*), and justice
has been done to its historical importance ; but any "amusing" quality which it
may possess is strikingly different in kind from that of the *Letters,* and would
certainly not have been taken gratefully by the author. His compilations, editions,
quasi-historical work, etc., are also not without importance, nor without refreshing
quality ; but they cannot be dealt with at length here.

At first it is—unless by some special favour of
Jove or of Apollo or of Minerva—rather difficult not

Macaulay
once more
recensendus. to take the view of " Horry " which has
been the usual one, and which was put
in its crudest form, again as usual, by the
cocksure dexterity of Macaulay. He was, according
to this, a man of some cleverness, but a wilful
dilettante possessed of, or at least willing to use,
no solid judgment and much rococo taste, with, in point
of moral character, a selfish and spiteful temperament,
chequered by some rather irrational personal friendships. It is all the more difficult to get rid of this
estimate, that it cannot be said to be entirely or even
mainly false : on the contrary there are few letters of
any length, perhaps even few pages, which do not
contain what may be pointed to as some justification
of it. Yet, if not the hasty or unthinking reader, the
careful student, must soon perceive that it is very
largely inadequate. The moral side of it is least so ;
but even that is unduly coloured and weighted. Horace
was selfish and he *was* spiteful ; but he was capable of
taking a great deal more trouble for other people than
many who go through life without any imputation of
selfishness would take ; and his spitefulness was not
seldom an odd sort of chivalry reversed. He would
probably never have thoroughly appreciated either
Fielding or Johnson ; but he would, as probably,
never have spoken contemptuously of either if they
had not lampooned Sir Robert. The immediate
occasion of his most offensive remarks on the great
novelist, who was more than his equal in birth and far
his superior in genius, was that some of Walpole's
friends (who apparently thought a gentleman and
a magistrate was a sort of ticket-porter to do their
bidding) had not found Fielding compliant
enough. He not unfrequently did generous
things ; and though his taking upon himself the
whole, or nearly the whole, blame of the quarrel

The real
" Horry."

with Gray, is not quite beyond the detraction of a clever Devil's Advocate, impartial judges will still give him a good deal of credit for it. His relations with Chatterton were [1] more unfortunate than blameworthy; and if he did set up that rather ineffectual person Conway as a sort of new-fangled and human Janus, with one face of a heroic general and another of a heaven-born statesman—if his senile admiration of the Miss Berrys had something of senility in the worse sense, neither could be said to be an unamiable weakness. In fact he had rather what is called a genius for friendship, though he certainly could be distinctly offensive in speaking of those whom he chose to regard as his *un*friends.

But these " moral sides " of men of letters are never the most satisfactory aspects for the contemplation of lovers of literature, though it must be admitted that in Walpole's case they cannot be wholly neglected. His taste, his judgment, his attitude to men, books, and things, his strictly literary gifts, and so forth, still remain to be considered. And they are still more difficult subjects for correct evaluation.

In the first place there is the problem—continuous and never to be neglected — of the amount of seriousness, *at the moment*, in Horace. Some would have it that he was always posing; but that is part of the shallow and slapdash view of him which we declined to take before. He certainly was, very often; and to entire strangers he was perhaps never quite sincere. The Mann letters, again, were avowedly written for preservation, if not definitely for publication; and this inevitably destroys complete sincerity. But in others, as, for instance, those to Lady Upper Ossory (the

The central problem of his sincerity.

---

[1] At least they seem to have been so; for there is a lack of impartial evidence on the subject. But the less painful side of the matter supplies an interesting instance of Horace's ignorance of older English letters. He told Chatterton, with delightful innocence, that he did not understand " the Saxon language." It is at least certain that Alfred or Ælfric would have been equally puzzled by the Rowleian lingo.

ex-Duchess of Grafton), there is little of the kind ; and in a good many the real Horace and the Horace whose mask he chooses to assume, speak in a complication rather bewildering to unravel. On one subject he is nearly always genuine, unless he is obviously not so, and that is " Strawberry." On some others it is not at all easy to " make him out," or, as they say over there, " reckon him up."

Perhaps his weakest point was in logical faculty. He had, when he chose not to be flighty or poco-To be deter-
mined by
estimate of
his logical
powers. curantish, not inconsiderable common sense ; but his arguments are absolutely childish, and his opinions, tastes, judgments, have no consistency or common " bottom," as the time would have said. Macaulay, in making fun of his Whiggism, was not merely throwing up the lights of his portrait in his usual fashion, but disembarrassing his own party of a most inconvenient and damaging partisan. Eighteenth-century Whiggism indeed—though Macaulay himself would have been the last to admit this—was very seldom logical. Even in Gray, who had a much stronger head than his friend, it is difficult to discern anything but sheer party spirit. One might alter, for the benefit of both, but especially of Horace, two famous lines into—

> On our side are Virtue and Wisdom,
> On yours are but Folly and Guilt.

It is even hardly fair to say that the French Revolution made Horace swallow his principles ; for he really had no principles to swallow. His seventeenth-century idols did not cut off Louis XVI.'s head ; and therefore, in the Horatian logic, " *Major* Charta " (otherwise King Charles's death-warrant) could not be in the least appealed to as justifying Robespierre and Danton. We certainly need not look back as far as himself to find examples of this curious state of mind ; but his example is at least capital.

It is, however, of much less importance to us in itself (for, as has been said, no one can possibly take Horace for a serious politician) than because of the light it throws on other sides of his character which are important. These concern his interest in and attitude to the lighter and more personal aspects of politics themselves ; but they also concern literature, art, society—things to us very important indeed. At an early age Horace Walpole found himself in a rather peculiar position. Succession to his father's title and estates was several stages off—might, in all probability, never happen : and as a matter of fact never did happen till he was an old man.[1] His father indeed provided for him amply at the expense of the nation ; but these provisions were sinecures, or at least offices entirely dischargeable by deputy. He was for a long time a member of Parliament, but had fortunately as little taste as he had capacity for active politics. He took to no profession. Although fond enough of pleasure, society, and to some extent, though a mild one, of the special delight of that society, gambling, he was, by disposition and health alike, disinclined to any of the more active forms of debauchery. But, though an idle, he was not a lazy man, like his friend Selwyn ; and he wanted something more to interest him besides society itself, its gossip, and its gaming-tables. He found it in what had, after being sporadically and slowly developed in the seventeenth century, become a common mania in the eighteenth, " collecting." At first—naturally enough as a result of the usual education of the day and the Italian visit which for a time

---

[1] I venture to "inscribe myself in false" (to use a charming French idiom), though with considerable diffidence, against a notion, entertained by some great ones, that we ought to make large allowance for Horace's "aristocratic" feelings. That he had them is clear ; that he was entitled to have them is, to me, not so. The Walpoles themselves were an old and good but by no means a very distinguished family : they were merely on a level with half the upper squirearchy of England. As for the Shorters, one trembles to think what even Mme. de Sévigné, still more Madame de Grignan or Saint-Simon, would have said of *them*. From his father's premiership Horace might derive position as well as places, but certainly not " aristocracy."

wrecked his friendship with Gray—his bent was chiefly classical and artistic; but before very long he extended and specialised it, concentrating himself more or less, though with considerable fringes and excursions, on the mediæval period, which had been and still was a stumbling-block or foolishness, or more generally both, to his contemporaries and predecessors.

"Strawberry" and its contents did not in fact confine themselves, especially at first, to the Middle Ages, admitting goldfish, and china to contain them, from the East, the pipes and hats at which Macaulay laughed from the modern West, and " curios " of all kinds, all times, all countries. But upon these ages Horace gradually concentrated himself more and more. Nor can it be said offhand that he never did so according to knowledge. At least he took a good deal of pains to acquire such knowledge as to arts and crafts, as to history, and even—in " a sort of kind of, as it were " way—as to literature. Unfortunately, though he has been followed almost to the present day by too many others, he paid least attention to the last, which should have been his first object. It would indeed have been pretty difficult for him (though, as Gray showed, not impossible) to obtain any knowledge of Old or Middle English, more difficult still to master Old French and the older Scandinavian (though Gray again and Percy did something here), and most difficult of all to acquaint himself with the older German, a language which, even in its modern form, was then very rarely tackled by Englishmen.[1] But it was not so much in positive ignorance of mediæval letters that Horace showed his disadvantages; it was in the inability

(margin note: " Strawberry" as a symbol.)

[1] We know this positively from Chesterfield (who recommends it to his son as a rare and valuable accomplishment) as well as from other sources. It may seem odd, considering the circumstances of the English throne and the constant continental entanglements which they involved. But French had anticipated these as the language of diplomacy : and our two German Kings were, even with their partisans, by no means popular enough to induce a devotion to things Teutonic.

(arising from that want of logical and consecutive thought which has been noticed) to see that his own ideas as to literature, religion, and the whole region where intellect and emotion reign, in Brentford fashion, were utterly foreign, indeed hopelessly hostile, to those of the Middle Ages themselves. In matters of taste and criticism, with some exception as to the arts of design, there is no more extreme representative of the hopeless Philistinism which has been unjustly charged on the century at large than Horace Walpole. Of real poetry, real romance, real mystery, and even real passion of any kind he had no share—no inkling even. It is pretty certain that if Gray had not been a personal friend, and especially if he had been an anti-Walpolian, Horace would not have admired even his poetry ; as it was, one shrewdly suspects that he thought Mason's quite as good. How utterly ignorant, though historically beneficial, his adoption of romance was has been shown already in regard to *Otranto*. In respect to any sign of religious feeling Chesterfield himself is a person of sincere piety compared to Horace ; [1] and his study, imitation, and collection of Gothic sacred things had as much reverence or sympathy in it as the exhibition of the spoils of the Temple in Titus's triumphal procession.

Yet it was his freedom from logical encumbrance which enabled him to collect, to build, to write *Otranto*, to encourage a kind of research into matters mediæval, and so to help one of the great " returns to the ancient mother " which have brought about the best parts of the history of mankind. And what is more to our purpose, this very inconsistency, preposterous as it is

---

[1] He is said to have had a passing phase of something like Methodism at Cambridge in his youth ; and Pinkerton gives Pinkertonian testimony to a very handsome disapproval of actual atheism by Horace in his age. He himself, with equally Frank-Churchillian handsomeness, declared that he would not allow guests of his to talk of the Old Testament as his French *philosophe* hosts talked before their servants " if a single footman were in the room." This is very satisfactory as far as it goes ; but how far that is every one must judge for himself. I know nothing in the letters that carries us an inch farther.

if you look at it in the wrong way, almost shocking as it may be to those who pursue that wrong way to its farthest, is productive, not merely of a variety, but of a clash and conflict of interest which is the main cause of the abounding vitality and refreshing character of the *Letters*. Their *farrago* is not only endless ; it is full of the small surprises which make the joy of life. Although he gives himself, as in duty bound, every now and then the airs of an *ennuyé*, one suspects that Horace, perhaps because he took great pains not to be so, was never bored ; and he certainly never bores us, perhaps because he is so " promiscuous." Behind all the unceasing " business " of his book—the great show-pictures of the parliamentary struggle, and the last tragedy of the 'Forty-five, and the Coronation ; the innumerable small sketches—Patty Blount trudging past his window in the rain with faded blue eyes and garments thriftily disposed to meet the atmospheric conditions ; flighty and sometimes more than flighty ladies like Lady Caroline Petersham, the " pollard Ashe," and the unbelievable Duchess of Kingston ; hands at faro that would have paid the Cæsar's debt if Horace had been playing the great game ; the feminine charm, in different grades of society and manners, from Lady Suffolk to Kitty Clive ; the broad jokes of Sir Robert and that other almost inconceivable, but not quite undelectable dame Etheldreda Harrison, Lady Townshend ; the finer ones of Chesterfield and others ; the interminable iniquities (here boredom approaches nearest) of Margaret Rolle, and the inconvenient personalities of her husband and son, Horace's brother and nephew ; the virtues and charms of the Conways and the Waldegraves, whom blood and friendship save from the Horatian vinegar-cruet ; Vauxhall and Ranelagh, Oxford and Stowe ;[1] endless

The labyrinthine and inexhaustible joys of the Letters.

---

[1] It is noteworthy that Bath, which figures so largely in most eighteenth-century lives, has very little place in Horace's panorama. He thought it did not do *his* gout any good ; but the reasons of his secession or abstinence are quite as likely to have

other things with which one might fill a chapter, sum-
marising them in this bald fashion,—all these relish the
better, stand out the more because they have among
them the *pièce de resistance*, behind them the continual
background (the figures of which occasionally advance
and take part in the movements at the front) of the
interest in genealogy and stained glass, in mullions and
carved oak, in mouldings (be they only plaster) and
tapestry, in altars and oratories, and what not.   Something of the dream-quality, which is, if not the one thing
needful, one of the things most delightful in life, and
which might seem in a sense to be wholly absent from
the Walpolian character and personality, is perhaps
imparted by this contrast.   At any rate the atmosphere
is never oppressive ; the society never tires or teases.
You do not violently like or dislike anybody, though
any dislike to Horace himself which you may have
begun with will probably dwindle ; you are not intensely interested in anything, you can leave off the
book almost anywhere without the too common mutter
of naughty words against the disturbing business or
person.   You have not been in an Earthly Paradise ;
there is no Matilda there, and most certainly no
Beatrice.   But you have been " in society " ; society
sometimes a little unedifying but never very bad, and
almost always amusing.   You have the key of it, and
you can return when you like, and have time.   There
is no book that I at least know of in the nineteenth
century, and most certainly the twentieth has as yet
produced none, that occupies a similar place.   The
best biographies, especially Lockhart's, come nearest ;
but they are essentially different in volume and variety,
and they have their analogue in Boswell, not in Horace.

   In a phrase too often used loosely, and sometimes
without any appropriateness at all, the book " is like a

---

been mere whim, determining him not to do what everybody did—or even the fact
that Pitt was an actual denizen, Chesterfield a constant haunter, and the arch-enemy
(albeit acquaintance) Pulteney a sort of landlord of the place.

novel," and it helps us perhaps a little to understand why the novel itself was practically a product of the same time. It has indeed no plot; but then some of us are heretical enough to think that plot is, of all the requisites of the novel, that which can be most easily dispensed with. It is very long; and a good novel (the contrary opinion is one of the most pitiable errors of the present day) cannot be too long. Of character there are innumerable touches, and one continuous, curious, not too obviously intelligible life-panorama. Description abounds, and of the best and most varied, while the whole is a sort of monologue-dialogue of a character different from that of the stage or that of the actual novel, but partaking of the character of both. If the old game of selecting a thirdsman for " The Bible and Shakespeare " in a library of three were resuscitated, Horace Walpole's Letters might be, by no means in mere joke, put forward as a candidate. It is certainly a striking contrast to the other two, and it cannot be said to duplicate anything that they contain. But it supplies the mere pastime which one of them at least does not pretend to offer, and almost everything in which it is wanting or faulty one or other of them will furnish or correct.

The century is deservedly famous for letters, memoirs, and all the other more or less personal literature which France had initiated in its
Mrs. Thrale —an attempt at a fairly detached study. predecessor, and to give an account of them here from Hervey to Wraxall would be impossible, and at least proportionately out of place. Something, however, may be said, before coming to Gray and Cowper—the chiefs of the department next to or with Horace Walpole —of a personage whom the writer has found it amusing and profitable to study—Mrs. Thrale. Some new *Thraliana* (though it is believed not all that are or were available) have recently been recovered;

but they seem not to add very much to Hayward's almost classical collection, and to the older documents in Boswell, Madame D'Arblay, and elsewhere. "Thralia dulcis" is certainly one of the most interesting, if not of the most fascinating, studies of the whole century. Nobody, so far as the present writer knows, has yet done her justice : and the reasons are pretty clear, though they require a certain amount of disentangling, and cannot perhaps be fully understood without reading the odd compilations of her later days. For Hester Lynch Salusbury - Thrale - Piozzi was possibly the most feminine person who ever lived—with the prerogative exception of Eve—and the circumstances, as if they were under the command of some malicious fairy, brought her femininity out in the most rainbow fashion of lights and shadows. It was a "Welsh fairy " too, as Falstaff prophetically observed, and an exceptionally "cenfigenous " [1] one. She was of one of the best families of the kingdom ; but of the kind of provincial bestness which has its drawbacks. She was very pretty, very clever, very good-natured ; but her prettiness was without dignity (the two qualities are by no means necessarily disjoined), her cleverness was desultory and undisciplined, and her good-nature, as it frequently is, was combined with something which, though you cannot exactly call it ill-nature, was capable of doing things very questionably amiable. There can be little doubt that she was unfortunate in her marriage —though it would have been a very exceptional person with whom she would have been more fortunate.

Of Thrale himself it is difficult to form a solidly based estimate, though he himself has often been called " solid." His widow's portrait of him as of a sensual tyrant, not indeed cruel, but treating her chiefly as something between a mistress who could not " resign "

---

[1] The word has Borrow's authority or responsibility. It signifies that peculiar quality of " bad blood "—jealousy, spite, etc.—with which the inhabitants of the Principality have been justly or unjustly labelled or libelled.

and a servant subject to the same disability, unfaithful, and so forth, is too obviously drawn to excuse her own conduct after his death not to require large " salting," regarded as evidence. But if you put it into correlation with Johnson's idea of her as " kept in order " by her husband, and with touches derived from Miss Burney and others, it is possible to form something like a notion of " My Master " as having been a little too much of My Master—as having sat on the safety valve too hard and too long. When the weight was withdrawn, though fortunately not before, it " ended in a blow up," to use the phrase which Marryat's schoolmaster affected, and which was visited upon him. She was not old, but unluckily she had several marriageable, or nearly marriageable, daughters, a fact which did not in the least prevent her from regarding herself as marriageable: and she characteristically looked upon her widowhood as a sort of deferred virginity, in which she might please herself, as she had not been allowed to do twenty years earlier. Her behaviour to Johnson will wear very different aspects according as we regard it from his side and from hers, and as we naturally prefer to take the former, it looks rather bad. Why she selected Piozzi, a respectable person enough it seems, and of a respectable family in his own country, but neither young, nor handsome, nor to outsiders specially attractive, is a mystery, but one to be left alone with myriad others of the kind. Why, many years later still, she nearly made a third husband of the person whose name was Rugg, and who called himself Conway, is no mystery at all. To the end of her eighty years she was a girl of eighteen—a sort of Miss Hester Thoughtless. The only bad thing she ever did was the handing over of the ancestral property of the Salusburys to an Italian connected with her second husband. And this was rather like a girl of eighteen too.

She had, however, very considerable brains—as of the feminine gender of that organ—and she showed them—if not in the curious book-making [1] of her later years or in her Della Cruscan exercises—in her letters and reminiscences throughout, and in the anecdotes of her which others, by no means always with friendly intentions, tell. Her formidable guest and quasi-lover used to charge her with inaccuracy, but he probably liked her all the better for it. Who, putting Aristotle out of the question, expects a lady, except in the unnatural relations of examiner and examined, which have come in since, to be accurate? and who desires it? One might as well expect and desire her to have a beard. Mrs. Thrale herself has no doubt " confused the record," sometimes by her deficient memory or care and her superabundant liveliness, but what does that matter? Boswell of course hated her as a rival favourite *in esse* and a rival biographer *in posse*; and she no doubt disliked Boswell as an inconvenient and excessively ill-mannered guest.[2] But in the anecdotic kind of history she is nearly if not quite his equal, and she never descends to the pure silliness which he sometimes intermixes. Her letters of all times are extremely interesting; though they are, as might be expected from her general character, an olio of acute remarks, conventional banalities, trivial things, things important, and in fact almost everything, good and bad. It has been already said or implied that she never grew old. There are some inconveniences and some possible absurdities about the possession of this gift; but there are more than counterbalancing advantages, not merely for the actual possessor. It confers perhaps some additional happiness (if also something not quite that) on the individual, and it leaves a faculty of interesting posterity. The vitality indeed which it connotes is observable in Mrs. Thrale from first to last—from her

---

[1] *British Synonymy* (1794) and *Retrospection* (1801), the latter a singular medley of ladies' learning "without the accents." Her account of her honeymoon or honey-year travels with Piozzi is unequal; but the " Johnsoniana," with all (and partly because of all) their uneasy self-defence, are delectable.

[2] Nothing in Boswell is more inexcusable than his well-attested habit of hovering at Johnson's elbow with a notebook in other people's houses.

vivid if perhaps not quite " achromatic " account of
the first meeting with Johnson to her indignation sixty
years or so later when the folk in Weston-super-mare
were distrustful of cheques on London (an interesting
touch a hundred years later still), and her unwearied
passion for entertaining at Streatham, at Bath, at
Clifton, wherever she was. The character of " Mrs.
Arlbery " in Madame D'Arblay's *Camilla* is admittedly
studied from Mrs. Thrale, nor is it exactly a caricature.
But " character-monger " as she might be, Fanny did
not quite grasp Hester, who shocked alike her prudery,
her conventionality, and the curious kind of family as
well as personal egotism which Mrs. Thrale herself
shrewdly detected in her friend.

" My Mistress," though much talked about, has,
as was said, not been very much or very carefully
studied ; it is otherwise with the two most
remarkable poets and letter-writers, who,
though her elders, have been postponed to her, not on
the principle of *place aux dames* so much as on that
of leaving the more important figures to the end, if they
have not been taken in the beginning. Gray and
Cowper have been almost universally admitted to be
among the first of our epistolers ; yet that would not
be a good reason for leaving them out, or dismissing
them with only brief notice here. Except in bulk, they
rank with Walpole as very treasuries of pastime ; and
one of the charges sometimes, though not perhaps very
critically or necessarily, brought against his, cannot even
be hinted in reference to theirs. It is not impossible
that Gray's rather incomprehensible toleration of
" Skroddles " would have been seriously interfered
with had he known that the said Skroddles (whom bored
men call Mason) would publish [1] his letters ; and though

Gray.

---

[1] Even Mason should have his due in both ways. In one he may have it elsewhere ; in the other and more favourable it should be said here that he has been
credited with something like the invention of that most important form of biography
in which letters are incorporated with text. He garbled these letters abominably it
is true, but the general principle was valuable.

Cowper did not enjoy, or suffer from, Gray's disdainful hatred of publicity, it is certain that he hardly ever [1] wrote for effect or to be read by any one save his actual correspondent. It is impossible again to conceive more distinct sets-off to Horace's worldliness and his dilettantism than Gray's retired leisure and study, Cowper's seclusion, family affection, and spiritual disturbance. Both were much better writers of English than Horace from the strictly literary point of view, though indeed it is difficult to write " better " than in a manner exactly suited to your subject, character, and purpose—as Walpole, for all his Gallicisms, etc., certainly did.

Although Gray, as above mentioned, was very badly served by the first edition of his *Letters*, the result gave rather an incomplete than a false view of his character. But the incompleteness extended much farther, as concerns the mere enjoyment of his work. Additions, corrections, extensions have been freely and repeatedly made since; and one hears of probable additions (which will be welcome if wisely chosen,[2] as they are likely to be) even to the late Mr. Tovey's admirable reissue. Meanwhile this is something to be thankful for. Until the issue of it, it was difficult for any one, and impossible for those who had not a rather wide antecedent knowledge of eighteenth-century persons, things, and books, to form a probably correct conception of Gray. The most concrete or synthetic attempt, that of Matthew Arnold, had been —as Matthew Arnold's estimates were wont to be too often—conditioned by that ancient disease, the desire to

Necessity of a careful reading. The Arnoldian view dangerous.

[1] The most suspicious exception is the letter giving account of the friendship with Lady Austen after its breakdown—the most questionable thing that Cowper ever wrote or did. But it may be admitted that he was rather " in a cleft stick."

[2] The dictum, old and new, that there was " a good deal of the schoolboy in Gray " has no little truth in it ; and among these schoolboy characteristics was a certain fondness for " Fescennine " writing, which has led to the destruction of some, and the mutilation of others, of his MS. letters, while yet others are said to be unpublished for this cause. The habit was common at the time.

make other people out either in doubt, agreement, or
hopeless dissidence with oneself, and by the writer's
curious and, in such a critic, most uncritical weakness
for taking a catch-phrase and working it to death.
" Gray never spoke out," said some unlucky friend at
his death, and Mr. Arnold seized on these innocent
words, undoubtedly descriptive of a peculiarity of the
living man in society, and wrought them into a pervading and overshadowing scheme of Gray's life and
literature, connecting them with a supposed radical incompatibility of man, time, and surroundings.   Now it
is quite true that Gray was, to some and even a considerable extent, what Mr. Arnold himself has called in
another context, a " shy trafficker."   He wrote extremely little ; he had a most unfortunate habit of
leaving what he did write unfinished ; and he was undoubtedly influenced, in the character of his work, by a
singular conflict of traditions, tastes, and the like, which
will be further handled when we come to deal with his
poetry.   But, as all careful and impartial readers of his
letters know, he often " speaks out " in them quite loud
and clear.   It would be rather interesting to be certain
to what extent Mr. Arnold knew them.   It was not, as
we know from a curious example in regard to Heine, by
any means a necessary part of the Arnoldian method
to acquire exhaustive knowledge of the documents of
your subject.

We have, however, greater advantages than those
of which Mr. Arnold did or did not choose to avail
himself, and we can judge Gray, not indeed as a poet—
that has been open to anybody with the necessary
equipment for the best part of two centuries—but as
a man and a letter-writer accordingly.   He is not,
indeed, an easy study.

The abysmal depths of personality

are not to be readily plumbed in his case, if indeed they
are in any which is worth plumbing at all.   But at

least part of the copious and various delectation to be found in his letters comes from the problems as to their author's character which they offer ; while, alike for those who take an interest in such problems and for those who do not, there is in the one case an abounding *bonus*, in the other a far more than sufficient alternative, of simple pastime—of things varied, interesting, human—and admirably told.

" Is your brother an agreeable man ? " asked David Copperfield of Peggotty, and she had no difficulty in answering enthusiastically and truly. It might be difficult to affirm positively that Gray was either agreeable or even amiable *simpliciter*. From his Eton days onwards he seems to have been infected, like his associate Walpole, with the virtue-vice of " chummishness "[1]—a quality which is not entirely virtuous even in regard to the chums, and which is apt to be, in more senses than one, very vicious indeed towards those who are not in the chummage. He, again like Walpole, but in a much more passionate degree, seems to have had the gift of friendship and of enmity in a wider sense than that of mere " chumming." One sometimes does not know quite what to make of his friendships ; and Horace himself could hardly be more spiteful when some one he dislikes dies by overeating himself, or when some political, academical, or other opponent is concerned in any way.

On the other hand, few things in the history of friendship are brighter than his relations with Wharton (who seems to have amply deserved it) and Wharton's family, and even with Mason, who was not worthy of it. One differs reluctantly with Mr. Tovey about Gray,[2] but it certainly does seem to the present writer that he had more than a sort of belated calf-love for Miss Speed, and that something beneficial to him

---

[1] This of course is part of the " schoolboyism " noticed above.

[2] The views expressed above seldom show such difference ; and though I believe I may claim to have formed them before Mr. Tovey wrote, they were greatly strengthened and enlarged by his work.

might have come of it. All this there is in the *Letters*,
and much more, for people to trace who like tracing
such things, as well as the further portrait of a scholarly
and scientifically-minded recluse (Gray's combination
of these too often incompatibles was remarkable), the
indications of one of the first discoverers of the real
picturesque [1] and many other things. But nobody
whose appetite and intelligence can deal with anything
above halfpenny picture papers or sevenpenny and
fourpenny-halfpenny novels (however indisposed he
may be to trace and analyse and conjecture and the rest)
can fail to find an ample store of amusement in Gray's
letters. As every poet who is a poet from the first
must do, he " takes notice ": as every man of letters of
his nature must be able or must learn to be able to do,
he is able to express that notice in words. He has not
a very wide range, but on the other hand he has a range
which in comparison with Cowper's, for instance, may
be said to extend from horizon to horizon. Cambridge, London, Stoke Poges, his travels abroad early
and at home late, give plenty of scene and background
to one who can, almost first of all Englishmen, perceive, conceive, and reconceive for literary presentation
a sunrise over sea on the Kentish coast. Acquaintances
of various ranks kept up his interest in men and his
knowledge of them. Acquaintance with different
literatures, ancient and modern, more remarkable perhaps in its combination of width and critical character
than any man in Europe then possessed, adds its quota.
And a fondness for natural science (strictly " natural,"
for it was mainly botany) should neutralise those bad
but vague effects of exclusive devotion to literature of
which one hears so much—and sees so little.

These things supply, in all but the greatest variety,

---

[1] It is of course quite true that "Estimate" Brown "discovered" the Lakes before
Gray, and I should not be at all surprised to find that somebody else discovered them
before Brown. That "nobody ever did anything for the first time" is a proposition
which has quite as much serious spirit as burlesque expression in it. But Gray was
the first Englishman of genius to go in for the picturesque, and the passage referred
to below is a point of reference for ever.

and in a style constantly increasing in merit, not much fewer than four hundred letters (excluding a few from other people to him), cover- *The constant interchange of interest be- tween nature and man.* ing a period of nearer forty than thirty years, though the earliest of these were not very productive. Gray was always afraid of " fine writing " in them ; he makes quite unnecessary apologies for something like it in some of the earliest and some of the latest. At first, as was natural, considering his age and the age, he is slightly stilted and artificial now and then ; but after he returned to England and began to live his own life, this almost entirely disappears. He may have pushed his very remarkable and essentially true dictum that, except in French, " the language of the age is never the language of poetry," [1] too far in his own poetic diction ; but it certainly says very much for " the language of the age," if we may judge it from his familiar prose. The same thing recurs, with a slight time-allowance in the younger man's favour, in Cowper. There is absolutely no parade about Gray's letters, and though he attributes to himself (not by any means without reason) a sort of " kittenish disposition " which sometimes scratches, there is no overdone jocularity. That he had fits of melancholy is certain—it would have been strange if a man of his poetic temperament, of weak health, and leading, though entirely by his own choice, a quasi-monastic life, with absolutely no fixed duties or occupations had not had them. But that this melancholy was no *Weltschmerz*, no anticipated Jacopo-Ortism or Obermannishness, that it had little or nothing to do with any feeling that the time was out of joint or that he was out of joint with the time, the present writer has long been convinced, and he therefore joins himself to the Toveians rather than to the Arnoldians

---

[1] It seems likely that it was this dictum, even more than Gray's poetical practice, which made Wordsworth unjust to him. It is certainly a remarkable indorsement of Dante's view (which Gray may or may not have known) and an anticipatory cut-direct at " W.W." 's.

as to Gray. In poetry he may be, and is, and will be here treated as one of the " disturbers of the Happy Valley " ; in prose he is nothing of the kind.

It has just been said that the life which Gray led was entirely of his own choice; and it is believed that this statement can be proved up to the hilt. People abuse his father, and he may have deserved the abuse ; but Gray never, during the whole of his life, seems to have done anything (or at least much) else than the thing he would. The—to modern conventional ideas —rather bewildering mixture, in his surroundings and connections, of millinery, financial business, Eton masterships, postmistress-ships, and other experiences, acquaintance with burgomasters and great oneyers, position—first in one college, then in another —neither as undergraduate nor don, but as a sort of " paying guest," and resembling that of the ladies and gentlemen who boarded in French monasteries, refusal or acceptance of more or less lucrative offices, and calm neglect (when they were accepted) of his duties— all bears directly on the general characteristics of the time, which have been so much misunderstood. The popular idea of the eighteenth century (still existing to some extent, it would appear) is as of a period of ill-recognised industrial progress indeed, but the scene of an aristocratic if not yet plutocratic tyranny, when wicked lords in stars and garters murdered and violated and persecuted as they would ; when baser but almost badder baronets ran away with every virgin they could find ; when every squire bullied and robbed his tenants ; and every justice abused or sold the law. To those who know it was a very different period. Abuses of authority and strainings of law were perhaps a little more common and more likely to escape with impunity than they are to-day ; though the laws themselves were generally better. It was left to the twentieth century to set any class above the law ; while, as for individuals, the name of Lord Ferrers, a gentleman

R

not only as good as the king but, as the saying
goes, a little better, for actual punishment, and
those of Lord Baltimore and the notorious Charteris
for narrow escape of it, suggest arrest of judgment
on the blacker parts of the indictment. The evidence
of the " greyer," as one may call them, is drawn
chiefly from novels. And though it is somewhat surprising that the warning should be needed, it may be
as well to say—on the faith of a person very well
acquainted with novels and not quite unacquainted with
life—that no documents are more misleading.

This, however, though not irrelevant to our general
subject, lies a little outside the present division of it.
What is germane to both is the position which Gray
attained mainly by help of a system which has been
more maligned and more misunderstood than most
things—the old English system of grammar school
and university education. The present writer, who
has been educated, educating, criticising education, and
educating again for nearly all his threescore and ten
years, with an outside variety of positions and interests
which makes prejudice impossible, believes that this
system, in itself, was the best ever heard of from the
beginning of years to the present day, and infinitely
superior to that of the present day itself. Like all
things genuinely English of the old kind, it was so
" individualist " that it admitted of great abuses and
was freely abused ; but it had the qualities of its defects.
The great accusation brought against it is that it did
not provide universal education ; and the experience
above mentioned has convinced one person that mankind are not even universally educable, while if they
were, it would be very unwise to educate them all equally.

However this may be, Gray was a shining example
of the good effects of the system. He profited amply
by the opportunities of scholarship which it gave him ;
and showed, once for all, if there had not been innumerable other witnesses, that it prepared men and stimu-

lated them for studies far beyond its own immediate curricula.   He profited by it further in the well-known direction of formation of friendships, and by the determination it gave him to a life of familiarity with the best society and, at the same time, of academic study. Gray's position at Peterhouse and Pembroke, after his emergence from the state pupillary, was, from modern points of view, rather anomalous, though it is a great question whether it would not be wise to restore it. He was certainly at first a fellow-commoner, that is to say an undergraduate with certain privileges. What he was later, especially after his flight to Pembroke, nobody seems quite to know.   In modern times each college would probably have made him an honorary fellow, with a right to (or at least a gift of) rooms, and membership of common [combination] room, but without emoluments or governing powers.   This might now be justified by the blessed word " research," and though Gray certainly took matters in a very leisurely way, his single *Metrum* is, considering time, place, and circumstance, more than many " research fellows " have done from morn to night of their researching career in recent times.

But of course Gray was, as Mr. Tovey has contended and made out, emphatically a man of his time, though a man of genius not very common in that time.   It is quite certain that he did not write the *Metrum* with any desire to compensate or excuse the hospitality of Peterhouse or of Pembroke.   It is exceedingly likely that he refused the Laureateship, not more out of the high-courageous superiority to an inferior position, which, from first to last, was perhaps as much affected as real, as from a consciousness that he never could bind himself to the then not inconsiderable and rather disgusting *corvées* of the office.[1]   And we know that, for the Professorship of Modern History which he actually held,

[1] There is said to have been a proffered understanding that he was to be excused. But Gray was a very shrewd person ; and he probably suspected that (as afterwards actually happened in Southey's case) the understanding would not hold.

and which he was perhaps as well qualified as any man in Europe to adorn, he never did a single stroke of solid work.[1]

Some have even ventured, in opposition to Mr. Arnold, to speculate what Gray's career would have been if he had actually been blessed with Arnoldian surroundings ; and had carried into them that sympathy with classical standpoints in literature, Liberalism of a kind in politics, and a Middletonian latitudinarianism in religion, all of which conciliated him to his critic. These heretics have been audacious enough to conjecture that his career would have been, with the necessary *mutandis mutatis*, very much what it was. To retain his position at the University he would have had to obtain an actual fellowship, and could have done so easily unless he had very bad luck ; he would have performed (let us not say " scamped ") a little college work to enable him to hold it ; or in default of this he would have taken rooms in London. The increased opportunities of periodicals would have made his prose publications—very improbably his verse—rather larger, but probably not much. He might have edited some classics instead of merely annotating them. The *Metrum* (and it would have been a great gain) might have become a book instead of a fragment. But he never could have been a prolific poet ; and it is exceedingly doubtful whether he would have written even as much prose as did Mr. Arnold or Mr. Pater, both persons to whom he had close affinities.

Moreover, as we have a rather pathetic warning in Mr. Arnold's own case, anything that he did do would probably in these ways have drained off interest from his *Letters*, if he had left any. As it was, to compensate for the very small amount of his verse, and the few fragmentary examples of unpublished prose that he has bequeathed us, we have the not inconsiderable bulk of

[1] He is said to have begun some notes, but they never came to anything, though, comically enough, he did a supererogatory ode for Grafton.

' epistolary correspondence " now under discussion.
To grumble at it as an inadequate substitute for rows
of serious volumes is an obvious and perhaps a respectable temptation ; to reconsider the grumble and say,
' We are much better off " is, for the reasons just
given, probably the more excellent way. Gray has
indeed — and his contemporary, Lessing, distinctly
claimed no more for his own " serious " work—*fermenta
cognitionis*—suggestions and hints of thought and learning scattered freely over these letters of his. You have
in them, as it were, the texts of whole critical treatises,
the sketches and scantlings of elaborate picturesque
tours, the chapter-heads and a little more of comedies
(sometimes scandalous) of academic and other life,
specimens of scientific papers, friendly warnings and
advices, unfriendly skits and snapshots—an extraordinary pepper-boxful of seasoning, and no niggardly
provision of solid substance. But it is all put at the
service of the letters themselves. Gray has much more
art than to " praelect " for a certain time, and then to
turn the page and trifle. His ingredients are almost
as well mixed as those of Walpole himself, though they
are sometimes very different in character. And therefore it is the case with him, as it is *not* (except to a
very small extent) with Lady Mary, with Chesterfield,
or again with Walpole, as it is not at all with Mrs.
Thrale and with others who have not been dealt with
here at length, that we have a body of familiar letters
combined with one of pure literature for those who
choose to accept it, a body of almost pure pastime for
those who are otherwise minded.

It takes some time, perhaps, before this curious
diversion of possible books into actual letters is perceived ; there have been notices of Gray's
correspondence in which it comes in for
hardly any attention. But the saturation
of the Letters themselves with it is a fact ;
and it brings about in them an equally curious com-

*Leading to
one between
literature and
life.*

bination of the Letter and the Diary. The famous
motto of *Sibi et amicis* applies no doubt to most good
letters, more or less ; but it applies to few better than
to Gray's, and to his perhaps earliest of all English
examples. One takes a volume up—absolutely and
honestly at random—and opens on Letter Two
Hundred, addressed to Wharton. It begins with a
more or less striking reflection—at any rate rather an
original one—that to find oneself business is the great
art of life, with the corollary—a little amusing now
that we have changed all that—that women have always
something to do because they can sew. Then there is
some scandal about the Duke of Cleveland and his
family, then a duel with another duke in it, then an
account of Lord George Sackville's trial and sentence,
then (it is true that the hour helped the man with extraordinary liberality in this instance) one of that of Lord
Ferrers, with, in it, mention of the nickname " Rugged
[Gray has R*a*gged] and Dangerous," of which Scott
made one of his felicitous uses in *Redgauntlet*. Frederick the Great's shoddy poetry and *Tristram Shandy*
turn the subject to letters in the other sense ; and the
epistle closes with Miss Speed's lucky thirty-thousand-
pound legacy, and some gossip about friends and
weather. Of course, as has just been said, accident—
it was perfectly genuine accident—brought a bumper
here to the *sors Graiana*. But a letter or two before we
have a first-hand outburst of enthusiasm for an " Ossianic " specimen, chequered by a touch of Gray's almost
infallible criticism as to its possible spuriousness ; and
the very next one to this has curious details about non-
inflammable silk-rag paper for writing and hanging
rooms ; and the very next after CC. contains a placid
enough notice of Colman's and Lloyd's poor parodies
on his own *Odes*. For Gray, unlike Johnson in so
many things, was at least like him in being quite in-
vulnerable by his inferiors.

And so it is always. By dint of variety of interests

and faculty of reporting them, he made as humdrum a life as has fallen to the portion of most men, not doomed to actual drudgery, perennially interesting to other people. Now he is " buck-washing " Mason's balder-dash, now recounting some of Newcastle's absurdities, now looking at the Lakes with cunningly framed glasses to get more " picturesque " out of them. Despite his poetic flights, and his various fancies, and his occasional spitefulness, nobody has more of the admirable common sense of the century than Gray. He is not a particularly orthodox person ; but his disgust at the rabid and childish atheism of the French *philosophes* is again nearly as great as Johnson's. He is himself a vale-tudinarian and uses strict regimen, yet he protests against Horace Walpole's whimsies of absolute " tem-perance " and abstinence from warm clothing. Just before his death he is almost as enthusiastic about Isocrates as he had been, thirty years before, about Crébillon.

In short, in these letters we have some of the greatest requisites of interest. The writer never goes out of his way to be interesting, but always manages to be so. Paucity of newspapers and the slowness of the transmission of such news as does get abroad may help him a little, the more human and less headlong fashions of travel a little more, other circumstances of time and place and circumstance more still. But, as in all art, the treatment not the subject is the thing ; and the treatment here is well nigh perfect.

That Gray's melancholy appears in (or rather be-hind) the letters is perfectly true ; but it has perhaps been exaggerated, even by those who have not fallen into the other and Arnoldian exaggeration of his being born out of due time. It is so difficult not to confuse the worker and the work that most people, no doubt, and even some of the elect sometimes, will have the subject, or hero, or whatever he is to be called, of the *Elegy* to be Gray himself. That they had something in common—and not a very little something—it would be folly to deny. Gray, who does not seem to have had much even of the quasi-dramatic faculty possessed by many poets who have not written and probably could not write good plays, could not have written the poem if they had not. But there is a great deal in the *Elegy* man that was not in Gray, and there was a great deal more in Gray that is not in the *Elegy* man. Also, though it is not an unamiable it is surely an uncritical fancy to discover in Gray " sweet serenity." He was indeed not always or very often so *un*sweet as when he gloated over the five mackerel full of roe and the huge turbot that finished poor Dr. Chapman ; but if he had, lover of botany as he was, taken a plant for his crest, it should certainly have been dulcamara rather than meadowsweet. Cowper, when not subject to his peculiar " horrors," or fussing about some political matter that he did not understand, was often sweetly serene: one doubts whether serenity is exactly the word for Gray's quiescence or quietism, even putting " sweet " out of the question. It was rather a variety of that essentially eighteenth-century quality of *not* " making a fuss," which we have seen and shall see in so many forms, and which is not the least commendable of its merits, and one of those which most deserve the crown which we are endeavouring to weave for it here.

In passing from Gray to Cowper himself, we come to one who perhaps may be said to have been the most popular, and to be still the best known, of all the eighteenth-century letter-writers. This popular estimate has more to say for itself than is always the case, though if it said anything, that thing would probably be more of an actual than of a logical reason for the preference. Lady Mary and Lord Chesterfield are rather " far off " for the average reader, and they want warmth and colour for him. He feels, as was felt respecting two estimable but ill-fated ladies immortalised in a

Cowper. His small-beer not a poor creature.

famous schoolgirl epigram, that "they are not like *us*" that "their hearts cannot feel"; while, even if this sentimental objection be got over, they need a certain preparation and adjustment which he does not feel able or inclined to give. Something of the same prejudice of unfamiliarity and want of sympathy may extend to Horace Walpole and even to Gray, while at least some part of the latter's attraction is only, or mainly, for those who have some share of his own scholarly interests. But in Cowper all these obstacles are smoothed away. He also was a scholar, but of the most undonnish and unpedantic character.[1] He is pathetic to most, and sympathetic to nearly all, except very superior and Nietzschian persons. If his range of subject is somewhat small-beerish it is the freshest and most refreshing, the most delicately tasted, and the most enlivening if not stimulating small beer that ever came from honest malt and hops and pure water. You cannot dislike anything in Cowper, and it must, again, be a very peculiar and unenviable person who despises anything in him. There is—how there comes to be may be discussed presently—extraordinary variety, monotonous as a mere abstract of his life may seem. All attractions, or all except the—

> Grand, epic, homicidal, six-feet-high

dignities, and the half or wholly illicit allurements of the letter kind are there. He has neither history nor scandal, neither passion nor deliberate fun-making; but he has almost everything else.

But for those who can look deeper, or at any rate further than "the subject," there is far more reason why Cowper deserves perhaps the highest place among English letter-writers—certainly a place equal to the highest. It is simply that he had the art of letter-writing —the secret of epistolary presentment—as hardly

---

[1] One half laughs and half shudders to think what would have happened if the notion he at one time entertained, of taking pupils, had been carried out.

anybody else has had it. His epistles delight because there is in them an infinite virtue of delectation—a formula in respect of which Molière, of all people, was least likely to be blind to the valid as well as the ludicrous side of it. It is curious, or at any rate noteworthy, that the great tragedy of his life seems hardly to have affected this power in the very slightest degree, except by suspending its exercise. He had it to some extent from the very first, and he kept it and improved it to the very last, whenever he was sufficiently in possession of his faculties to write letters at all. This art is of course present in all or most of those who have been discussed earlier, but nowhere is it in such quintessence as in Cowper. All of them, even Gray, are laboured sometimes, or if laboured is too strong a word for him, slightly self-conscious. Cowper never is, while on the other hand he never even approaches that most offensive of attitudes—over-innocence, super-simplicity,—in its various forms of trifling, gush, and other objectionable things. To some extent this may have been a result of the very limited society in which he passed the later part of his life. Speaking under correction, one does not remember much positive evidence as to how he *talked* after the halcyon " giggling and making giggle " days were over. It may be an injustice or a mere whim, but one does not fancy Mrs. Unwin as much of a talker or much of an enjoyer of talk.[1] Lady Austen undoubtedly was both, and the fact was apparently part cause of trouble. Lady Hesketh probably was ; her sister, if she talked as she wrote in the few but famous words which we have of hers, must have been an adorable talker. But Cowper saw the first rarely till late, the second—" the lost woman of his youth "—never at all after he had lost her. The detestable habit of reading aloud in which he is known to have indulged, and which was so common in the

---

[1] Why is it difficult to be enthusiastic about Mrs. Unwin? One ought not to be influenced by Rose's unlucky admission that her face was not angelic.

eighteenth century as to be one of its worst blemishes, is of course murderous to talk. But the gift of familiar expression was probably in the family. And Cowper, debarred by choice or circumstance from free oral use of it, turned the stream on to paper, writing as nobody else, except Madame de Sévigné, has ever written. The femininity in him is of course undeniable, and he showed it sometimes rather unfortunately. But he made the very best use of it here. Something, as part cause of his supremacy, may be perhaps also allowed to his double character of poet and letter-writer, a conjunction which has proved fertile and fortunate in later times. Lady Mary, Chesterfield, Horace were not poetical, though the first two wrote brilliant and the third tolerable scraps of *vers de société*. Gray was a poet certainly, but he wrote so little poetry and that of so peculiar a kind, that, except in the " Cat " piece, the " Long Story," and one or two more, his subjects never clash with anything that could be properly epistolary. But, except during those sad periods of his life when prose and verse were alike impossible or unlikely, Cowper always had the two modes of expression at his command, and availed himself of both freely. Nay, he did so sometimes when the evil angel himself was hovering over him. The grim " Sapphics " might have found expression in a prose letter, and would then have been simply horrible or perhaps even rather disgusting ; while the verse-expression of them acquires and communicates the true " terror and pity." The pietism of the *Hymns* might (there are, fortunately, other examples) have been effectively and admirably expressed in prose ; unfortunately there are many other examples still which show that it might have been cloying and in bad taste there, while the magic of verse purifies it.

The constituents of its quality.

How glad one is to be free or almost free in the letters (it appears there but seldom) from the windy and ignorant rhetoric of the satires and didactic pieces !

Much of *The Task* is itself charming stuff, which might have been also charming in letter form, but it admits treatment which, quite welcome in verse, might in prose have approached that " fine writing " which is very rarely in place anywhere, and which the style of the century did not suit.

On the other hand Cowper, who was not in the least a professional poet, never, good as he was at occasional verse, dreamt of manufacturing it to order out of the ordinary details of his life ; and so had all or most of these, except when the occasion called for verse-celebration (as in the various cat-anecdotes, the tributes for fish, and others), for material of the letters themselves, which were sometimes half in verse.

With what astounding art [1] he made these materials up has already been observed. The public fastened early on the hares ; but the quality of the treatment there noticeable is practically ubiquitous. Cowper is like Harpagon's ideal cook, he does not need a hare to make a succulent and varied dinner of. Anything will do ; the most trivial incident of village life ; the mishaps or repairings of house and household goods ; a present—clothing, eatables, what not—there never was any one so little of a parasite and yet ready to accept any gift kindly offered as Cowper. It may almost be said that he can make a letter out of nothing at all but his own wits, without any of the antics of those who have written elaborately on Nothing with a capital N. As he never excites, so he never cloys. He

---

[1] His own slighting but felicitous notice of this art is one if not the most commonly quoted of his poems—the *Poetical Epistle to Lady Austen* (he follows it with a more ambitious description of poetical writing)—

> Dear Anna—between friend and friend
> Prose answers every common end ;
> Serves in a plain and homely way,
> To express the occurrence of the day ;
> One's health, the weather, and the news,
> What walks we take, what books we choose,
> And all the floating thoughts we find
> Upon the surface of the mind.

" trifles " (in the good sense [1] which is now almost
obsolete) with most if not all things ; he never trifles
with any in the bad. He can deal with serious matters
quite seriously, though not in the least dully, as in the
curious batch of critical letters to Thurlow and some
of those to Hill. He can be extremely interesting—
more so, to speak frankly, than he is in the works themselves—in writing about his translations. No one has
hit off such a scene as the visit of a canvassing parliamentary candidate better, while no one has more
poignantly expressed the difficulties [2] of a bachelor
(permanent or " grass " it does not matter) in catering
for himself.

In the "candidate" letter, a faculty, for which he has
perhaps not always had full credit given to him, displays itself more obviously than usual. Cowper's
irony is a curious study—one of many for which the
letters give subjects. It was of course a quality very
prevalent and not a little cultivated in the century of
Swift and Fielding ; in fact it was one of that century's
main gifts, strikingly distinguishable from the cheap
paradox, the pinchbeck epigram, and the " platitude
reversed " which have taken its place. In Cowper
himself it was probably restrained to some extent by
his pietism, and hindered in development by the
retired life he led. But it is the considerable dose of
it in his humour which makes that humour so delightful
—mixed as it is with good nature—and he can exercise
it on all sorts of things and persons, including, till the
great collapse, himself. Nothing is more curious—
though from another point of view few things can be
sadder—than the obviously clear and decidedly ironical
conception which he had of the fool-rascal Teedon's
folly, if not of his rascality, so long as he retained control enough of his own faculties to see it, and until the

---

[1] Cf. Borrow, who is fond of using it of the after-dinner enjoyment of wine.

[2] Yet these difficulties were, in his own case, lessened by the fact that, at the
time, he had not given up the usual eighteenth-century appendage of a " man " to
wait on him. But perhaps this official was on board-wages.

general paralysis of his mind set in. When he talks nonsense it is generally, of course not quite always, in verse ; and, whether in verse or prose, it generally comes from some actual ignorance of facts, or from some distortion of prejudice which his withdrawal from books and persons has prevented from being dispelled. Of the century's most precious possession, Common Sense, Cowper, once more, has an ample share ; if ever he seems to lack it we may be sure, once more also, that the special conditions which have prevented him from bringing it to bear are precedent.

Miss Burney's letter and diary work has been already dealt with in connection with her novels, and it

Some miscellaneous writers. Gilpin and White. would probably be superfluous to extend notice to others, though the abundance of matter of the kind from this time has been recently shown by the publication of fresh documents from her friend and "Daddy" Crisp and his circle. But there are two writers who, though the one is only a letter-writer in form and the other not even that, come so close to the kind of literature dealt with in this chapter that they had best figure here. One is the famous and constantly reprinted "White of Selborne," the other the much less known, and since his own days never reprinted, but most readable William Gilpin of the Picturesque Tours. To say much about White would almost be as impertinent as to say nothing would be unpardonable : but perhaps nowhere was that equable and intelligent but untiring " curiosity," which was one of the century's gifts, better displayed in reference to a special class of subjects ; and here at least posterity has made any argument for its rest and refreshment-giving powers perfectly otiose. It is, on the other hand, a great pity that so few people now read Gilpin. His bulky and rather clumsy volumes, with their paper that is rather too like blotting paper and their often foxed aquatints, are written on principles which are supposed to have been antiquated by Mr. Ruskin, and which have not been rehabilitated by those who have since scoffed at Ruskinism. Probably, too, they underlie the objection commonly felt to " old guide-books " in common with old almanacks and old newspapers. But this view is quite mistaken, and those who take it deprive themselves of much very agreeable reading. Gilpin could see and he could write—two faculties which are by no means invariably found together, and which are sometime found together without a third which he also possessed—that is to say he could think. The " tour " form has often been combined with that of the letter or diary, and is never, except in unimportant details, far from them.

Attempts have sometimes been made to attribute the peculiar excellence of letter-writing and of other writing akin to it (such as the examples just noted) in these eighteenth-century writers and in a few later examples, such as Lamb and FitzGerald, to various causes—freedom from the necessity of earning a living, and various other forms of relief from care, even bachelorhood. But there have been few better letter-writers than Scott and Southey, though the excellence of the latter has been obscured by the very clumsy fashion of editing from which he has suffered. Both of these were " family men," and both among the hardest workers (in Southey's case at least by necessity) of all time. Even Lamb, though he may have taken it easily, had thirty years of office drudgery. What seems to be more of a *vera causa* may be found in " eighteenth-centuriness " itself ; for Lamb, Scott, and Southey were all grown men before that century came to an end, and all show other signs of its influence ; while Byron, another good epistoler, though much younger, was a declared admirer of the age of his actual birth. As for FitzGerald, he was too absolutely individual to be brought under any generalisation. But it is a mere

Suitableness of the time for this kind of work.

commonplace that the goodness of letter-writing has
died off since ; and putting this down to postcards,
telegrams, or even to the penny post itself, is a very
hasty and insufficient explanation. A good deal, no
doubt, may be allowed for some other mechanical or
quasi-mechanical conditions—multiplication of newspapers and rapidity of communication of their news *is*
a true cause. People who have the letter-writing
spirit in them—for it is not extinct—do sometimes
discuss news, but are often dissuaded even from this
by the feeling that it may be stale or contradicted before
their letters reach their readers. Now a very large
proportion of Walpole's and Gray's letters is occupied
by matter of this kind. The element of travel has also
been cut at in a similar way, and so have others.

But though, as has been admitted, the letter-
writing spirit is not dead, it has, as the old Puritan
lingo went, " no freedom," or little freedom as a rule
to express itself. Business, though, as we saw, it did
not keep Scott and Southey from being copious
epistolers, interferes much, the strenuous idleness of
multiplied amusement more. But most of all is there
wanting, in a new sense, what we may call the *dimidium
animae*, the indispensable half of the spirit itself, which
was supplied by the " eighteenth-centuriness " referred
to above. This is not the will to write or even the
knowledge how to do so ; but the atmosphere, the
temperament, the *milieu* proper to the occupation.
Good sense (there may be plenty of fooling in a good
letter, but the slightest silliness is fatal) ; good temper
(bad temper never looks so bad as on paper, though
it may be in other ways least offensive there) ; leisure—
a very good letter, except of the passionate kind, which
stands by itself, and though it can be produced from
the eighteenth century, is not of the staple there, can
seldom be written in a hurry, never in a flurry ; a
genuine interest in many different things — all are
wanted. This last the century called " curiosity," and

possessed in striking contrast to the particular mono-
mania and the general indifference and ignorances of
other times.   So with many other phases and concomi-
tants of that wisdom which is its crowning attribute.
A fool sometimes does a good deed, but it is almost
impossible to imagine him (perhaps it is just possible
to imagine a very amiable *her*) writing a good letter.
It is quite astonishing, especially at a time when—

> Whene'er we take our walks abroad,
> How many fools we see,

to think how few there were in the eighteenth century.
Its wisdom was of course rather strictly limited ; perhaps this limitation was a property and cause of it ;
but, such as it was, it was justified of nearly all its
children in a way lamentably absent in more high-
flying ages.

CHAPTER VI

SOME GRAVER THINGS

OF course if anybody thinks that there can be no rest
or refreshment in grave things—as appears to be the
Gibbon and opinion of a very prevailing party, which
Burke. as soon as it gets out of the picture-book
takes to the picture-house—this chapter is not for
him. The writer of it saw, the very day before
writing these words, " Gibbon " used as a token or
counter to express " something quite unreadable " by
any one in search of pastime. Now, as a matter of
fact, large parts of Gibbon are a great deal more
interesting, in the simplest and most guileless sense of
that word, than most modern novels. One may be
perfectly orthodox and yet enjoy the wicked wit—
Voltairian of course in quality and probably in suggestion, but with little of the vulgarity which spoils
Voltaire—of the Chapter of the Heresies. It is
impossible not to admire the spirit with which the
story of Islam in its early days is told; and again and
again it is possible to see that Gibbon anticipated some
of the best points in the historical novel—if one may
not almost say that some of the best points in Scott's
handling of fiction owe a little, and not so very little,
to Gibbon's handling of fact. One cannot perhaps
say quite so much of Burke. It is difficult to imagine
any one, however much he may admire Burke, reading
him for amusement's sake; though a sort of transferred
interest may arise from intellectual appreciation of his

arguments, sympathy with his objects, and the temper
in which he pursues them, and the like. But these
latter are not the matters with which we are really
busying ourselves. Nor has Burke much to do with
" peace." Admiration he excites to any extent ; but
he hardly provides rest or (except in a very peculiar
sense) refreshment.

The most barren, for our purposes, of all departments of literature in the century is no doubt the
Theology, pulpit, or, to speak more exactly, the spoken
philosophy, and written theology of the time. Queen
etc. Caroline is said to have taken Butler's
Analogy for light boudoir and dressing-room reading,
but divers interpretations may be put on that story.
Neither the tone nor the style of sacred writing during
the period can give anybody nowadays the sort of positive satisfaction, quite apart from edification, which is
given by Donne and Taylor in the seventeenth century,
or by Newman in the nineteenth. But the *ancilla
theologiae*, philosophy, is somewhat more attractive,
as has been observed by the wicked in unmetaphorical
relationship—the maid is better worth attending to
than the mistress. With perhaps only two exceptions,
eighteenth - century philosophy has a bad name for
shallowness ; but it is curious that these two exceptions
are, in part of their work at any rate, eminently readable
and enjoyable by any fairly intelligent person. The
more esoteric work of Berkeley may perhaps hardly
answer to the description, but *Alciphron* may be read
again and again with positive pleasure, and as for *Siris*,
I wish I knew of a pocket edition of it ! Hume
perhaps relies rather more upon his substance—a
substance, too, not quite so easy to get at as it may
seem to be—but his *Essays* can in almost every case
be read, and read with pleasure, without bothering
oneself much about anything but their readableness.
This is hardly the case with Reid and others ; even
Adam Smith, though readable enough, is hardly likely

to be read for mere pleasure, and the æsthetics (Gerard and his followers), after you have once laughed at them, are very poor creatures.[1]   But some of the more out-of-the-way and eccentric books of philosophy possess quality of the kind we are seeking for in a most eminent degree, and the chief of these perhaps is Abraham Tucker's *Light of Nature Pursued*.

Somebody stole—or at any rate I lost—my Tucker years ago, and I was so fond of the book that I have never liked to put another copy in its place ; *A less well-known instance— Tucker.* but I remember it perfectly well, and if I ever enjoyed retired leisure, with a few books only, I should certainly acquire it.   Hazlitt is said to have abridged it, which is one of his few positive literary crimes—almost a worse one in fact (for it is tampering with, if not poisoning, the sources) than his denigration of Sidney and the Caroline poets, and his blasphemy against Scott and others of his own time. Abraham Tucker (or " Ned Search," as he chose to call himself) is essentially unabridgeable.   His life covered the greater part of the century in which it was included, and after he left Merton College, Oxford, he seems to have spent his wealth, obtained in commerce by his father, on the purchase of a country estate near Dorking, and to have lived there reading, fancying, and writing without disturbing himself about anything else.   This is the true eighteenth-century *diathesis*. That he was praised by Paley, as one is tediously told in every regulation notice of him, matters little or nothing at all to the present purpose.   Paley himself has been much too much abused for many years—a result partly of the fact that he was inflicted upon generation after generation of Cambridge men desperately against their grain (one read him at Oxford or not as one liked, and therefore judged him justly when one did judge him), partly because of his faults—which

---

[1] Although it may seem blasphemy, I am afraid this applies even to the great Mr. Burke, as far as *The Sublime and Beautiful* is concerned.

did exist in a certain ledger-and-weighing-machine treatment of matters escaping those implements—and partly because of his merits, which translated themselves into a hard but logical orthodoxy, disgusting to the sloppy agnosticism of the last half-century.

But Tucker was a man of a very different kidney from his eulogist. The contemporary for the greater part of his life, though his senior, to whom he bears most resemblance, is " John Buncle " Amory ; his newest successor in the resemblance at a long interval, is probably the late Samuel Butler the second, author of *Erewhon*. But Tucker was free from the excessive eccentricity of both these writers and also from the touch of bad blood in one of them—no matter which. He is perhaps our most remarkable type or expression of the *intellectus sibi permissus*—the mind allowed to roam and play pranks as it pleases—though conditioned in its gambols by certain characteristics of the time. In some ways he reminds one of the most *un*commonplace writers of the seventeenth century, from Burton and Browne to Urquhart and Alexander Ross ; but " prose and sense " do not entirely let go of him as in some of the other cases, and his *O Altitudo !* is never concerned with anything very lofty or very deep.

The liveliest part of his book, according to common estimates of the time, is a long account of certain " vehicles " or soul-bags, as one may call them, which, in another world or department of the world, represent distinguished and undistinguished persons among the dead, and possess the faculty of administering pleasant or unpleasant shocks by contact. This is his furthest excursion in the direction of concrete fancy. But almost everywhere in his huge book he does pursue the light of nature—deviously indeed, but with a curious originality and fertility of observation. Not that he disdains guides. He follows, as long as it suits him, now Locke, now Hartley, now Hume ; he has no " enthusiasm " ; he is thoroughly of his century on one side of it, in a mild scepticism which dominates him throughout. But if he doubts conclusions, and seems to think that thinking is a circular process which merely brings you back to the point where you started, he is quite pleased to accomplish the circumambulation for all that, and at least the right sort of companion will be equally pleased to accompany him. You may find histories of eighteenth-century literature in which he is not named, and histories of philosophy in which he is rather poohpoohed. Sir Leslie Stephen called him "half-trained," and, though he could not fail to see Tucker's humour, was apparently unconscious that what he meant by training would probably have stifled this humour itself. They call him a Utilitarian! If so he was the only Utilitarian humorist, and one of the very few of the school who can write delectably. But the fact is that he ought to be taken out of the hands of specialists altogether. Tucker has something of the universal, and wherever the universal is there is rest and refreshment.

In his senior, Shaftesbury, some at least find very much less of this delight. He was of course at one time very popular,[1] and there is a most
Backward glances. Shaftesbury, etc. attractive little edition of him in 32mo, or some size of that kind, very clearly printed, which would make one like him if anything could. But Shaftesbury, clever as he is, is thin and acid reading. To anybody who knows all the texts, his thought will never recover the calm but pitiless examination of part of it given by Berkeley in *Alciphron*, nor his style the unceremonious tousling that it received from George Campbell in *The Philosophy of Rhetoric*. To couple him with Temple as an example of "the genteel style" was monstrously unfair to Temple; to make him a model of it in the less favourable sense of the adjective is not unfair at all. He

[1] G. H. Lewes's book has been ungraciously called "A *Popular* History of Philosophy," but why does not some one write a *History of Popular Philosophers*? Perhaps it is too early—for they yet live.

may be interesting in the history of moral philosophy; in that of delightful literature one has very little use for him.

For another of the unorthodox philosophers or philosophasters, Mandeville, one may have a little more. The *Fable of the Bees*, with some at least of its telescope-like prolongations, is not " dull " reading ; and though in his other works Mandeville never quite " comes off," he is very near to success occasionally, and undoubtedly possesses a sort of savage but vigorous satire, which contrasts not unfavourably with the sickly simper of Shaftesbury. But like most writers mentioned in this chapter, he stands in our " last provincial " company. One would never undertake to give the eighteenth century the place which is here challenged for it on the strength merely or mainly of its various contributions to didactic literature. It is really worth while to contend—and in the case of Gibbon and Tucker one may contend very strongly— that it is not an abode of dulness and shallowness even here. Its inadequacy in certain directions may make itself felt, but within its range it can still do not a little.

What some one has well called " the ferocious appetite for information," which alternates in modern times with mere frivolity, objects to the historical and other " informative " writing of our century on the score of its out-of-dateness, inaccuracy, and so forth. From the literary-hedonist point of view which we are taking, this matters once more very little. Gibbon has been already mentioned as a shining example of the highest scholarship combined with very high artistic merits— of science and literature, instruction and delight wedded. Until quite late in the century we shall find indeed few to keep him company—even in the attempt to unite these things—and nobody at all who succeeds as eminently as he does. But as almost everybody— except those who write new novels, and not all of them— admits that you may read old tales, why should you not

The " obsolete hack work"— Dr. John Campbell.

read old histories, accurate or not, if they have the power of amusing ? Now I do not hesitate to say that these antiquated volumes, which you may buy, in solid and sometimes handsome bindings, for sixpence or a shilling apiece at the stall, are very often, if not always, much better reading than their esteemed successors. I know, of course, that Hume is sadly partial, and to modern ideas impudently inexhaustive, in his dealing with documents ; but he is much better to read than Lingard, and oh ! *how* much better than the highly extolled Samuel Rawson Gardiner ! History was not Smollett's province, and I have never found much delectation in Robertson. But that treasury of hack-writing, the *Universal History*, in which wrote Dr. John Campbell (who once drank thirteen bottles of port at a sitting,[1] and never passed a church without taking off his hat, though he did not often go in, and made the first really comfortable income by sheer honest journey work in letters, and deserved it) and George Psalmanazar (most pious, most industrious, and most learned of impostors), and other good brethren of the pen — the *Universal History*, I say, is full of good matter well put, and one might be very happy with it (the standard test) in the country inn on wet after-noons, even though one might be able to make cor-recting notes as to fact on every page one read.

I cannot, I suppose, expect many people to share my own opinion that there is a great deal of positive diversion in the abundant critical literature of the century ; but, however I may be left crying in the desert, I shall continue to say that there is much good reading in what some call a desert of Sahara. Spence's *Anecdotes*, I

Critical mis-cellanea— Spence, Edwards, etc.

---

[1] It was a very long sitting, as he admitted to the puzzled and perhaps envious Boswell. Perhaps the "militia officer" who was his compotator, and, as he said, tied with him in number, really drank six and a half of them : or perhaps there were more militia officers and fewer bottles, who and which got confused with one another in the later stages. Hallucinations of various kinds are possible long before the thirteenth bottle. But Dr. John Campbell was certainly a "good fellow" in almost every sense. And there are many complaints that bottles were then small, while thirsts were really great.

suppose, would be admitted as an oasis even by the severest, while on the other hand I do not commend my respectable predecessor Blair, except to experts at once in criticism, skipping, and the exercise of humour. It is not necessary to be an expert—it is sufficient to be a moderately intelligent and curious amateur—to find plenty of amusement in Kames's *Elements*, of what seems to some so dismal a science, and a little in Edwards's *Canons* thereof, while Edwards's principal " subject " (in the dissecting-room sense), Warburton, whether he is himself criticising or theologising, is a very curious and interesting study, far too much neglected of late years. " The inestimable *Estimate* of Brown " requires, of course, a certain knowledge of and interest in history and other things to make it go down. But it is, after all, the first or almost first elaborate expression in English literature of that quaint delusion about everything " going to the dogs," which alternates with the other about everything being nearly the best in almost the best of all possible worlds—at any rate a world which can look back, now on mediæval, now on Victorian times, with a mixture of pity and contempt. The mistily famous " paper Lord " Monboddo had perhaps better be left alone by most people, though the courageous may plunge into the mist and emerge with some booty; and for my part I would much rather be left *tête-à-tête* with Vicesimus Knox, or Johnson's rather ill-treated " Sherry," not to mention others, than with some very popular writers of to-day. For, if I did meet with platitude in them, it would not be the platitude that apes originality ; I should find no mere silliness and no positively bad taste, though I might find much limitation of good. I should be in an atmosphere where Daylight Saving Bills were unthinkable and Spelling Reform confined either to the significantly called " retreats," private or public, or to the studies of a very few eccentrics.[1] There would be

[1] Let it be frankly owned that Tucker himself was something of a spelling reformer. But then he *was* an eccentric, and so privileged.

little cant—that only came in late in the century—and no " rotting," which only came in late in the next. When there was nonsense it would be good nonsense— sound, fresh, and refreshing—and when there was sense it would be at least sound.

In one curious division of literature, whose *seria* are deliberately mixed with *nugae* for a special purpose, the century has long been, not unjustly, credited with a certain pre-eminence ; and this justice, not always even so fully done, has recently been embodied, to the surprise and pleasure of some at any rate, by a chapter in the Cambridge *History of English Literature* [1] on " Children's Books," from the hand of one not only to the matter born but, one may say, " ancestried." Mr. Darton's account takes in, of course, a good many things that cannot be noticed here, and it was not his business to insist on the curious attraction which these old children's books possess for " old children " in another sense. But a sentence in the tail of his paper has a sting which may or may not have been intended ; but which may be utilised here. He says, speaking of the change of things in the second quarter or thereabouts of the nineteenth century, " Education was henceforward divorced from pleasure."

It had been the object of the writers of children's books, even for mere amusement, from the commencements in the earlier century, and of those who later wrote books of instruction with honey, not poison, smeared on the leaves, to effect the marriage which suffered this divorce at the hands of their successors. The decree *nisi* took a long time in being made absolute, and the old nursery and schoolroom classics held their place in most cases till the 'fifties, in some even till the 'sixties of the nineteenth. And not only these, which

Children's books.

---

[1] Vol. xi. ch. xvi. For the benefit of those unversed in the history of " The Trade " it may not be impertinent to explain that Wells Gardner, Darton and Co. are the lineal successors of the great Newbery—first in almost every sense of children's booksellers.

actually amused, and instructed, and certainly did not harm, the childhood of persons still living, but others older still, retain for some a curious attraction. The most famous of all the indirectly educational works, *Sandford and Merton*, is defended by Mr. Darton rather half-heartedly. Some of us would make a much stronger fight. Even in the case of Mr. Barlow, who has been the cause of so much wit, might not some of those who have exercised it on him be all the better for some of his own methods, and for those from which he indeed abstained, but which his fellows affected so freely?[1] The fight with Master Mash has conciliated the most unregenerate, and is of course the gem of the book, but those who do not require to be always taken by force may receive almost equal pleasure from such things as the much-abused Harry's polite refusal of Mrs. Merton's offers because " he was not dry." To drink, but not unless you are dry, and to punch heads, but not unless they richly deserve it—how good and, allegorically, how far-reaching a rule of life is this ! The book is really delectable throughout ; you can laugh at it and with it in a most agreeable *carillon* of alternative- and change-ringing. But it is only the best of its kind, and some of the merits of that kind are carried into other books, the main and not the secondary object of which is instruction, such as Joyce's *Scientific Dialogues*, a book not indeed published till after the end of the century, but written by a man who was between forty and fifty at the time of publication.

The reasons of the practical goodness of these nursery and schoolroom books, and of their controlling **Their** theories, are closely connected with the **importance.** characteristics which are being pointed out in eighteenth-century literature generally. There is in

[1] The modern divorce of education from the stick as well as the sugar-plum has to be taken into account. It concerns us less here : but if ever bigamy was justifiable and double divorce disastrous it was and is in this case—especially as new wives or concubines of much worse character have been introduced.

them a curious mixture of good sense and good feeling
—the latter even including an unpretentious but very
genuine " charity " in almost the apostolic sense of
the word—which wishes at once to do good and to
give pleasure to other people, and takes personal
pleasure in doing both. The strong *domestic* character
of the time likewise comes in ; but perhaps the most
important qualification is the absence of pedantry,
actually combined as it is with the presence of peda-
gogic interest. The eighteenth century might sometimes be called priggish, though it would be well for the
person who calls it so to make quite certain that he is
not another kind of prig himself, and so merely feels
that jealousy which constantly prevails between species
of the same genus. But pedantic, with of course some
exceptions, it seldom is. The seventeenth had been
so, though in a gorgeous and stately fashion, united
with quaintness, which sometimes wholly and almost
always to some extent transcends pedantry. The
nineteenth very soon began to breed pedants freely,
and the most abominable of human weaknesses has
become more and more a standing disease, especially
in this very matter of education. There was a fanci-
fulness about the Rousseau-and-Marmontel-and-Edge-
worth-and-Day-and-Mrs. Trimmer systems which excused much not quite so good in them, and provided
a perennial something to survive when the other parts
were obsolete. Moreover, the eighteenth century had
not, though it saw a great birth of " science," allowed
that science, in the narrower sense, to neglect, to oust,
still less to control literature, and art, and morality, and
religion, and politics. There was as yet little if any
specialisation. " Periods " and " lines " and other
swaddlings in the cultivation of the mind were remote.
The eighteenth century might have laughed or stared
and even frowned at such a question as " Describe the
geographical importance of snow," but it took care that
anybody who studied geography should, as far as its

maps went, be able to carry a pretty good one of most parts of the world in his head.[1]

The result of all this was the peculiar—and, as it has been represented and is to some people, attractive— humanity of this educational literature, contrasting increasingly with the arid scholasticism (in the very worst sense of that sometimes abused word) of much of what has followed, and the futile aspirations of much else.

---

[1] Cowper says in a letter (Sept. 7, 1780), "Lord Spencer's son, when he was four years of age, knew the situation of every kingdom, country, city, river and remarkable mountain in the world," from having had "printed maps as toys." The age makes the person somewhat of a "prodigy son" but the achievement is unexceptionable. In modern times the possessor of this knowledge at his tender years would probably be ploughed in a geography examination—the candidate who passed highest there would probably not know whether there is more than one Wellington or Marlborough in England, and if so where they are.

CHAPTER VII

THE GARDEN OF MINOR VERSE AND THE LATER
DRAMA—ANSTEY AND SHERIDAN

THE last chapter was something of an *excursus* ; but it
at least endeavoured at the grace of being " a very
little one." The present also need not be long, but it
returns to the divisions of the subject more obviously
germane to our title. Something has already been said
—in the chapter which dealt with Pope and " Grub
Street " and some other matters affecting poetry—of the
minor poets of the classical dispensation ; and the most
really refreshing writers of its verse are necessarily
reserved for the next. So also in regard to drama—
the subject has received some attention, but it requires
a little more. And two remarkable writers, one in
each division, may be taken for more detailed notice.

There can be no harm in repeating that whoso
knows not " Dodsley " and his continuator Pearch
misses a literary region of some extent and considerable
amenity, while he who knows this, and does not, if he
has the opportunity, extend his explorations into
authors and work not there collected, is not completely
wise. The caution is no doubt too likely to be addressed to deaf ears—ears suffering from the very
worst kind of deafness, that of the will ; you may still
commonly see the whole subject brushed away with
some such remark as " that the minor poetry of the
eighteenth century (well if ' minor ' is not missed) is a
matter which has now lost all interest outside of lecture-

rooms," or something of that sort. One can only retort
that the ignorance which is the only possible excuse
for such a judgment is very much the reverse of a
justification of it.

Few serious pieces of note and interest escaped or
will escape treatment either in the chapter just referred

Light poets
of the looser
sort—
Williams,
Stevenson,
Wilkes.
to or in that which will follow this ; but
something may still be said on the lighter
verse. In this the century had been so
brilliantly initiated by Swift and Prior that
it had no excuse for not keeping up to the
mark ; nor, to do it justice, did it discredit these famous
artists and teachers. It has been noted how men like
Chesterfield, Pulteney, and even Horace Walpole, how
women like Lady Mary and Mrs. Greville, on no
single one of whom could the reproach of professional-
ism be for a moment planted, could, with apparently
no difficulty, knock off epigrams and slight "copies of
verse" of almost, sometimes of quite, the first class.
The kind, of course, though not necessarily, still owing
to the laxity of language and manners of the time, and
also to the actual example of the two great leaders
themselves, lent itself to license ; and this was in some
cases carried to a pitch, rebuke of which need be neither
ultra-squeamish nor partly hypocritical. Chesterfield's and Walpole's common friend Sir Charles
Hanbury Williams has had attributed to him (whether
with justice or not in the worst cases is a question
which has never been critically settled, or even, I think,
critically examined) some excessively coarse and at
least equally dull ribaldry ; Sterne's ally, John Hall
Stevenson, was certainly guilty of more ; and the case
of Wilkes is notorious. But if anybody cared to use
the pitchfork and turn over the pitch, a good deal of
amusing stuff could be found in Williams, and some,
though less, in Stevenson.[1]

[1] Keeping the stuff well aloof with this useful implement, one may at least
remark as to the third case, that there is about it (and perhaps better so) some mystery.
It seems at least doubtful whether the actual *corpus delicti* exists, or at any rate, if

But the fact is that the later eighteenth century, in England at any rate, was incapacitated alike by its defects and its qualities from doing this sort **Anstey.** of thing with the kind of naughty grace which alone makes it tolerable, and which Prior could still impart. As far as broad coarse fun went it did not hesitate, pretty often indeed, to indulge itself. But the great bulk of its light verse is harmless enough, and, rather after the middle of the century, Christopher Anstey, availing himself of, but not exceeding, the more moderate license just described, put his time upon a new way of comic poetry, which has been, with varying success of course, constantly trodden since. The *New Bath Guide* owed, of course, something, even in its management of the loose, continuous anapæst, to both Swift and Prior. But while these great elders had chiefly taken older fabliau-stories, or, as in Swift's *Hamilton's Bawn* and Prior's *Down Hall*, single incidents or episodes without much elaboration of scene and character as subjects, Anstey made a sort of novel in verse, or even a versified and narrated drama, out of his subject. This was the then familiar and fashionable scenes, customs, company, and so forth of the beloved city of the West, where Comus and Hygeia sat as reconciled King and Queen, and where everybody, like Mr. Pickwick [1] later, " felt a great deal better " and

---

it does, whether it has ever been reprinted. The contraband matter surreptitiously current does not in the least answer to Macaulay's description of what he had apparently seen, and is itself such utter balderdash of merely dirty language, without wit, or point, or attraction of any kind, that one cannot imagine a man of Wilkes's wit and manners being guilty of it. As for the two others, Williams has less brains and less reading than Stevenson, but more humour and much more good humour.

[1] " Whereat," the text continues, " his friends were very much delighted, though they had not previously been aware that there was anything the matter with him." Dickens did know Bath, before he used to go and see Landor there ; but if he always, as by Forster's account he and Dickens sometimes did, made flying visits (day coach or railway down, dinner at Bath, and then night train or coach up), it is not wonderful that he confused it with Bristol as to " Park St.," and that he put the immortal scene of Mr. Winkle's unwilling provocation of Dowler in the " Crescent," where it could hardly occur, though it might in the " Circus." If he had known Bath better he would not have made the joke just quoted. You can't help " feeling a great deal better " in Bath, whether there is " anything the matter with you " or

merrier the longer he stayed, unless he succumbed to certain temptations. Anstey wrote many other things (none of them of much value) and lived in Bath itself nearly forty years. He saw—later—the follies of the "Bath-Easton vase," when the side of the century which we are now contemplating was getting withered and in its dotage, when it had not learned to be Romantic, and had entirely forgotten how to be in any good sense Classical. But this his book neither attempts to be the one nor fails to be the other. It is pure *burla* of almost the best kind, and for the person who cannot be amused by it one can only be sorry.

Its influence was undoubtedly very great, both in spirit and in form, the latter it should be observed **Importance** being by no means confined to the anapæst. **of the** *New* To some extent, as was almost inevitable, **Bath Guide.** its family was deplorable ; for it started a fashion of couching private letters in rickety doggerel which lasted for a long time, and, though it sometimes produced amusing scraps, was more likely to be productive of boredom. It had not a little to do with the still remembered *Dr. Syntax* (partly parodied on Gilpin) and with the numerous other forgotten works of that singular person William Combe—a typical eighteenth-century character, though he lived till nearly the end of the first quarter of the nineteenth—whose neglected wilderness will repay exploration by the intelligent.[1] Nor was it in all probability without influence on that

---

not. In fact you sometimes feel better when you are not better at all. The true Waters of Oblivion (see an early *Keepsake* in crimson silk which these eyes have not seen for some fifty years) are those of Bladud. And if this seems impertinently dithyrambic let it be remembered that Bath and the eighteenth century are in a way one, and that both are haunts of peace.

[1] One may be allowed to smile when, in looking up Combe in a well-known and most useful book of reference, one finds his best-known work described as "letterpress" to Rowlandson. In a sense no doubt it is, as also in a sense *Pickwick* also was, at least at first, "letterpress" to Seymour. But otherwise there is food for quiet laughter in the phrase. Literary critics on art are often no doubt inadequate, but art-critics on literature are not seldom absurd. Perhaps Rowlandson was, in his own line, somewhat more of a genius than Combe in his. But where shall we find a critical calculus which can exactly evaluate the rather Dutch-doll Blowzalinds of the artist against the somewhat slipshod octosyllables of the poet ?

extraordinary outburst of political verse which will figure in a future chapter.

It was said earlier that the later eighteenth-century drama offers no very delightful pastime, but a little more detail must here be given to it, if only for the sake of another single "amuser" greater far than Anstey. Goldsmith's work has been noticed, and as literature it certainly stands above all other contemporary compositions of the kind except Sheridan's. But pleas have been, sometimes justly, put in for others. Eighteenth-century tragedy is indeed hopeless from whatever point of view we look at it, though persons who are able to isolate purely theatrical situation from literary expression have been known to "speak up" for Lillo's *Fatal Curiosity*. The same writer's infinitely more notorious *George Barnwell*[1] is one of the not very numerous things (yet still rather surprising in their number) which exceed in absurdity all possible parodies of them. The stroke of justice and genius combined which enabled Thackeray also to combine the foibles of eighteenth and nineteenth century sentimentality—to transfix Lillo and Bulwer on a single spear—may induce some people to turn to the original. It will be strange if they get through it, though some still stranger criticism has assigned to Lillo "force," "nature," and even "style." Some pathos he has, but any other merit can only be attributed by the desperate effort "to be different," which has made some attempt to rehabilitate Kirke White. Moore's *Gamester*, sometimes praised as a naturalisation of French *tragédie bourgeoise*, is less absurd, but scarcely more interesting.

The later Drama.

---

[1] The first half of the title (*The London Merchant, or G. B.*) is practically never used and would probably escape identification if used alone. It may be mentioned that what makes the play so certain to provoke irresistible and inextinguishable laughter is not merely—not perhaps so much—its combination of priggishness and sentimentality as that other *macédoine* of limp or stilted prose with limper or more stilted blank verse, all mish-mashed into one, which the (perhaps unconscious) imitation of Dickens and the elaborate satire of Thackeray have made perennially ludicrous.

It is, however, of course true that the comedy is better, and (almost of necessity) more amusing. Writers of such talent as Colman and Garrick, especially in combination, could hardly be dull ; and *The Clandestine Marriage*, which, after long exclusion from the stage, was successfully revived with some alteration a few years ago, is anything but a bad play, and by no means a bad piece of literature. Yet, as a rule, the *British Theatre*, and other collections of the drama of the time, are hard reading, whether in tragedy, in comedy, or in farce, despite the famous names, in the last-named kind, of Foote and O'Keefe.

Great as Sheridan's reputation has always been, it may be doubted whether it has been as great as he

Sheridan. deserves, when he is considered solely as the author of *The School for Scandal*, *The Rivals*, and *The Critic*. To any one who cannot concentrate his attention upon these he undoubtedly "carries *over*weight." His political record is none too creditable ; and though deliberate dishonesty is nowhere proved against him, his behaviour in money matters was reckless, and in other branches of ordinary conduct questionable. *Pizarro* [1] is rubbish : and *The Duenna* and *St. Patrick's Day* are not at all worthy of him. But the three masterpieces—all written before he was thirty—are, each in its own way and calibre, masterpieces pure and simple—of higher and lower comedy and of pure or partly pure farce. The *School for Scandal* has roundly and often been pronounced the best comedy in our tongue. These unqualified superlatives are generally rash ; and there could hardly be a rasher one than this, because comedy subdivides itself into so many different kinds. It would be as ridiculous to say that *The School for Scandal* is better than *Twelfth Night*, or *The Alchemist*, or *Love for Love*,

---

[1] It can be urged, of course, that he only "put his name" to this, and was not really its author. But the process of "putting your name" to things is doubtful in itself, and that of putting your name to rubbish is hardly pardonable.

as to say that a perfectly succeeded bottle of Lafite is better than one of Clos Vougeot, or of one of the best vintages of port. The things are different; even in the case of Congreve's play,[1] which comes nearest. In construction, Sheridan has the advantage; in sheer wit Congreve. But if, instead of this unsatisfactory fashion of comparison, we take the things by themselves, or in comparison only with the ideals of their kinds, a sensible person will want *at the time* nothing better than these adventures of the Teazles and the Surfaces. Of course the reproach of artificiality, which belongs to the whole school, is not to be utterly repelled. Theatrical presentation is a thing so essentially artificial in itself that, except in stages like those of the early Greek and the Elizabethan, when precedents have had no opportunity to accumulate and establish themselves, convention will force itself in. Playwrights imitate playwrights, actors are trained by, or (which is almost worse) deliberately avoid imitating, other actors; nay, the very audience, in some mysterious way, exhibits the effects of heredity in what it will accept and what it will not. Again, Gray, as we noted above, said and said rightly, that the language of the actual time and country is never that of poetry. He might have added that the behaviour of the actual time and country is never the behaviour of the stage, though posterity constantly makes the mistake of thinking it so. If you turn from *The School for Scandal* to the contemporary diaries of Fanny Burney (who was so properly shocked

His quality as illustrated in the works. at Sheridan's part in the Hastings trial), you will find how people, from princesses to professional men's daughters, really talked, and that it was not in the least like the conversation of the characters of the play: just as if

---

[1] Some of the knowing ones, including my friend Professor Brander Matthews, prefer Farquhar as an "aged" horse to try Sheridan with. This match is certainly more level in point of good temper and decency. But in *diable au corps*—that quality which Voltaire declared to be necessary in everything—Congreve and Sheridan are nearer to each other.

you turn to Anthony Trollope's novels you will find
how people really talked in the 'sixties, and may contrast it advantageously with the lingo of Mr. " Tom "
Robertson's dramas. But Sheridan is almost as little
asphyxiated by " the odour of sawdust " as can be
expected, and the result has justly been a continued
life for the play during nearly a century and a half,
with little prospect of its ever becoming entirely
obsolete. This is due partly to the fact that it really is
a masterpiece of its own kind of art or " imitation,"
and that such masterpieces, of whatever kind or time,
assimilate to some extent the vitality of nature itself; partly to the other fact that Sheridan has introduced no very small dose of actual and perennial
nature, fixed by humour and wit ; but yet partly also,
one may surely think, to the general moderating and
preservative effect of some characteristics of the eighteenth century itself.

The School is perhaps better to see than to read ;
The Rivals, though it can be seen with joy even by
At large and persons who do not regard the theatre with
individually. extraordinary affection, is even better to
read, not merely because you can then skip Falk-
land and Julia if you choose.[1] That it is quite free
from artificiality nobody in his senses would, again,
maintain. But Sheridan has had the wit to give this
artificiality itself that touch of burlesquing sincerer
examples of it which saves everything. The piece is
a kind of *féerie* ; it might not improperly conclude
with a transformation of the good old kind, and an
immortal harlequinade, in which Sir Lucius and Lydia,
Sir Anthony and Bob Acres would find their places
ready cut out for them, while Mrs. Malaprop would

---

[1] Of course they have, since their earliest days, when their appeal to " sensibility "
actually conciliated audiences, been, as a rule, mercilessly " cut " in representation.
But I am told that some modern criticism objects to this, holding that Sheridan
attached importance to the contrast they made. There may be something in this
as far as the stage goes, though our modern dramatic critics seem to have got
" contrasts " and " conflicts " and so on rather on the brain.

add a new star to the cheerful old constellation of the
commedia dell' arte. It must be from lack of the
imagination, which can see the presence at once of fairy-
tale and farce, that anybody finds fault with its plot, and
fails to discover in it the " brilliancy " allowed *The
School for Scandal*. The fact is that there is nothing
else quite like *The Rivals*; and the complaints of
plagiarism, etc., are even more imbecile than usual.
You must indeed be clever if you can parody without,
in a manner, plagiarising. *The School for Scandal* and
the third piece to which we are coming belong to
classes; and in the wise way, though not in the unwise
above referred to, they may be compared. *The Rivals*,
as has been said, is like nothing else—at least nothing
that came before it. Malapropism may go back through
the recent work of Smollett (associated likewise with
Bath), through Swift to Shakespeare; the testy father
is as old, even in criticism, as the *Epistle to the Pisos*, and
Heaven knows how much older in drama; the comic
Irishman, though he only now comes to his own, is,
though in another sense, of almost as ancient a house
as he could himself claim, and Bob Acres's ancestors
were born with the comic drama. But in all the
immense bulk and range of our theatre you will find
no whole piece of quite the same kind; nor will you,
if you extend the search to the houses of Molière or
of Calderon. And as Sheridan had here no predecessor
in fee, so he has had no exact successor, despite the
immense popularity of the thing and the, beyond all
doubt numerous, attempts at imitation. His sole heir
(as it seems to the present writer, though he puts
forward the suggestion humbly and diffidently), and
that in a transformed fashion, was the late Sir William
Gilbert.

The Critic, it has been confessed, is less of an *a-per-se*.
Considering the originality shown in *The Rivals*, it
would be rash to say that it could never have existed if
The Rehearsal and *Tom Thumb* and *Pasquin* had not

preceded it. But that as a matter of fact they not
only preceded it, but, especially in the case of *The
Rehearsal*, showed it the way, there can be no doubt.
Still, Sheridan bettered his patterns very considerably.
The Rehearsal is amusing in parts, but it is very unequal; the principal character, Bayes (admittedly a
jumble of two caricatures intended to lampoon Dave-
nant and Dryden), fails in personal verisimilitude, and
Dryden's own retort that Smith and Johnson are
" cool and insignificant " is perfectly true. Sheridan
had the wit not to make *The Critic* merely a personal
lampoon on Cumberland; and the power to extend the
pungency of his satire over the whole piece and all the
characters—except the opening " nag " between Mr.
and Mrs. Dangle, which is stale and heavy, but can
be very easily omitted.[1] Perhaps the most remarkable
thing about the play is the way in which the pure farce-
burlesque of the close is united to the higher comedy
of the Sir Fretful part by the character and deliverances
of Puff. There is here, in actual fact, something like
the transformation-scene suggested as possible in the
case of *The Rivals*.[2]

But still the three plays belong to distinct classes (if
in the case of *The Rivals* to a class of one only), and this
increases one's admiration of the achievement of their
author, who thus at eight and twenty had fixed himself
with each of them on the treacherous and rarely
" holding " ground of the stage, not to be dislodged for
more than four generations. And we may hark back
for a moment to what was said of the most important
of these pieces, the connection of its merit with certain

[1] We are told, though the original " book " does not seem to have survived, that
the initial failure of *The Rivals* itself was due, not merely to the inadequacy of the
first Sir Lucius, but to the presence of much superfluous matter, which was thinned
out after the first two nights.

[2] Some readers may not know the story, often as it has been told, that this delightful conclusion was literally extracted from the author by durance, though not
exactly durance vile. They lured him into a room with a plate of anchovy sandwiches and a magnum of claret, and locked him up till he had finished the provant
and the play. And seldom perhaps was even the best wine better justified of its
work in producing literature of the particular kind.

characteristics of the time—that curious " standardisation " which distinguishes it, and which, on the eve as usual of a return to flux and confusion itself, fixed certain things after a fashion not even yet disturbed.

CHAPTER VIII

THE FUGITIVES FROM THE HAPPY VALLEY

A CAPTIOUS person may attempt to cavil at the inclusion,
especially in the proposed space (which should be considerable) of any persons likely to be indicated by the above chapter-heading ; but
the objection can be promptly disallowed. It is not
merely—it is not nearly so much—the peace which the
Augustans enjoyed, the rest and refreshment which
they themselves took, as the supplies of these excellent
things that they afford to posterity, which it is the
object of this book to unfold and uphold. Moreover,
as a matter of fact, there is no person to be discussed at
any length here of whom it may not be said that
eighteenth-centuriness is as obvious in him as the
fact that he is trying, in some respects, to get beyond
or outside of his century. Perhaps none of them
actually returned to the Happy Valley itself, as did
Rasselas and Nekayah ; but that was because, in the
vast majority of cases, they had not consciously or
definitely left it—a fact which further establishes their
claims to abide here. We shall indeed have to re-
linquish one poet of whom the present writer at any
rate could never be tired of speaking—Blake. And
it will probably be unnecessary to say much about
Burns. But from the obscure and wholly unconscious
beginnings to the work of men like Cowper and
Crabbe, we shall find plenty of subjects—subjects
contributing, no doubt, to some tastes the most refresh-

ing matter of the whole ; to none, one would fain think, matter wholly *un*refreshing. In a few important cases, too, we shall have the opportunity of completing—as in reference to the poems of Gray and Cowper— notices only partially given before of writers of the first rank among their fellows ; while in others, the most remarkable of which are probably Macpherson and Chatterton, we can touch on things much written about indeed, but scarcely of late years much read, and still, it would seem, subject to much misconception.

It has been from the first allowed that one of the dangers of the century—especially and naturally so during its early years—was self-complacency. A good conceit of yourself is perhaps a stimulant ; but stimulants (as we all ought to know from the abundant admonitions we receive on the subject) must be used with caution. And it was also pointed out that this self-complacency too often took the worst and commonest of all forms [1]— that of contempt of predecessors. After his very early youth the great Mr. Addison was too polite for contempt ; but the feeling in his case took the forms of condescending patronage or august disapproval, as in the cases of " Chevy Chase " and " False Wit " respectively. But this buckram of conceit was at- tacked—insidiously, one might say, if it were not pretty certainly a fact that there was no conscious or inten- tional treachery or indeed hostility—by that very in- nocent and harmless study of older literature which Addison himself had thus to some extent chaperoned. The prejudice continued late—we have noted how a good-natured person and a true man of letters like Goldsmith could, when the meridian of the century was turned, speak unadvisedly about Drayton ; and how Horace Walpole, who all but touched the next age, and

The begin- nings of the rebellion.

---

[1] It may of course be contended that the perfectly self-complacent man, who is also, in the good Greek sense, self-sufficient, *need* not despise anybody. But this perfection is rare.

who had been a lifelong coquetter with things
mediæval, never had any real tincture or enjoyment of
mediæval or any literature much before Dryden.   We
may be quite sure that when Tom D'Urfey and (apparently) "Namby-Pamby" Phillips in England,
when Watson the printer and Allan Ramsay in Scotland unearthed and reprinted ballads and (in the Scotch
case) old poetry of various kinds, they were not plotting
against the tastes or the orthodoxy of their time.   Tom
was trying to turn a more or less honest penny, and (to
do him justice) indulging and trying to let others indulge a wholly honest love of music and song ; Namby
may have been endeavouring to follow the lead of his
revered master Joseph as to " Chevy Chase " itself ;
the Scotsmen were patriotically Scotticising.   But all
the same they were unconsciously introducing, if not a
Greek horse, a whole stud of Greek ponies into the
Trojan citadel.

We must not, however (with one or two exceptions,
where something more than mere reprinting went to
the matter, as in the case of Percy's *Reliques*),
poach, for the benefit of the eighteenth century
itself, on these older and merely " brought forth "
stores ; but turn to what the popularity and the imitation of them produced, to important manifestations like
the poetry of Gray and Collins.[1]   The compared and

[1] It may seem that default is being made in regard to some names on which
something was promised above—those of Lady Winchelsea, Parnell, and Dyer.   But
the passages to be noted in the two former are few, and have of late
years been frequently dwelt upon ; while in the case of Dyer, beautiful as *Grongar Hill* is, and astonishing as is the difference between
its cadence and even its diction and those of his contemporaries,
it is but a single and short composition.   If by any chance it
had perished, we should have thought of the author of *The Fleece* and *The Ruins of
Rome*, and even of that curious study for, or spoilt replica of, the masterpiece, *The
Country Walk*, as a *perruque* of the *perruques*, having only in *The Country Walk* itself
something of the cheerful ease of *The Spleen*.   But the extraordinary beauty of
Grongar Hill itself can never be staled with fit readers.   The poet, as if of malice
prepense, takes two of the most hackneyed catchwords of the poetic lingo of the time,
"nymph" and "purple," in his very first two lines ; and *un*hacks them into propriety and as it were personality.   He varies his cadence as nobody had done in the
metre since Milton ; he fastens idiosyncrasy to the single words "lonely" and
"van," whether the latter means only promontory, or (as has been suggested) refers

*Note on some
minors,
especially
Dyer.*

contrasted character of these two poets has long been, and must always be, a rather favourite and a wholly legitimate exercise of criticism and literary taste; but this again is hardly for us here, though it belongs, legitimately enough again, to what may from different points of view be called the *hors-d'œuvre* or the dessert of the feast to which we invite readers. It is in themselves that we must contemplate them.

The probable error of making Gray a sort of wanderer, dweller in the tents of Kedar, and some **Gray.** such " exile " as is depicted in O'Shaughnessy's most beautiful poem,[1] has been pointed out in speaking of his letters; but it is perfectly obvious from the poems themselves. Mr. Tovey perhaps pushed his own thesis too far when he questioned the Wordsworthianism of the unfinished *Ode to Vicissitude*; but this is the only piece, and almost the only passage, where the poet really uses a language —perhaps the only one where he really breathes a spirit—essentially non-eighteenth century. He knows and has read much more than his eighteenth-century

---

to the actual use in the neighbourhood of " Van " for the Welsh transliterated " Ban." Just after a commonplace eighteenth-century line—

> Big with the vanity of state

you come upon something so far from commonplace as—

> A little rule, a little sway
> A sunbeam on a winter's day—

and, not much further, upon one of the alms for Wordsworth's theory—

> Like human life to endless sleep.

But no scraps can do justice to the piece; to its strange interpenetration of the placidity and quiet of the century generally with a depth and intensity of feeling usually foreign thereto; its combination of music and *decorato* both usually so absent at the time.

> [1] A common folk I walk among;
> I speak dull things in their own tongue :
> But all the while within I hear
> A song I do not sing for fear—
> How sweet ! how different a thing !
> And when I come where none are near
> I open all my heart and sing.

" I waited for the train " once, not at Coventry but at Oxford, and quoted that to a great expert in poetry who happened not to know it. His " Who on earth wrote that ? " was satisfactory, and made me think of Colomba's " Qui a fait cela ! "

fellows; he sublimates their poetic diction into something much higher and finer than they commonly know how to use; he extends his curiosity into regions of literature which they have never yet attempted; and, above all, he rejects their most popular forms of poetry and adopts others of his own. He thus justifies rather the charge of not being fully contented with the Happy Valley of couplet and convention, of stock phrase and reasonable satisfaction, than that of being absolutely discontented with it. He will almost certainly point others to ways which he does not himself tread far; yet after all he checks his own footsteps.

Yet the handful of verse which he chose to leave us is one with which few persons who care for poetry *The general* would part. The two elaborate Odes would *character of* perhaps be resigned with least dissatisfac-*his verse.* tion, if it were not that no such lover could ever dream of parting with anything to which the name of poetry can really be applied. The inordinate person who said—

> Je voudrais boire tout le vin,
> Et baiser tout le monde

was inordinate because indiscriminate. It would have been difficult to find fault with him " in the abstract " if he had restricted himself to all the good drinkable wine and all the nice kissable world. So, also, many as are the mansions in the House of Poetry, a lover of poetry itself could not be content *not* to have access to any one of them.[1] But the *Progress of Poesy* and *The Bard* he would perhaps more rarely visit than others. Their form is not one that really suits English,[2] the elaborate correspondences escape attention, or when attended to produce an uneasy effect of constraint and mechanism, from which one flies for relief to the *Epithalamion* or *Lycidas*, to " Constantia Singing " or

---

[1] It may be remembered that to the denizens of the *Paradiso*, though they had special spheres, all Heaven from the Moon to the Rose was open.

[2] Gray knew and admitted this.

the " Grecian Urn " or the " Lotos Eaters," nay, in comparison with which one finds more satisfaction even in " Mrs. Anne Killigrew." To this stiffness of form they add another, not indeed of thought (as some of their contemporary readers strangely fancied), but of diction and phrase. It is essentially rhetorical poetry ; and some of the figures and " machines " which it employs are rather childish, especially the behaviour of Gloucester and Mortimer, the latter of whom seems to have had " an attack of nerves." But as a sort of poetical *feu d'artifice* the things are fine.

Very much more agreeable, though still artificial, is the Eton Ode, Johnson's objections to which are among the least worthy of him. It is not *The minor odes.* for nothing that so many of its phrases have fixed themselves in the memory ; the imagery and even the ornaments (a thing which Johnson seems to have strangely forgotten) are essentially proper to the scene and subject, and the whole has that fitness, that obvious sense of sympathy between writer and writing and theme which, though it will hardly or not at all dispense with technical excellence of expression, reinforces and animates that expression notably. " Spring " and " Adversity " on the other hand, especially the first-named, relapse towards the qualities of defect in the two greater odes, and contain some of the worst examples of that cut-and-dried personification which is undoubtedly one of the greatest faults of eighteenth-century verse.[1] Contrasted with the unfinished *Vicissitude*, they certainly show what an enemy the " might

[1] That Gray hardly escaped from being a mere eighteenth-century poet, as common estimation holds eighteenth-century poets, is shown by the ambitious but fortunately discarded fragment on " Education and Government" which is of the class of Johnson's, Goldsmith's, and the earlier Cowper's poems of the same kind, but infinitely below *The Vanity of Human Wishes*, far inferior to *The Traveller* and *The Deserted Village*, and not so good as the best parts of *Table Talk* and its companions. Mason's description of its one jewel—

> When love could teach a monarch to be wise
> And Gospel-light first dawned from Bullen's eyes

—as " much too beautiful to be lost " is ridiculous. It is a fair mixture of smartness and prettiness certainly, but nothing more.

have been " is to the " was." But still, even as regards these, how many but the very best poets even of
the nineteenth, even of the sixteenth-seventeenth
centuries have given better things? The defects
disappear and the merits increase as we come to the
" Elegy," the " Long Story," and the " Cat."

There are few more saddening things to a sensitive
if considerate critical mind than the dissidence of the
elect on the subject of Selima's epitaph,
which, it seems, ought to have been Zara's
or Fatima's. As for Johnson, prejudice against
everything but the *Elegy* here, for once, leads that
great man not merely to injustice—he was not seldom
unjust in a way—but to something near positive
stupidity. At least, though the stupidity may be on
my side, I cannot even guess what he means by saying
that " the azure flowers that blow " show how " a
rhyme is sometimes made when it cannot be found." [1]
And one of the best of logicians and not the worst of
humorists seems again to have bid good-bye to both
logic and humour when, after objecting to " nymph "
and thereby showing that he did not see the burlesque
so admirably blended with the pathos, he says of the
two famous lines—

> What female heart can gold despise?
> What cat's averse to fish?

that the first applies only to the nymph and the second
only to the cat. *Ex hypothesi Graiana* the cat was a
nymph and the nymph was a cat; the two lines fit the
twynatured creature in both its natures.

Others, while they condescend to give exact reasons
for dislike, seem to regard Gray as brutally indifferent
to poor Selima's fate.[2] Now the present writer adores

[1] For it is surely impossible that a man of the doctor's combined sense and
humour could have meant that porcelain flowers do *not* actually " blow." If he did,
he was for the moment on a par with the North Britons who represented to Lamb
the impossibility of Burns's joining their party.

[2] This may also have affected Johnson; for we know that he rightly loved cats.
But he should not have said, *before* Hodge, that he had had finer cats than him, for

cats ; they are the only animals (except bull-dogs) for whom, when they are alive, he really cares. He adds his tears to the water that drowned Selima ; but that does not prevent him from admiring the lightness, the vividness, the economy and sufficiency of detail, the slight satire on the ways of the time, and the admirable instance of its command of light verse that the little piece gives.[1]

The " Long Story " is a poem of curious effect, at least on some people. Johnson apparently did not *The Long* know of it, or thought it beneath his notice ; *Story.* but there were moods of his to which, if it had been anybody's but Gray's, it might have commended itself. Mason tells us that, of its readers in MS., and of those later when it was printed, some thought it " a masterpiece of original humour " and some " a wild and fantastic farrago." There have even been persons who called it " dull." Yet on the whole, with the " Cat," the fragments mentioned in a note, and many things in the letters, it *does* support Walpole's dictum referred to below, that Gray " never wrote anything naturally but things of humour," and it commends itself the more to one the more one reads it. Never was there such an absolute " Much Ado about Nothing," such a tale of a toy tub ; and if the actual thirty or forty stanzas had been reinforced by the missing " five hundred " it never could have been anything else. It is crammed with quotations—that is to say, things quotable and quoted since ; but scarcely one of these has anything to do with such story as it does not tell, and it would be possible, by judicious garbling, to make it look like a poetical account of Strawberry Hill itself, or what " Strawberry "

---

whom he bought oysters. The possibility of inferiority is never admitted by a cat —any more than by another kind of living creature—and the suggestion of it is never forgiven by either.

[1] The " Posthumous Fragments " include not a few other pieces supporting Walpole's theory that Gray's real strength was in humour. But scarcely any one is thoroughly finished ; and some are ill-natured,

would have liked to be. It is in fact almost as much pure *fatrasie* as anything in Sterne; but with the honey of poetry added, with no merely mechanical tricks, and with no *immunditiae* lurking in corners.[1]

As for the *Elegy*, scores, no doubt, and possibly hundreds of people have prefaced any observations which they have been (or have thought themselves) obliged to make on it with some such phrase as, " It is of course vain to attempt to say anything new about it," and have then proceeded to attempt the vanity. Something of the same feeling seems to have been experienced by Johnson himself when he wrote the famous words which almost constitute a palinode to the whole of the rest of his notice: " In the character of his *Elegy* I rejoice to concur with the common reader; for by the common sense of readers uncorrupted with literary prejudices, after all the refinements of subtilty and the dogmatism of learning, must be finally decided all claim to poetical honour. The ' Churchyard ' abounds with images which find a mirror in every mind, and with sentiments to which every bosom returns an echo. The four stanzas beginning, ' Yet even these bones,' are to me original; I have never seen the notions in any other place; yet he that reads them here persuades himself that he has always felt them. Had Gray written often thus it had been vain to blame and useless to praise him." The stately simplicity of this memorable confession is at once a warning bell to these critics who " consider too curiously," and a remarkable example of criticism itself, condensed in form, but far-reaching in scope and quality.

Perhaps the common sense of later generations has not invariably deserved the compliment which Johnson justly paid to that of his own contemporaries. The

The Elegy.

---

[1] The " Amatory Lines," " With beauty and pleasure surrounded to languish," which were in the possession of the younger heroine of the " Story," Miss Speed, and were pretty certainly addressed to her, have been generally taken as playful or feigned. I am not so sure: there is a curious throb—if not even a sob—in them.

U

Elegy has had, if not exactly " its exits and its en-trances," its ups and downs.   From a very early period, and inevitably, it has been bound as a burden on the back of youth ; and youth, if not wisely, yet excusably, has been apt to shake that burden off, and loth to take it up again, even when it would not be a burden at all. To excitable and high-flying, as well as still more to would-be cynical fashions of thought, it has seemed commonplace—*vulgaire* in the French sense, in which Madame de Staël, to the not always well-informed horror of some, applied that word to Miss Austen.   No doubt it does seem to the moods that resent morality too moral, to those which despise religion too religious, to others other things that they do not like.   Although the statement may seem merely an attempt to galvanise a dead subject, it may be questioned whether there are still many better tests of a real critical nature, well trained, than a clear and reasoned conception of the faults or at least defects (for it has hardly any positive faults) of Gray's *Elegy*.   And it is much " for thoughts" that a critic like Matthew Arnold, who had a very high idea of Gray, " shies " at the *Elegy*, thinks that, though a beautiful poem, it has received praise too unbounded, and in fact says very little more about it.   It is signi-ficant also that Mr. Arnold bestows much higher and more evidently heart-felt praise on the far more artificial, and, one may boldly say, far inferior *Progress of Poesy*. That Gray himself was, it is said, rather annoyed at the immense comparative popularity of the *Elegy*, and declared that it was merely due to the subject, need not trouble us very much.   This kind of thing is one of the commonest of the little ways of the irritable kind. Poets, like mothers, care less for the praise bestowed on the one child than for the neglect of the rest of the family which they think to be implied.

The difficulty lies, for us at least, in the very peculiar character of such excellence as may be rightly attributed to the piece.   It is quite possible that Gray may have been right in thinking that his contemporaries liked the poem more because of the subject, just as they liked *The Bard* and *The Progress of Poesy* and the *Fatal Sisters*[1] less on the same account. But though this judging by subject and love of subject is, alas! not less rife now than it was then; though it is even celebrated as a virtue by some priests of Baal, this is not the sort of subject that has, for a great while, been popular. On the contrary, some clever folk have long been accustomed to class it, with other examples of " the obvious," as merely or nearly contemptible. Even those who are wiser, those who know that all great subjects are obvious, even those wisest who do not judge by the subject at all, may miss the charms of the poem because of its form of expression. This is of a kind which is really very hard to judge, and has perhaps been getting harder for the last hundred years and more. It is impossible to assign to Gray that poignant and surprising power of clothing or bodying thought with musical and picturesque form— that almost supernatural gift of *exploding*, as it were, from the narrow case of a lonely word, or a small group of words, volumes of suggestion and association of beauty—which belongs to the very highest poetry. The kind of stupor on the one hand, of enthusiastic flush on the other, which is caused by the rarest things, in Homer, Æschylus, Lucretius, Dante, Shakespeare, Milton, Blake, Wordsworth, Coleridge, Shelley, Keats, Tennyson, Browning, Swinburne, Heine, Hugo, never comes from any verse or line or word in him, here or elsewhere. Collins, as we shall see, had, or came near to having, this power. Gray never showed it. And this one cannot but set down as a defect—as a defect of course serious and to its own extent fatal.

But it is easy to give too great positive weight to

---

[1] Of this and *The Descent of Odin* I shall not say much. Their matter was precious then; their manner now may seem hardly " brought off." But their earliness is a great possession for them.

this defect; and one is sometimes inclined to think that critics during the last seventy or eighty years, if not more, may have been tempted to do so. The paradise of the *Elegy* is not apocalyptic or ravishing, but it is a very fair earthly paradise, with a prospect of Heaven not excluded; and it is perhaps only after very long exercise in all kinds of poetry that one perceives its perfection as regards that " conformity to its own ideal," in which one class of perfection certainly consists. For one thing Gray has almost—not quite—discarded the heavy and distasteful phraseology of his other best known and most ambitious poems. There is still some personification which we could willingly spare; an abstract Ambition mocking and an abstract Grandeur smiling are much more likely to bore than to impress us now. We had rather he had not apostrophised us, or somebody, as " Ye proud." But these things are comparatively rare; and hardly even Spenser has achieved a fashion of rhythm and phrase more suitable to the matter he wishes to convey, and the effect he wishes to produce. All or almost all is subdued, half-toned. There is no exaggerated gloom as in Blair's *Grave*. *Sunt lacrimae rerum*, but the tears are not accompanied by shrieks or gesticulations. The greater and later single line of a greater and later poet of Cambridge—

To where, beyond these voices, there is peace

sums up the whole. It has been said of the *Elegy* that it has probably given to a larger number of persons, who are fitted to enjoy poetry somewhat " below proof," but genuine, more pleasure than any other piece of the same length. If there seems to be something a little patronising in this its author would no doubt disclaim any such intention. It is in reality very high praise. It may be added that if any one fails to taste the poem because he wants a higher strength, his taste must have been vitiated by poetical dram-drinking, and indeed probably never have been of the most delicate or sensitive kind.

Gray's, in more senses than one immortal, companion Collins offers no such difficulty ; but he is still a very curious study, and some people find him even more delectable than Gray, much more delectable than Gray found him,[1] or than Cowper afterwards did.[2] This incompatibility among poets will only surprise those who do not know the poetic " ropes," especially the leading case of Keats and Shelley. But it may act as a pointer to one main feature of the curiosity above referred to—that while neither Cowper nor Gray has anything like the extremer weaknesses of Collins in eighteenth-century kind, neither of them betrays any such likelihood of being an almost totally different poet in a different time.

It is, however, with what he was at this time that we are concerned. Some one has, I think, said that Collins has never been a popular poet ; and editions of him have certainly been far from numerous, while comments, with fewer exceptions, have been strangely inadequate. The well-known and slighting criticism, referred to above and quoted below, may receive an additional explanation, though hardly an excuse, from the fact that Gray was still youngish, and that his naturally somewhat disdainful soul was still full of that youthful partisanship which has its bad as well as its good effects. Johnson's affectionate notice of the man and unfavourable criticism of the work is

[1] He allowed Collins "a fine fancy" and "great variety of words," but called his "ear" bad (Gray's own is harsh and tuneless compared to it), and denied him any "choice of images." Finicalness, and perhaps a little inter-university jealousy (for Collins was an Oxford man), may account for this to some extent ; but it certainly reads ill beside the liberal laudations bestowed on that wretched stuff of Mason's which he so unweariedly buck-washes. As to Mason himself it will be sufficient here to repeat what I have said of him elsewhere, also in a note—for he deserves no text-notice : " His couplets are tinsel ; his blank verse is wood ; his Hudibrastics are straw ; and his odes are plaster."

[2] He took, indeed, great interest in Collins's piety as recorded by Johnson. But as for his work he dismisses him as "a poet of no great fame," of whom he himself had never previously heard.

Collins.

intelligible on other grounds ; for what we like best in
Collins, the " irregular " verse, the intense lyric quality,
and some other things, were not Johnson's doxies.
Cowper, as has been said, did not, apparently, care for
him. Nor was he much luckier in his eulogists.
Somebody—one is not quite certain who—has ap-
pended to the reprint of the Poems and of Johnson's
Life in Chalmers's *Poets* some " Observa-
The contrast tions," which even those who try as hard as
Eclogues and they can to observe courtesy to predecessors
the Odes. may be tempted to call fatuous. The
Eclogues (which, with the rarest exceptions, can only
escape the contempt of a lover of poetry because of the
extreme curiosity of their having proceeded from their
author) receive this crown from the Observator, a
crown which would hardly be too decent in colour
or fragrance, in substance or art, if bestowed upon
Lycidas or *Adonais* : " In simplicity of description and
expression, in delicacy and fitness of numbers, and in
natural and unaffected tenderness, they are not to be
equalled by anything of the pastoral kind in the English
language." The detailed conclusions with which this
dictum is supported are sometimes delightfully comic,
but their character may be judged from the fact that
the critic admires, beyond everything, perhaps the most
absurd expression that a really great poet ever permitted himself—

> Their eyes' *blue languish.*

A palette of " languishes," ranging through the
spectrum order from red to violet, would indeed be
interesting.

It was impossible that, with the Romantics, Collins
should not at least partially come to his own ; but here
the opposite objections to his personification, to his
poetic diction, and others began to count.[1] Even more

---

[1] Wordsworth pitied and praised, but in his own very earliest period. As a matter
of fact, the abuse of Gray in the famous Preface hits Collins with tenfold force.
Shelley, I think, knew Collins well ; but I remember no special reference to him.

recently, when Mr. Swinburne took him up with his usual enthusiasm, that enthusiasm was unfortunately directed in part to, and might seem to ill-disposed readers to be inspired by, Collins's schoolboy or undergraduate Republicanism. The present writer is sensible to the fullest degree of the fashion in which Collins exposes some of the worst defects of the poetry of his century, and is under no delusion whatever, ethical, poetical, or historical, as to Harmodius and Aristogeiton ; but he has always been far more sensible of the depth and purity of the poetic inspiration which breaks through the clumsy trammels of " nymph " and " shell " and " scene," dignifies the puppet-show of abstractions and personification, and turns to poetic glory the tawdry rags of conventional liberty-mongering.

Some people may think that it requires the Cyclopean or Ogreish taste of a critic to find " rest and refreshment " in work of which he can only speak with something like contempt as a rule. But this is the usual injustice that our slighted art meets with. Collins's *Eclogues*, from another than Collins, would be stuff too dull for a lively, and too poor for a generous, mind to regard with satisfaction of any sort. But when, in company with things like " blue languish " and others, which may be noticed presently, you come (let us for the moment suppose it to be verse of an author of which you know nothing) upon flashes like—

> Cold is her breast, like flowers that drink the dew,[1]

curiosity, and desire to find out the secret of such strange society, should certainly give a certain zest to the search for other work of the same uncertain kind. You find that work in the few but partly magnificent Odes which Gray half patronised and half sneered at ; [2]

---

[1] A flash that lights memory down to Rossetti and *Rose Mary*.

[2] It has been pointed out by the most faithful Graians that he was not above taking hints from the poet who, he thought, " deserved to last some years but [would] not," and who in fact has lasted and will last as long as himself. The " Ode to

but you find their magnificence accompanied by slips quite worthy of " blue languish " itself. Then the curiosity is whetted still more, and bare individual satisfaction is accompanied by positive æsthetic pleasure, though also (till the not very deeply hidden secret is discovered) by continued puzzlement. The poetic analysis of the *Odes* yields a result which may be said to be, in a fashion, that of the *Eclogues* upside down, though the proportions do not quite entirely correspond. The *Eclogues* contain about a halfpennyworth of sack to an intolerable amount of mouldy bread. Almost every one of the Odes is wine of Dionysus, but there are too often sops of the old mouldy stuff floating in it.

These *Odes*, which ought to be a perpetual delight, though of the most mixed and peculiar kind, to every lover of poetry, fill, in the " Aldine " edition (with miscellaneous additions seldom of much value) about eighty, and without these appendages about sixty, small pages, many of them half-blank from the beginnings and ends of poems, and not even at their fullest containing more than some five - and - twenty lines. In Chalmers's large pages and compressed printing, they barely exceed the half score, and do not reach the dozen. Yet in them—side by side, it is true, with some of the worst follies and flatnesses of the poetic diction of the time— we find what their contemner called, in verse much more artificial than their own, " gems of purest ray serene "—gems that, to use a different order of words and thought, " make a sunshine in the shad*iest* place "—phrases and passages that you can murmur to yourself for luxury and for consolation, for example of poetic life and instruction of poetic manners, as you can do with nothing else written in the eighteenth

(side note:) The *Odes* themselves.

Simplicity" (to which I should add its next neighbour, that "On the Poetical Character") cannot possibly have been without influence on the "Progress of Poesy." On the other hand, Collins cannot possibly have learnt anything from Gray.

century till the very close of it, except one or two
given by Chatterton and a considerable number by
Blake. The most unfortunate, and to modern tastes the
most unattractive, of the snares of his time into which,
for reasons to be discussed presently, Collins fell, was,
it has been said, Personification. This figure of speech
—to which, if he had not been under her spell himself,
Milton might nowadays have applied the same rude
language which he used to Plurality—is undoubtedly
of an ancient house, and has always proved a very
Circe or Delilah to poets, it being one of the most
humorous touches in literary history to find Wordsworth, after using language of almost Miltonic strength
about her, writing " Odes to Duty," and personifying
to the nth in most of his best poems.

In fact the lady is very difficult to get rid of. Ancient
mythology almost consisted of her representatives, and
therefore ancient poetry abounded with them. The
Middle Ages, in their devotion to allegory, revived her
in myriad forms. The Renaissance, finding her so
classical, never resented the mediæval stain (as they
thought it in other things), and passed her on with full
license of enjoyment to the seventeenth century,
whence she proceeded serenely to the eighteenth. To
skip that period for the moment, Wordsworth's pre-
cept of objection has been much less minded than his
adoption in practice since. Personification is not
" widowed " yet, while looking back to the earlier and
the later stages of purely Victorian poetry, we shall not
find better things among Tennyson's earliest poems
than the " Ode to Memory," and almost the very finest
of Rossetti's sonnets—

Under the Arch of Life

is a constellation of personified Qualities and Circumstances.

Personification herself, therefore, is a personage ill
to speak ill of; but it must be admitted that the per-

sonifications of the eighteenth century, and especially those of Collins and Gray, are not the most attractive avatars or representations of this demi-goddess who has made herself familiar to so many generations of poets. There are too many of them, they are too obtrusive, they are clumsily badged and uniformed, and there is a rhetorical touch about them which suggests the same actor or actress executing a " quick change " and presenting half a score of different parts. Gray's unfinished " Vicissitude," Mrs. Greville's " Indifference," [1] Collins's own " Evening " above all, and at least the opening of his " Liberty " escape this suggestion of " the boards," and retain the vagueness which is convenient to abstractions. But it must be admitted that too many passages do not either escape the one or attain the other, while Gray's most celebrated examples, if not his *Elegy*, sometimes almost deserve the censures of Johnson and of Wordsworth— an ominous conjunction.

Some of the worst faults of the kind and type occur in the first of the Odes, that " To Pity." In its very first stanza comes one of many misuses of the word " scene," which Collins frequently commits, and which culminated long afterwards in that strange blot on Campbell's famous poem—

Some detailed criticisms of their faults,

> Then the might of England flushed
> To anticipate the *scene*.

" Turtles " for " doves," the curiously unhappy phrase for the temple of the Goddess, "its southern site," which is not only prosaic, but does not really give the meaning, " aspect " being required ; " picture's toils " for " the art of the painter," and the crowning false note—

> To hear a British *shell*,

---

[1] This is called a " Hymn "—but the eighteenth-century Ode and the eighteenth-century Hymn are often " as like as my fingers to my fingers."

the word [1] being intended to convey the idea of an
English " voice " or " musical instrument," or
" poetry " generally—all these things may in different
moods annoy or amuse, but they can hardly in any
genuine sense please. And, yet the total result of the
thing, with all its faults, *is* pleasure ; you feel that
here is a poet who has a new and sweet song to sing—
if only he could prevail upon himself not to quaver
and shake and falsetto it into absurdity.

The " Ode to Fear," which follows, is more ambitious and contains better things, but is not yet
faultless, or provided only with those faults which
enhance the beauties. Collins had been contented to
sing of Pity in the old *rime couée* (8 8 6 8 8 6), which,
for some reason or other, the eighteenth century preferred to all the simpler old-fashioned lyrical measures.
Here he attempts the regular Pindaric, though, instead
of the more usual arrangement, he sandwiches the
epode between strophe and antistrophe, and does not
observe an equal number of lines in these two latter.
Part of this piece is rather too much in Ercles' vein—

> The fiends who near allied,
> O'er nature's wounds and wrecks preside,

and would be better away. But the " epode," in
alternately rhymed decasyllabic quatrains, has that
singular sweetness which has just been noticed, and
which is more Greek than most English-Greek things.
There is again much of this in " Simplicity," where he
returns to the regular stanza (but a slightly larger one),
and uses a good deal of Milton's phrase. Nor is there
much false diction, though the inevitable and abominable " scene " reappears, in worse plight and in worse
company than ever—

> Nor olive more nor vine
> Shall *gain thy feet to bless the servile scene*.

---

[1] It must be remembered that the certainly very audible military " shell " had
been commonly employed for a good hundred years in Collins's time, so that the
équivoque was obvious, while the " musical instrument " sense is a cheap and clumsy

The " Ode on the Poetical Character " is interesting
not merely in itself, but, as suggested above, in connection with Gray's much more ambitious *Progress
of Poesy*. In elaboration, critical correction, display
of reading, and other things, the Cambridge poet has
of course the clear advantage. But for poetical *je ne
sais quoi* Collins completely distances his follower.
" Mercy," consisting of a strophe and an antistrophe
without epode, intends greatly, but perhaps does not
quite achieve ; and then we come to the first thing in
which Collins shows his real powers, the famous
" Liberty." Undoubtedly the subject has conciliated
some judges ; but such conciliation is by no means necessary to bring out not merely enjoyment, but enthusiasm.
You may feel inclined to mutter with Tennyson—

> And I think we know the hue
> Of that cap upon her brows.

You may even be abandoned enough to sympathise
with Mr. Carlyle when, in words authenticated by tradition, he was so far left to himself as to remark that he
" didn't care a *dom* for Leeberty," at least in the sense
in which Collins uses it. You may know all about
Harmodius and Aristogeiton and the real facts of their
case ; and may wonder how any scholar could possibly
regard the shattering of the clay-and-iron tyranny of
Rome by northern tribes as a blow to Freedom ; and so
on. But if you care for poetry in the least truly, the
very sound of the lines—

> Who shall awake the Spartan fife,
> And call in solemn sounds to life,
> The youths whose locks divinely spreading
> Like vernal hyacinths in sullen hue,

will make you indifferent to anything else but the
poetry itself. The rest is not quite up to the over-

---

classical importation which should have been left to schoolboy " copies of verse "
and have been crossed out there, in English, by any judicious schoolmaster like
Coleridge's Boyer not much later.

ture, but it is such stuff as no one else then living
could, even in his dreams, have written ; and it has
and beauties. itself that dreamlike quality, something of
which must always enter into the greatest
verse, and the absence of which is too often obvious in
Gray.

The spirit of the thing is vigorous enough, and yet
it is expressed in that true poetic fashion, " softer than
sleep," which only those very words themselves—a
triumph of poetry in Greek and Latin and English alike
—fitly describe. Except Spenser, who was perhaps
Collins's chief master, and Tennyson, it is difficult to
think of any other English poet who has this miraculous
softness ; while Musset once or twice (especially in *À
Saint-Blaise, à la Zuecca*), and Heine often, are almost
the only foreigners since his day who have equalled it,
unless, like the Italians, they use a language in which
it is, so to say, ready-made and almost mechanical.
It is Collins's great gift, and is shown partly in the
popular and unequal " Ode on the Passions," fully in
the exquisite " How Sleep the Brave " (whereto so
many thoughts must have turned recently when men
read the awful doggerel and drivel which, with rare
exceptions, the present war has produced), the magnificent " Evening," the graceful and tender piece on
Thomson's grave, and that less universal and more
contemporary but still charming " Dirge in Cymbeline," against which some critics have raised their
hoofs.

These half-dozen poems, with the inchoate and
rather puzzling " Superstitions of the Highlands,"
constitute Collins's poetic documents or diploma-
pieces. Their bulk is small enough (it does not in all
reach the five-hundredth line, about half of it being
occupied by the unfinished " Superstitions "), and even
in them the faults of the time, here so strange, crop up
occasionally. But the quality just mentioned is so
pervading in them, that it can be missed by no real

lover of poetry ; and it is hardly fanciful to regard it
as a sort of consecration by that Spirit of Poetry itself
which, repress it as you will, must have its way sometimes, of the very quietness and peace which have been
assigned here as the gift of the actual century.   In one
sense the second stanza of " How Sleep the Brave " [1]
could have been written in no other time, and it takes
some of the colour of that time upon it.   There is the
personification, there is a little primness and Quakerism
of language ; but what ineffable grace and sweetness
accompany and excuse the mannerism !

The present writer is by no means enamoured of
unrhymed verse, outside the continuous decasyllable,
in English ; but there can be no question that if all
our unrhymed lyrics were like Collins's " Evening,"
Johnson's sentence on his rival's *Elegy* would have
simply to be repeated.   We might spare " paly " and
" sheety " with some feeling of relief ; the sacred
hunger of the critic for alteration might dispense
with the last three stanzas [2] and prefer an ending at
line 40—

> Thy dewy fingers draw
> The gradual dusky veil.

But was ever any poem, by the very greatest master,
written in tone and colour more absolutely and finally
predestinated for the subject ?   Did ever any, except
again the greatest, conceive and formulate such an
epithet—hard to find, "inevitable" when found,—
for flowing water at evening, distinguished from the
same at morn, as " thy *solemn* springs " ? or in a different and perhaps less winsome key, that of " reserved "

---

[1] By fairy hands their knell is rung ;
  By forms unseen their dirge is sung ;
  Here Honour comes, a pilgrim grey,
  To bless the turf that wraps their clay,
  And Freedom shall awhile repair
  To dwell, a weeping hermit, there !

[2] They are good in themselves ; but rather of the nature of a "moral" tacked on
to the unrivalled "curtain" of the distich given above.   The difference between the
versions of the poem illustrates Collins's tendency to revise, but minute discussion of
it would perhaps hardly be in place here.

for the nymph of Evening herself? For my own part I hunger and thirst for rhyme throughout the poem, and yet I cannot refuse to admit that there is something in it in the strength of which one can consent to go hungry and thirsty.

The Thomson Ode and the Cymbeline Dirge are less absolute things than the " Evening " or than " How Sleep the Brave " ; but the same poetic honey abounds in them. And when we reach the " Highlands " piece the attractions—not universally felt, but by some very considerably—of a *crux* are added to the mere charms of poetry itself. Here, of course, more than anywhere else, we see how far Collins's mind and taste reached beyond the age, of which, nevertheless, he so constantly exhibits the influence in diction, imagery, and so forth. None of Gray's excursions into mediæval literature, or exercises in fancies of his own, approaches this piece of Collins's in genuine " Romantic " spirit, in personal not bookish [1] sympathy with ghost-story and folk-lore and fairy-tale, with the scenery that suits all these, and with the history that half or wholly turns them into fact. The exact text remains, it would seem, unsettled ; and though nobody has spent much pains on the matter, documents for settlement seem to be wanting. The few pieces of evidence we have about it are not only doubtful but contradictory, as, for instance, the statement of Warton that Home (" My Name is Norval " Home), to whom, having met him in England, Collins addressed the poem, " kept no copy," and another, that the imperfect copy found later at Edinburgh was a sketch preserved by Home. As for the fuller text usually printed, nobody seems to know where it came from when it was first published in 1788.[2]

---

[1] It is important to remember that it was written years before *Ossian*; though a hint or two may have been given by Thomson's *Winter* and by the " Hebrid Isles " passage of *The Castle of Indolence*.

[2] The argument that it must be all right because it was dedicated to the Wartons (Collins's schoolfellows and most intimate friends) and they made no objection,

Collins, who was nearly as prone to alter his work (though unluckily he had not the same chances) as Tennyson, would probably have made a very different thing of this Ode had he had life and faculty. The very spirit of " curiosity " indeed—of enquiry into new and unfamiliar things—which it exhibits, may have interfered at first, though it might have done so less in revision, with that almost unearthly and essentially dreamlike placidity which has been noted in his other best poems. But this curiosity itself, and other signs of it not yet mentioned (such as the enthusiasm for Tasso, or at least for Fairfax [1]), add to its interest for the modern reader.

Still one may fall back on the suggestion that in Collins we have the most accomplished exponent of what is here put forward as the century's crowning grace—the special solace of its possible sins. He is not the greatest poet *in* the eighteenth century—that position was reserved for Blake ; [2] but he is the greatest poet who, in any but a chronological sense, was *of* it. Nor does it militate against this estimate to hold that

seems to be rather a " figwood prop." If either of them ever saw the poem it must have been forty years earlier ; and Thomas Warton at least, infinite as is the honour due to him for his *History* (*vide infra*), has never been regarded as a very accurate or a very trustworthy authority on texts.

[1] I have never been quite so certain as some are that the striking phrase—

Prevailing poet ! Whose undoubting mind
Believed the magic wonders which he sang,

refers to the Englishman not the Italian, the translator and not the "maker." But it may be so.

[2] Some of Blake's best things in his earliest work are however Collinsian, such as the exquisite—

Speak silence with thy glimmering eyes
And wash the dusk with silver.

A good many other resemblances will reward the enquirer. But I do not remember that Blake ever mentions Collins. Chatterton, poor boy ! has been supposed to have spoken unadvisedly about the senior of the trio which he and Blake completed, and which vindicated their common century from the charge of possessing no representative of poetry pure and simple. But the sneering references to " Collins " in " February " and " Kew Gardens " contain nothing either certainly identifiable with, or probably referring to, our poet ; and most likely apply to some of the numerous local nobodies on whom Chatterton wasted his spleen in the dreary *non*-Rowley poems. Collinses of some literary notoriety were numerous in the eighteenth century ; and one was the butt of a quaintly titled skit which I have often seen catalogued but have never read, *Collinso Furioso or Matters to Tatters.*

at another time he would have been better and greater than he was.[1]

Of the remarkable group of four books which, in the early 'sixties of the century, made a sort of false

The Mani-
festoes of
Romanticism.
Hurd's
Letters.

dawn—if indeed it was false—of Romanticism, we have already noticed the *Castle of Otranto*. The others — Percy's *Reliques*, Macpherson's *Ossian*, and Hurd's *Letters on Chivalry and Romance*—form an odd trio, the oddity of which is increased in quartette by *Otranto* itself. As the least delightful to the average modern reader, Hurd's book may be treated first. Its author was, though after a fashion a respectable, a not very amiable, or even admirable person in more ways than one ; and some have even tried to deny his originality as regards the views expressed in the *Letters*. In rigid exactness no views are original ; and you might tack together almost everything that Hurd says in defence of the " unity of Design," the different principles and objects of classical and romantic literature, and the like, out of the Italian critics of the sixteenth century—perhaps out of more modern writers still. But nobody in his time had exposed, in such solid and forcible fashion, the fallacy of erecting the practice of one particular period or style of literature into a code of salvation and damnation for all time to come ; and the exposure came with peculiar effect from one who was not a poet or a skirmisher in letters of any kind, but a typical don and " learned Theban." To anybody who takes any but a most superficial interest in literature, both Hurd's *Letters* and his *Dialogues* are very good reading ; and the latter had a great literary influence—

[1] It may seem to some readers hard that Beattie, who has previously been noticed only or mainly as an imitator of Spenser, should not be reintroduced here. If we were definitely dealing with the ushers of Romanticism as such, he would deserve to be so. But as a provider of rest and refreshment, he seems to me to have been sufficiently dealt with. We know to our sorrow that his great pattern " mostly sent to sleep " no less a person than Landor, and sleep is certainly restful and refreshing. But some of us Beattie does not send to sleep : he only sends us to another book.

not least perhaps on Landor, though Landor's curious and most clay-footed, though by no means golden-headed idol, Parr was Hurd's bitterest enemy.

It may be, though for obviously different reasons, nearly as difficult to get the modern reader to tackle *Ossian* as to grapple with Hurd. But few

Ossian.

people can be unaware that no such difficulty was felt by original readers of that singular compilation, which, if not real poetry itself, inspired poetry in two generations at least (the second of these being one of the most poetical in the world's history), and spread its influence all over Europe. What seems necessary on the controversial side—and that is but little—may be said below ;¹ we must here take *Ossian* simply at its "face-value," though that face-value itself varies as we look at the obverse and reverse of the coin—the face which appeared to contemporaries who did not question its genuineness, and that which it bears to us when we leave the technical question of genuineness more or less—altogether if possible—out of sight and mind.

It has been said that it requires considerable critical exercise or expertness to appreciate, in any critical fashion, the charm of Gray's *Elegy*. It may be added that even greater preparation is required before any modern man can really appreciate *Ossian*. The penalty of enthusiastic and unhesitating acceptance, at once, of such a work of art as this by any generation has—not quite universally but almost so—been future

---

¹ If not the whole truth, the best conclusion of this infinitely debated matter seems to be the statement which ends the last paragraph of the article on *Ossian* in Chambers's *Encyclopædia*, by my late friend and colleague Professor Donald Mackinnon, admittedly one of the most careful, and certainly one of the most enthusiastic, of Gaelic scholars : " The truth seems to be that these so-called translations (*Fingal*, *Temora*, etc.), are essentially the compositions of James Macpherson ; and that the Gaelic texts subsequently published were prepared with or without aid from his friends, but how and when we do not now know." The body of the article while, of course, insisting on the fact that Ossian (Oisin), Fingal (Finn), and others were actually traditional heroes of Irish and Scotch Gaelic story, points out that the *form* of the English *Ossian* has nothing to do with any ancient Gaelic poetry, that its vague and abstract treatment is in direct opposition to an almost prosaic concreteness in actual Gaelic poetry, and that the Gaelic versions referred to are essentially modern, and, as slang says now, " bad modern at that."

distaste if not disgust. The extraordinarily fashionable almost inevitably becomes the irreconcilably un-
fashionable. With singular felicity or singular cleverness (he showed himself, in fact, in all relations of life,
except his exceedingly foolish and rash attempt to
bully Johnson, a very clever man indeed) Macpherson
managed to shoot his bolt with just that aim, a little
ahead of the object, which is sure to hit as the object
itself progresses. His recipe (to change the metaphor)
was exactly what the crude and indiscriminate but
greedy appetite of the last third of the century de-
manded without knowing its own demand, and con-
sumed ravenously when it was presented with the
supply. But this very description implies a certainty
of satiety, and its usual consequences, later.

To the modern reader, then, for some generations
past, *Ossian* has been a shot bolt—a fashion out of
fashion—a food which is turned from, if not exactly
with loathing, at any rate with no appetite. Even such
things as " Celtic renascences " have done it little if
any good, because of its less than doubtful genuineness
and its perfectly certain adulteration, even if there is
any genuineness in it at all. For readers of some
reading its countless bad imitations,[1] and the trail
which these imitations left upon succeeding literature,
have put it still more out of favour ; and to the comparatively illiterate (no disrespect to them) it offers few
present delights.

These considerations can hardly lose their force ;
and many as are the changes which the student of the
The power and the influence of Macpherson's work. history of literature has seen, it is very difficult to imagine eager and intense enjoyment
of *Ossian* reappearing at any time. Yet the
person who neglects it entirely, loses something. For the actual student—not a " researcher,"

---

[1] Even more wonderful than the imitations are the attempts made by some honest
devotees to do more " justice " to Macpherson's Gaelic " originals " by retranslating
into modern English verse or prose of a kind. You lose what at its best, though
" faked " and rococo, is literature—sometimes very nearly very fine literature. You
get balderdash and drivel.

but an intelligent reader—whom we have frequently had in view, the immense influence of the book or books, the evidence given of the desires and needs of the time, and other such things, would make *Ossian* readable, even if it were savourless in itself. But it is not. Actual forger as Macpherson may have been and probably was ; charlatan and " faker " as he was beyond all doubt—he was, after all and before all, an actual Highlander: he had, at a time when not many had done so, traversed and observed the Highlands pretty thoroughly, and he had, beyond all question, if only by the combined instincts of the native and the " literary gent," succeeded in grasping and expressing the local colour in a singularly effective and original way.[1] His history is patched and colourless myth ; he has no connected romantic story to tell, and does not show much sign of being able to tell it if he had ; while his characters are hardly even shadows. But no one who has watched the snakes of mist coil and twine and mock round the summits of the Coolins ; no one who has seen the black rocks sleep and the brown rivers plunge and foam ; no one who has trudged over leagues of moor and peat-hag in search of some " Burn of the Deceivers," [2] which is almost impossible to find, and acts up to its name as a guide when found,— can admit that the scenery and atmosphere of *Fingal* and *Temora* and the rest are merely theatrical. There is more in it than any scene-painter, even if he be a very Stanfield, can give ; more even than the most accomplished artist, with no taint of the theatre about

[1] The late Mr. Tovey, discussing Gray's eager tumbling to the bait at first, and his rejection of it afterwards, thinks it strange that the English poet did not notice indebtedness to his own *Bard*. I cannot see very much of this, though if Macpherson's restless industry had led him to explore the recesses where the MS. of Collins's *Superstitions of the Highlands* was lying *perdu*, he might have taken important hints. Perhaps he did, for he had much dealing with Home, and was a very Ulysses in policy. Gray himself saw resemblances to Thomson. (*N.B.—Ossian*, though always used, is not an *original* title for *Fingal*, *Temora*, etc.)

[2] " Allt-na-Gallagach " or " Gealgach "—a name the repeated occurrence of which in the Highlands has suggested to the brutal Saxon deductions suitable to his brutality.

him, has given—the charm of "the word" expressing the experience and the emotions of the senses and the soul.

This, though the gift referred to may perhaps have obtruded itself in too overwhelming measure, and have been made to do duty for a great many other gifts, the want of which is only too much felt, is a great thing to say of any book or book-writer. There may be added to it another and more questionable attraction—that of the curious verse-prose in which the composition is couched. To different persons—even to the same person in different moods—this will of course appeal differently. It will sometimes tease; it will very frequently seem, what the scenery has been denied to be, theatrical; it must be admitted to be unequally managed. But it sometimes suits the peculiar description itself very well; and it must be admitted to be a very clever mask and " pass " for the shadowiness of figure, the insufficiency of character, and the absence of story, which plain prose would set ruthlessly in the daylight, and to which almost any regular form of verse would be almost equally dangerous. Of course any one may say that this brings us back to the central fact that *Ossian* is after all (as somebody once punned it) a mere " *mis*tification." It is, except for some definite purpose, an impossible book to read through; and in any case a very unlikely book to which to recur often. But almost everybody who cares for the Humanities of modern as well as ancient literature should read it, or a good part of it, at least once; and it would be surprising if some such readers did not sometimes turn to it again, if only as to a shrine (to talk in the vein of its own century), desolate and unlit now, but once thronged with worshippers and fragrant with glowing incense.

Far less allowance, though some, and that of a kind which once more, as in the case of Collins, fixes the subject in its place here with a curious combination of attractions, is required for Percy's *Reliques*. This, except the great pioneer

Percy and his *Reliques*.

novels perhaps, is the most epoch-making contribution of the century to literature before its last year but two, and the most purely delightful of its productions, except the novels again and some of the letters and lighter things. Its inestimable compiler may have deserved the hackneyed praise-blame of " building better than he knew " ; and may, beyond all question, have built wood and hay and stubble into the marbles and the precious stones of his structure. But he meant well, and he did even better than he meant ; and he has, on the whole, received by no means a very liberal amount of thanks, and in some cases a great deal of positive and rather black ingratitude. Personally, he seems to have had a few weaknesses. He was, like some nine-tenths of his cloth in the century, a good deal of a toady, and perhaps a very very little of what has been later called a snob. He was, again after a fashion of his time, to which hardly anybody but Gray was superior, strangely indifferent to what we now consider literary " good form " ; and garbled, patched, borrowed, altered, and generally " faked " after a fashion horrific to the more prudish kind of scholar. But, on the other hand, he seems to have been entirely free from the bad blood which is so frequent in scholars,[1] and from the donnishness which affects others, as has been noticed in Hurd ; he never, as it is to be feared that Hurd did, " left his first works," but on the contrary lived to welcome Scott. He bore Johnson's, it must be said, rather ignorant and ill-judged contempt for the most part good-humouredly ; he did not lose his dignity over the virulent attacks of the half-lunatic Ritson. It has sometimes, one must admit, been a little disgusting to find him treated with magisterial or patronising admonition by mere hacks of literature, and abused by persons respectable enough in themselves, but after all mere profiters by the generations

[1] He is accused of a " violent temper," but he certainly, as is remarked above, did not show it (though he did sometimes show a " proper spirit ") to Johnson, and I do not remember any bad instance of it authentically vouched for.

of improved knowledge which have come since Percy
wrote.

For, if he was not a great man, he did a greater work
than scores of greater men put together have been able
to accomplish.   He seems from the first to
Unimportance
of the faults
found with
him. have been gifted with that excursive " curiosity " which was exactly the thing required
to break the bonds of artificial neo-classicism.
He began with Chinese, no doubt " in translations,
sir ! in translations " ; but, it would seem, with
translations from real Chinese, not with the imaginary
philosophy and literature of the usual eighteenth
century Fum Hoams and Lien Chi Altangis.   He
went on to Norse ; and it has been contended, with some
if not full appearance of truth, that Gray was largely
and directly, if not exclusively, indebted to him for his
own knowledge of the subject.   And then—stimulated
perhaps by Shenstone and Warton and others ; and
almost miraculously helped, and not behaving himself
quite in too comely fashion to his miracle, by the folio
MS. ; under whatever conditions anybody may think
fit to add—he issued the *Reliques*, and *ipso facto* did more
than any single man to revolutionise, by restoration
not destruction, the poetry of England.

It is so easy now that Old English and Middle
English are taught in almost every school ; now that
literary history is a drug in every university ; now that
the principles of editing, elaborated by a long series
of mistakes and corrections of mistakes, have become
vulgate, and that texts of meticulous and often in more
than one sense painful accuracy are on shelves accessible to almost everybody who will take the slightest
trouble ;—it is easy to belittle, or denounce, or at best
patronise, the book.   The *moles* of disinterring and
rebuilding its constituents was somewhat greater in
difficulty ; and the value of the result is, as has been
said, almost infinite.

It is in fact hardly necessary, except for the sake of

justice and completeness, to say anything more about
the charges brought against Percy. That his idea of
the duties of an editor was not only not ours, but was
an indefensible idea as soon as it came to be examined,
has been allowed, and, except out of mere paradox-
hunting, can never be denied ; [1] but, as has also been
said, there were few people then living upon whom its
impropriety had dawned, and the error was certainly
grounded upon an excellent though mistaken intention
of conciliating readers—of giving them something not
too much unlike what they were accustomed to and
would expect. That Percy jumbled incongruous
things together is a positively frivolous cavil. None
of the things that he gave was familiar to the readers
to whom he gave them ; and they were all, in varying
measure, suited to give the required and inestimable
shock of unfamiliarity. His " Essays " are, of course,
to a large extent out of date, in consequence of the
very investigations to which they themselves led ; and
they contain not a few things which have turned out to
be errors. But they are highly creditable for their
time, in respect of mere information ; and they often
display much more real critical power than later
writers, with large advantage, have shown. In short,
without going quite so far as that Perceian stalwart, who
declared that the publication, some half-century ago,
of the actual Folio had " redoubled his admiration
for the excellent Bishop's poetic gift," we may, with
a clear conscience, pronounce most of the obloquy with
which he has met unnecessary and pedantic.

Despite its scores of editions and the innumerable
references to it in books of all sorts, from the most
learned to the most popular, it is doubtful whether the
collection itself is read as much as it ought to be—the

---

[1] The least excusable part of his conduct concerns the refusal to let the actual
MS. be known during the half-century of life which remained to him ; and if it
was his doing, the continuance of this which kept the world in ignorance for
another half-century afterwards. But at first this was no doubt due to the insensi-
bility above admitted ; and, as public opinion changed, reluctance to incur ever-
increasing disapproval would complicate the matter.

omission being partly due, no doubt, to the fact that almost all, if not quite all, its contents are accessible in other collections of poetry and editions of poets brought up to date.   Even persons who might, without too much fatuity, call themselves men of letters, have sometimes had to be reminded that such and such a thing is "in Percy."   But it is of course only by taking the book as it stands that its real merit and delight can be appreciated ; and even then there is perhaps necessary some rather unusual knowledge, of what its time did not know before it, to make the appreciation complete.   But without such knowledge sufficient satisfaction may be got out of this most precious reliquary by an ordinary reader, though the original fashioner of it was so afraid of unfavourable censure for having "bestowed attention on a parcel of old Ballads," that he drew up a mighty list of " men of learning and character "—including even that rather less than half-hearted ally Johnson himself—as compurgators, and that it might serve " as an amulet to guard him."

It was natural enough ; but he need not have looked for " amulets " beyond the store of " grandam gold," [1]

Intensity and immortality of the virtue of the book.
wrought into all manner of rings and torques and owches, that he had actually collected. It would almost have been worth being alive, ordinarily ignorant, but of years of tolerable literary discretion, in 1765, to have read the *Reliques* fresh from the press.   The reader, if he had had any tincture of letters, would have known " Chevy Chase," as well as not a few of the Elizabethan and seventeenth-century contributions.   A few more he might have picked up out of the earlier ballad- and song-books mentioned before ; [2] or, if he was really a book-

---

[1] An agreeable phrase of Dryden's.

[2] I venture to call attention to this, lest any reader should think that I put Percy too high.   Philips, Durfey, and the Scotch reprints have been already mentioned.   There is fair matter in the so-called Dryden's *Miscellanies*, and other names might be indicated.   But they are all scattered and scrappy as compared with the *Reliques*.

worm, out of the original editions. But much he could hardly have known, and a great deal more we may be quite certain that he did not know ; so that in a cursory survey of the wealth which lies along this " rich strond," one need not make pettifogging distinctions between absolute novelties to all but bookworms themselves, and other pieces.

Some fantastic persons have imagined clinical thermometers, of a kind different from those of ordinary science, and measuring human passions and emotions. If one could devise such an instrument as would accurately gauge poetic susceptibility, it would be very interesting to apply it to a suitable subject as he read for the first time, without any previous knowledge, the refrain of Percy's fourth piece, given to him by Sir David Dalrymple, otherwise and later Lord Hailes. There may not appear to be anything very wonderful in the words :

Edward, Edward,

which might be shouted by any slatternly mother or careless nurse to a truant or misdoing urchin. I do not myself take the least delight, and I do not think much of anybody who does, in z for y, or in the other characteristics of not very accurate Scots dialect. The unimpeached and not too " bellettristic " authority of the late Professor Child warrants the poem as itself " unimpeachable " as " one of the noblest and most sterling specimens of the genuine ballad " ; and it is impossible, though one may have been familiar with it from early youth, to avoid the thrill given by the mounting horror of the details, the infallible adjustment of the verse, and the dæmonic accompaniment of the (as has just been said) almost banal refrain, with its varied possible echoes of disguised suspicion, rising anxiety, and anticipation of the final curse on the subject of its counter-refrain, " Mither, Mither ! "

" King Estmere " gave our neophyte nothing so

intoxicating; but a good meal of ballad-stuff. And then he came to "Sir Patrick Spence" (or Spens). Anybody who says anything at length about "Sir Patrick Spens" at this time of day must have an extraordinarily good conceit of himself, or some entirely new information. Let us only observe that if the book had held nothing else it would have been "good value" for any price the publishers put on it. A new or presumedly new Robin Hood Ballad followed, and then the precisians are shocked by an "incongruous" admixture of Skelton and Hawes. The reader might have had worse pastime in 1765, when Glovers and Masons were alive and *scribent*, which is worse than rampant. One may of course wish that Percy had not amplified and watered "The Child of Elle" (one of his Folio windfalls) so extensively, and it is certainly a pity that he left out what seems to be originally part of it—the exquisite if not uncommon fancy of the rose and briar springing from the lovers' grave, and substituted a commonplace happy ending. But we must put ourselves in his readers' place and only think how infinitely good *for them*[1] it was to read :

> Now Christ thee save, thou little footpage,
> Now Christ thee save and see—
> O tell me how does thy lady gay
> And what may thy doings be,

at the time when even the great Mr. Gray, even the in some ways greater Dr. Johnson, were framing dead if correct Pindarics, and uttering rhetorical couplet verse.

To go right through the *Reliques* would be pleasant but inexcusable. Before, however, selecting a few
A variegated others of their constituents for comment, it
selection. may be observed that the promiscuity so much objected to by certain stop-watch critics—

---

[1] "He is important *for us*," said Sainte-Beuve to Matthew Arnold about Lamartine.

the way in which after a ballad, probably not much altered (except for some of Percy's patchings) since the fifteenth century, you come across an entire pastiche of his own, a scrap of Beaumont and Fletcher, or Daniel, or Lovelace, a genuine antique of the oldest, like the " Lewis Battle Song," or a golden windfall like " The Nut-Brown Maid "—this way will hardly be objected to by anybody who is not a hopeless, bloodless pedant. Such a quartet as " Sir Aldingar " (no matter what Percy did to it), " The Gaberlunzie Man," the virulent, though not undeserved, satire on Thomas Cromwell, and " Harpalus," which actually follow one another, must (though no one of them is positively of the first quality) have done infinite good to an eighteenth-century reader, if only because of the multifariousness of the shaking-up they must have administered to him. If he failed to observe the distinctions between them, he may have suffered a little— not much—harm ; but they were all poles apart from the Masons and the Glovers, even from the less good characteristics of Collins and Gray.

There is certainly not much good in " Hardyknute " after the first two lines ; but it is at least interesting as probably the first deliberately " faked " ballad we have, and as having borrowed something from that noble original which did not come into Percy's hands :

> King Easter courted her for her lands,
>   King Wester for her fee,
> King Honour for her goodly face
>   And for her fair bodie.

But the ring of this very stanza was frequent through Percy's originals, even when they were mishandled. Some even of his imitations could not fail to wake the dormant spirit of poetry from the effects of the soothing syrup of the antithetic couplet. How immensely better must our man of 1765 have been for reading the " Heir of Lynne," which is one of the

happiest examples of Percy's Watertonisings [1] of
ballads.

> He told him forth the good red gold—
> He told it forth with mickle din ;
> The gold is thine, the land is mine
> And I'm once more the Heir of Lynne.

The sweep and the rush of it are like the actual wind
clearing the atmosphere. That day you read no more
of the Glovers and the Masons.

A muddle of inferior yet still not unwelcome things
follows, including that libellous and blundering ballad
which (or something like it) had suggested to Peele
to mix up Eleanor of Guienne with Eleanor of Castille,
and, in one of the ugly fits in which patriotism sometimes indulges, to stain the memory of—

> Her who knew that Love can vanquish Death,
> Who, kneeling with one arm about her King,
> Drew forth the poison with her balmy breath
> Sweet as new buds in Spring.

But " The Beggar's Daughter of Bednall Green " and
" Sir Andrew Barton " and " Young Waters " and
" Mary Ambree " and " The Brave Lord Willoughby "
and " The Spanish Lady " — how infinitely better
must have been the state of a man of any mark or
likelihood in ways literary after, as compared with
before, his reading of these ! There are nine " Books "
in the *Reliques*, and we have got past the centre with the
end of the Fifth ; but there is still plenty to be thankful
for. The *Essay* on Langland's verse, which opens the
Sixth, is of course unillumined by many of our later
lights ; but there are some things in it which show that
mother-wit can sometimes dispense with book-lore.

---

[1] As that excellent and humorous, but perhaps now by some forgotten, Yorkshire
gentleman, traveller, and taxidermist, used, by his skill in the last-named art, to fashion
fantastic or appalling creations, appropriately stuffed from nature, so did Percy here
finish off, or rather introduce the finish, of the older piece by the very striking
incident of the lonesome lodge and the attempted suicide, which he took from a
wretched late chap-book form. The difference between the scholar and the pedant
could hardly be better shown than in Child's frank and reasoned acknowledgment
of this " improvement " as being really a great one.

The Book itself is a *macédoine* of mostly modern things ;
but "The Braes of Yarrow" and some others save it
from insignificance ; and Book Seven is introduced by
another of the Editor's Essays, this time on "Metrical
Romances," which pedantry scorns and literature
loves. In it, and in the following Book Eight, comes
in "the sweet of the night," the night of more than
Arabian magic that this country parson and town
courtier had conjured up. No matter that the old
peccatum or at least peccadillo of "faking" continues ;
that some, especially of the Arthurian pieces, are from
late and inadequate forms ; that, as a rule, Percy has
rather given the broken-down ballad-romances than
the pure ballad or the actual romance—which latter
indeed it was none of his purpose to give. Here is
that strangely unforgettable oath of "Glasgerion" :

> By oak and ash and thorn,

which has fired the hearts and brains of some good men
at least in every generation since. Here are "Child
Waters" and "Little Musgrave" and "Lord
Thomas" and "Gil Morrice," with, in a lower and
comic vein, "The Boy and the Mantle" and "The
Marriage of Sir Gawaine." All these are in the
Seventh Book. In the Eighth follow "Barbara
Allen" and "The Bailiff's Daughter," the ineffable
"Waly Waly," with "The King and the Miller of
Mansfield" for contrast, and a "stuffing" of not
disagreeable oddments. The Ninth, as might perhaps
be expected, is more a thing of shreds and patches, of
chips and sweepings, than the others, some of the con-
stituents being so recent as to come from Mallet and
Tickell. But he must be too much of the following of
Momus who quarrels with a miscellany containing in
one kind "The Dragon of Wantley" and in another
Lovelace's "Lucasta."

One may indeed very seriously question whether
at the time, and even to some extent since, this *pot-*

pourri character of Percy's work, which allows the delightful but almost contemporary " Winifreda " of Lewis (or somebody else) to appear side by side with much older matter, was not an almost unmixed good. For what was wanted (one may doubt whether the want does not persist in spite of all our teaching of literature) was to get people to recognise the continuity of things literary, and especially things poetical, in English History — to banish from their heads the accursed and Philistine notion that modern things alone were worth attention. It was not yet possible to do this thoroughly—to put " Deor " and " The Ruin," " Alison " and " E.I.O." on the exhibition board beside " Under the Greenwood Tree " and later verse. But Percy did a good deal towards this, and he poured—if not quite in " neat " condition—abundant doses of Ballad life-blood into the parching veins of his time.

We may go further and say that, with all respect to the labours of some six generations since, with all critical shortcomings that we can so easily point out, Percy's *Reliques* remains, and probably always will remain, one of the very best books of its kind, if not an almost unique book in that kind for rest and refreshment, for inspiration and delight. It would be easy to draw up a list of the great things from " The Ancient Mariner " onwards, that but for it we might not, or certainly should not have had ; but it does not require this additional consideration. " Take it and read it for itself " is, once more, the most important thing that need be said.

If anybody wrote, in the extensive and fearless old fashion, a *Dissertation upon Torture as applied to Books*
Warton and *and Authors*, a most interesting section might
his *History*. be allotted to the question " Which has suffered hardest things from the racks and pincers of modern scholarship—Percy, or his friend, follower, and in a manner complement, Thomas Warton ? " Most

people would probably prefer Percy's fate, for he has
only been abused and punished for his reticence as
to the actual contents of the Folio, by having those
contents made public. Warton's *History of English
Poetry* has been more cruelly treated. Percy's actual
work has been left pretty much to itself; Warton's
has been more than once severely re-edited—on the
last occasion with a virtuous but ruthless thoroughness
which leaves hardly a thread of the original in un-
disturbed contact with its comrade thrum. No one
whose pleasure it has been to study—still less any one
whose duty it has been to teach—our earlier literature,
can fail to be grateful for assistance received from the
forty-year-old work of Mr. Hazlitt, Dr. Furnivall,
Professor Skeat, and others, including the ever-helpful
Thomas Wright, his namesake the late Vice-Master
of Trinity, Sir Frederick Madden, Dr. Morris, and in
fact all the " Elder Statesmen " of Mediæval English
at the time and long before and after. As a thesaurus
the book has long been, and still is, invaluable. But
Warton's own work has been " translated " in it—not
indeed Bottom-fashion, but in a way which leaves its
original literary and artistic features almost unrecog-
nisable. As a book of reference, that original may be
allowed to have been totally antiquated by this rude heir
who has almost, as in the old joke, blotted out *Resurgam*
from its hatchment, and substituted *Requiescat in Pace*.
Any one who wishes his own refreshment and rest from
it must needs go back either to the actual *princeps*, or
to Price's edition, which, though adding and correcting, does not bury or disfigure the original.

The abundant citation of the book provides much
curious pasture, of a kind similar (though of course
more scrappy) to that furnished by the
Parallels between their character and fortune. *Reliques*, even for the laziest and most self-
indulgent of literary libertines, who merely
cares to skim the pages for it. But to a
person a little more advanced in knowledge, and a

little more industrious in gratifying taste, the whole is easily and delightfully legible. In Warton's actual critical faculty, as in that of his elder brother Joseph, there were indeed curious flaws; and, leaving the *History* for a moment aside, Joseph's *Pope* and Thomas's own *Spenser*, both extremely interesting books, show the fact strikingly and, to a reader who comes to them without much previous knowledge, it may be almost unintelligibly. Such a reader has heard the Wartons spoken, and rightly spoken of, as being among the foremost of romantic pioneers. He finds Joseph denying poetry to Donne, and after apparently planting and even using his batteries to drive Pope out of his pride of place altogether, readmitting him by a sort of postern. He finds Thomas picking holes in the Spenserian stanza. But these very inconsistencies and contradictions are valuable and interesting, because they show us the vacillation and uncertainty of the mind of the time. To remove that vacillation and uncertainty there could be no better way than—there could not be any half so good as—that provided by Warton's *History*—the way of exhibiting what earlier English poetry in all kinds, except drama, really was. It is immaterial that Warton does not always see the beauty of what he has unearthed, and that, still more frequently, he adopts a sort of mild patronising and apologising attitude towards it which is rather exasperating now. Probably it was the reverse, was actually conciliating, then.

And, once more, his judgments, whether in individual instances or in the *Dissertations* which, like Percy's *Essays*, suffer from the infancy of the study, are not the important part of the matter; though his central principle—that the palmy day of poetry up to his own time had been the Elizabethan—would make up for any deficiencies. He may have been sometimes inaccurate, though when we consider that (except Gray, who died before the *History* began to appear) the ground which he worked was hardly *terra cognita* to a single other person in England, we shall be slow to bring such accusations against him. He, like Percy, but on a wider scale, " fished the murex up " ; he pointed and blazed the way ; he brought back samples of the grapes of Eshcol which had been so long allowed to remain unknown in the true old domain of English literature. Since the institution of a British Academy some unknown but generous and intelligent person has instituted a lecture in Warton's honour on subjects connected with his and under his name. Sixty years earlier Thomas Wright and other good people started a " Warton Club," for publishing texts, which did excellent work, but died soon. On the whole, however, it may be doubted whether anything like sufficient honour has been paid to him. He has been accused of want of method ; but it may be questioned very seriously whether, in his time and for his purpose, method was the principal thing. It may be all very well, when the *materies* is really *publica*, to dispose it according to the views of a certain arranger, though even then there is the danger that the arrangement will be more thought of than the facts. In this case there was a huge neglected body of facts—much of it very precious —to be rummaged out, exposed, made accessible. It may be doubted whether, to be cumbered about too much serving, as actually happened in the case of Gray, would not have meant that the dinner would never have been served at all.

Chatterton could not have read Warton—a Fury rather than a Fate with abhorred shears had made that impossible. There has been, I think, some
Chatterton. speculation as to the effect which might have been produced on him by reading Percy, as he could have done and (pretty certainly) did not. That effect might have been an immense improvement ; it might have been complete silence. But the other might-

have-beens surrounding him—in a less picturesque and gracious fashion than the abstractions grouped round Keats in Shelley's apotheosis—are too many and too sinister to make it either pleasant or profitable to argue or to speculate upon them. Chatterton, if anybody in our literature, is *un grand peut-être* (or if any one insists on logical grammar "un grand *pouvait-être*"), with a note of interrogation after it. But it is practically of little use to talk about him from that point of view in our present connection. In those things of his that can be read easily he is simply not worth reading—as how should he be? What possible good can there be in the *vers de société* of a boy not yet eighteen, who had seen nothing that can be called society?—In the political and other satire of one who could know nothing about politics, and who had one of the worst patterns in the world—Churchill—before him?—In the miscellaneous writings of a stripling writing for bread at the commission of a gang of the lowest gutter-journalists? Outside "Rowley" Chatterton does not exist, for literature or for delight. I have never known—possibly there is something about it in *Notes and Queries*—whether there is any connection between Chatterton's inventions and the famous refrain—

> With a Rowley powley *gammon* and spinach,

but there is in the other sense both gammon and spinach—and they are two good things—in Rowley. Unfortunately, not only the endless controversy about genuineness, but other things interfere with one's quiet enjoyment of this excellent dish.

Controversy is the least part, if indeed it is any part at all, of the purpose of this book; and though it will be impossible to omit altogether, we must shorten as much as possible some remarks on available texts of Chatterton. To the present writer it seems a most unfortunate thing that the late Professor Skeat, in

Some hardships of his—not in his lifetime.

giving what is otherwise by far the best edition of Chatterton, should have modernised almost the whole of the Rowley poems. I have no veneration for " printers' spelling," and I hold that practically everything since the invention of printing, certainly everything since Elizabethan times, is better printed without the observance of forms now out of fashion. But Chatterton's spelling in " Rowley " was a definite part of the plan of the composition (" imposition " if anybody prefers the word), and you cannot judge the poetical value of his work without it. Professor Skeat's motive and object were of course purely philological ; he was horrified at the idea that any one should take Chatterton's bastard jargon for genuine dialect of any time. But his object might surely have been attained, if not by printing original and modernisation opposite each other throughout, which would perhaps have been the counsel of perfection, by taking a few poems and analysing the lingo used. At any rate it may be laid down peremptorily that no one can in the least appreciate the effect which Chatterton wished to produce ; or the effect which he actually produced upon his actual readers ; or, to be very bold and go further still, the permanent poetical value of the poems themselves, unless he reads them in the original spelling.

Unlucky, however, as Professor Skeat's proceeding seems to me, it is better than the almost incredible action of the late Mr. Watts (afterwards Watts-Dunton), who, in his selections from Chatterton for Mr. Humphrey Ward's *Poets*, actually presented a composite text framed out of Chatterton's own, Chatterton's " gloss words," and, when neither of these hit his own fancy, corrections of his own, *à la* Bentley, or *à la* Pemberton with Milton, besides as a rule modernising spelling.

It is all the more important to insist upon " neat " Rowley, because it is on Rowley pure and simple, in

the best sense of the latter adjective, that judgment
of Chatterton for enjoyment and refreshment must be
based. The inevitable paradox-monger has,
I believe, now and then endeavoured to
question the condemnation which qualified
judgment passes on the modern poems, and to discover signs of genius in the miscellaneous fragments.
It is one of the vainest of these usually vain pranks.
One can indeed hardly avoid wishing that all the
rubbish, prose and verse, could be utterly swept out of
possession and memory.   Always dull, always trivial,
often dirty, usually ill-natured, raw in taste and judgment to an extent rather pardonable than excusable
even in an underbred and half-educated boy — the
songs and miscellaneous pieces touch the lowest level
of eighteenth - century poetastry ; the satires are
Churchill-and-dirty-water ; the *Letters* are full of that
same vulgar coxcombry which disgusted Mr. Stevenson
(as it had others before him) in the not much later ones
of Burns.   One forgives them because of the intense
pathos of their writer's fate, and because of the flashes
of genius in Rowley.   But if ever a literary executor
would have been justified in what, no doubt, in
the abstract is the high treason of destroying work
committed to him—it would have been the man who
happened, as none actually was, to be in a position
enabling him to burn every scrap of Chatterton's
writing outside " Rowley."

> And much rubbish in him.

Yet the attraction of the Rowley poems is, after all,
a much more mysterious thing than most of the Rowley
controversialists have seen even afar off.   It
is partly metrical ; Mr. Watts made some
atonement for his meddling with the text by
stating what, it seems, nobody had definitely
stated before, that Chatterton, especially in *The
Tournament*, had anticipated Blake and Coleridge
in introducing trisyllabic substitution into the octosyllable after the example (probably) of Spenser.   But

> But Rowley —in Row-leian form— indispensable.

this is only very occasional. It is in the atmosphere—
an atmosphere produced by some magical combination
of thought, imagery, metre, diction, and the very
spelling itself—which he succeeds in communicating
to the Rowley poems (and to these only) that his secret
consists. The instance of the " Romance of the
Knight," with which he cajoled Burgum the pewterer
in both ancient and modern form, is critical in more
ways than one. The Rowley piece itself is not good
Rowley—the considerable Mephistophelian touch in
Chatterton probably took care that it should not be.
But, even as it is, it is better than the " gaudy, blabbing,
and remorseful " eighteenth-century phrase into which
the author has translated himself. In the highest
passages of all such, as the famous " Dirge in Ælla,"
the magic is unmistakable ; even Collins has not got
it, and you must go to Blake to find anything equal or
better. There is not much of the same quality elsewhere. The " Ballad of Charity " has been rather
overpraised, but there is some of the charm there ; and
where he got it Heaven or the Zeitgeist only can tell.
After all, as so constantly happens, there is nothing
better to do than to fall back on Johnson. He never
wrote anything formal on Chatterton ; there were
many reasons which may have prevented him, ranging
from the poor boy's vulgar, silly, and ignorant abuse of
himself to his own profound sympathy with a fate which,
if he had not been a man and a Christian, might have
been his own. But we know that he went down to
Bristol with Boswell, looked at the scenes and some of
the documents of the case, and came, as every rational
and instructed person has come, to the all but inevitable
conclusion. Yet he said, " This is the most extraordinary young man that has encountered my knowledge. It is wonderful how the whelp has written such
things." *And it was so*—" extraordinary," " whelp,"
" wonderful," and all.

The protest made in favour of " Rowley neat "

springs from no affection for Rowley's spelling in and
for itself. It is of course, when considered in isola-
tion, absurd—an eighteenth-century and schoolboy
exaggeration of the worst period of tricks in ortho- or
pseudography (the fifteenth and early sixteenth century)
ever known in English or French till Spelling Reform
came in. And the vocabulary which is bedizened with
it is, too often, worthy of the bedizening ; but both are
an essential part of Chatterton's work, and you might
just as well paint out the costume of any actual picture
as the artist drew it, and work it up to some modern
pattern, as interfere with this spelling and diction. In
the weaker parts of the poems it is of course merely
an additional nuisance. In the stronger and better it
does not interfere with their enjoyment, because it is
an integral part of them. In every case there is or
must be shifting of values of the most audacious and
possibly the most fatal kind, if any attempt is made to
interfere with it or with the diction.

Take a few examples. " Robes " is put for
" gites," " hardy " for " prevyd," " recompensed " for
" meeded out," and " represent " for " corven them " !
Now surely any one with an ear must see that the total
effect of phrase and line, where the words or groups of
words occur, is altered utterly by these substitutions.
How can a broad *o* like that in " robes " replace a sharp
i like that in " gites " ? How hopelessly different is
" corven them " from " represent " ? The modern
ignorance of what was well known so long ago as the
time of Dionysius of Halicarnassus—that phrase and
word, yea, actual syllable and letter, are indissolubly
connected with the expression of thought—could
hardly be better illustrated than here.

It is not altogether easy to decide, in the case of some
writers, whether they should come in this chapter or in
the next : but on the whole it has seemed desirable to
separate those already noticed here from their followers,

or in some instances contemporaries. To some persons it may seem that the change went on unhastingly, unrestingly, from the earliest pipe of half-awakened birds in Parnell and Lady Winchelsea to the unmistakable trumpet of the *Lyrical Ballads* ; others may admit an interesting and, though scarcely so in intention, a beneficent interruption, or reduction to muffled music, in the twenty or five-and-twenty years' domination of Johnson. But that the facts of the case, gnostically but impartially surveyed, require a certain " turning over " at different stages of the century, will hardly be denied. And here it appears that such a turnover is desirable.

CHAPTER IX

THE SETTING OF THE AUGUSTAN SUN

IT must have struck many people as more than a coincidence that Wordsworth was born in the same year in which Chatterton died, and Coleridge in that which saw the death of Gray. By less striking but still notable freaks or facts of chronology, Tom Warton had only been dead two years when Shelley was born, while Joseph lived till Keats was five years old and till the *Lyrical Ballads* themselves were getting into their second edition, with a certain famous Preface to it. Too great attention to such chronological casualties is no doubt idiotic: whether too great neglect of them does not merit an adjoining classification may be at least suggested. At any rate the dates, if contemplated with a very little thought, show that the last quarter of the century, speaking widely, must have been one of those periods big with change, which diversify and render interesting all kinds of history. There are those of course who would interject, " Why ! there was the French Revolution ! " and consider that a sufficient explanation of everything. For myself, I do not see how the French Revolution can have caused Wordsworth and Coleridge to have been born nearly twenty years before it occurred, though I do see how Gray and Percy and Warton may have influenced, in metaphysical as well as physical manners, their literary development. But we have here nothing

The last quarter of the century—its curiosities.

directly to do with Wordsworth or Coleridge. We have to do with that remarkable and interesting, if in most of its productions second- or third-rate, period of rather less than twenty years, which intervenes between the appearance of Cowper, Crabbe, Blake, and Burns, and the end of the century.

It has been called second- or third-rate, and perhaps these epithets demand an explanation, if not an apology.

Full of faults but too much decried. Gibbon is not second-rate, nor is Burke, in the work of this time, nor is Blake, nor is Burns, each in his own department, nor are some things in Cowper. But, as has been said already, we are not going to treat Blake or Burns in any detail; what has seemed necessary has already been said about Burke and Gibbon; and scattered excellences of the time, such as *Vathek*, have also had their turn. And on the whole it is, though full of interest, a distinctly second- or third-rate time, and what is more, its greatest interest is essentially alien from, if not actually rebellious to, the temper of the main body of the century—rebellious in a fashion particularly opposed to one at least of the terms of our title. A time of refreshment it still is; all times of literature are times of refreshment, if not to those living in them, to those who live after them, and know how to take the goods provided by the gods. But a time of rest it certainly is not; rather of fermentation, of effervescence, of much flowing of ginger-beer, of the bursting of flawed and feeble ginger-beer bottles, if also of the *cuvage* of strong wine to come. We have dealt with the novels and we have dealt with the dramas, the former the most promising, the latter as a whole the least so of the literary results of the time. We have spoken at least of its more serious work. There remain to be noticed here, with the restrictions already announced, the members of the great poetical quartette, and some at least of the small fry who play round them.

Although few people who have given any real attention to the subject can have wholly missed the
Cowper. point, it has perhaps not been so generally recognised as it might have been how unique Cowper is as a Rip van Winkle of literature. The bare fact that he was about twenty years older than the three other poets with whom he has been yoked, and who all began to publish at about the same time as he did, is of course generally known, if not generally realised ; and the other fact that this gap of twenty years was occupied in his case by mental disease, religious melancholy, and seclusion, not in the widest or farthest, but in something like the deepest depths of the then hardly accessible country, everybody also is supposed to know. But only a rather unusually attentive reader of the *Letters* can know—what the *Poems* only indirectly suggest—that during these twenty years Cowper read hardly anything, and during the next ten or twelve—the period of almost all his compositions and on the whole the best time of his life —not very much. The thoroughness of his groundings in the only education—that of the classics—which has any real " grounding " effect ; the liveliness of the society in which he passed his few years of youthful sanity ; and his own genius, together with the excellent use he made of such books as he had, disguise from us what, in some other circumstances and antecedents, would have been almost illiteracy. That he had apparently never heard of Collins till, thirty years after Collins's death, he read about him in Johnson's *Lives*, is only a fair specimen of the narrowness of his reading even before his breakdown. This narrowness no doubt accounts to some extent for the strange limitations and prejudices which meet us everywhere in his poems. But it also makes him, when it is taken in connection with those more favourable features above referred to—his birth, his breeding, his education, his society as far as it went, and so forth—a very useful

specimen of his age in extraordinary "preparations," using that word in a scientific sense. The stories of children, isolated purposely to observe the progress of their natural development, receive here a striking variant in actual experience. Nor does his unhappy infirmity destroy the value. When Cowper was not mad he was perfectly sane—a great deal saner than some people who are never technically mad at all.

The results of this singular physiological-literary adventure or experiment are to some extent ghastly— His value as explaining and explained by the character of the century. physiological experiment too commonly is. But they are not always so, and are almost always very instructive and very interesting. Before his occultation by an appalling blend of religious and other mania, Cowper seems (and it must be remembered that the occultation itself did not happen very early) to have been a rather ordinary kind of creature of his time—a gentleman (that he always was, except in one instance perhaps), a " wit and Templar," not of a " foolish face " at all, but of a very fair staple kind, a giggler and a maker of giggling when he could get agreeable subjects and companions in gigglement, as are most people who are good for anything, and a great many people who are good for nothing. He could write trifles very tolerably, and he had an early eye for scenery. (He discovered the beauties of the neighbourhood of Southampton before Gray and long before Gilpin.) Then there was the frightful drop of the curtain, which was never really lifted till the appearance of his first volume of *Poems*—for the *Olney Hymns* only represented lucid intervals ; and the lucidity was due to a kind of " hair-of-the-dog-that-bit-you."

I should be very sorry if the words just used were interpreted into a sense adverse to religion. I am myself quite sure, much as I admire Lucretius, that religion has never caused a thousandth or a millionth part of the ills that it has remedied ; and for my part

I am content—presumptuous as it may be—to take my chance with Hooker and Herbert, with Berkeley and Johnson, with Keble and Pusey. I know that the irreligiosity, and even the unorthodoxy, of the eighteenth century has been exaggerated. I am prepared to admit, on the other side, that the Church of England failed lamentably in its duty. But that the special influences under which Cowper fell were influences very much less of God than of the enemies of God, I, knowing something of their works and ways, will steadily maintain. In literature the Evangelical School was not quite despicable ; it gave us, besides Cowper's own hymns, many great ones of Charles Wesley's, and Toplady's " Rock of Ages," and some other real poetry, though its prose was very inferior. But its evil works were innumerable ; and I am nearly sure that Cowper would have been not only immeasurably happier, but a greater figure in English literature, if the Reverend Mr. Newton had been early conceded to the sharks to whom, no doubt, he had chucked so many (let us hope dead) slaves.

The *Hymns* require no long notice here, though there is astonishing quality in them. When we come *His extra-* to the first volume of the *Poems* the problem *ordinary* is of greater interest, though the actual *training.* satisfaction is less. The twenty years of unquiet sleep have evidently exercised on the author something of the strange effect which ordinary sleep exercises in the ordinary human being. He has grown, things have ranged themselves in his brain, too, tired as it has sometimes been ; he is in a way ready to grapple with them. But, as always happens, he wakes to some extent under the conditions under which he went to sleep, and he has had no experiences meanwhile to teach him better. *Truth* and *Expostulation* and the rest are much maturer than the scraps of verse, and the portion of respectable but seldom remarkable prose, which were produced before the catastrophe.

But the author has naturally enough taken bad models, especially his dead schoolfellow Churchill ; and, with much more than Churchill's general ability and poetical gift, he is writing without any glimmer of Churchill's knowledge of the actual world—its men, its things, and its circumstances.   His objects are far higher and better than Churchill's ; he has no personal or vicarious spite to gratify, and only in a respectable and honourable, if sometimes mistaken, way any personal or partisan axes to grind.   But he is writing essentially " in the air," and, what is more, in the air of a time which is not that of the actual day.   He has not found his way in form—he is still under the domination of the couplet ; he has not found his way in subjects ; he is still fumbling with the barren didacticisms and conventional abstractions which had sufficed Akenside and his fellows ; he has not found his way in treatment. Being what he is, a man of genius, he cannot help making this genius felt across the hampers and limitations just mentioned.   But if Cowper had written nothing except this Newton - endorsed collection he certainly would not have had the place he occupies here.   *Vile damnum* perhaps, but significant in a way.

Lucid intervals, and the still more *lucida sidera*—Lady Austen and Lady Hesketh—by whom they benefited, changed all this for a time ; and to Lady Austen and Lady Hesketh we owe the Cowper that " almost drove " Marianne Dashwood " wild," and that (though his effect on us, who are not feminine or seventeen, or at the junction of the eighteenth and nineteenth centuries, is quieter) still excites the emotion which poetry and poetry only can give.   To speak familiarly, Lady Austen was the box upon which Cowper struck, and to her, directly or indirectly, we owe not only *John Gilpin* and *The Task*, but almost everything else.   To Mrs. Unwin we owe, which is certainly something, the earlier prolongation of Cowper's existence ; but also that innocent but prolonged worry of his later years, which almost certainly brought about the fatal close. An ordinary scapegrace may be permitted his Elvine and his Fifine ; an extraordinary person like Shelley may be at least allowed his Mary and his Miranda. But a slightly effeminate and very pious gentleman had perhaps better not write both

> The star that shines on Anna's breast

and

> My Mary !

Nor, without any " perhaps " at all, should he give outsiders to understand that " Anna " had pushed herself into his and " Mary's " society till she became a nuisance.

But it is with the effects of these various situations on Cowper's poetry, and the singular correlation of those effects with the progress of poetry itself during the century, that we are concerned. He has, let it be once more remembered, read little,[1] and when Hill sends him the *Lives of the Poets* as they appear, they are a sort of revelation to him. But he has his old classical grounding to go upon ; and when he resumes attention to this, the pseudoclassicism of the century seems, whether as a result of his own nature or of the progress of the years, to lose not all but much of its hold upon him. He had been born when Pope was undisputed monarch of English poetry : and when he first retired from the world, though Pope had been dead for some years, nobody had appeared as his successor, while such hints at rebellion as Warton's were made in a gingerly fashion, and generally regarded as flat heresy. There is no evidence—and considering his almost complete booklessness at Huntingdon and in the earlier Olney years, it would have been strange if there had been any—of his knowing much of Gray ;

And his unparalleled literary position.

---

[1] He refers more than once to a library of some value, coming from his father and brother, which he had possessed while living in the Temple, and which had somehow disappeared in the trouble of his madness ; but this does not go for much.

we have seen that he knew nothing of Collins ; and he seems not to have taken any interest in, even if he knew anything of, the *Ossian* and Chatterton controversies or the two chief *promi* or storekeepers of romantic knowledge, Percy and Warton. Yet he has found out for himself the central lever for setting the new poetry in motion, that is to say, discontent with Pope's couplet. And when, under the influence of the Anna to whom he behaved so shabbily, he found and turned to one of his truest vocations, description of country, he showed at once that he was not in the least a mere pupil of Thomson. Justice, it is hoped, has been done to Thomson here. But his "nature" had been treated either in rather wide sweeps of the brush or in minute touches like that of—

> The yellow wallflower stained with iron-brown,

which, observe, is after all *generic* rather than individual. And you will not find in *The Seasons* anything like this other touch or combination of touches :

> Hence *ankle deep in moss and flowery thyme*
> We mount again, and *feel at every step,*
> *One foot half-sunk in hillocks green and soft,*
> Raised by the mole—the miner of the soil,

or the distinctive sketches of trees [1] so interesting to compare with the shorter labels of Chaucer and Spenser, which follow this within some twenty or thirty lines of *The Sofa*.

But additional accuracy and suggestiveness of description was not the only, if it was not the least, thing that Cowper gained from that " strange and shaken " night of twenty years—so little fertile directly—indirectly so much so. The qualities of the century—its placidity, its not altogether profound but at any rate not quite superficial meditativeness, its pleasantry, its homeliness, and some other of its good things, he had had,

His style, criticism, versification, etc.

---

[1] Gilpin's elaborate tree-studies in prose were subsequent to Cowper's.

as it were, " cellared " into perfection. But the cellarage had developed new qualities, of which there are only prophetic signs in those writers who were writing when he " left the herd." In *John Gilpin* itself what a curious combination of attractions, hardly to be recognised at all without a considerable acquaintance with the history of literature! The peculiar ballad form is one of these. It has been said that Cowper does not show much influence of Percy. Yet before the *Reliques*, even with the assistance of " Namby's " collection, it would hardly have been chosen. Dryden, though much too great to disdain it, would have found it out of fashion. Pope would have let the fashion influence him. Gay and others, though they might have utilised it, would have not known what to do with it in this particular connection. Cowper has got it as nobody, except Gray in " The Long Story," had got it before, and there are a world of differences between them (besides Gray's double rhyme). Take the thing on the face of it, like the " Story," and it is a " tale of a tub," a history of nothings, which ends very much as it began, except for the fate of the two regretted bottles of what was too probably, in Fielding's language, " win*d*," rather than " win*e*." Taken as a caricature of the ballad, it is an utter failure, because it is too good. But as getting out of a form, and to some extent under its strict conditions, every ounce of its possibilities—as a lasting masterpiece of the comic kind, it is, as the unbiassed and unsophisticated judgment of five generations has held it to be, perfect. And it may be doubted whether it could have been written in any other conjuncture of man, time, and circumstance than the later period of the century which produced " Molly Mog " and the " Long Story " itself, and the *Reliques*.

The far-flooding influence of recent poetry on form and mood appears in Cowper elsewhere fitfully, and with a strange intermixture of that of the time of his

z

birth. Of the one great curse of the century, its
" poetic diction," he never got cured, and it was almost
impossible that he should, since his later studies were
mostly in Milton, the god who, by admixture with
very inferior daughters of men, begat that gigantic
error. To some extent, no doubt, he saw the absurdity
of it, but he somehow never could prevail on himself
to give it up, except where, as in *The Castaway*, supernal
or infernal fire burnt the rubbish out. The Thing
(for it really deserved Cobbett's capital T in another
case) never released its clutch on him. When at Bath,
in his seventeenth year, he wrote—

> This ponderous heel of perforated hide,

it may have been a joke. When at fifty-four he mentioned in *The Sofa*—

> The pangs arthritic that infest the toe,

the joke may have persisted. But when, six years
later, or later still, on the eve of the final occultation
(save for the terrible gleam of *The Castaway* itself) he
wrote his own greatest poem,—one of the greatest of
the whole century, and a clear prophecy of the still
greater things to come in the next,—and hung upon the
guiltless branches of *Yardley Oak* the frippery of—

> Excoriate forks deform,

he would have been guilty of an impossible lapse of
taste if there had been any burlesque intention. The
habit had maintained itself and prevailed.

Yet in these last few years of at least occasional
happiness—happiness which might perhaps have
lasted had it not been for the diabolic conduct of
Newton, the crass idiocy and charlatanism of Teedon,
and the most unfortunate illness of Mrs. Unwin—
extraordinary signs of poetic progress are visible,
even outside the two masterpieces just referred to.
The unmatched urbanity of the eighteenth century
appears everywhere. It is a pity, no doubt, that he

adopted from Gay and Byrom and Shenstone what
has been more truly than kindly called the " rocking
horse " metre of the triple anapæst, which can be so
easily mended, as Byron and Praed and Mr. Swinburne have shown, into a stately and magnificent
measure. His subjects were occasionally inadequate ;
he was right to be fond of fish, but a poet who can
celebrate halibut must lack some of that discrimination
which should be a characteristic of the poetical character. In the eighteenth century dwellers inland had
to take what they could get in the way of what the
French delightfully call *marée*—a term which sur-
rounds the actual fish with the sound and the sight and
the smell of the sea. But when there are not only
salmon and trout, turbot and brill, John Dory and
mullet, but whiting and whitebait and sole and herring
and flounders and sprats—nay even plaice and bass
and skate and gurnet and other worthy if second-
rate fish—to eat and to celebrate in verse a thing which
is at best a cooked cotton counterpane, is shocking.[1]
But let us set against this slip of Cowper's his memorable dictum on wine. He had no foolish scruples on
that point—the Evangelicals of his time never had—
and his friends were commendably assiduous in stocking his cellar. But he tells Lady Hesketh that he had
never found any wine that really suited him except
port ; and there can be little seriously wrong with a
man who says that, either in taste or in purely physical
constitution. There may be narrowness and exclusive-
ness in it—they were faults of Cowper's age, creed,
and perhaps character: but as far as it goes and on
the positive side, it is admirable.

What Cowper might have been as a poet is perhaps
only shown in *Yardley Oak* and *The Castaway*. The
rest—even *John Gilpin*, even the best passages in *The*

---

[1] It is comforting to remember that Peacock, who seldom goes wrong on such
points, has solemnly, through the competent and canonical mouth of Dr. Opimian in
Gryll Grange, excommunicated this abominable Brobdingnagian dab.

Task and the prettiest of the smaller poems—is second-rate of various degrees,[1] from the very " best second " to something much above the average.　These two are first-rate, though they differ remarkably in individual quality.　The last, as is often the case with last words, has more of the older fashion in it—the first

The Castaway and Yardley Oak. that of the time which was to come.　In the magnificent and terrible *Castaway* there is nothing outside the eighteenth century except a certain concentration and intensity which are rarely found there, and which rather sublimate and transform the usual phenomena than add anything to them.　It is all quite quiet ; the diction, while not offensively " poetic," is ordinary, and to some extent conventional ; it has a concrete subject, a story of the time which you could illustrate easily in the charming fashion of that time.　A vignette heading of the ship with bursting canvas, and a tailpiece of " the cask, the coop, the floating cord " almost impose themselves.　But the " maniac's tongue," the " hopeless hand " of Mrs. Browning's graceful threnody has infused or superimposed something quite different in and upon this " language of ordinary life."　If the doctrine of *furor poeticus* is to be pushed so far that nobody is to write poetry unless he is in an access of actual delirium, and if *The Castaway* is a fair sample of what will result, almost might one become a Wordsworthian.

　　It is strange that these two, as masterpieces of Cowper, should both suggest Wordsworth in however different ways.　*The Castaway* suggests the doctrine which he so carefully abstained from carrying out in all his own triumphs ; *Yardley Oak* suggests the spirit which helps to give these masterpieces, relieved as they are of the doctrine's burden, their inexhaustible charm.

---

[1] Perhaps *Boadicea* is first-rate : and some might claim that rank for *The Royal George*.　But in each the subject (*i.e.* what is given to, not by, the poet) claims a very heavy royalty on the value.

That the poem was not finished is an open allegory.
There was no reason in the author's health or other
circumstances why it should not be ; for his mind did
not break down finally for more than two, and nearly
three years, after the portion we have was written ; and
he had composed not a little verse, good if not supreme,
meanwhile. But Fate denied metaphysical aid for the
conclusion, and left it to the younger man, who, before
it was actually written, had composed the *Evening
Walk*, who at twenty-three, when its author might still
have finished it, was writing the *Descriptive Sketches*,
and who was to publish *Tintern Abbey* before Cowper's
death. There are few instances in literary history of
such a handing on of a very special torch of poetry
with no gap of darkness.

It is rather the fashion, I believe, just now to
belittle *Yardley Oak*, at any rate to deny that it, to
any considerable extent, anticipates Wordsworth. This
last point need not be argued at any length here, for
it is in a way out of our bounds.[1] But the value of
the poem itself is not. There is a combination of
massiveness and " atmosphere " about the piece which
I at least do not know where to match earlier in the
actual century, and which, out of Spenser and Shakespeare, I cannot remember having been reached by any
other earlier English poet, for Milton could hardly
have taken the point of view. And as we read it,
besides enjoying its poetical excellence, we have to
remember how many of the minor influences coming
on the century it embodies or at least suggests—the
historic sense, hitherto unknown, the imaginative
envisagement of everything, the half-pantheistic feeling
of the community of man and nature and God. The
poem, as has been hinted before, perhaps outruns the
eighteenth century proper a little ; but it may be

---

[1] It may be enough to say that the denial is an interesting instance of that
uneasy " revaluation of old values " in others which often distinguishes those
incapable of enlarging their own actual capital.

claimed by that century as its own, not merely in sheer chronology, not merely in virtue of the diction, which could be spared, but in virtue also of a certain *justesse* and moderation of thought and phrase which are essentially Augustan.

Although Crabbe and Cowper (putting aside what may be called the latter's " antenatal " work) began to write, or at least to publish, practically at the same time, and although the eighteenth century in some ways is as strong in the younger man as in the older, the difference of their circumstances was immense. There is an old French story, the authorship and origin of which escape one, but in which the prosperous father of a not obviously ne'er-do-well, but unprosperous, son is asked why that son and his wife have never got on in the world. The answer is, " They began with the chicken "—the not very recondite explanation being that the father and mother had begun life in very narrow circumstances, and had gradually advanced till they could afford that " chicken in the pot " which, as far back as Henri Quatre, has been the legendary ideal of the French peasant ; whereas the younger pair started with this, and with habits in a concatenation accordingly. How does this apply to Cowper and Crabbe ? Marry, tropically. Cowper started, not indeed in great prosperity as far as actual means went, but with indefinite but most promising prospects, in an atmosphere of gentility and giggles and the chances in love which, if they were not fortunate, were made unfortunate, to speak kindly, by his unhappy affliction, to speak unkindly, by his want of application, of self-command, and of " the stalk of *carle* hemp " generally. He ended, not merely in despondency and madness, but in what, but for the charity of relations, would have been utter poverty. Crabbe was, as the phrase goes, nursed in a much sterner school ; and for a time nearly as long as that of Cowper's fallacious semi-prosperity

Crabbe.

and wasted chances, he wrought hard, loved hopelessly,
tried every way to exercise his proper vocation, and was
only admitted to that exercise at last by the fairy-tale
goodness of Edmund Burke. He was prosperous
ever after; and if he was not entirely happy in the
marriage which followed pretty soon, the causes of his
unhappiness do not appear to have been of the worst
kind. The last twenty years of his long life seem to
have been actually happy almost without alloy.

But either the crosses and disappointments of his
youth, or the dreadful though very scantily recorded year
of struggle which he passed in London before
A knell to his luck with Burke, would seem to have
cheerfulness: made an indelible impression on him. And
but not some light is thrown upon his temperament
always.
by a further comparison with Cowper, and also with
his own nearer contemporary, Chatterton. Chatterton,
after a struggle of the same kind, but less prolonged and
apparently more chequered with gleams of hope than
Crabbe's, committed suicide. Cowper, between fear
of what would happen to him after death and fear of
reading documents before the House of Lords in life,
attempted it. Crabbe, we know, walked during the
whole night, between lodging his letter to Burke and
getting an answer to it, about and on Westminster
Bridge; but there is no suggestion of his being
tempted to throw himself over it. So much the better,
no doubt; but the harder and manlier temperament is
likely to retain longer the impress it has received in
youth. Cowper could at times quite forget his woes,
in actual pleasantry or in temporary but quiet comfort;
one is not sure about what Chatterton might have done
if he had tided over the fatal moment. Prosperity
might not have been much better for him than adversity: for there was a good deal in him which reminds
one of his predecessors Savage and Churchill, though
he had far greater genius than both put together. In
no case, however, can one imagine him a serious and

rather gloomy realist. That is what Crabbe is, and as
such he strikes a new note—and one fatal to the
Augustan peace—in the chorus of the Augustan poets.
Of course there had been *Night Thoughts* and *The Grave*;
of course people had meditated among tombs, and so
forth. But most of these things had been done either
from a definitely religious point of view, or with regard
to the end of life, and the various other old moralities
of a general kind. It was reserved for Crabbe not
merely to write " the annals of the poor," but to deal
with the seamy side of ordinary life, the disappointments of ambition, the vanity of wishes—neither in the
copybook fashion of the preacher,[1] nor in the yet-to-
come extravagances of Byronism, *maladie du siècle*,
etc., but with a deadly verisimilitude—similar to, and
perhaps to some extent partly derived from, that which
the novelists had more cheerfully put in practice.

From all former handlings of his own class of matter,
Crabbe's stood almost startlingly distinct and separate.
With the old swain-and-nymph, Hobbinol-and-Bum-
kinetta business, his verse has nothing to do—in fact
that was out of fashion—even for parody—by his day.
But his handling of country subjects and common town
life stands—if not in quite such glaring contrast—
almost as clearly distinguished from Goldsmith's in
The Deserted Village not long before, and Cowper's in
The Task not long after he himself began. It is
amusing, though in rather a grim way, to body forth
a Sweet Auburn, *before* its misfortunes, as it would have
been painted by the author of *The Village*; and
though " Crazy Kate " and one or two other passages
show us that Cowper was neither indifferent to, nor
ignorant of, the sufferings of the poor, his treatment of
them is still idealised and conventionalised in adjustment with actual scenery; while in dealing with that
actual scenery, though he realises more, he almost always
beautifies wherever it is possible. Crabbe never does

---

[1] *Not* the author of *Ecclesiastes*.

this ; he seems indeed to have little sense of beauty at all.[1] Nor does he confine his realist dealings to mere " tales of mean streets," of mean cottages, workhouse, or fishing-boat hells. Consider his masterpiece, that wonderful picture of autumnal sadness which has collected so many eulogies of greater as well as smaller men—the landscape seen by the foolish and luckless hero of " Delay breeds Danger," who has bartered love for patronage and lucre. Observe the Dutchmanship with which he depicts low tide, and the mudbanks, and the dismal wreckage of the shore at such times, the slimy mooring-posts, the broken boats. Consider again that study of " The Natural Death of Love," which is at once so characteristic of the century, and yet so unlike any treatment of the subject that you would be likely to find earlier.

> Right little mirth there is therein, God wot !

and yet you cannot say that there is actual lamentation and mourning and woe, for everything is too quiet. There are no *alti guai* in Crabbe: if there were, his eighteenth centuriness would be gone. But it may perhaps be admitted that, just as his life was extended far beyond the confines of the century itself, and though his best work was at least published (the exact dates of its writing are rather uncertain) during this latter part of it, so the colour of this work, never losing its eighteenth-century basis, took further tints and shades from his later circumstances. Although the eighteenth century itself was thoroughly real, it was seldom real*ist* ; it would hardly have been as restful and refreshing if it had been. Its melancholy, up to all but the last, had but been the " leucocholy " of Gray, or the (mostly religious) dread which ran to madness in Cowper, and sometimes

---

[1] It is possible that this may be misunderstood. His art is sometimes admirable as in the passages mentioned and others ; and it may be contended that where there is admiration there is beauty. On the other hand where there is ugliness there can sometimes be love, as Tassoni showed long ago, and as Ausonius had formulated long before Tassoni. But you cannot, at least I cannot, love anything in Crabbe though you really admire it. And beauty should draw both admiration and love.

threatened madness in Johnson. And though it seldom, save in exceptional personages like Collins and Blake, touched fantastic beauty, it never liked mere ugliness.

Burns, and Blake himself, falling out for reasons already mentioned, and the novelists, the historians, Burke, and some miscellaneous writers of the last twenty years of the period having been already handled, we are left with a curious class or group of work, in which this double decade stands alone or almost alone, as producing first-class work of a special and peculiar kind difficult to parallel elsewhere. This is the curious outburst of satiric verse—mainly political but to a certain extent literary and general—which began with *The Rolliad* and culminated in the *Anti-Jacobin* on the political side, and which extended towards the literary, sometimes in the very same pieces by the very same persons, and sometimes in more specifically titled and intended things like Gifford's *Baviad* and *Mæviad* and Mathias's *Pursuits of Literature*. For sheer amusement this shelf-ful of work is difficult to beat ; and it blends itself, in a truly English and Shakespearian manner, with the more romantic and the more serious work of the time.

Omission of Burns and Blake—the Satirists.

In fact, it may be said (without any of that exaggeration for a special purpose which is too common) to be a very notable outcome of the ways, circumstances, and character of the century as an earlier whole.

Of course neither political satire, nor literary satire, nor even the combination of the two, was a new thing in English ; and Churchill and Mason, if not even Addison and Pope, had already extended the range of the scourge of verse to other arts—acting, music, painting, architecture, etc. *Hudibras* had been an English Classic, and Dryden's Popish plot satires still more so, for over a hundred years when *The Rolliad* was published. Shorter and lighter " skits " in verse had not been

Curious causes of this development.

unknown, either in the seventeenth century or in the earlier eighteenth, when Chesterfield, Pulteney, Walpole, Williams, Stevenson had been adepts at them. But *The New Bath Guide* had more recently had a great effect, popularising easy verse of all sorts ; journalism, and its foster-child, the professional man of letters, had increased and multiplied ; and lastly, politics, with the appearance of the younger Pitt first, and the rage aroused by him in the so long dominant Whig faction, and then the French Revolution, had become less and less of a " civil game " of persons and interests, more and more of a deadly struggle of principles and passions. Meanwhile, in literature, divers new absurdities were making their appearance as a result, now of the romantic now of the revolutionary spirit, and now again of the fossilising and self-caricaturing of eighteenth-century conventionality and sentimentalism. Light horsemen like the lampooners of *The Rolliad*, a born Ishmael like " Peter Pindar," whose hand was almost impartially against any one in whom he saw a possible butt—George the Third, his Queen, that Queen's chief bedchamber-woman, the Royal Academy, Sir Joseph Banks and scientific " collecting," Mrs. Piozzi, Boswell, everybody and everything ; critics of half-pedantic good sense and wholly pedantic temper like Gifford and Mathias ; " gentleman-and-scholar " defenders of law and order and social happiness against the Tophet-let-loose of Jacobinism, like Canning and Frere—all found their subjects ready for them, and all flew upon the spoil.

That things which seem very funny at one time may seem very dreary at another is a sufficiently hack-neyed truism ; but it is equally true that there are funny things which never lose their fun. If, for anybody, the political and miscellaneous satire of 1780–1800 is not in this latter case, it can only be due either to the incapacity of the individual, or to a drawback which undoubtedly does apply, too often, to this class of literature. It some-

Some details on them.

times, if not usually, needs, for people of ordinary reading and ordinary memory, a great deal of explanation. Even in its own days Mathias had, or thought he had, to overload his text with notes in a manner which was even then considered rather a nuisance, and which now makes what is perhaps itself the least amusing book of the whole shelf duller still, if still not quite dull. Even the unsurpassed brilliancy of the best *Anti-Jacobin* things is not quite free from dependence on annotation. But this has been supplied in some cases ; it would be easy to do, and would be worth doing, in those of the whole *Rolliad* and even of Wolcot. In fact something of the same kind as the well-known and invaluable *Répertoire* of Balzac's characters could be executed in no very great space, and would apply to all the matter here dealt with. For, as was said above, there is nothing quite like this group. The habit continued during the earlier nineteenth century, and produced good things on both sides, especially in the hands of Moore. It was revived at intervals later by Praed and Mansel and H. D. Traill, and there is one young living practitioner of it who deserves very high praise.[1] But for concentration, during a manageable period, on nearly the same set of events and persons, by a few but eminent hands, there is nothing like it in our own, nor, I think, in any literature. The atmosphere is indeed not exactly peaceful, and the battle is not always one of flowers or even of pretty hard *confetti*. But the records of it provide as good refreshment as any one need desire.

Except for singularly unintelligent or uninterested folk (and it is almost safe to say that, as is the intellect so is the interest), not the least part of the refection derivable from this curious department of literature should be given by the subjects and circumstances of the satire. On the political side we must not be too discur-

Especially the character and position of the younger Pitt.

[1] Mr. Ian D. Colvin ("I. C." or "Rip van Winkle ").

sive.   It is sufficient to remind, or to inform, readers
who do not want to go much into detail, that, for
some half-century in England, after the great and to
this day not entirely explained collapse of the Tory
party during the death-agony of Anne, the Whigs,
though quarrelling violently with each other, and losing
all or almost all grasp of principle in regard to politics,
had been masters of the political situation, and had
done practically what they chose.   It would be very
agreeable to the present writer to say a good deal on
this head ; but it would be irrelevant, and irrelevance
on serious matters is worse than the sin of witchcraft,
because it is not attractive as that sometimes is.   When
George the Third came in, and there once more was a
chance for Toryism, it was handicapped for a long time
by the unpopularity of Bute and the what-shall-any-
man-in-a-single-word-call-it of North.   Then came
Pitt the younger, and the Whig hell trembled to its
centre.   At first Pitt was no more a Tory than his
father had been, and he never became one in consistent
theory ; it is perhaps one of the greatest misfortunes
in English history that he did not.   But he set himself,
from the very first, against the Whig principles—if
they can be called principles—of corruption, place-
hunting, family influence, indifference to the general
welfare of the country, and the kind of silly academic
republicanism which has been noticed in Horace
Walpole.   That intense patriotism which Macaulay
conceded to his father, and which it is surprising that
a Whig like Macaulay [1] should have been able even to
recognise, burnt in Pitt the younger with a less brilliant
but an even intenser flame ; and the mere wood, hay,
and stubble of party interests and party shibboleths
disappeared in it like straw in a furnace.

It is not difficult to imagine the surprise, the horror,

---

[1] He was of course a peculiar Whig, and had been a Tory.   It was the remains
of the Tory that showed here, and in *Horatius* and in *Marston Moor* and in *The
Armada* and in the *Jacobite's Epitaph*.

and the gradually concentrated wrath which such a phenomenon must have caused in the occasionally buzzing and swarming, but on the whole tranquil, hive of Whig placemen and partisans. They had their own chief, Fox, a person of pleasant manners, loose but not offensive life, plentiful brains, some scholarship, and a perfect readiness to let England go to the devil if he could win a party triumph, make a telling speech, receive if possible a lucrative place, and spend his revenues (and a great deal more) on wine and cards and women. Pitt did not object to Bacchus, but he was *parcus et infrequens cultor*, if not an absolute enemy, of Venus; he did not gamble; and though perhaps in rather different ways he was at least as good a scholar as Fox, he was indifferent to general literature, and till he fortunately met with the concurrence of Windham, lost a great deal in that way.

How he daily grew a portent and an abomination to the Whigs can be readily appreciated on general grounds; but perhaps only those who are old enough to remember the general election of 1874 can know how the mere possibility of a Tory domination struck the holders, as they thought seriously, of power ninety years earlier. These political epoches [1] are not only important but very amusing; a man must perhaps have seen the faces of his Liberal friends when they turned from the club telegraph boards forty years ago, to grasp completely what the Foxites must have experienced.

But this political explanation and exploration must be accompanied by a literary one, if we are really to Literary revolution-aryism. appreciate the entertainment provided by the matter on which we are now engaged. In the very year of the appearance, or at least the conception, of *The Rolliad*, Johnson died, and a great change came over the literature of the century. The sceptre, or at least the ferule, fell into no other

---

[1] The form is Dryden's, and sometimes fits better than the shorter one.

hand ; and the literary Israel for a time was masterless.
Some persons who had actually come within Johnson's
circle were to stray rather terribly afterwards. Many
have shuddered in thinking what words he might have
addressed not many years later to that Helen Maria
Williams (who was indeed a very pretty girl, and not
a bad writer now and then) instead of the famous
" Madam, if I am very ill when you are near me, what
should I be were you at a distance ? " Alas ! Helen
Maria became not merely a Jacobin, but a poetastress ;
and other poetastresses and poetasters sprang up like
mushrooms, as soon as the devastating tramp and
scythe of the great dictator were removed. The promotion (just at the time, and connected with the idea
of the *Probationary Odes* that followed *The Rolliad*) of
Tom Warton to the Laureateship was an excellent thing
in itself ; but was certain to result in an efflorescence of
pseudo-romance, as well as of romance proper. *Thralia
dulcis*, now no longer Thralia, fleeing to Italy in
not immoral but rather ignoble company, had already
forgathered with the egregious Merry and his Della
Cruscans. At home the ineffable Hayley was maundering and twaddling, and the (in some ways) respectable Darwin was elaborately reducing to the absurd the
whole theory and practice of standard eighteenth-
century diction, versification, and handling of subject.
In other directions people were beginning to " have a
taste "—of a kind quite different from those tastes which
Pope had satirised, and different again, though there
was more connection between old and new here, from
those of which " Strawberry " had become at once the
temple, and the museum, and the symbol.

Let us for a minute suspend the survey, or rather
re-survey it from different points of view. It is im-
The total portant for the reader to realise the situation.
" moment." A political revolution, for the time only of a
party character, but destined before half a dozen years
had passed to be at once intensified by and merged into

the most momenotus European cataclysm which has
happened till our own time, and of a character somewhat unusually wide-reaching.   The dissolution of a
literary dynasty, and as yet the appearance of no
legitimate successor—only a sort of welter of *minimities*.
One eminent figure, with some personal weaknesses, in
politics; a King, who though far stronger and better than
was thought, had some vulnerable points, and was to
have, for unscrupulous assailants, more; an unpopular
Queen; one of the most virulent instances (chiefly
due to Fox's unsportsmanlike devices) of the habitual
enmity between King and Heir Apparent; undecided
but considerable social changes.   Add to this a literary
convention, still not overthrown, which had established itself for generations in ways very largely
satiric; an education—common to all men on both sides
of politics, and to the aristocracy, the upper and middle
class generally — which enabled men thoroughly to
enjoy a certain kind of this satire; a comparatively idle
upper class, abundantly sinecured; a professional class
keen for promotion and skilled at literary arms; a
rising trade of men of letters from almost the highest
to almost the lowest class, ready to play Swiss of
Heaven (or the other place) for pay as great as they
could get, but almost as small as would keep them alive.
No very great writers in any popular department of
literature to carry off attention.   No religious controversy of a serious kind to divert that attention.
Everything, in short, propitious for a fool-hunt in
politics, literature, and a fringe of other interests.

   " The Hunt was up," as mentioned above, with *The
Rolliad*, and the *Probationary Odes*, on the vacancy in
The Rolliad, the Laurel arising from the death of that
   etc.   innocuous William Whitehead—" Clean "
Whitehead, as a nineteenth-century epigram on another
pair [1] has been transferred to him—of whom nobody
need say anything very bad, and of whom the by

---

[1] The Broughs.   " Clever " Whitehead was Paul.

no means heedless charity of Mr. Austin Dobson has contrived to say something rather good. The quarry was, in one direction, Pitt and his followers, from Jenkinson and Dundas down to public butts like Sir Joseph Mawbey and Sir Cecil Wray, through intermediates, of whom the chief was the wealthy and powerful Devonshire squire Rolle, of the same family as Horace Walpole's detested sister-in-law Margaret, and to the Whigs a very Goliath of Toryism in the West. On the other side were the real or supposed candidates for the Laurel, from Warton, the destined possessor, to any (and sometimes the same) literary and political scrubs who might have incurred the lampooners' wrath or contempt. Exactly who the chief huntsman was is not certainly known, but the post is generally conferred upon the Irish civilian French Lawrence— a Winchester and Oxford man of great ability, and an intimate friend of Burke,—who is said to have made to him the confession that he thought the famous " Windsor Castle " passage his own finest, and to have illustrated from it his theory as to such passages, that they should contain a thought, an image, and a senti- ment intertwined. The whippers-in, or in proper phrase, " prickers " (a peculiarly appropriate title here), and the general meyny of the hunt included Sheridan now and then, Richard Burke, Richard Fitzpatrick (brother of the second husband of Horace's favourite, Lady Upper Ossory, ci-devant Duchess of Grafton), Lord John Townshend, Burgoyne, who could write rather better than he could fight, Tierney, a rather wandering star of some brightness, who afterwards refused to follow the Foxites into treason, and Ellis, who also " found salvation," and was a stauncher Tory than Tierney later. It will be seen that this squadron of light horsemen —most, though not all of whom were Irish—had, in abundance, qualifications for a literary-political guerilla; and he must be a very violent and perhaps not a very intelligent partisan who declines to be amused at their

2 A

feats because they were on the Whig side. In fact
a Tory admirer can hardly claim much credit for
catholicity, inasmuch as the strife was of such a purely
party-personal character that very few questions of
principle came in. Nothing indeed could contrast
more strongly with the life-and-death struggle in which,
some fifteen years later, Ellis once more engaged on the
other side. They used some ceremony in attacking the
King, and the Prince was of course on their own side,
fortunately for him, for though the faults of " Gor-
gius " have been exaggerated, and his merits obscured,
by other satirists, from Moore (when the Prince had
changed sides) and Thackeray downwards, there has
hardly in history been a public personage more exposed
to the arrows of such authors as the merry men of
the Rolliad. But everybody else, on the other side,
came in for showers of not always too clean water, and
of not perhaps lethal but sufficiently stinging shots.
Never quite foul-mouthed in the Williams-Stevenson
fashion, they preserved at least Anstey's license ; and
Pitt's supposed indifference to " the fair " was re-
morselessly and ceaselessly ridiculed. Aristocratic
morgue, as in Portland, or silliness, as in Salisbury and
Mountmorres, met with no more mercy, though the
group could hardly be said to have any particular fancy
for " the people." In the *Probationary Odes* especially,
their skittishness took the widest range, and, except in
Sheridan's own plays, you may look in vain at the time
for such a dazzle and rattle of wit. A shilling *Rolliad*,
with its appendages and fair annotations, would keep
one amused from London to York. Of course there
is the drawback—not merely, I should suppose, from
the Tory point of view—that the thing represents mere
random mischief, work—

> Without a conscience or an aim,

except, in the latter case, to keep Taper out and get
Tadpole in.

But there are consolations ; themselves of an emin-

ently eighteenth-century kind, even from a tolerably
serious, at least not merely Puckish point of view. To
say that the fun is always good-natured would be
excessive, it is sometimes much the reverse ; but that
there is a certain good humour about it all is eminently
true. The older Irish character—which the events of
the last forty years have unfortunately obscured, if
they have not actually killed it—is evident almost
everywhere. I am not certain, well as I know Thackeray—whether he ever mentions the *Rolliad*; although
it was in a way on his own side he perhaps took politics
rather too seriously, in his Colonel-Newcome-like
style, to be able to sympathise with it thoroughly. But
nobody has expressed its spirit better than he in his
Irish " intromittings." The spirit which is certain
that its sister Anna Maroia poisoned her husband, but
under other circumstances, such as a considerable
legacy to Anna Maroia, would be quite willing to admit
that the same husband richly deserved it, and to take
the said sister to its heart and home, is largely present
in the *Rolliad*. You see the effects in Tierney's actual
conduct, if not in Ellis's. Moreover, the famous and
much debated defence of Restoration Comedy applies
(though it was very soon not to apply) to this division
of literature perfectly. It is, to a very large extent
at any rate, " make believe," puppet-show work, or
political pantomime. Half if not all the men concerned
had been quite content that Fox should coalesce with
North, and some of themselves were quite content
afterwards to coalesce with Pitt. But, as literature,
the thing is admirable, and some of the Ossianic imitations, extending, unlike some earlier parodies, from
Ossianic into pure Whitmanese, are instinct with new
and original genius. But though the thing is almost
pure literature itself, references to things literary are
for the most part indirect and occasional, and the time
was not favourable for more. Cumberland, the universal whipping-boy, comes in for castigation. But

other literary victims and scapegoats, Hawkins, Wraxall, etc., are poor creatures.

The very best thing that John Wolcot, otherwise " Peter Pindar," ever did was his already-mentioned *Bozzy and Piozzi*, a combined satire on the lady's *Anecdotes of Johnson*, and (not on Boswell's *Life*, which was not yet published, but on) the *Tour to the Hebrides*. Wolcot's Muse is not only far too often draggle-tailed and (as Horace Walpole did falsely say of Fielding's) " bunter," that is to say, drab-like, but also verbose, careless, and unequal in every respect. Here she becomes, though still a pert enough minx, apparently neat, well-behaved, and ostentatiously respectful, though relentlessly observant of absurdities. The rivals take the amœbean style, not so much answering each other as uttering passages of their respective books antiphonally in stanzas. The metre and even phrase are in no way extravagantly burlesque, though they skip along in a flowing popular style which any beaver can well understand. But all the weakest parts of the books themselves: the egotism of the two writers, Bozzy's childish digressions about his ancestry and personal proceedings, Thralia's small-beer chronicle and peevishness, the trivial details which both give about their hero—every one, in short, of the lapses in which the Laird of Auchinleck abounds and the lady of Bach-y-Craig is by no means deficient, are arranged, exposed, and delivered with a wonderful mixture of grimace and gravity, hardly to be surpassed in its own line.[1]

To few, if any, other things of Wolcot's can such unmixed praise be given, and if his work be taken as a whole [2] (though it is, even in that state, much better worth reading than appears to have been for a long

Peter Pindar.

---

[1] The same qualities occur, less eminently, in his skits on the Royal Academy, and on scientific *virtuosi* like Banks, but are there accompanied by much more personal feeling and general " street-Arabism." But if Opie was a fellow West-countryman, and not exactly a Reynolds or a Raphael, he was at any rate better than West.

[2] As an actual whole it is said never to have been fully collected. The present writer is acquainted with it in four fat little volumes of smallish print, and in five statelier but still not thin ones of standard type.

time thought), the general mark for "cleverness," which must still be accorded to it, has to be qualified with so much blame that the compound may seem to some severe judges actually little better than base metal. Peter is sometimes very dirty, and seldom quite clean. In his long series of personal satires on George the Third there is indeed less positive ill-nature than he displayed against other foes.[1]   But the very title of the most elaborate of them—the *Lousiad*—could not, even at his date, have been adopted and carried out by any but a "vulgar fellow."   And in fact—though Peter was a doctor of Physic, a clergyman (not to its credit certainly) of the Church of England, and not entirely unscholarly in other ways—it is impossible even to think of calling him a gentleman.   The epithet "savage" which Macaulay has applied to him is perhaps exaggerated as regards his satires on the King, but is deserved elsewhere, especially in relation to Gifford, who, however, was quite capable of outsavaging Peter or anybody.[2]   When he is in this mood he is seldom very good ; and when he is "serious" in another way (*i.e.* non-satiric) he has been said with truth to be like, and about as bad as, Hayley.   But in a large portion of his work, where he is simply mischievous, he is generally clever and sometimes extremely amusing.   He was, in the circumstances, naturally on the Whig side, until, in the stress of the Revolution, he was either frightened or bribed to neutrality ; but there are no signs of any Whig principle in him, and not much if any definite partisanship, except of the personal kind. He will speak as irreverently of Burke and Burgoyne as of Pitt ; and though, as he says himself, he—

Wrote *Will*ippics on administration,

he was in fact a mere *frondeur*.

[1] It was his whim to assert that the King rather enjoyed these lampoons ; and, as George was by no means destitute of humour, there may have been some truth in this.

[2] They are said to have actually come to blows, and to have rolled each other in the gutter.

It is really a pity that one of the useful persons who make cheap selections of older literature in shilling series does not set to work to make an anthology of this period's verse.[1] There has been no room for many extracts here ; but one or two must be subjoined to show the senile dotage and the childish prattle of the setting and rising age. Hayley, indeed, need hardly be drawn upon, for he is simply dull and silly ;[2] Helen Maria is a sort of ancestress of the Miss Bunions of the nineteenth century ; but a note from them may show what Gifford and Mathias, Ellis and Canning and Frere had as subjects, while others, Sir James Bland Burges, for instance, must go quite untouched.

The literary victims—Hayley, Darwin, the Della Cruscans, etc.

These however are, so to speak, colourless and negative as compared with the astounding drivel poured forth in the *British Album* by the Della Cruscan school proper—Merry himself, Mrs. Cowley, the powder manufacturer " Benedict," " Arley," " Cesario," " The Bard," and Heaven knows how many other aliases and *noms de guerre*. It is, I fear, impossible to give adequate evidence of this here, though I had intended to do so. The stuff is so incredibly silly that a few specimens would strike almost anybody who did not know the book as probably unfair ; and it would be

---

[1] Some very excellent discussion and citation of it will be found in the late Mr. Armine Kent's *Otia* (London, 1905). The political part had been dealt with earlier in the present writer's *Twenty Years of Political Satire* (*Macmillan's Magazine*, March 1890, and *Essays in English Literature*, Second Series, London, 1895).

[2] Perhaps Hayley may be allowed to commit suicide in a prose passage of his Preface to *The Triumphs of Temper*. " I wished indeed, but I fear most ineffectually, for powers to unite some touches of the sportive wildness of Ariosto, and the more serious sublime painting of Dante, with some portion of the enchanting elegance, the refined imagination, and the moral grace of Pope ; and to do this, if possible, without violating those rules of propriety which Mr. Cambridge has illustrated."

And Helen Maria shall bind her fate to his, but in verse :

> While Hayley wakes thy magic string
>   His shades shall no rude sound profane,
> But Stillness on the folded wing,
>   Enamoured catch his soothing strain ;
> Tho' genius breathe its purest flame
>   Around his lyre's enchanting frame ;
> Tho' music there in every period roll—
>   More warm his friendship and more pure his soul !

impossible to give more than a few. Let me only repeat a crucial instance, which I have already used elsewhere, " Anna Matilda's " (Mrs. Cowley's) two lines :

> A feast so dear to polished taste
> As that thy lyre correctly flings.

If any one will kindly ponder, for only a minute or two, " feast," " polished," " lyre," " correctly," and " flings," he can hardly require any commentary to bring out the (beforehand inconceivable) absurdity of the whole thing.

Nor should we omit, before describing the torture-chamber, the greatest, at least the most imposing of **Example of** the victims, Erasmus Darwin, whose real **Darwin.** faculties of a certain kind, and whose ancestorship of a greater than himself still, I believe, make some people reluctant to see him treated as he in strictness deserves. The following passage will show not only his delinquencies, but the extraordinary cleverness of his caricaturists in the *Anti-Jacobin*, who have managed, with practically no exaggeration, to emphasise his unparalleled frigidity :

> So where the Hummingbird in Chile's bowers
> On murmuring pinions robs the pendent flowers ;
> Seeks where fine pods their dulcet balm distil,
> And sucks the treasure with proboscis bill :—
> Fair Cypripedia with successful guile
> Knits her smooth brow, extinguishes her smile !
> A spider's bloated paunch and jointed arms
> Hide her fine form and mask her blushing charms ;
> In ambush sly the mimic warrior lies,
> And on quick wing the panting plunderer flies.[1]

---

[1] *The Botanic Garden* (London, 1791). A most delightful 4to, printed and margined luxuriously, and decorated not only with engravings of flowers, and coins and the Portland Vase, but with the more imaginative sprouts of the brains of Fuseli and Blake ; possibly also a respectable record of science. But such a monument of fustian, false taste and (once more) frigidity in the pure Greek sense as literature hardly possesses elsewhere. It is only fair to add that Coleridge and Southey, in their early work, sometimes nearly equalled the silliness, and both of them, with Wordsworth also, the frigid grandiloquences of their contemporaries. But they "dived and rose far off " ; the personages of the text still wallowed in the pool of Dulness.

This gang of strange creatures, more than one of whom, as has been said, showed in other conjunctures distinct talent, though in this they were yoked with others who were fools pure and simple, had their appointed punishment from divers hands ; especially from two curious persons, differing in nature and genius, but each singularly well qualified to act the parts of Barbariccia and his companions in the Inferno. If this seems a somewhat unsavoury, if not a worse still, comparison for an unblushing Tory to make of two men who were good Tories in their time, no great apology is necessary. William Gifford is entitled indeed to large allowance for early hardships, for undaunted struggles to overcome his apparently evil destiny in his earlier life, and for ill-health in his later. He was a fearless, and, as it seems to the present writer, a sound politician. He made himself a good scholar ; and his edition of Ben Jonson, though disfigured by the faults to be noticed immediately, is one of the best performances of its kind in the whole range of English literary study, while those of Massinger, Ford, and (a beginning only, finished by Dyce) Shirley are hardly inferior. He could write with vigour, point, and a certain polish both in verse and prose. He was perfectly honest. But even Scott, the most good-natured of men, on the same side with Gifford politically, and a person too important for even the editor of the *Quarterly Review* to take liberties with, called him a " cankered carle " ; and the description suits him only too well and only too constantly. He had received from nature, and had perfected by art, that peculiar fault-finding, fault-seeking, and generally aggressive character which a critic has only too many opportunities of displaying, and which has been only too commonly, though most foolishly, thought to be rather appropriate to the critic as such. In his affrays with Wolcot and even Hazlitt, who were *de même farine et pareil bran*, this sort of

Their torturers— Gifford.

Tasmanian-devil attitude was not out of place; and Gifford was never so undignified as Hazlitt in his famous Letter to the Editor. But he never could ask himself the question, " Is the work good ? " without previously laying down literary and unliterary stipulations and specifications with which it had to comply or be damned.

Fortunately, as far as the Della Cruscans and some other writers of the time were concerned, his violence and his acerbity, though perhaps the old tag of the butterfly and the wheel might come in, were hardly out of place. His two satires, *The Baviad* and *The Mæviad*, in which he attacked them, were not such good poetry as parts of *The Dunciad*, and they were not so witty as more of it. But whereas Pope (see above) had been attacking persons who had no business to be where they were, and persons who had no business to be anywhere, Gifford was trying to squash,[1] and to no small extent succeeded in squashing, a really fashionable school of poetastry, which was all the more dangerous because it threatened to pollute and adulterate the greater school that was just beginning to arise. True, Gifford in this sense was doing good unawares and (had he known the whole state of the case) against the grain. He had no love for Wordsworth or Coleridge, even after their conversion; he pretty certainly would have had none for Shelley or for Keats if they had been converted politically, or even had never needed conversion. But here was a small and useful thing to be done, and Gifford did it—did it thoroughly, effectually, and almost artistically, certainly in a craftsmanlike fashion. The proportion of means to ends, and the pompous style of the satire, prevent it indeed from being so amusing as *The Rolliad* before or the *Anti-Jacobin* (which Gifford himself edited) afterwards. But it *is* amusing, and it

[1] They used then, and Scott used it of this very case, the longer and perhaps compounded form *squabash*.

[2] See note above on the early work of the Lake poets.

heightens, and is heightened in zest by, the folly of its subjects.

Numerous as were the terms of abuse applied to Gifford, no one who used words with any propriety could have called him a prig. Nor, though **Mathias.** he was often called a pedant, was he exactly that. But both of these injurious applications might have been bestowed upon Thomas James Mathias, author of the once widely read, and still in a way famous, *Pursuits of Literature*. Mathias also had his good points. He was the best Italian scholar of his day in England, and his enthusiasm for Gray (he also was a Cambridge man) made him nearly ruin himself over a luxurious edition of that poet. In keeping with these two tastes, and perhaps parent of both, was his scholarship in the older classical sense. But *The Pursuits of Literature* was quite modern—extremely " up to date," as has been said since. Its satire has been called " audacious " and " reckless," and De Quincey, among some abuse, has allowed its author " a demon of originality." On the other hand, it has been stigmatised as tedious, dull, and so forth. The truth as usual lies between. Mathias had at least the wit to select victims who had a good deal of the wind-bag about them—Godwin, Parr, " Monk " Lewis, Payne Knight, and others ; and he let fly some pretty sharp arrows at them, some of which hit, pierced, and let out not a little of their wind. The book is really a sort of complement of the *Baviad* and *Mæviad*. Like Gifford, Mathias exaggerates, is indiscriminate, and sometimes (De Quincey has selected some instances) distinctly unfair, if not definitely dishonest. But his greatest fault—one which he again shares with Gifford but displays in far greater volume—a fault which was common at the time and itself a just subject for satire— was the immense profusion of learned or quasi-learned annotation. It is difficult to see where Mathias's " audacity," in attacking divers not very exalted or

saintly persons, comes in,[1] and his method is too ponderous to be called reckless. But he has a certain
satiric force, and, if the least amusing of his group,
fairly belongs to it.

To pass from the least good to the best is always
pleasing, and the *Poetry of the Anti-Jacobin* is the best
The *Anti-* of its kind *sans phrase*. Well-intentioned
Jacobin. "informationists" sometimes painfully point
out, and partisans who, a hundred years after, feel
their party stung scornfully reassert, that this famous
" Poetry " is only the cream of a bulky collection of
violent, unequal, and sometimes positively dull journalism. It certainly is so. But of the " Poetry "
itself, which was isolated early, and has been constantly reprinted since, it is almost equally difficult to
say and not to say too much. That modern Radicals
still sometimes profess to find it ignoble, disgraceful,
inhuman, not true satire, and so forth, is only interesting
because it shows how hard and true—with what lasting
effect—Canning and his friends hit perennial weak
places. Those of us of course who cling to the Tory
house, though we may fairly plead that we do not feel
in the least indisposed to acknowledge the literary
merit of *The Rolliad* or of Wolcot, of Shelley or of
Moore, may, no doubt, be to some slight extent handicapped, though not at all disqualified, by the fact that
while our midriffs are enormously tickled, our withers
are not in the least wrung. How hard the wringing
was is shown by the fact that Southey, a good fellow
and a good humorist, as well as a strong Anti-Jacobin
himself later, never could get his withers into comfortable order. It is the weakest point in him ; but
it is a very strong one for the " Anti-Jacks."

The devotees of the " time, place, and circumstance "

---

[1] One should, however, no doubt beware of the "outrages of time." Parr unquestionably once seemed a Titan if not a god ; and Godwin's influence at least is
undoubted. De Quincey's famous diploma-piece on Parr may be compared with, and
corrected by, an admirable and far too little known judgment by the late Rev. S. H.
Reynolds (*Studies on Many Subjects*, London, 1898).

formula, if their wit were of a lighter order than it usually is, ought to rejoice in the *Poetry of the Anti-Jacobin*. For from Aristophanes downwards there is no better thing of its kind, and from Aristophanes downwards there are few instances in which the quality of time, place, and circumstances must be more freely admitted as influencing, if not exactly causing, the idiosyncrasy of man and work. Some of us will still hesitate to admit that, given the French Revolution and its history, given the English eighteenth literature and its character, without Canning, Ellis, and Frere, *The Poetry of the Anti-Jacobin* must have resulted. Few should be so stiff-necked as not to acknowledge that all these things and persons were, with the *Poetry of the Anti-Jacobin*, in a concatenation most remarkably according.

Let us take these " factors," as the theorists themselves would call them, in reverse order. George Canning was one of the most typical ex-

Its creed. amples of the type of English- (in his case English-Irish) man of the not quite uppermost class whom the eighteenth century produced,[1] whom it handed over to the nineteenth to preserve as best it could, and whom the nineteenth has further handed on, not quite spoilt, to the twentieth. His family, actually ennobled later in more than one branch, would already have been called noble in France ; but his immediate division of it had " had losses." He himself, however, fully enjoyed the public school and university education which had so much to do with the formation of the type itself, and his school position at Eton, not merely in the ordinary classical scholarship, but in English writing (the *Microcosm*) is well known. Both there and at Christ Church he made many friendships.

Canning has been labelled " rat " because he fell at first into Whig circles, his uncle belonging to that

---

[1] *Vixere fortes*—of course indeed *fortissimi*. But this particular type was post-Restoration—even Clarendon and Evelyn do not belong to it—and almost post-Revolution—though Halifax shows something of it.

party. But as has been pointed out more than once, and quite recently, the Whiggery of the eighteenth century, till the great touchstone of the Revolution was applied to it, was a most indeterminate creed, and for the most part meant only that your father had held it before you, that it was your ticket or *symbolum* for a place, and that you had a vague idea that nothing much mattered before 1688. But the touchstone came, and Canning was found true blue, and not buff and blue. The tradition that his conversion was effected by an effort on the part of that Pecksniff-Pangloss Godwin to convert him the other way, is at any rate humorous.

John Hookham Frere fortunately needed no conversion, but was one of those over whom there is more joy in earth than even over convertites. Except in regard to some prosodic will-worship (and even there you could not call him bad), Frere was an almost impeccable person in politics and scholarship and letters. He must have somehow inherited much of the spirit of the great Greek Tory dramatist and satirist whom he later translated so admirably; and some of the very best parts of the joint work are his. Ellis has been spoken of already. He, like Canning, had to come out of Philistia, and had even fought for it, but the touchstone again found him true. His metal was rather lighter than that of the others; but they all "shot close together" at the foe, and Ellis's independent work on English poetry and Romance was, for the time, first-rate.

Three such men as these, associated together for such a purpose and professionally captained by such a Their method. fourth as Gifford, with not a few others to help them, were not a little formidable. The Scriblerus Club in the earlier days of the century had indeed greater geniuses, and so had "those about Johnson"; but the former had more restricted objects, the latter had no common object at all, and some members of both were neither men of affairs nor fully " men

of society." Ellis's earlier confederates of the *Rolliad*
might claim both these descriptions in a way; but in
scholarship, intellectual weight, and definite purpose
they were nowhere in comparison. Chesterfield and
Bolingbroke may suggest themselves, but they came
too early, and were in a way belated *grands seigneurs*
playing at literature. Canning, Ellis, and Frere were
gentlemen in every sense—Frere's family in particular
was one of the best in Norfolk—but a kind of professional man-of-letters-ship had by their time come to
be regarded as quite compatible with the position of a
gentleman. Indeed the whole status of writing had
risen.[1] Grub Street was mainly a tradition; the
victims of Gifford and Mathias were, at least for the
most part, quite out of the reach of Pope's ignoble
satire on dinnerlessness and holes in coats. So that
the adventurers of the *Anti-Jacobin* found themselves
in a position strengthened and made more formidable,
in a rather surprisingly different number of ways, by
the events and circumstances of the century. They
had its great literary patterns before them; they could
avoid (and were inclined to avoid) its conventions when
they chose, retaining them equally at pleasure; they
had connection as well as scholarship, a certain position
as well as wit, and they were able, by new ways and
means, to attain and maintain that attitude of scornful
superiority which Dryden had only reached by dint of
genius, and which Pope, despite his genius, never did
reach, while men like Savage and Churchill raged and
reviled far below.

But they could hardly have done what they did
without the unique opportunity with which their
adversaries supplied them. "Thou hast given a
handle," said their ancestor in Athens; but the re-
volutionaries gave as many handles as those which
grew up in the *Île des Ferrements*, ready for irons to be

---

[1] Its revenues not quite equally. To give every dog its due, it was the *Edinburgh
Review* that effected that life-preserving dead-lift.

fitted to them. On one side were the actual crimes of
the Jacobins ; on another the traditional enmity between
England and France and the usual excitements of
warfare ; on yet another the material and the taste for
sarcastic political argument ; on a fourth the fantastic
absurdities which attend many great political cata-
clysms, and which were peculiarly abundant then. The
available points and methods of attack were indeed
so numerous that there might have been no small
danger of that attack itself being frittered away, of its
becoming too serious at one time and too frivolous at
another. It was here that that combination of the man
of letters with the man of affairs which has been mentioned, and of which Canning and Frere at least were exceptional representatives, came in.[1] It has sometimes
been said—perhaps with some truth—that, in England,
attacks of mere persiflage, especially when continued
long, do little harm to the persons or things attacked,
and are apt to recoil on the assailants. But no one
could say that the Anti-Jacobins never took politics
seriously. The great and just-silenced fulminations of
Burke were not in their way, but they had their own
way of serious as well as light dealing. " The horror
and the hell " of the Jacobin tyranny was fully kept
in view, as if in a mediæval theatre, behind the scoffs at
German Romanticism gone mad and English Rights-
of-Man-ism gone silly.

The results ought to be perennially delectable,
except to those whose conviction of the majesty of the
murder of Marie Antoinette, or the delicate
*A slight
anthology for* delights of the Feast of Reason, prevents
critical pur- enjoyment. Some of the fun is almost non-
poses. political, and a great part of *The Rovers*
should be enjoyable by everybody. Such an entire
and perfect peacock spinel (to give the chrysolite a
rest) would be hard to find elsewhere, in and out of

---

[1] Of Canning one need say nothing more ; but some readers may have forgotten
thas Frere discharged to admiration one of the most arduous and ungrateful tasks in
diplomacy, that of English minister with the Spanish Junta during the war.

English literature. A pair to it could have been produced by those benefactors of the third and fourth quarters of the nineteenth century, Calverley, Dodgson, Gilbert, and Traill, who were the next group of recurrent stars to fill the sometimes quite vacant Heaven of this kind of poetry; but no one or more of them actually duplicated it. As with all the greater things of the kind, knowledge of the parodied originals, though it may increase, is not absolutely necessary to the enjoyment of the composition. *Stella* and *The Stranger* and *Count Benyowsky* and the curious onomatology of Goldoni (and of some greater continentals than Goldoni) need not be hunted up in order to draw almost the fullest amount possible of delectation from Beefington and Puddingfield, from Cecilia and Matilda, from the sufferings of Rogero and the machinations of the mysterious waiter, from the immortal simplicity of—

> She was the daughter of my tu—

and the cunningly concocted melodies of—

> This cherry bounce, this loved noyau.

The thing is not only roaring fun—that admirable nonsense which Hazlitt, on the duller side of politics, elsewhere had the wit to recognise and the sense to champion as the special gift of Englishmen—but it is something more. It has the true aristocratic quality which Aristophanes was the first to show in any Western literature—the scorn too utter to be anything but quiet, though it may take noisier partners, for vulgarity, stupidity, commonness on one hand and crankery on the other. The tone is what poor Nietzsche meant by the word *vornehm*, though he was misguided enough to think that the Romans (hardly one of whom ever was a gentleman) had it, and to hold it up to his own countrymen, whom God had condemned to severance from it for ever and for ever.

It is, however, possible that there may be too much of the farcical element in *The Rovers* for some people. The unique Even the lovers of the play will admit that Mr. Higgins. *The Loves of the Triangles*, and *The Progress of Man*, and *New Morality* are in some ways of a higher strain, and that they show this noble and royal scorn—the essential quality of the *kalokagathos*—in a less equivocal manner. The height of the strain rises, though its comic spirit does not fall, as we pass from one to the other. The *Loves* are still ascribed to that priceless *eidolon*, Mr. Higgins of St. Mary Axe, the playwright of *The Rovers*, for whom no one original has ever been found, though he has a little of a good many real people, Godwin, Thelwall, Payne Knight, Horne Tooke, etc. etc., and must surely have been a sort of city cousin of Mr. Nicodemus Easy of Forest Hill, in the county of Southampton. Even Swift's prefatory matter to the *Tale of a Tub* is less grave and chaste than the prose controversy with Mr. Higgins, which introduces the poem: and the philosopher is always treated with almost Castilian courtesy by his editors, whether he is laying down the great principle that " Whatever is is wrong," is nevertheless maintaining infinite Perfectibility, or is promising a versification of the Encyclopædia in the style of Dr. Darwin. He begins with mathematics, and the reader finds himself, in the necessary intervals of *bonne fine rage de plaisir* at them all, wondering whether the arguments, the notes, or the verses themselves are the most exquisitely absurd—into which of them " Divine Nonsensia," who is solemnly invoked in the classical measure, has infused the greatest quintessence. We learn how—

> Wanton optics roll the melting eye ;

how—

Water when pressed by a moderate degree of heat has been observed to simper or " simmer " as it is more usually called. The same does not hold true of any other element ;

2 B

how—

> The conscious fire with bickering radiance burns,
> Eyes the rich joint, and roasts it as it turns.

One piece of audacious inconsecutiveness, the envy and despair of all later satirists, is the note on—

> Not thus Hyperbola ; with subtlest art
> The blue-eyed wanton plays her changeful part.

Note Hyperbola.   Not figuratively speaking, as in rhetoric, but mathematically : *and therefore blue-eyed.*

The reflections on the Spanish asses, and other well-known but never to be hackneyed jewels, wait to fill those who are new to them with " undisguised delight," and those who know them with the charms with which *usus concinnat amorem.*

Mr. Higgins's second absurdity, the *Progress of Man*, gets " warmer," as they say in the old game: and also comes nearer to a single victim, among those named above,—that very questionable person Payne Knight, who may possibly have been saved by his respectable friendships, but who certainly had some very disreputable tastes.   Payne Knight had published, the year before, an exceedingly worthless and contemptible poem on *The Progress of Society*, and the satirists dedicated to him another " in forty cantos " on the *Progress of Man*.   Specimens only were of course given, and at intervals ; but the authors, beginning with harmless generalities, closed in after a deadly fashion with Payne Knight's well-known fondness for " curious and disgusting " subjects.   The Variety of Nature supplies the innocent overture and suggests the matchless lines—

> The feathered race with pinions skim the air,
> Not so the mackerel, and still less the bear,

on which distich a whole volume of commentary might be hung.   The next canto attacks Society, and we are not surprised to find Mr. Higgins denouncing the

abominable institution of marriage. How charming
were the manners of Otaheite! where—

> Each shepherd clasped with undisguised delight
> His yielding fair one in the captain's sight,

with a note on " Shepherd " which is almost equal to
that on " Hyperbola."

But, in both of these, ridicule rather than righteous
wrath rules the roast, and the objects " squabashed,"
as the time said, are at best butterflies, at
worst black beetles. The *New Morality* is
in deadly though never dull earnest ; and a
great deal of it is dreadfully apposite to the
present day and minute, though of course some
parts are obsolete, and the whole tone may, by
persons who have not got an easily adjustable ear, be
thought too rhetorical if not too dithyrambic. But,
except *The Dunciad* close, with that of *The Vanity of
Human Wishes* and some of Juvenal and Victor Hugo,
there is little in literature to beat the final pages and
the earlier " Hymn " of the Jacobins—

The union of force and lightness in satire.

> *Couriers* and *Stars* ! sedition's evening host !

No matter that some of the persons stigmatised repented of their folly and developed unexpected greatness ; no matter that others were scarcely worth the
blasting they received. But this very blasting force,
combined with a general serenity of style, Dryden
himself never surpassed, as in

> Still blasphemous or blackguard, praise Lepaux,

and

> All creeping creatures, venomous and low.

The *vis superba formae*, with a wider sense for *forma*
than Secundus had meant in using the phrase, appears
here in a perfect exemplification of the other two words.
One sees the vermin wriggling, hears their canting
whine, and sees and hears at once the rush of the
arrows of Apollo as they speed against the prey.

Shortness, however, is to some a special grace in this kind of poetry; and the *Anti-Jacobin* is no less justly famous for its lyric than for its didactic and dramatic skits. Two famous things, the *Knife-grinder* and *Mrs. Brownrigg* (which, as above mentioned, Southey was weak enough never to forgive), have the general verdict, and perhaps not without justice, though the dactylics on another of the same poet's experiments—

Come! little drummer boy; lay down your knapsack here,

which are much less frequently quoted, are nearly as good, and have the, in English, rare merit of being *really* dactylic. A second attempt at the metre is much less successful.

In fact most people who love the *Anti-Jacobin* have their special favourites. The Elegy on Jean Bon St. André—

[Who] fled full soon on the First of June
But bade the rest keep fighting,

has many partisans. The sweet simplicity and unadorned nature of—

Beware the Badger's bloody pennant,
And that d——d invalid lieutenant!

appeals to others. But there is something for everybody who is not a Jacobin, as well as in the other sense " something " for everybody who is.

A year after the appearance of these delectable ebullitions of the best kind of *alma sdegnosa*, one of the persons lampooned in them—and another who certainly would have shared that fate if the lampooners had known that, for some time at any rate, he was almost a Girondist if not a Jacobin—put forth another book of verse of a remarkably different character. It would, no doubt, be an odd kind of person who would rather have the poetry of the *Anti-Jacobin* than *Lyrical Ballads*, but it would be an odder who should not say, " Both, please ! " As it happened, the volume of 1798 was—some unimportant things excepted—almost entirely of the future ; it was chronologically just within the eighteenth century, but logically and psychologically quite out of it.   On the other hand, as has been partly shown already, the *Anti-Jacobin* poems, though making a distinct assault on some characteristics of the eighteenth century, in the main came from them, and represented them.   Some further remarks on these characteristics themselves, in a short Conclusion, may wind up this book.[1]

---

[1] I notice, rather late for reparation in text, that neither here nor in the "Novel" chapter have I included *Zeluco* Moore—a great favourite of my own, and not only in his most famous book a real *provedor* of our commodities.

CONCLUSION

IF the foregoing pages—such of them at least as have
not been devoted to pure history—have not also been
filled with merely idle and fanciful matter, they may,
it is hoped, have gone a little way to establish a view
of the eighteenth century,[1] in its literary aspect, which
differs widely, both from the estimate which it formed
of itself, and from that which was generally entertained
of it for a long time after its close, and is still to some
extent held now.

Like most centuries, and most individuals, the
eighteenth century was (it has been said and shown)
"bumptious" in its youth and (as is almost always
the case) bumptious about the wrong things ; while,
unlike most centuries, and nearly all individuals who
are not fools, it unluckily did not quite unlearn this
bumptiousness in its middle age. It had indeed one
enormous defect, which is, and no doubt always will
be, charged against it, till a similar period returns. That
defect has been perhaps not quite correctly or happily
defined as the lack of wonder. The eighteenth century wondered at many things ; but, once more, not
at the right or the most right ones. It wondered at the
British Constitution ; at the growth of Trade and Com-

---

[1] An objection has been made, and may probably be shared by not a few readers,
that to take the century "solid" as "Augustan" is a liberty—that about Pope's
death a severance was made by some god, and that the star of Anna and the first
Georges quailed before the more unquiet captain of the dreams and actions of the
subjects of George III. It is of course true that something of the sort happened ;
but I had meant to warn readers of the fact in the chapter on the "Fugitives from
the Happy Valley." And it seems to me that these never quite lost its characteristics,
even in the stormy and unequal period with which we have just been dealing.

merce; at a good many other objects. It was even
so enthusiastic about them, that though it deprecated
enthusiasm about divers important matters, want of
that quality *per se* is again not to be justly charged
against it. Its infirmity was that it did not understand
the subject of a book which it professed to admire.
It knew not "The Sublime." Shelley, one of the
children of its old age, and the greatest incarnation of
difference from and rebellion against it, defined, as no
doubt many have seen, in perhaps his most famous
lines, the opposite of its ethos. "The desire of the
moth for the star," with all that follows, puts, in immortal words, exactly what the eighteenth century did
not desire. It was not a moth; but a comfortable solid
creature. It did not neglect or despise the stars; but it
liked best to make orreries of them. It was not night
but cheery day—good for working and playing in;
and if it was religious it thought it sinful, if not idle, to
care much about the morrow. It was not sorry—at
least "no more than reason"; and things remote
and afar appeared to it neither "business" nor "the
game."

But all this, for which we have hectored it, or lec-
tured it, or ignored it in superior fashion, or regarded
it with a more or less mild pity which has sometimes
come very near indeed to contempt, was only the sin of
its solace—if indeed it was a sin at all, and not a mere
necessity of its own quality. It is not a sin for a potato
not to be a peach, or not to be sorry because it is not one
—though it may be admitted that some peaches in these
improved days taste uncommonly like potatoes, and
so suggest possible development, in the other direction.

The list of its deficiencies is no doubt long and
heavy; but it may be most unparadoxically questioned
whether mere deficiencies are to be charged as faults
against any period. The question is, what it has of
positive to offer, what is its own contribution to that
glory of the past which, as was once said finely in about

the last place in the world where one would expect such a sentence, is irrevocably ours. No matter that those two great burdens which the prophet has put in imperishable words, " the burden of the valley of vision " and the " burden of the desert of the sea," were refused or ignored by most of its children. Even here it provided, in Blake, a visionary who could see for whole peoples and generations ; and it peopled and tinted the " desert of the sea " itself with actual glories which can never be forgotten, though degenerate generations may affect to be shocked at them. But if it did not like or did not know some burdens, it could, as in the cases just alluded to, wrestle with and overcome others with astonishing stoutness. Some of its accomplishments we may regard with mixed feelings ; but as accomplishments they can hardly be too much admired. One may wish that England had never had a " manufacturing system," and so had escaped the minor curses of irregular employment, occasional distress, and dangerously unequal distribution of wealth, as well as the major disfigurement of land and life, and the *maximum* abomination of Trades Unions. But that it was a great deed, if not a good one, to establish that system itself, nobody can deny who possesses any catholic estimate of greatness. Some people may have a horror of aristocracy, and others may regard representative government as the vainest of vain inventions ; but, again, no one with brains, and knowledge, and some faculty of detachment, can deny that, with its astonishingly illogical practicality and its marvellously practical want of logic, the English eighteenth century made the best of both these things, and of the one through the other, in a fashion which is unparalleled in the history of the world, though unfortunately the achievement has led half the world into mischief by clumsy attempts at once to rival and to spoil it.

The charge of defect of Idealism is, again, one which it would be absurd to deny *simpliciter*, or indeed to deny at all. But it is one which, for the particular purpose of this book, it is specially proper to examine. Idealism in itself, like all other terms of the kind, is susceptible of extremely various interpretations. If you go back to the origin it means the magnificent if unprovable (I do not say improbable) conception of Plato, wherein all things are reduced, or exalted, to functions of the Divine mind. If you take it as used in defence of Welsh disendowment recently,[1] it means an uncontrollable desire for other people's property. Now if the eighteenth century cannot be credited with it in the one sense, it certainly cannot be discredited with it in the other.

But, adopting the crude working opposition of idealism and materialism, it is of course undeniable that, both in strict philosophy and in general temper, our century inclined to the materialist side. Its attitude to Berkeley, its attitude to the Methodists, the inability of a man like Garrick (whose French blood must, however, count for something) to understand a poet like Gray, its " tapeyard infidelities," as no more orthodox a person than Mr. Swinburne accurately described them — these and many other things remain to its discredit. But they are all more or less covered by the reminder ventured at the beginning of the last paragraph.

In fact one of the uglier aspects of the subject contains or concerns one of the most interesting phases of the virtue of the Augustans, and the phase itself is particularly well worth studying in connection with the literature of to-day and the more immediate yesterday. The Augustans were free-spoken, and to a certain extent also foul-spoken ; but they were not, with the exception of Sterne, Williams, Stevenson, and one or two more, as well as of persons like Cleland, who do not come within our direct purview here, dirty. Indeed their sense of humour and of the true irony—

[1] In the debates on the Welsh Disestablishment Bill, July 1913.

both of which things have been so lamentably eclipsed of late—prevented them from being so.   The situation had been touched off finally, with their own combination of the said humour and of common sense, quite early in the period by the famous, " Do you see that little fellow ?   He has been committing adultery."   Our novelists, or some of them, for the last thirty years (Heaven forbid that I should be so impertinent as to call them " little fellows ") have fallen back upon whatever source of interest may be found in the way of committing adultery.   Hobbs makes his hero or heroine do it once ; Dobbs, greatly daring, does it twice or thrice ; Nokes outdares Stokes' varieties and extravagances of things inconvenient and forbidden. And the critics say, " Do you see this Great Man ?   He has received a sudden illumination.   He has outgrown the fear of Mrs. Grundy.   He is ' candid.'   He faces the facts of Nature.   Oh ! what a great man he is." When, at the beginning of this curious period, a hero of the gutter-press suddenly astonished the public by turning the contents of the gutter itself into " copy," a minor dignitary of the Church wrote to him with a feverish anxiety to know when he was going to let ordinary vices alone and come to extraordinary ones—a pyramidal monstrosity of unconscious humour which could hardly have occurred in the eighteenth century. They certainly had their Wilkeses and their Potters, they had also their Smolletts and their Churchills, as well as their Johnsons and their Berkeleys.   But they took good care not to confuse the kinds.

So let us, if it may indeed be so, hear the conclusion of the whole matter.   The eighteenth century had faults : what time, what man has not ?   But even in the direction of those faults, which have been too often and in too many other places recapitulated to need further recapitulation here, it had, throughout, veins of saving quality in matters of soul and sense, of art and of science, of philosophy and even of religion.

There is no real break in the higher inspiration of poetry (though the band may, as in the case of the White Lady of Avenel, have grown thin), from Lady Winchelsea to Wordsworth, in the higher metaphysic (where it was something stronger, though of less pure gold), from Berkeley to Coleridge. If these things and similar things were kept down and made less apparent, it was by an overlay of stuff which was only in small part bad and in much greater part almost wholly, if not universally, good. Its humour, its sometimes rough kindliness, its absence of insincerity and pose, above all, its massive and impregnable common sense, provided a school—something like the actual schools of its own time—which bred *men*. It was sometimes coarse perhaps, but it is better to be coarse than to be super-fine. Even while not exactly coarse, it was not much haunted by fine fancies ; but it could play the game and face the music, and win a victory without crowing too much, and take a beating without whining at all. Its statesmen were not immaculate ; but if you compare their faults with the utter scoundrelism which, one fears it must be allowed, was common among the great men of the sixteenth and seventeenth, with the whims and fancies and fads of those of the nineteenth, with the class hatreds and vote-catching tricks [1] of not a few of the twentieth, they become, if not white, at least a cool and inoffensive grey. Its churchmen did not always remember the elementary fact that if you take pay for preaching certain doctrines it is not well to deny or ignore them ; but for each Conyers Middleton, or Hoadley, or Herring of that time how many are there now ? But it is scarcely necessary, though it would be both easy and agreeable, to continue this line of argument.

Yet nothing, as it seems to me, is gained by such

[1] Why was it hopelessly wicked of Sir Robert Walpole to bribe one man's support with five hundred pounds which belonged to the nation, while it is perfectly pardonable (if not virtuous) of Mr. Anybody to bribe five hundred, or five hundred thousand, men's with money belonging to their employers or their employers' customers ?

over- and misvaluation of the Augustan period, as has (again, of course, as it seems to me) been consistently maintained by one excellently scholarly friend of mine, or as has been suggested in a somewhat different fashion by another. The judgment of literature should be conducted by means of a double criterion, which may in fact become a triple one. The first aspect of this trine looks towards the positive quality of the work of each period, the second towards its comparative quality, and the third to the manner in which it affects the critic. That perfect judge of Mr. Pope's—who perhaps never existed in perfection, but whose quality we should all aim at—would bring his estimate under each head to the utmost point of fineness, but would never allow these estimates to interfere with each other. Every division of English literature—Old, Middle, the despised " Transition " or Fifteenth Century, the Renaissance or major Elizabethan, the Augustan, the First Romantic, and the Victorian—has its own merits, and these are what are most to be studied under the first head. Under the second the character of the defects, which of course should not escape notice in the first enquiry, assumes still greater importance, for it is by these chiefly that the comparative position of the periods is to be judged. And then there comes the difficult and dangerous process of adjusting the judging to the liking. If you keep this latter out altogether, the total will be, as for instance in the case of Hallam, unsatisfactory and jejune, however respectable ; if you allow it to prevail too much, as in the case of Mr. Swinburne, it will be agreeable and stimulating, but a little untrustworthy and perhaps cloying. It would be absurd, indeed fatuous, to claim a complete power of initial severance between the duty of the examiner and the feelings of the lover, but I may at least claim to have tried to separate them. It would be more so to assert a complete adjustment of the results. But such an adjustment has been at least attempted.

I believe that, since the latest phase of medical science, the word " alterative " has become rather obsolete. You don't " alter " a *Staphylococcus pyogenes aureus* or a *Spirochaeta pallida* ; you kill these unpleasant infinitesimals. But literature is not science ; and the whole history of literature shows that the regimen of alteratives is the secret of beneficent treatment. For the present, and for some time to come, I can see nothing so admirable as the exhibition of a course of eighteenth-century specifics for our twentieth-century measles. For the really bad cases of this disease the great early Romantic period, 1798–1830, is no use ; they play their own tricks on it, and convert Jehovah into Dagon. 1830–1880 is, as the doctors say, or used to say, " badly borne " ; it would be sovereign if they could or would take it, but it is rejected. The latest nineteenth century could only give " auto-intoxication," and this does not do in literature, which, as has been said, is essentially different from science. The older ages, greater and smaller, are too far off for strictly practical effect. They have become names—to quote an author whom it is unsafe to mention. You will see one person write about Shakespeare, evidently without the slightest suspicion of the part which Shakespeare, if he had taken the trouble to " put him in " at all, would have assigned to him ; and another patronise Milton without the faintest idea of the company (see the *Sonnets*) to which Milton would probably have consigned him. Further back still there is—or at least there ought to be—more chance of peace. But the most mentally active and adroit of us, however we may enjoy Chaucer or the Romances, or Layamon or *Beowulf*, cannot put ourselves in the skins of the writers and the persons written about. The sea, if not salter, has grown more unplumbed and more estranging, and can only be bridged by purely scholarly or purely æsthetic communication, or, in happiest cases, by a combination of both, which leaves the visitor a " stranger yet."

It is not so with the eighteenth century. Much, for good or for evil, has gone ; but much remains, and there is no unbridgeable gap even between what has gone and what does remain. Enormous as are the changes between 1700 and 1915, they are, especially as regards literature, changes rather in detail than in essence. It has been pointed out that there are sentences in Swift's letters to Stella which might have been written to-day, that there are more in Chesterfield and Lady Mary, more still in Horace Walpole, most in Madame d'Arblay. The *frames*, at least, of politics, religion, other things, still exist recognisably. And the period is free from that unfortunate but undeniable prejudice which affects its successor. The " hard heir " need not at any rate " stride " offensively about this domain, which has passed through several hands before it came to him from the still not positively antediluvian ancestor. And we have endeavoured to show that the study of the old survey or *terrier* must have some useful lessons and some not unpleasant pastime.

But these may be, it is hoped without fatuity, foreseen, and it may not be quite improper to try to parry an objection of the *ad hominem* kind. " If you extol the eighteenth century so highly, why have you (here the possible fatuity comes in) in other works extolled other periods far above it ? " Or, to bring the matter home, " Would you like to have lived then ? " It does not seem that the question or questions are irrelevant, and it does seem that some discussion of them is admissible. I certainly do not think that if any one were, like the Blessed Damozel, contemplating the ages and worlds and their progress " from the gold bar of Heaven," he would choose the eighteenth century, for its literature or for its life, as the ideal compartment or phase. That " rascally comparative "—in designating which thing Shakespeare and Falstaff did not show the least of their genius—shows its full rascality here. The deficiencies of the century were enormous, and when you come to look at them without their compensations, almost appalling; but he who judges on defect without an accompanying specification of quality is himself deficient in the primary qualities of judgment. It is for what it had, and not for what it had not, that a somewhat new evaluation of the century's literature is offered to those who may care to consider it.

As for *living* in the eighteenth century, there is here a sufficiently obvious fallacy, which ought not to need much baffling, in both the old and the modern senses of that word. The profoundest of Dryden's many profound though constantly undervalued or neglected utterances—

> Who would live past lives again?

becomes more striking, if not profounder, when you gloss it into the form—

> Who would live other people's past lives again?

One has not proved these things; it is almost impossible to transvaluate the advantages and the defects. One has not with impunity, as another great saying of a worse person has it, more than a hundred years of change behind one. Some of the advantages, both negative and positive, of eighteenth-century living are indeed clear; some of these have been pointed out in passing. Its peculiar negative excellence is perhaps nowhere better observable than in those two all-important departments of politics and religion, in regard to which one of its most characteristic representatives made perhaps his most characteristic expression of quietly mordant irony. Its politics and its religion have been violently attacked or scornfully dismissed by turns. But one thing about both has been singularly little attended to. Nobody, I suppose, in spite of Berkeley and Butler, in spite of the two Pitts and Burke, can esteem them very much. But both deserved what, if not the highest, is one of the most valuable and not the commonest praises : they destroyed nothing. The Church of England was kept "in a cool barge" for resuscitation and restoration when the time came; and the State of England was handed on to the nineteenth century very little worse, and in some respects better, than it had been in 1700. There never was a century which did less harm than the eighteenth in England.[1] That it might have done more good is quite possible; but that is another matter. The growth of the industrial element which led to so much mischief was its misfortune, not its fault. On the whole, things did go very well then, though perhaps we have paid the penalty of their going so well since.

There are of course many things for which you must not look in the century, many sources of rest and refreshment from which you will be cut off. In vain will you look for (I quote from a book-catalogue which reached me while I was writing this chapter) "the glittering prose and extraordinary power of perfect expression of which Mr. —— is complete master. Open the volume where you will, and the romantic glory of the printed word makes reading as ecstatic as the joy experienced in listening to a highly-trained orchestra." There was nobody in the eighteenth century who could produce sensations of this sort; nor indeed was there anybody who would have expressed himself in such a manner about a writer who did produce great prose effects. I fear greatly that our Augustans would have been inclined to ask the gifted and generous critic whether "prose" and "power" are correlative expressions, and whether a power of "perfect" expression requires the epithet "extraordinary." I fear further that they might have thought "the romantic glory of the printed word" nonsense.

[1] Even the aristocracy, who were certainly more to blame than any other class for not making the most of almost unique powers and opportunities, made themselves, as the general attitude towards them showed when the cataclysm came in France, not positively unpopular, and deserved little unpopularity.

It is indeed astonishing how many small zests to
life this keeping of eighteenth and twentieth century
contrasts in mind will provide for the ingenious. For
another instance you read, in another book-catalogue,
the following exceedingly flamboyant puff of work,
which, as it happens, could very well dispense with
it — that of James Thomson the younger — the
James Thomson who did not live in a Happy Valley
of any kind. " When he speaks it is classical oratory.
When he depicts it is moulded sculpture. When he
plans his city of nightmare it has all the form and con-
sistence which happier dreamers have given to their
cities of the sun." How cheerful is it to consider the
differences (not always to contemporary advantage)
between the old Grub Street and the New! In the
old Grub Street indeed they did not write quite so
beautifully. But a good many of them had been to
schools where they would have had a good chance of
the birch if they had muddled painting and statuary.
Also nearly all of them " knew their Rabelais," and
would have been restrained from suggesting a very
famous and quite Pantagruelian passage by the formula, " When he does " this or that. But the study of
the genius whom we quote was probably but little in
Master Francis ; and he knew not the description by
Xenomanes of Quaresmeprenant.

Yet after all there is no necessity to finish with any
kind of poor mouth ; and the mouth of recrimination is
always poor. The century's own most characteristic
monarch might have asked, with some reason, why it
needs apology ? If other periods have record of higher
achievement, few have any of such solid and continuous
and abundant work. It began in what is, perhaps,
though the least obviously, the most certainly auspici-
ous way—without very much to show for itself. At
the end of its first lustrum, even a very acute judge,
who might have had the wits to recognise the extraordinary and dæmonic quality of *A Tale of a Tub*

(published the year before), must have confessed that there was little or nothing else to which such epithets could be applied. But if, for the moment, it was not paying high dividends, it had what it would itself have called a very solid " stock," and a " family," or staff, quite competent and very willing to improve that stock. It was not, as some periods have been, overshadowed by survivals of past greatness, nor was it distracted and weakened by a foolish revolt against such greatness. Dryden had got everything ready for it that it most wanted ; and it was not too proud to avail itself of this rich and varied if not absolutely unlimited inheritance. Swift might resent his great cousin's too true censure of things that should never have been written ; but all his own greatest things—things that it would have been a crime to have left unwritten—were in a tongue which Dryden had first freed from stammering ; and the very spirit of them, though concentrated and sub-limed, was that of Dryden's own satire. Addison in prose and Pope in verse " carried on the business " in their different administrations, but in the same spirit: and as this absence of revolution did not prevent the presence of development, founded that business with a strength and solidity to which there are few parallels in literary history.

Of the two great new products, the periodical essay and the novel, which it before long turned out with the means that Dryden had bequeathed to it, enough no doubt, perhaps too much, has been said in detail. But as a rule people are far too little grateful to the savers and the sowers of that seed from which flowers and fruit of so many kinds have proceeded since. It surely should not be difficult, for some at least of any " company of warm young men " (to borrow once more Dryden's own delightful phrase) to understand that though perhaps nothing—not even Aphrodite in her original appearance—came absolutely new into the world, an interruption of the chain of alterations is fatal to continuance. The " Coverley Papers " and the *Polite Conversation* were not absolutely without ancestors: nor were they, between them, certain progenitors of *Esmond* or of *The Egoist*, to give different tastes their choice. But it is not rash to say that, without the " Coverley Papers," and the *Polite Conversation*, or without something in their places which might or might not have been provided by Fate, *Esmond* and *The Egoist* could hardly have come into existence. Moreover, as we have seen, the eighteenth century did very much more than save and sow seed ; it carried the plant through generations of crossing and development and improvement of all kinds. There are still fogies who hold that the novel as a structure (a " toy-like structure," though some others may call it) and as a repertory of essential character has not got much beyond *Tom Jones*, though the details of the pattern may be varied *in aeternum*. A paper in the *Tatler* or the *Spectator* may look, to some eyes not yet of Odyssean experience, prim, jejune, stilted, what not ; yet in the same way it holds the position of—

That without which a thing is not

in regard, not merely to its own immediate and long-lived imitations, but to the magazine and review articles of more recent times, whether they be signed by Coleridge or Hazlitt or Lamb, by Ruskin or Arnold or Pater, by Robert Louis Stevenson or by Andrew Lang.

It may be thought, once more, that enough and too much has been said about eighteenth-century poetry ; but as this is the point which assailants attack hardest, it may surely be vigilantly defended, especially as there is one point as to which not merely positive attack, but almost unintelligible misunderstanding, seems to prevail. I have known persons—from whom I certainly should have expected better things—to lay it down almost or quite categorically that if a man speaks highly of Dryden he is practically unfit to admire—

cannot indeed *really* admire—Milton ; while others go
so far as to say, or imply, that eighteenth-century
poetry, with the exception certainly of Blake, more
doubtfully of Collins, Gray, and Chatterton, is not
poetry at all. With these last it is probably useless
and possibly impossible to argue. They either understand what they are saying or (which is more probable)
they do not. If they really have a reasoned definition
of poetry (not an easy thing to find or frame, and one
which the present writer has never seen from any of
them), which excludes Pope and Prior and everybody
save the exceptions, who are not always excepted, down
to Cowper and Crabbe, it is no use talking ; while if
they themselves talk so loosely that they cannot say
what they mean by poetry, it is perhaps equally useless.
It may, however, even with some of this last class—
and with a much larger body of persons who have no
reasoned opinion on the subject, only inherited and
borrowed prejudices—be permitted to ask them to
give the despised pudding at least a fair chance of
proof by eating. This, in the present case is, one
suspects, not often done, and indeed is not very easy
to do.

People are too lazy or too hurried now to read
Anderson or Chalmers ; and though no rational person can want anything better for actual reading than
such editions as those of the " Globe " or the " Aldine "
collections, these do not extend to all even of the major
poets, and certainly to hardly any of the minor.[1] It
would take some trouble, and some time, money,
and shelf room to get together a really representative
body of individual authors. Then the current antho-
logies, reflecting the prevailing taste or distaste, are
inadequate, excellent though they may be as far as
they go. It is certainly not because I myself contributed to it that I think the appurtenant volume of

---

[1] The Cambridge University Press has in recent years done great service by
publishing collected and enlarged editions of Prior and Crabbe.

Mr. Ward's *Poets* as good as it could be in the space: but the space itself was not sufficient for the purpose I have in view. Something like Mr. Miles's *Poets of the Nineteenth Century* (though no doubt not quite so bulky) would be wanted for a fair view of the greater and the smaller, the lighter and the more serious things, the poets and the poetesses, the " long tunes and short tunes " of this voluminous, varied, rarely perhaps consummate, but constantly ingenious, often amusing, sometimes touching, body of verse. It has been suggested above that at least an acquaintance with the whole of " Dodsley and Pearch " is a *sine qua non* ; till you have read those ten little volumes you do not know whether eighteenth-century poetry is worth reading or not. But if any one has read them, and going further, has examined the work, not included in them, of Prior and Gay and Swift and Pope, of Shenstone and Thomson and Dyer and Green and Akenside and Young, of Gray and Collins and Chatterton and of others, some referred to in the text and some not, till Goldsmith and Cowper and Crabbe ; if he has supplemented all this with the lighter work also not to be found in Dodsley or his continuator—the best things of Williams and Stevenson and Anstey, and the unsurpassable political verse of the time described in the last chapter—if he has done all this and then declares that all is barren, or even if he asserts that it is not worth going through so much to find so little—why, there is nothing for it but to accept his declaration and disable his judgment. Not merely the true critic, but the true lover of poetry requires the eyes of Argus and the ears of Fame ; while if he does not require tongues to match, his single tongue needs a sensibility of the most catholic and unbluntable kind and power. If he has these necessary gifts he will not find it hard to see the beauties, to hear the music, and to taste the sweetness or the tartness, the bitter and the salt, of Augustan poetry.

Of the general and miscellaneous prose there is no need to speak in like fashion. In so far as it has retained notice at all it has escaped—possibly because it appeals to a different sort of public—the ignorant ingratitude which the fiction and the essay-writing still sometimes suffer. Philosophers have not forgotten Berkeley and Hume, nor perhaps even Hartley ; the theologian who forgets Butler is only a theologaster, and the economists have perhaps, as a rule, rather remembered Adam Smith too well than too wisely. But to that delightful literature of letter and memoir and allied kinds, which the century, though it did not quite see the birth of it in England, matured into perfection almost as much as it did the Essay and the Novel, only negative injustice has been usually done. People have not read it nearly enough ; and that is all. Moreover, this neglect has had one good result, that the minor paradoxer and verdict-reverser has as yet done very little to defile or damage the graves of these prophets. One cannot read all the literature of the oven that arises each day, and so some efforts in this direction may have been missed. Dick may have pointed out that, though objections to Chesterfield's morals and to his views on religion are of course absurd, he was, as a matter of fact, a writer of bad English and a person almost Victorian in the puerility of his wit. Tom may have observed that though it might be possible to defend Lady Mary against Pope and Horace Walpole, such dull stuff as her ladyship's letters and such feeble deliverances as her ladyship's criticism really made both attack and defence quite superfluous. Harry may have hastened, in the best compound of Paterian and Meredithese to relegate the frivolity and the rococo of "Horry" himself to the dustiest of dustbins and the most omnivorous of paper-mills. But the general judgment does not err or fool about the matter so much as it abstains.

It is this abstinence—this " taking-for-granted "—

of the literature of the eighteenth century as a thing
estimable perhaps, but negligible and certainly not
very delectable, which has existed too long, still exists,
and ought to be abolished. What a store of pleasant
material this literature provides for all times, and of
profitable literature very specially for this time, the
present volume has endeavoured to point out. There
are divisions of this literature, especially the political
and theological, of which little has been said here for
reasons which may be tolerably obvious ; but the
profit, if not the pleasure, by no means ceases there.
In some ways it actually increases, and though to a
much less extent, the same is the case in what may be
called the " old almanacks," the members of the
scientific and other admittedly " out-of-date " departments. Their facts may be antiquated, their opinions
sometimes may be shown to be not only erroneous,
but made even a little ridiculous, by that most unsportsmanlike operator Time. But over the whole,
or at worst again and again at intervals throughout
the whole, there will be found something of those
delectable and profitable qualities on which we have
endeavoured to insist here—the calm unhurried
judgment, the absence of excitement and flurry and
phantasm and fad, the curiously all-pervading good
nature which, combined as it was with rough " knock-
about " manners, contrasts so strikingly with our own
ill-blooded effeminacy and humanitarianism. We can
indeed still fight—it will be a total *Finis Angliae* indeed
when we cannot do that—and they could already cant,
for that less admirable faculty was a development of all
Teutonic nations at a very early date. But they made
much less fuss about their fighting than we do, and
their cant had less of the disgusting quality about it
which is too evident in most of ours.

It is, however, with the pure literature that we have
had most to do, and with it that we should finish. If
a man cannot be satisfied with a body of verse and prose

which begins with Swift and Addison, with Pope and Prior, which proceeds through Collins and Gray, Hume and the novelists, Johnson and Goldsmith, which ends with Gibbon and Burke, Cowper and Crabbe, Beckford and Canning, dozens of other names being omitted all through, he is a person sincerely to be pitied.   If, being competent to enjoy them, he lets laziness or fashion or what not prevent him from attempting the enjoyment, he is somewhat to be contemned.

INDEX

Addison, 2-4, 11-19, 36, 39, 43, 50, 65, 67, 93, 95, 106, 107, 147 *note*, 167, 210, 211, 282, 346, 386, 387
Adventures of a Guinea, The, 156
Adventures of an Atom, 132
Akenside, 83-85, 87
Alciphron, 259, 262
Alma, 56
Alwyn, 170
Amelia, 119-130, 154 *note*
Amory, T., 150-153, 158, 159, 261
Analogy (Butler's), 259
Anna St. Ives, 170
Annals of the Parish, 176 *note*
Anstey, 77, 272-274
Anti-Jacobin, The, 346, 363-373
Arabella, 148
Arblay, Mme. d'. *See* Burney, Fanny
Arbuthnot, 22, 92
Argument against abolishing Christianity, 28, 82, 236 *sq.*, 290
Aristophanes, 33, 364, 368
Aristotle, 10 *note*, 29
Armstrong, 69
Arnold, Matthew, 7, 8
Aurengzebe, 13
Ausonius, 62, 345 *note*
Austen, Miss, 12, 16, 29, 123, 143, 149, 155, 161, 168, 290

Bage, R., 170, 171
Bagehot, 128, 129
Baltimore, Lord, 242
Balzac, 212 *note*
Barham Downs, 171
Barnaby Rudge, 220 *note*
Barry Lyndon, 122
Bastard, The, 96
Bath, 272 and *note*, 273

Battle of the Books, The, 2
Baviad, The, 346, 360, 361
Bayly, Haynes, 82
Beattie, 73, 74, 305 *note*
Beaumont, Sir J., 5, 6
Beckford, 171-172
Beggars' Opera, The, 41, 58, 59
Behn, Aphra, 106 *note*, 107, 150 and *note*
Bentley, 11, 324
Berington, S., 146
Berkeley, 21, 146, 259, 262, 377, 385
Blackmore, 2
Blair, Robert, 64, 293
Blake, 21, 152, 212, 281, 304 and *note*, 325, 326, 330, 336, 359 *note*, 376, 388
Boileau, 65
Bolingbroke, 47
Bonstetten, 198 *note*
Borrow, G., 159, 232 *note*, 253 *note*
Bossuet, 36
Boswell, 178-197, 204-206, 208, 230, 234, 326
Boyse, 95-99, 218
Bozzy and Piozzi, 356
Brooke, H., 158, 159
Brown ("Estimate"), 239 *note*, 265
Browne, Sir T., 8, 9, 193, 261
Browning, 56
Browning, Mrs., 340
Brydges, Sir E., 198 *note*
Bulwer, 169, 274
Bunyan, 106 *note*
Burke, 217, 258, 260 *note*, 330, 343, 346, 353
Burney, Dr., 76
Burney, Fanny (Mme. d'Arblay), 76 *note*, 119 *note*, 145 *note*, 146, 160-165, 232-235, 254, 276

393

THE END

Printed by R. & R. CLARK, LIMITED, *Edinburgh.*

In Four Volumes.   Post 8vo, 7s. 6d. net each.

Vols. I. and II. Ready.   Vols. III. and IV. in the Press.

THE

MISCELLANEOUS WORKS

OF

JOSEPH ADDISON

EDITED BY

A. C. GUTHKELCH, M.A.,

Senior Lecturer in English, King's College, London.

Vol.   I. POEMS AND PLAYS.

Vol.   II. PROSE.

Vols. III. and IV. CORRESPONDENCE, INTRODUC-
TION, COMMENTARY, BIBLIOGRAPHY,
APPENDIX OF DOUBTFUL AND SPURIOUS
WORKS, INDEX.

"A man who was loved and praised in his life, and for 150 years
after death, as Addison was, cannot be denied the position of a
national classic. . . . It would be difficult to over-estimate the effect
his writings have had on English literature, English character, and
English life.   So it is right that we should have, what we have not
yet had, a complete and scholarly edition of his work; and so far as
can be judged from a single volume, this is what Mr. Guthkelch is
giving us."—*Times.*

LONDON: G. BELL AND SONS, Ltd.

I

SWIFT'S WORKS

THE CORRESPONDENCE OF JONATHAN SWIFT. Edited by F. ELRINGTON BALL, Litt.D. With an Introduction by the Most Rev. the ARCHBISHOP OF DUBLIN. Now complete in six volumes, with copious Index. Demy 8vo. 10s. 6d. net each.

"This is the most important venture in the literary history of our country upon which any publisher is at present engaged."—Mr. EDMUND GOSSE in the *Morning Post.*

"We have repeatedly expressed our admiration for the editor's high standard of accurate research and verification. We shall not again weary him with reiterated praise, beyond saying that in these last two volumes there is no falling off from his scrupulous ideal of scholarship, and that the whole work, an arduous and severe labour, has been carried out with a tenacity and a thoroughness that could not be surpassed, nor probably equalled, by any other scholar. Dr. Ball has conferred a munificent boon upon students of eighteenth-century life and letters, and has earned our thanks and warm congratulations on the conclusion of his devoted task." —*Athenæum.*

SWIFT'S PROSE WORKS. Edited by TEMPLE SCOTT. With a Biographical Introduction by the Right Hon. W. E. H. LECKY, M.P., and full Bibliography and Index. With Portraits and other Illustrations. 12 vols. 5s. each.

Vol.   I. A TALE OF A TUB AND OTHER EARLY WORKS.
Vol.   II. THE JOURNAL TO STELLA.
Vols. III. and IV. WRITINGS ON RELIGION AND THE CHURCH.
Vol.   V. HISTORICAL AND POLITICAL TRACTS—ENGLISH.
Vol.   VI. THE DRAPIER'S LETTERS.
Vol.   VII. HISTORICAL AND POLITICAL TRACTS—IRISH.
Vol. VIII. GULLIVER'S TRAVELS.
Vol.   IX. CONTRIBUTIONS TO THE "EXAMINER," "TATLER," "SPECTATOR."
Vol.   X. HISTORICAL WRITINGS.
Vol.   XI. LITERARY ESSAYS.
Vol.   XII. BIBLIOGRAPHY, INDEX, ETC.

"Messrs. Bell are to be warmly congratulated on the completion of their edition of Swift's Prose Works. Of the care and thoroughness of all concerned in it—editors, contributors, publishers, and printers—we cannot speak too highly. For the first time the student has a really complete and satisfactory edition of Swift's Prose Works, sufficiently annotated and provided with the needful bibliographical apparatus, issued in a very convenient form and at a very moderate price. Type, paper, portraits, are all that can be wished in such a work; the volumes are light in the hand, and remarkably free from blemishes of any kind."— *Athenæum.*

SWIFT'S POEMS. Edited by W. ERNST BROWNING. 2 vols. With Portraits. 3s. 6d. each.

"Swift, indeed, is himself so vital a figure, whether in Irish politics or in English literature, that everything he wrote—even the most occasional verse—is worth eager reading, and Mr. Browning is to be thanked for so ably editing these volumes in the complete Bohn edition of Swift's works. The hundreds of skits, satires, epigrams, and friendly epistles which they contain are an indispensable aid to all who wish for a detailed and satisfactory portrait of Swift in his different and often conflicting aspects. They are expressive trifles of a great man."— *Daily News.*

LONDON: G. BELL AND SONS, LTD.

BOHN'S LIBRARIES

"Bohn has soared above criticism. It is a national institution."—*Daily Chronicle.*

Complete Catalogue sent post free on application.

AUGUSTAN LITERATURE

A SELECTION FROM THE FAMOUS "LIBRARIES"

ADDISON'S WORKS. With the Notes of Bishop Hurd, Portrait, and 8 plates of Medals and Coins. Edited by H. G. BOHN. 6 vols. 3s. 6d. each.

BERKELEY'S WORKS. Edited by GEORGE SAMPSON. With Biographical Introduction by the Right Hon. A. J. BALFOUR, M.P. 3 vols. 5s. each.

BOSWELL'S LIFE OF JOHNSON, with the Tour in the Hebrides and Johnsoniana. Edited by the Rev. A. NAPIER, M.A. 6 vols. 3s. 6d. each.

BURKE'S WORKS AND SPEECHES. 6 vols. 3s. 6d. each.

BURKE'S SPEECHES ON THE IMPEACHMENT OF WARREN HASTINGS. 2 vols. 3s. 6d. each.

BURNEY'S EVELINA. By FRANCES BURNEY (Madame D'Arblay). With an Introduction and Notes by A. R. ELLIS. 3s. 6d.

BURNEY'S CECILIA. With an Introduction and Notes by A. R. ELLIS. 2 vols. 3s. 6d. each.

BUTLER'S (JOSEPH) ANALOGY OF RELIGION, together with Two Dissertations on Personal Identity and on the Nature of Virtue, and Fifteen Sermons. Edited, with Analytical Introductions, Explanatory Notes, a short Memoir, and a Portrait. 3s. 6d.

BUTLER'S (JOSEPH) SERMONS. Edited, with Introduction, Notes, and Analyses, by the Rev. W. R. MATTHEWS, M.A., B.D. 3s. 6d.

BUTLER'S (SAMUEL) HUDIBRAS. With Variorum Notes, Biography and Index, and numerous Illustrations. 5s.

CLASSIC TALES, containing Rasselas, Vicar of Wakefield, Gulliver's Travels, and The Sentimental Journey. 3s. 6d.

DEFOE'S NOVELS AND MISCELLANEOUS WORKS. With Prefaces and Notes, including those attributed to Sir W. SCOTT. 7 vols. 3s. 6d. each.

FIELDING'S ADVENTURES OF JOSEPH ANDREWS AND HIS FRIEND MR. ABRAHAM ADAMS. With CRUIKSHANK'S Illustrations. 3s. 6d.

FIELDING'S HISTORY OF TOM JONES, A FOUNDLING. With CRUIKSHANK'S Illustrations. 2 vols. 3s. 6d. each.

FIELDING'S AMELIA. With CRUIKSHANK'S Illustrations. 5s.

GIBBON'S DECLINE AND FALL OF THE ROMAN EMPIRE. Complete and unabridged with Variorum Notes. Edited by an English Churchman. With two Maps and Portrait. 7 vols. 3s. 6d. each.

GOLDSMITH'S WORKS. A New Edition. By J. W. M. GIBBS. 5 vols. 3s. 6d. each.

GRAY'S LETTERS. Including the Correspondence of Gray and Mason. Edited by the Rev. D. C. TOVEY, M.A. 3 vols. 3s. 6d. each.

JOHNSON'S LIVES OF THE POETS. Edited by Mrs. ALEXANDER NAPIER, with Introduction by Professor HALES. 3 vols. 3s. 6d. each.

JUNIUS'S LETTERS. With all the Notes of Woodfall's edition, and important Additions. 2 vols. 3s. 6d. each.

LONDON: G. BELL AND SONS, LTD.

MONTAGU. THE LETTERS AND WORKS OF LADY MARY WORTLEY MONTAGU. Lord WHARNCLIFFE's edition, revised by W. MOY THOMAS. With 5 Portraits. 2 vols. 5s. each.

PERCY'S RELIQUES OF ANCIENT ENGLISH POETRY, consisting of old Heroic Ballads, Songs, and other Pieces of our earlier Poets, together with some few of later date. Collected by THOMAS PERCY, Lord Bishop of Dromore. With an Essay on Ancient Minstrels, and a Glossary. A new edition by J. V. PRICHARD, A.M. 2 vols. 3s. 6d. each.

POPE'S POETICAL WORKS. Edited by ROBERT CARRUTHERS. With numerous Illustrations. 2 vols. 5s. each.

POPE'S HOMER'S ILIAD. Edited by the Rev. J. S. WATSON, M.A. Illustrated by the entire Series of Flaxman's Designs. 5s.

POPE'S HOMER'S ODYSSEY, with the Battle of Frogs and Mice, Hymns, etc., by other Translators. Edited by the Rev. J. S. WATSON, M.A. With the entire Series of Flaxman's Designs. 5s.

POPE'S LIFE, including many of his Letters. By ROBERT CARRUTHERS. With numerous Illustrations. 5s.

SHERIDAN'S DRAMATIC WORKS. Complete. With Life by G. G. S. 3s. 6d.

SMOLLETT'S ADVENTURES OF RODERICK RANDOM. With short Memoir and Bibliography, and CRUIKSHANK's Illustrations. 3s. 6d.

SMOLLETT'S ADVENTURES OF PEREGRINE PICKLE, in which are included the Memoirs of a Lady of Quality. With Bibliography and CRUIKSHANK's Illustrations. 2 vols. 3s. 6d. each.

SMOLLETT'S THE EXPEDITION OF HUMPHRY CLINKER. With Bibliography and CRUIKSHANK's Illustrations. 3s. 6d.

SMOLLETT'S GIL BLAS, THE ADVENTURES OF. Translated from the French of Lesage by SMOLLETT. 24 Engravings on Steel, after SMIRKE, and 10 Etchings by GEORGE CRUIKSHANK. 6s.

SMITH'S (ADAM) THEORY OF MORAL SENTIMENTS; with his Essay on the First Formation of Languages; to which is added a Biographical and Critical Memoir of the Author by DUGALD STEWART. 3s. 6d.

SMITH'S (ADAM) THE WEALTH OF NATIONS, AN INQUIRY INTO THE NATURE AND CAUSES OF. Edited by E. BELFORT BAX. 2 vols. 3s. 6d. each.

SWIFT'S PROSE WORKS. Edited by TEMPLE SCOTT. With a Biographical Introduction by W. E. H. LECKY. With Portraits and Facsimiles. 12 vols. 5s. each.

SWIFT'S POEMS. Edited by W. E. BROWNING. 2 vols. 3s. 6d. each.

WALTON'S COMPLETE ANGLER. Edited by EDWARD JESSE. With Portrait and 203 Engravings on Wood, and 26 Engravings on Steel. 5s.

WALTON'S LIVES OF DONNE, HOOKER, ETC. New edition, revised by A. H. BULLEN, with a Memoir of IZAAK WALTON by WM. DOWLING. With numerous Illustrations. 5s.

WHITE'S NATURAL HISTORY OF SELBORNE, with Observations on various Parts of Nature, and the Naturalist's Calendar. With Notes by Sir WILLIAM JARDINE. Edited, with further Notes, a Biographical Sketch, and complete Index, by EDWARD JESSE. With 40 Portraits and coloured Plates. 5s.

YOUNG'S (ARTHUR) TRAVELS IN FRANCE DURING THE YEARS 1787, 1788, and 1789. With an Introduction, Biographical Sketch, and Notes by M. BETHAM-EDWARDS. With a Portrait. Small post 8vo. 3s. 6d.

YOUNG'S (ARTHUR) TOUR IN IRELAND, with General Observations on the State of the Country during the years 1776-9. Edited by A. W. HUTTON, Librarian National Liberal Club. With Complete Bibliography by J. P. ANDERSON, of the British Museum; Index and Map. 2 vols. 3s. 6d. each.

LONDON: G. BELL AND SONS, LTD.